Beginning Oracle SQL

For Oracle Database 12c
Third Edition

Lex De Haan
Tim Gorman
Inger Jørgensen
Melanie Caffrey

Beginning Oracle SQL

ISBN-13 (pbk): 978-1-4302-6556-6

ISBN-13 (electronic): 978-1-4302-6557-3

President and Publisher: Paul Manning
Lead Editor: Jonathan Hassell
Technical Reviewer: Yelena Cohen
Editorial Board: Steve Anglin, Mark Beckner, Ewan Buckingham, Gary Cornell, Louise Corrigan, Jim DeWolf, Jonathan Gennick, Jonathan Hassell, Robert Hutchinson, Michelle Lowman, James Markham, Matthew Moodie, Jeff Olson, Jeffrey Pepper, Douglas Pundick, Ben Renow-Clarke, Dominic Shakeshaft, Gwenan Spearing, Matt Wade, Steve Weiss
Coordinating Editor: Mark Powers
Copy Editor: Rebecca Rider
Compositor: SPi Global
Indexer: SPi Global
Artist: SPi Global
Cover Designer: Anna Ishchenko

Distributed to the book trade worldwide by Springer Science+Business Media New York, 233 Spring Street, 6th Floor, New York, NY 10013. Phone 1-800-SPRINGER, fax (201) 348-4505, e-mail orders-ny@springer-sbm.com, or visit www.springeronline.com. Apress Media, LLC is a California LLC and the sole member (owner) is Springer Science + Business Media Finance Inc (SSBM Finance Inc). SSBM Finance Inc is a Delaware corporation.

For information on translations, please e-mail rights@apress.com, or visit www.apress.com.

Apress and friends of ED books may be purchased in bulk for academic, corporate, or promotional use. eBook versions and licenses are also available for most titles. For more information, reference our Special Bulk Sales–eBook Licensing web page at www.apress.com/bulk-sales.

Any source code or other supplementary material referenced by the author in this text is available to readers at www.apress.com/9781430265566. For detailed information about how to locate your book's source code, go to www.apress.com/source-code/.

Contents at a Glance

Contents

About the Authors

Lex de Haan studied applied mathematics at the Technical University in Delft, The Netherlands. His experience with Oracle went back to the mid-1980s, version 4. He worked for Oracle Corporation from 1990 until 2004, in various education-related roles and ended up in Server Technologies (product development) as senior curriculum manager for the advanced DBA curriculum. In that role, he was involved in the development of Oracle9i Database and Oracle Database 10g. In March 2004, he decided to go independent and founded Natural Join B.V. In 1999, he became involved in the ISO SQL language standardization process, as a member of the Dutch national body. Lex passed away on February 1, 2006.

Tim Gorman began his information technology career in 1984 as a C programmer on UNIX and VMS systems, working on medical and financial systems as an application developer, systems programmer, and systems administrator. He joined Oracle Corporation in 1990 as a consultant, then became an independent consultant in 1998, and has worked for Evergreen Database Technologies (EvDBT.com) since then. He is the co-author of Oracle8 Data Warehousing, Essential Oracle8i Data Warehousing, Oracle Insights: Tales Of The Oak Table, and Expert Oracle Practices: Database Administration From The Oak Table. He specializes in performance tuning, as well as data warehouse design and implementation, backup and recovery, architecture and infrastructure, and database administration in challenging scenarios. He is a frequent Oracle conference speaker.

After a Languages Master degree (English and French) **Inger Jørgensen** started working at Oracle Denmark teaching SQL and PL/SQL as well as database administration from Oracle version 6 onward with a five-year period in between of teaching developers Forms, Reports, and Graphics. Inger spent 18 years at Oracle Corporation and is presently a teacher and a consultant at Oracle Gold partner Miracle A/S in Denmark.

Melanie Caffrey is a senior development manager for Oracle Corporation, providing front-end and back-end Oracle solutions for the business needs of various clients. She is co-author of several technical publications including Expert PL/SQL Practices for Oracle Developers and DBAs, and Expert Oracle Practices: Oracle Database Administration from the Oak Table (Apress), and the SQL 101 series of articles for Oracle Magazine. She instructed students in Columbia University's Computer Technology and Applications program in New York City, teaching advanced Oracle database administration and PL/SQL development. She is a frequent Oracle conference speaker and a member of the Oak Table network.

About the Technical Reviewer

Yelena Cohen is a strong database administrator with a broad range of skills in all aspects of the management of Oracle products. She likes to address performance, capacity planning and provisioning, and many other design issues and troubleshooting activities. During her career, Yelena has worked as a senior DBA for big enterprise companies and has supported implementations of big scale projects for telecommunication, advertisement and media, retail and marketing.

Acknowledgments

Working with professionals like Melanie Caffrey and Inger Jørgensen is an amazing experience, not only because of their generosity and shared respect for the SQL language, but also in our shared admiration for Lex de Haan. Seldom are three people in such close agreement. This book was one of Lex's favorite projects and it shows in every word, every sentence, even after translation. I am honored to have participated in keeping his work moving forward as the Oracle database moves forward. I thank our colleagues at Apress, I thank Yelena Cohen for her technical review, and I appreciate the support from my partner in life, Kellyn Pot'vin.

—Tim Gorman

To this I would like to add thanks to Lex's widow, Juliette, for letting us keep this book alive and up-to-date. Even though we have added to it, I still feel I can hear Lex's humorous and competent teaching in the tone of the book.

—Inger Jørgensen

I would like to thank my co-authors Tim Gorman and Inger Jørgensen for their wisdom, collaboration, hard work, and generosity. Without them, the current edition would not be taking place. I'd also like to thank Mark Powers, Rebecca Rider, Jonathan Hassell, and Jonathan Gennick at Apress, and our technical editor, Yelena Cohen, for keeping this important work in circulation, their invaluable insights and careful attention to detail, and for being so easy to work with. And I'd be remiss if I did not thank my family and friends for their unwavering support and enthusiasm, and for understanding when I didn't return phone calls right away. Additionally, thanks go to my husband, Tom, who serves as a constant reminder that the most interesting people you will ever meet always find work that they love and make it their own.

This naturally brings me to Lex. I'd like to thank Lex de Haan for putting together a work that continues to teach new and current Oracle students with each subsequent revision. It is an honor to be able to contribute to his extraordinary book series. The contributors who help to keep his books alive do so because they feel lucky to have been able to spend time with such a genuinely well-esteemed individual. I count myself among the lucky.

—Melanie Caffrey

Introduction

This book was born from a translation of a book originally written by Lex de Haan in Dutch. That book was first published in 1993, and went through several revisions in its native Dutch before Lex decided to produce an English version. Apress published that English version in 2005 under the title "Mastering Oracle SQL and SQL*Plus". The book has since earned respect as an excellent, accurate, and concise tutorial on Oracle's implementation of SQL.

While SQL is a fairly stable language, there have been changes to Oracle's implementation of it over the years. The book you are holding now is a revision of Lex's original, English-language work. The book has been revised to cover new developments in Oracle SQL since 2005, especially those in Oracle Database 11g Release 1 and Release 2, and Oracle Database 12c Release 1. The book has also been given the title "Beginning Oracle SQL". The new title better positions the book in Apress's line, better reflects the content, fits better with branding and marketing efforts, and marks the book as a foundational title that Apress intends to continue revising and publishing in the long term.

About this Book

This is not a book about advanced SQL. It is not a book about the Oracle optimizer and diagnostic tools. And it is not a book about relational calculus, predicate logic, or set theory. This book is a SQL primer. It is meant to help you learn Oracle SQL by yourself. It is ideal for self-study, but it can also be used as a guide for SQL workshops and instructor-led classroom training.

This is a practical book; therefore, you need access to an Oracle environment for hands-on exercises. All the software that you need to install Oracle Database on either Windows or Linux for learning purposes is available free of charge from the Oracle Technology Network (OTN). Begin your journey with a visit to the OTN website at:

```
http://www.oracle.com/technology/index.html
```

From the OTN home page, you can navigate to product information, to documentation and manual sets, and to free downloads that you can install on your own PC for learning purposes.

This edition of the book is current with Oracle Database 12c Release 1. However, Oracle SQL has been reasonably stable over the years. All the examples should also run under 11g Release 2. And most will still run under Oracle Database 10g, under Oracle Database 9i, and even under Oracle Database 8i, if you're running software that old. Of course, as you go further back in release-time, you will find more syntax that is not supported in each successively older release. Oracle Corporation does tend to add a few new SQL features with each new release of their database product.

Oracle Corporation has shown great respect for SQL standards over the past decade. We agree with supporting standards, and we follow the ANSI/ISO standard SQL syntax as much as possible in this book. Only in cases of useful, Oracle-specific SQL extensions do we deviate from the international standard. Therefore, most SQL examples given in this book are probably also valid for other database management system (DBMS) implementations supporting the SQL language.

SQL statements discussed in this book are explained with concrete examples. We focus on the main points, avoiding peripheral and arcane side-issues as much as possible. The examples are presented clearly in a listing format, as in the example shown here in Listing I-1.

Listing I-1. A SQL SELECT Statement

```
SELECT 'Hello world!'
FROM dual;
```

One difference between this edition and its predecessor is that we omit the "SQL>" prompt from many of our examples. That prompt comes from SQL*Plus, the command-line interface that old-guard database administrators and developers have used for years. We now omit SQL*Plus prompts from all examples that are not specific to SQL*Plus. We do that out of respect for the growing use of graphical interfaces such as Oracle SQL Developer.

This book does not intend (nor pretend) to be complete; the SQL language is too voluminous and the Oracle environment is much too complex. Oracle's SQL reference manual, named the Oracle Database SQL Language Reference, comes in at just over 1800 pages for the Oracle Database 12c Release 1 edition. Moreover, the current ISO SQL standard documentation has grown to a size that is simply not feasible anymore to print on paper.

The main objective of this book is the combination of usability and affordability. The official Oracle documentation offers detailed information in case you need it. Therefore, it is a good idea to have the Oracle manuals available while working through the examples and exercises in this book. The Oracle documentation is available online from the OTN website mentioned earlier in this introduction. You can access that documentation in HTML form, or you can download PDF copies of selected manuals.

The focus of this book is using SQL for data retrieval. Data definition and data manipulation are covered in less detail. Security, authorization, and database administration are mentioned only for the sake of completeness in the "Overview of SQL" section of Chapter 2.

Throughout the book, we use a case consisting of seven tables. These seven tables contain information about employees, departments, and courses. As Chris Date, a well-known guru in the professional database world, said during one of his seminars, "There are only three databases: employees and departments, orders and line items, and suppliers and shipments."

The amount of data (i.e., the cardinality) in the case tables is deliberately kept low. This enables you to check the results of your SQL commands manually, which is nice while you're learning to master the SQL language. In general, checking your results manually is impossible in real information systems due to the volume of data in such systems.

It is not the data volume or query response time that matters in this book. What's important is the database structure complexity and SQL statement correctness. After all, it does no good for a statement to be fast, or to perform well, if all it does in the end is produce incorrect results. Accuracy first! That's true in many aspects of life, including in SQL.

About the Chapters of this Book

Chapter 1 provides a concise introduction to the theoretical background of information systems and some popular database terminology, and then continues with a global overview of the Oracle software and an introduction to the seven case tables. It is an important, foundational chapter that will help you get the most from the rest of the book.

Chapter 2 starts with a high-level overview of the SQL language. SQL Developer is then introduced. It is a tool for testing and executing SQL. It is a nice, fairly intuitive graphical user interface, and it is a tool that has gained much ground and momentum with developers. Free download and documentation can be found here:

```
http://www.oracle.com/technetwork/developer-tools/sql-developer/downloads/index.html
```

Data definition is covered in two nonconsecutive chapters: Chapter 3 and Chapter 7. This is done to allow you to start with SQL retrieval as soon as possible. Therefore, Chapter 3 covers only the most basic data-definition concepts (tables, datatypes, and the data dictionary).

Retrieval is also spread over multiple chapters—four chapters, to be precise. Chapter 4 focuses on the SELECT, WHERE, and ORDER BY clauses of the SELECT statement. The most important SQL functions are covered in Chapter 5, which also covers null values and subqueries. In Chapter 8, we start accessing multiple tables at the same time (joining tables) and aggregating query results; in other words, the FROM, the GROUP BY, and the HAVING clauses get our attention in that chapter. To finish the coverage of data retrieval with SQL, Chapter 9 revisits subqueries to show some more advanced subquery constructs. That chapter also introduces windows and analytic functions, the row limiting clause, hierarchical queries, and flashback features.

Chapter 6 discusses data manipulation with SQL. The commands INSERT, UPDATE, DELETE, and MERGE are introduced. This chapter also pays attention to some topics related to data manipulation: transaction processing, read consistency, and locking.

In Chapter 7, we revisit data definition, to drill down into constraints, indexes, sequences, and performance. Synonyms are explained in the same chapter. Chapters 8 and 9 continue coverage of data retrieval with SQL.

Chapter 10 introduces views. What are views, when should you use them, and what are their restrictions? This chapter explores the possibilities of data manipulation via views, discusses views and performance, and introduces materialized views.

Chapter 11 is about automation and introduces the reader to the SQL*Plus tool. SQL statements can be long, and sometimes you want to execute several in succession. Chapter 11 shows you how to develop automated scripts that you can run via SQL*Plus. SQL*Plus is a command-line tool that you can use to send a SQL statement to the database and get results back. Many database administrators use SQL*Plus routinely, and you can rely upon it to be present in any Oracle Database installation. Many, many Oracle databases are kept alive and healthy by automated SQL*Plus scripts written by savvy database administrators.

Oracle is an object-relational database management system. Since Oracle Database 8, many object-oriented features have been added to the SQL language. As an introduction to these features, Chapter 12 provides a high-level overview of user-defined datatypes, arrays, nested tables, and multiset operators.

Finally, the book ends with two appendixes. Appendix A at the end of this book provides a detailed look into the example tables used in this book's examples. Appendix B gives the exercise solutions.

About the Case Tables

Chapter 1 describes the case tables used in the book's examples. Appendix A goes into even more detail, should you want it. The book's catalog page on the Apress.com website contains a link to a SQL*Plus script that you can use to create and populate the example tables. The direct link to that page is: http://www.apress.com/9781430265566. When you get there, scroll down the page about halfway and click on the Source Code/Downloads tab, which will reveal the link from which you can download the aforementioned script.

CHAPTER 1

■ ■ ■

Relational Database Systems and Oracle

The focus of this book is writing SQL in Oracle, which is a relational database management system. This first chapter provides a brief introduction to relational database systems in general, followed by an introduction to the Oracle software environment. The main objective of this chapter is to help you find your way in the relational database jungle and to get acquainted with the most important database terminology.

The first three sections discuss the main reasons for automating information systems using databases, what needs to be done to design and build relational database systems, and the various components of a relational database management system. The following sections go into more depth about the theoretical foundation of relational database management systems.

This chapter also gives a brief overview of the Oracle software environment: the components of such an environment, the characteristics of the components, and what you can do with those components.

The last section of this chapter introduces seven sample tables, which are used in the examples and exercises throughout this book to help you develop your SQL skills. In order to be able to formulate and execute the correct SQL statements, you'll need to understand the structures and relationships of these tables.

This chapter does not cover object-relational database features. In Chapter 12 you will find information about Oracle features in that area.

1.1 Information Needs and Information Systems

Organizations have business objectives. In order to realize those business objectives, many decisions must be made on a daily basis. Typically, a lot of *information* is needed to make the right decisions; however, this information is not always available in the appropriate format. Therefore, organizations need formal systems that will allow them to produce the required information, in the right format, at the right time. Such systems are called *information systems*. An information system is a simplified reflection (a *model*) of the real world within the organization.

Information systems don't necessarily need to be automated—the data might reside in card files, cabinets, or other physical storage mechanisms. This data can be converted into the desired information format using certain procedures or actions. In general, there are two main reasons to automate information systems:

- **Complexity:** The data structures or the data processing procedures become too complicated.

- **Volume:** The volume of the data to be administered becomes too large.

If an organization decides to automate an information system because of complexity, volume, or both, it typically will need to use some database technology.

1

The main advantages of using database technology are as follows:

- **Accessibility:** Ad hoc data-retrieval functionality, data-entry and data-reporting facilities, and concurrency handling in a multiuser environment

- **Availability:** Recovery facilities in case of system crashes and human errors

- **Security:** Data access control, privileges, and auditing

- **Manageability:** Utilities to efficiently manage large volumes of data

When specifying or modeling information needs, it is a good idea to maintain a clear separation between *information* and *application*. In other words, we separate the following two aspects:

- **What:** The information *content* needed. This is the *logical* level and it represents the *information*.

- **How:** The desired *format* of the information, the way that the results can be derived from the data stored in the information system, the minimum performance requirements, and so on. This is the *physical* level and it represents the *application*.

Database systems such as Oracle enable information system users and designers/developers to maintain this separation between the "what" and the "how" aspects, allowing users of such systems to concentrate more on the first aspect and less on the second. This is because database system implementations are based on the *relational model*. The relational model is explained later in this chapter, in Sections 1.4 through 1.7.

1.2 Database Design

One of the problems with using traditional third-generation programming languages (such as COBOL, Pascal, Fortran, and C) is the ongoing maintenance of existing code, because these languages don't separate the "what" and the "how" aspects of information needs. That's why programmers using those languages sometimes spend more than 75% of their precious time on maintenance of existing programs, leaving little time for them to build new programs.

When using database technology, organizations usually need many database applications to process the data residing in the database. These database applications are typically developed using fourth- or fifth-generation application development environments, which significantly enhance productivity by enabling users to develop database applications *faster* while producing applications with *lower maintenance* costs. However, in order to be successful using these fourth- and fifth-generation application development tools, developers must start thinking about the structure of their data first.

It is *very* important to spend enough time on designing the data model *before* you start coding your applications. Data model mistakes discovered in a later stage, when the system is already in production, are very difficult and expensive to fix.

Entities and Attributes

In a database, we store facts about certain objects. In database jargon, such objects are commonly referred to as *entities*. For each entity, we are typically interested in a set of observable and relevant properties, commonly referred to as *attributes*.

When designing a data model for your information system, you begin with two questions:

1. Which entities are relevant for the information system?

2. Which attributes are relevant for each entity, and which values are allowed for those attributes?

We'll add a third question to this list before the end of this chapter to make the list complete.

For example, consider a company in the information technology training business. Examples of relevant entities for the information system of this company could be course attendee, classroom, instructor, registration, confirmation, invoice, course, and so on. An example of a partial list of relevant attributes for the entity COURSE_ATTENDEE could be the following:

- Registration number
- Name
- Address
- City
- Date of birth
- Age
- Gender

For the COURSE entity, the attribute list might include attribute items such as:

- Title
- Duration (in days)
- Price
- Frequency
- Maximum number of attendees

■ **Note**   There are many different terminology conventions for entities and attributes, such as *objects*, *object types*, *types*, *object occurrences*, and so on. The terminology itself is not important, but once you have made a choice, you should use it consistently.

Generic vs. Specific

The difference between *generic* versus *specific* is very important in database design. For example, common words in natural languages such as *book* and *course* have both generic and specific meanings. In spoken language, the precise meaning of these words is normally obvious from the context in which they are used.

When designing data models, you must be very careful about the distinction between generic and specific meanings of the same word. For example, a course has a title and a duration (generic), while a specific course offering has a location, a start date, a certain number of attendees, and an instructor. A specific book on the shelf might have your name and purchase date on the inside cover page, and it might be full of your personal annotations. On the other hand, a generic book has a title, an author, a publisher, and an ISBN code. This means that you should be careful when using words like *course* and *book* for database entities, because they could be confusing and suggest the wrong meaning.

Moreover, we must maintain a clear separation between an entity itself at the generic level and a specific occurrence of that entity. Along the same lines, there is a difference between an entity *attribute* (at the generic level) and a specific *attribute value* for a particular entity occurrence.

Redundancy

There are two types of data: base data and derivable data. *Base data* is data that cannot be derived in any way from other data residing in the information system. It is crucial that base data is stored in the database. *Derivable data* can be deduced (for example, with a formula) from other data. For example, if we store both the age and the date of birth of each course attendee in our database, these two attributes are mutually derivable—assuming that the current date is available at any moment.

Actually, every question issued against a database results in derived data. In other words, it is both undesirable and not reasonable to store all derivable data in an information system. Storage of derivable data is referred to as *redundancy*. Another way of defining redundancy is storage of the same data more than once.

Sometimes, it makes sense to store redundant data in a database; for example, in cases where response time is crucial and in cases where repeated computation or derivation of the desired data would be too time-consuming. But typically, storage of redundant data in a database should be avoided. First of all, it is a waste of storage capacity. However, that's not the biggest problem, since terabytes of disk capacity can be bought for relatively low prices these days. The challenge with redundant data storage lies in its ongoing maintenance.

With redundant data in your database, it is difficult to process data manipulation correctly under all circumstances. In case something goes wrong, you could end up with an information system containing internal contradictions. In other words, you could have *inconsistent* data. Therefore, redundancy in an information system may result in ongoing consistency problems.

When considering the storage of redundant data in an information system, it is important to distinguish two types of information systems:

- Online transaction processing (OLTP) systems, which typically have continuous data changes and high volume

- Decision support systems (DDS; often referred to as data warehouses), which are mainly, or even exclusively, used for data retrieval and reporting, and are loaded or refreshed at certain frequencies with data from OLTP systems

In DSS systems, it is common practice to store a lot of redundant data to improve system response times. Retrieval of stored data is typically faster than data derivation, and the risk of inconsistency, although present for load and update of data, is less likely because most DSS systems are often read-only from the end user's perspective.

Consistency, Integrity, and Integrity Constraints

Obviously, consistency is a first requirement for any information system, ensuring that you can retrieve reliable information from that system. In other words, you don't want any *contradictions* in your information system.

For example, suppose we derive the following information from our training business information system:

- Attendee 6749 was born on February 13, 2093.

- The same attendee 6749 appears to have gender Z.

- There is another, different attendee with the same number 6749.

- We see a course registration for attendee 8462, but this number does not appear in the administration records where we maintain a list of all attendees.

In none of the above four cases is the consistency at stake; the information system is unambiguous in its statements. Nevertheless, there is something wrong because these statements do not conform to common sense.

This brings us to the second requirement for an information system: *data integrity*. We would consider it more in accordance with our perception of reality if the following were true of our information system:

1. For any course attendee, the date of birth does not lie in the future.

2. The gender attribute for any person has the value M or F or O.

3. Every course attendee (or person, in general) has a unique number.

4. We have registration information only for existing attendees—that is, attendees known to the information system.

These rules concerning database contents are called *constraints*. You should translate all your business rules into formal integrity constraints. The third example (in the list above)—a unique number for each person—is a primary key constraint, and it implements *entity integrity*. The fourth example—information for only persons known to the system—is a foreign key constraint, implementing *referential integrity*. We will revisit these concepts later in this chapter, in Section 1.5.

Constraints are often classified based on the lowest level at which they can be checked. The following are four constraint types, each illustrated with an example:

- **Attribute constraints:** Checks attributes; for example, "Gender must be M or F or O."

- **Row constraints:** Checks at the row level; for example, "For salesmen, commission is a mandatory attribute."

- **Table constraints:** Checks at the table level; for example, "Each employee has a unique e-mail address."

- **Database constraints:** Checks at the database level; for example, "Each employee works for an existing department."

In Chapter 7, we'll revisit integrity constraints to see how you can formally specify them in the SQL language.

At the beginning of this section, you learned that information needs can be formalized by identifying which entities are relevant for the information system and deciding which attributes are relevant for each entity. Now we can add a third step to the information analysis list of steps you've learned thus far to produce a formal data model:

1. Which entities are relevant for the information system?

2. Which attributes are relevant for each entity?

3. Which integrity constraints should be enforced by the system?

Data Modeling Approach, Methods, and Techniques

The job of designing appropriate data models is not a sinecure and is typically a task for IT specialists. And although end users are not what you may think of as the parties responsible for assisting in data model design, it is almost impossible to design data models without the active participation of the future end users of the system. End users usually have the most expertise in their professional area, and IT specialists use this expertise to their advantage when designing data models. Additionally, a seasoned IT specialist ensures that the end users are also involved in the final system acceptance tests.

Over the years, many methods have been developed to support the system development process itself, to generate system documentation, to communicate with project participants, and to manage projects to control time and costs. Traditional methods typically show a strict phasing of the development process and a description of what needs to be done in which order. That's why these methods are also referred to as *waterfall* methods. Roughly formulated, these methods distinguish the following four phases in the system development process:

1. **Analysis:** Describing the information needs and determining the information system boundaries

2. **Logical design:** Getting answers to the three questions about entities, attributes, and constraints, the concepts presented in the previous section

3. **Physical design:** Translating the logical design into a real database structure

4. **Build phase:** Building database applications

Within the development methods, you can use various *techniques* to support your activities. For example, you can use diagram techniques to represent data models graphically. Some well-known examples of such diagram techniques are Entity Relationship Modeling (ERM) and Unified Modeling Language (UML). In the last section of this chapter, which introduces the sample tables used throughout this book, you will see an ERM diagram that corresponds with those tables.

Another example of a well-known technique is *normalization*, which allows you to remove redundancy from a database design by following some strict rules.

Prototyping is also a quite popular technique. Using prototyping, you produce "quick and dirty" pieces of functionality to simulate parts of a system, with the intention of evoking reactions from the end users. This might result in time-savings during the analysis phase of the development process, and more importantly, better-quality results, thus increasing the probability of system acceptance at the end of the development process.

Rapid application development (RAD) is another well-known term associated with data modeling. Instead of the waterfall approach described earlier, you employ an iterative approach.

Some methods and techniques are supported by corresponding computer programs, which are referred to as computer-aided systems engineering (CASE) tools. Various vendors offer complete and integral support for system development, from analysis to system generation (Oracle's SQL Developer Data Modeler is one example), while others provide basic support for database design even though their products are general-purpose drawing tools (Microsoft Visio is an example).

Semantics

If you want to use information systems correctly, you must be aware of the *semantics* (the meaning of things) of the underlying data model. A careful choice for table names and column names is a good starting point, followed by applying those names as consistently as possible. For example, the attribute "address" can have many different meanings: home address, work address, mailing address, and so on. The meaning of attributes that might lead to this type of confusion can be stored explicitly in an additional *semantic explanation* to the data model. Although such a semantic explanation is not part of the formal data model itself, you can store it in a *data dictionary*—a term explained in Section 1.3.

Information Systems Terms Review

In this section, the following terms were introduced:

- Entities and attributes

- Generic versus specific

- Occurrences and attribute values

- Base data and derivable data

- Redundancy and consistency

- Integrity and constraints

- Data modeling

- Methods and techniques

- Logical and physical design

- Normalization

- Prototyping and RAD

- CASE tools

- Semantics

1.3 Database Management Systems

The preceding two sections defined the formal concept of an information system. You learned that if an organization decides to automate an information system, it typically uses some database technology. The term *database* can be defined as follows:

■ **Definition**   A *database* is a set of data, which is needed to derive the desired information from an information system and maintained by a separate software program.

This separate software program is called the *database management system* (DBMS). There are many types of database management systems available, varying in terms of the following characteristics:

- Price
- Ability to implement complex information systems
- Supported hardware environment
- Flexibility for application developers
- Flexibility for end users
- Ability to set up connections with other programs
- Speed (performance)
- Ongoing operational costs
- User-friendliness
- Ability to guarantee data consistency
- Ability to support concurrent access by multiple users

DBMS Components

A DBMS has many components, including a kernel, data dictionary, query language, and tools.

Kernel

The core of any DBMS consists of the code that handles physical data storage, data transport (input and output) between external and internal memory, integrity checking, and so on. This crucial part of the DBMS is commonly referred to as the *engine* or *kernel*.

Data Dictionary

Another important task of the DBMS is the maintenance of a *data dictionary*, containing all data about the database (the metadata). Here are some examples of information maintained in a data dictionary:

- Overview of all entities and attributes in the database
- Constraints (integrity)
- Access rights to the data
- Additional semantic explanations
- Database user authorization data

Query Languages

Each DBMS vendor supports one or more languages to allow access to the data stored in the database. These languages are commonly referred to as *query languages*. SQL, the language this book is all about, has been the de facto market standard for many years.

OTHER QUERY LANGUAGES, REALLY?

SQL is such a common query language that very few realize that there were ever any others. In fact, few even comprehend the concept that there exist query languages other than SQL. But there are others. Oracle Rdb supports SQL, but Rdb also supports a language called Relational Database Operator (RDO). (Yes, you've heard it here: there was an RDO long before Microsoft took up that abbreviation). RDO is a language developed by Digital Equipment Corporation (DEC) for use in their own database management system. Oracle bought that system and continues to support the use of RDO to this day. The Ingres database, once a competitor to Oracle, also had its own query language. Ingres originally supported a language known as Quel. That language did not compete well with SQL, and Ingres Corporation was eventually forced to build SQL support into their product. Today, SQL is the dominant database access language. All mainstream relational databases claim to support it. And yet, no two databases support it in quite the same way. Instead of completely different languages with dissimilar names, today we have "variations" that we refer to as Oracle SQL, Microsoft SQL, DB2 SQL, and so forth. The world really hasn't changed much.

DBMS Tools

Most DBMS vendors supply many secondary programs around their DBMS software. The authors of this book refer to all these programs with the generic term *tools*. These tools allow users to perform tasks such as the following:

- Generate reports
- Build standard data-entry and data-retrieval screens
- Process database data in text documents or in spreadsheets
- Administer the database

Database Applications

Database applications are application programs that use an underlying database to store their data. Examples of such database applications are screen- and menu-driven data-entry programs, spreadsheets, report generators, and so on.

Database applications are often developed using development tools from the DBMS vendor. In fact, most of these development tools can be considered to be database applications themselves, because they typically use the database not only to store regular data, but also to store their application specifications. For example, consider tools such as Oracle JDeveloper, Oracle SQL Developer, and Oracle Application Express. With these examples we are entering the relational world, which is introduced in Section 1.4.

DBMS Terms Review

In this section, the following terms were introduced:

- Database
- Database management system (DBMS)
- Kernel
- Data dictionary
- Query language
- Tool
- Database application

1.4 Relational Database Management Systems

The theoretical foundation for a *relational database management system* (RDBMS) was laid out in 1970 by Ted Codd in his famous article "A Relational Model of Data for Large Shared Data Banks" (Codd, 1970). He derived his revolutionary ideas from classical components of mathematics: set theory, relational calculus, and relational algebra.

About ten years after Ted Codd published his article, around 1980, the first RDBMS systems aiming to translate Ted Codd's ideas into real products became commercially available. Among the first pioneering RDBMS vendors were Oracle and Ingres, followed a few years later by IBM with SQL/DS and DB2.

We won't go into great detail about this formal foundation for relational databases, but we do need to review the basics in order to explain the term *relational*. The essence of Ted Codd's ideas was two main requirements:

- Clearly distinguish the logical task (the *what*) from the physical task (the *how*) both while designing, developing, and using databases.
- Make sure that an RDBMS implementation fully takes care of the physical task, so the system users need to worry only about executing the logical task.

These ideas, regardless of how evident they seem to be nowadays, were quite revolutionary in the early 1970s. Most DBMS implementations in those days did not separate the logical and physical tasks at all; did not have a solid theoretical foundation of any kind; and offered their users many surprises, ad hoc solutions, and exceptions. Ted Codd's article started a revolution and radically changed the way people think about databases.

What makes a DBMS a *relational* DBMS? In other words: how can we determine how relational a DBMS is? To answer this question, we must visit the theoretical foundation of the relational model. Two important aspects of the relational model, relational data structures and relational operators, are discussed in Sections 1.5 and 1.6. After these two sections, we will address another question: how relational is your DBMS?

1.5 Relational Data Structures

This section introduces the most important relational data structures and concepts:

- Tables, columns, and rows
- The information principle
- Datatypes
- Keys
- Missing information and null values

Tables, Columns, and Rows

The central concept in relational data structures is the *table* or *relation* (from which the relational model derives its name). A table is defined as a set of *rows*, or *tuples* (pronounced like *couples*). The rows of a table share the same set of attributes; a row consists of a set of (`attribute name`; `attribute value`) pairs. All data in a relational database is represented as *column values* within table rows.

In summary, the basic relational data structures are as follows:

- A database, which is a set of tables
- A table, which is a set of rows
- A row, which is a set of column values

The definition of a row is a little imprecise. A row is not just a set of column values. A more precise definition would be as follows:

- A *row* is a set of ordered pairs, where each ordered pair consists of an attribute name with an associated attribute value.

For example, the following is a formal and precise way to represent a row from the DEPARTMENTS table:

```
{(deptno;40),(dname;HR),(location;Boston),(mgr;7839)}
```

This row represents department 40: the HR department in Boston, managed by employee 7839. It would become irritating to represent rows like this; therefore, this book will use less formal notations as much as possible. After all, the concept of tables, rows, and columns is rather intuitive.

In most cases, there is a rather straightforward one-to-one mapping between the entities of the data model and the tables in a relational database. The rows represent the occurrences of the corresponding entity, and the column headings of the table correspond with the attributes of that entity. See Figure 1-1 for an illustration of the DEPARTMENTS table.

Table: DEPARTMENTS

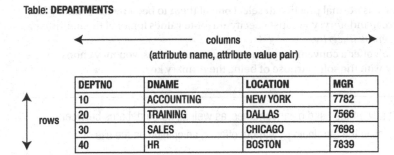

Figure 1-1. *The DEPARTMENTS table*

The Information Principle

The only way you can associate data in a relational database is by comparing column values. This principle, known as the *information principle*, is applied very strictly, and it is at the heart of the term *relational*.

An important property of relational datasets is the fact that the order of their elements is meaningless. Therefore, the order of the rows in any relational table is meaningless, too, and the order of columns is also meaningless.

Because this is both very fundamental and important, let's rephrase this in another way: in a relational database, there are no pointers to represent relationships. For example, the fact that an employee works for a specific department can be derived only from the two corresponding tables by comparing column values in, for example, the two department number columns. In other words, for every retrieval command, you must explicitly specify which columns must be compared. As a consequence, the flexibility to formulate ad hoc queries in a relational database has no limits. The flip side of the coin is the risk of (mental) errors and the problem of the correctness of your results. Nearly every SQL query will return a result (as long as you don't make syntax errors), but determining whether it is really the answer to the question you had in mind is up to you.

Datatypes

One of the tasks during data modeling is to decide which values are allowed for each attribute. You could allow only numbers in a certain column, or allow only dates or text. You can impose additional restrictions, such as by allowing only positive integers or text of a certain maximum length.

A set of allowed attribute values is sometimes referred to as a *domain*. Another common term is *datatype* (or simply *type*). Each attribute is defined to be of a certain type. This can be a standard (built-in) type or a user-defined type.

Keys

Each relational table must have at least one *candidate key*. A candidate key consists of an attribute (or attribute combination) that uniquely identifies each row in that table, with one additional important property: as soon as you remove any attribute from this candidate key attribute combination, the property of unique identification is gone. In other words, a table cannot contain two rows with the same candidate key values at any time and still maintain row uniqueness.

For example, the attribute combination course CODE and BEGINDATE is a candidate key for a table containing information about course offerings. If you remove the BEGINDATE attribute, the remaining course CODE attribute is not a candidate key anymore; otherwise, you could offer courses only once. If you remove the course CODE attribute, the remaining BEGINDATE attribute is not a candidate key anymore; otherwise, you would never be able to schedule two different courses to start on the same day.

In case a table has multiple candidate keys, it is normal practice to select one of them to become the *primary key*. All components (attributes) of a primary key are mandatory; you must specify attribute values for all of them. Primary keys enforce a very important table constraint: *entity integrity*.

Sometimes, the set of candidate keys doesn't offer a convenient primary key. In such cases, you may choose a *surrogate key* by adding a meaningless attribute with the sole purpose of being the primary key.

___

■ **Note** The use of surrogate keys comes with advantages and disadvantages, as well as fierce debates between database experts. The intent of this section is to explain the terminology, without offering an opinion on the use of surrogate keys.

___

A relational table can also have one or more *foreign keys*. Foreign key constraints are *subset requirements*; the foreign key values must always be a subset of a corresponding set of primary key values. Some typical examples of foreign key constraints are that an employee can work for only an existing department and can report to only an existing manager. Foreign keys implement *referential integrity* in a relational database.

Missing Information and Null Values

A relational DBMS is supposed to treat *missing information* in a systematic and context-insensitive manner. If a value is missing for a specific attribute of a row, it is not always possible to decide whether a certain condition evaluates to *true* or *false*. Missing information is represented by *null values* in the relational world.

The term *null value* is actually misleading, because it does not represent a value; it represents the fact that a value is missing. For example, *null marker* would be more appropriate. However, null value is the term most commonly used, so this book uses that terminology. Figure 1-2 shows how null values appear in a partial listing of the EMPLOYEES table.

Table: EMPLOYEES

EMPNO	ENAME	MSAL	COMM
7369	SMITH	800	
7499	ALLEN	1600	300
7521	WARD	1250	500
7566	JONES	2975	

Figure 1-2. Nulls represent missing values

Null values imply the need for a *three-valued logic*, such as implemented (more or less) in the SQL language. The third logical value is *unknown*.

___

■ **Note** Null values have had strong opponents and defenders. For example, Chris Date is a well-known opponent of null values and three-valued logic. His articles about this subject are highly readable, entertaining, and clarifying.

___

Constraint Checking

Although most RDBMS vendors support integrity constraint checking in the database these days (Oracle implemented this feature a number of years ago), it is sometimes also desirable to implement constraint checking in client-side database applications. Suppose you have a network between a client-side data-entry application and the database, and the network connection is a bottleneck. In that case, client-side constraint checking probably results in much better response times, because there is no need to access the database each time to check the constraints. Code-generating tools typically allow you to specify whether constraints should be enforced at the database side, the client side, or both sides.

■ **Caution** If you implement certain constraints in your client-side applications only, you risk database users bypassing the corresponding constraint checks by using alternative ways to connect to the database.

Predicates and Propositions

To finish this section about relational data structures, there is another interesting way to look at tables and rows in a relational database from a completely different angle, as introduced by Hugh Darwen. This approach is more advanced than the other topics addressed in this chapter, so you might want to revisit this section later.

You can associate each relational table with a table predicate and all rows of a table with corresponding propositions. *Predicates* are logical expressions, typically containing free variables, which evaluate to true or false. For example, this is a predicate:

- There is a course with title T and duration D, price P, frequency F, and a maximum number of attendees M.

If we replace the five variables in this predicate (T, D, P, F, and M) with actual values, the result is a *proposition*. In logic, a proposition is a predicate without free variables; in other words, a proposition is always true or false. This means that you can consider the rows of a relational table as the set of all propositions that evaluate to true.

Relational Data Structure Terms Review

In this section, the following terms were introduced:

- Tables (or relations)

- Rows (or tuples)

- Columns and domains

- Candidate, primary, and foreign keys

- Integrity checking at the database level

- Missing information, null values, and three-valued logic

- Predicates and propositions

1.6 Relational Operators

To manipulate data, you need *operators* that can be applied to that data. Multiplication and addition are typical examples of operators in mathematics; you specify two numbers as input, and the operator produces one output value as a result. Multiplication and addition are examples of *closed operators*, because they produce "things" of the same type you provided as input (numbers). For example, for integers, addition is closed. Add any two integers, and you get another integer. Try it—you can't find two integers that add up to a noninteger. However, division over the integers is *not* closed; for example, 1 divided by 2 is not an integer. Closure is a nice operator property, because it allows you to (re)use the operator results as input for a next operator's operation.

In a database environment, you need operators to derive information from the data stored in the database. In an RDBMS environment, all operators should operate at a high *logical level*. This means, among other things, that they should *not* operate on individual rows, but rather on tables, and that the results of these operations should be tables, as well.

Because tables are defined as sets of rows, relational operators should operate on sets. That's why some operators from the classical set theory—such as the union, the difference, and the intersection—also show up as relational operators. See Figure 1-3 for an illustration of these three set operators.

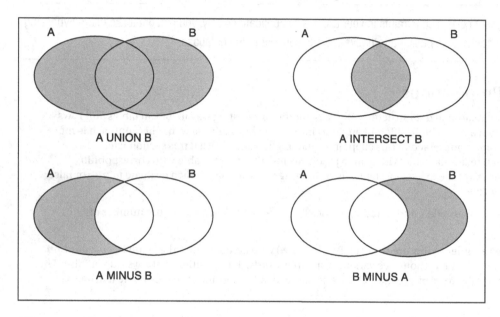

Figure 1-3. *The three most common set operators*

Along with these generic operators from set theory that can be applied to any sets, there are some additional relational operators specifically meant to operate on tables. You can define as many relational operators as you like, but, in general, most of these operators can be reduced to (or built with) a limited number of basic relational operators. The most common relational operators are the following:

- **Restriction:** This operator results in a subset of the rows of the input table, based on a specified restriction condition. This operator is also referred to as *selection*.

- **Projection:** This operator results in a table with fewer columns, based on a specified set of attributes you want to see in the result. In other words, the result is a vertical subset of the input table.

- **Union:** This operator merges the rows of two input tables into a single output table; the result contains all rows that occur in at least one of the input tables.

- **Intersection:** This operator also accepts two input tables; the result consists of all rows that occur in both input tables.

- **Minus:** Again, based on two input tables, this operator produces a result that consists of those rows that occur in the first table but do not occur in the second table. Note that this operator is not symmetric; A MINUS B is not the same as B MINUS A. This operator is also referred to as *difference*.

- **(Cartesian) product:** From two input tables, all possible combinations are generated by concatenating a row from the first table with a row from the second table.

- **(Natural) Join:** From two input tables, one result table is produced. The rows in the result consist of all combinations of a row from the first table with a row from the second table, provided both rows have identical values for the common attributes.

■ **Note** The natural join is an example of an operator that is not strictly necessary, because the effect of this operator can also be achieved by applying the combination of a Cartesian product, followed by a restriction (to check for identical values on the common attributes), and then followed by a projection to remove the duplicate columns.

1.7 How Relational Is My DBMS?

The term *relational* is used (and abused) by many DBMS vendors these days. If you want to determine whether these vendors speak the truth, you are faced with the problem that *relational* is a theoretical concept. There is no simple litmus test to check whether or not a DBMS is relational. Actually, to be honest, there are no pure relational DBMS implementations. That's why it is better to investigate the relational *degree* of a certain DBMS implementation.

This problem was identified by Ted Codd, too; that's why he published 12 rules (actually, there are 13 rules, if you count rule zero, as well) for relational DBMS systems in 1986. Since then, these rules have been an important yardstick for RDBMS vendors. Without going into too much detail, Codd's rules are listed here, with brief explanations:

1. **Rule Zero:** For any DBMS that claims to be relational, that system must be able to manage databases entirely through its relational capabilities.

2. **The Information Rule:** All information in a relational database is represented explicitly at the logical level and in exactly one way: by values in tables.

3. **Guaranteed Access Rule:** All data stored in a relational database is guaranteed to be logically accessible by resorting to a combination of a table name, primary key value, and column name.

4. **Systematic Treatment of Missing Information:** Null values (distinct from the empty string, blanks, and zero) are supported for representing missing information and inapplicable information in a systematic way, independent of the datatype.

5. **Dynamic Online Catalog:** The database description is represented at the logical level in the same way as ordinary data so that authorized users can apply the same relational language to its interrogation as they apply to the regular data.

6. **Comprehensive Data Sublanguage:** There must be at least support for one language whose statements are expressible by some well-defined syntax and are comprehensive in supporting all of the following: data definition, view definition, data manipulation, integrity constraints, authorization, and transaction boundaries handling.

7. **Updatable Views:** All views that are theoretically updatable are also updatable by the system.

8. **High-Level Insert, Update, and Delete:** The capability of handling a table or a view as a single operand applies not only to the retrieval of data, but also to the insertion, updating, and deletion of data.

9. **Physical Data Independence:** Application programs remain logically unimpaired whenever any changes are made in either storage representations or access methods.

10. **Logical Data Independence:** Application programs remain logically unimpaired when information-preserving changes that theoretically permit unimpairment are made to the base tables.

11. **Integrity Independence:** Integrity constraints must be definable in the relational data sublanguage and storable in the catalog, not in the application programs.

12. **Distribution Independence:** Application programs remain logically unimpaired when data distribution is first introduced or when data is redistributed.

13. **The Nonsubversion Rule:** If a relational system also supports a low-level language, that low-level language cannot be used to subvert or bypass the integrity rules and constraints expressed in the higher-level language.

Rule 6: Comprehensive Data Sublanguage refers to transactions. Without going into too much detail here, a *transaction* is defined as a number of changes that should be treated by the DBMS as a single unit of work; a transaction should always succeed or fail completely. For further reading, please refer to *Oracle Insights: Tales of the Oak Table* by Dave Ensor (Apress, 2004), especially Chapter 1.

1.8 The Oracle Software Environment

Oracle Corporation has its headquarters in Redwood Shores, California. It was founded in 1977, and it was (in 1979) the first vendor to offer a commercial RDBMS.

The Oracle software environment is available for many different platforms, ranging from personal computers (PCs) to large mainframes and massive parallel processing (MPP) systems. This is one of the unique selling points of Oracle: it guarantees a high degree of independence from hardware vendors, as well as various system growth scenarios, without losing the benefits of earlier investments, and it offers extensive transport and communication possibilities in heterogeneous environments.

The Oracle software environment has many components and bundling options. The core component is the DBMS itself: the *kernel*. The kernel has many important tasks, such as handling all physical data transport between memory and external storage, managing concurrency, and providing transaction isolation. Moreover, the kernel ensures that all stored data is represented at the logical level as relational tables. An important component of the kernel is the *optimizer*, which decides how to access the physical data structures in a time-efficient way and which algorithms to use to produce the results of your SQL commands.

Application programs and users can communicate with the kernel by using the SQL language, the main topic of this book. Oracle SQL is an almost fully complete implementation of the ANSI/ISO/IEC SQL:2011 standard. Oracle plays an important role in the SQL standardization process and has done so for many years.

Oracle also provides many tools with its DBMS, to render working with the DBMS more efficient and pleasurable. Figure 1-4 illustrates the cooperation of these tools with the Oracle database, clearly showing the central role of the SQL language as the communication layer between the kernel and the tools, regardless of which tool is chosen.

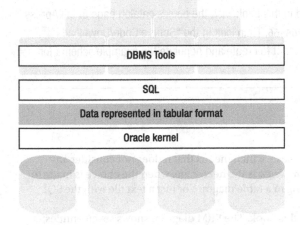

| DBMS Tools |
| SQL |
| Data represented in tabular format |
| Oracle kernel |

Figure 1-4. *Tools, SQL, and the Oracle database*

■ **Note** Besides tools enabling you to build (or generate) application programs, Oracle also sells many ready-to-use application programs, such as the Oracle E-Business Suite and PeopleSoft Enterprise.

The following are examples of Oracle software components:

- **SQL*Plus and SQL Developer:** These two tools stay the closest to the SQL language and are ideal for interactive, ad hoc SQL statement execution and database access. These are the tools we will mainly use in this book. SQL*Plus is a command line tool while SQL Developer is a graphical database administration and development tool.

■ **Note** Don't confuse SQL with SQL*Plus or SQL Developer. SQL is a *language*, and SQL*Plus and SQL Developer are *tools*.

- **Oracle Developer Suite:** This is an integrated set of development tools, comprised of the main components Oracle JDeveloper, Oracle Forms, and Oracle Reports.
- **Oracle Enterprise Manager:** This graphical user interface (GUI), which runs in a browser environment, supports Oracle database administrators in their daily work. Regular tasks like startup, shutdown, backup, recovery, maintenance, and performance management can be done with Enterprise Manager.

1.9 Case Tables

This section introduces the seven case tables used throughout this book for all examples and exercises. Appendix A provides a complete description of the tables and also contains some helpful diagrams and reports of the table contents. Chapters 3 and 7 contain the SQL commands to create the case tables (without and with constraints, respectively).

You need some understanding of the structure of the case tables to be able to write SQL statements against the contents of those tables. Otherwise, your SQL statements may be incorrect.

■ **Note** You can download a script to create the case tables used in this book. Visit the book's catalog page at the Apress website, at the following URL: http://www.apress.com/9781430265566. Then look in the "Source Code/Downloads" section on that page. You should see a download link containing a script to create and populate the example schema for the book.

The ERM Diagram of the Case

We start with an ERM diagram depicting the *logical design* of our case, which means that it does not consider any physical (implementation-dependent) circumstances. A *physical design* is the next stage, when the choice is made to implement the case in an RDBMS environment, typically resulting in a table diagram or just a text file with the SQL statements to create the tables and their constraints.

Figure 1-5 shows the ERM diagram for the example used in this book. The ERM diagram shows seven entities, represented by their names in rounded-corner boxes. To maintain readability, most attributes are omitted in the diagram; only the key attributes are displayed.

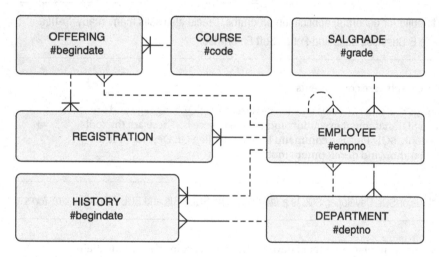

Figure 1-5. *ERM diagram of the case*

We have several relationships between these entities. The ten crow's feet connectors in the diagram represent one-to-many relationships. Each relationship can be read in two directions. For example, the relationship between OFFERING and REGISTRATION should be interpreted as follows:

- Each *registration* is always for exactly one course *offering*.

- A course *offering* may have zero, one, or more *registrations*.

Course offerings without registrations are allowed. All one-to-many relationships in our case have this property, which is indicated in this type of diagram with a dotted line at the optional side of the relationship.

Notice that we have two different relationships between EMPLOYEE and DEPARTMENT: each employee works for precisely one department, and each employee can be the manager of zero, one, or more departments. The EMPLOYEE entity also shows a *recursive relationship* (a relationship of an entity with itself) that implements the hierarchy within the company.

Each entity in the ERM diagram has a *unique identifier*, allowing us to uniquely identify all occurrences of the corresponding entities. This may be a single attribute (for example, EMPNO for the EMPLOYEE entity) or a combination of attributes, optionally combined with relationships. Each attribute that is part of a unique identifier is preceded with a hash symbol (#); relationships that are part of a unique identifier are denoted with a small crossbar. For example, the unique identifier of the OFFERING entity consists of a combination of the BEGINDATE attribute and the relationship with the COURSE entity, and the unique identifier of the entity REGISTRATION consists of the two relationships to the EMPLOYEE and OFFERING entities. By the way, entities like REGISTRATION are often referred to as *intersection entities*; REGISTRATION effectively implements a many-to-many relationship between EMPLOYEE and OFFERING.

An ERM diagram can be transformed into a relational table design with the following steps:

1. Each entity becomes a table.

2. Each attribute becomes a column.

3. Each relationship is transformed into a foreign key (FK) constraint at the crow's foot side.

4. Each unique identifier becomes a component of the primary key (PK).

This mapping results in seven tables: EMPLOYEES, DEPARTMENTS, SALGRADES, COURSES, OFFERINGS, REGISTRATION, and HISTORY.

Table Descriptions

Tables 1-1 through 1-7 describe the structures of the case tables.

Table 1-1. The EMPLOYEES Table

Column	Description	Key
EMPNO	Number, unique for every employee	PK
ENAME	Last name	--
INIT	Initials (without punctuation)	--
JOB	Job description of the employee	--
MGR	The employee number of the employee's manager	FK
BDATE	Date of birth	--
MSAL	Monthly salary (excluding bonus or commission)	--
COMM	Commission component of the yearly salary (only relevant for sales reps)	--
DEPTNO	The number of the department for which the employee works	FK

Table 1-2. The DEPARTMENTS Table

Column	Description	Key
DEPTNO	Unique department number	PK
DNAME	Department name	--
LOCATION	Department location (city)	--
MGR	Employee number of the manager of the department	FK

19

Table 1-3. *The SALGRADES Table*

Column	Description	Key
GRADE	Unique salary grade number	PK
LOWERLIMIT	Lowest salary that belongs to the grade	--
UPPERLIMIT	Highest salary that belongs to the grade	--
BONUS	Optional (tax-free) bonus on top of the monthly salary	--

Table 1-4. *The COURSES Table*

Column	Description	Key
CODE	Course code; unique for each course	PK
DESCRIPTION	Short description of the course contents	--
CATEGORY	Course type indicator (allowed values: GEN, BLD, and DSG)	--
DURATION	Course duration, expressed in days	--

Table 1-5. *The OFFERINGS Table*

Column	Description	Key
COURSE	Course code	PK, FK
BEGINDATE	Start date of the course offering	PK
TRAINER	Employee number of the employee teaching the course	FK
LOCATION	Location (city) where the course is offered	--

Table 1-6. *The REGISTRATIONS Table*

Column	Description	Key
ATTENDEE	Employee number of the course attendee	PK, FK1
COURSE	Course code	PK, FK2
BEGINDATE	Start date of the course offering	PK, FK2
EVALUATION	Evaluation of the course by the attendee (positive integer on the scale 1–5)	--

Table 1-7. *The HISTORY Table*

Column	Description	Key
EMPNO	Employee number	PK, FK1
BEGINYEAR	Year component (4 digits) of BEGINDATE	--
BEGINDATE	Begin date of the time interval	PK
ENDDATE	End date of the time interval	--
DEPTNO	The number of the department worked for during the interval	FK2
MSAL	Monthly salary during the interval	--
COMMENTS	Allows for free text style comments	--

In the description of the EMPLOYEES table, the COMM column deserves some special attention. This commission attribute is relevant only for sales representatives, and therefore contains structurally missing information (for all other employees). We could have created a separate SALESREPS table (with two columns: EMPNO and COMM) to avoid this problem, but for the purpose of this book, the table structure is kept simple.

The structure of the DEPARTMENTS table is straightforward. Note the two foreign key constraints between this table and the EMPLOYEES table: an employee can "work for" a department or "be the manager" of a department. Note also that we don't insist that the manager of a department actually works for that department, and it is not forbidden for any employee to manage more than one department.

The salary grades in the SALGRADES table do not overlap, although in salary systems in the real world, most grades are overlapping. In this table, we are keeping things simple. This way, every salary always falls into exactly one grade. Moreover, the actual monetary unit (currency) for salaries, commission, and bonuses is left undefined. The optional tax-free bonus is paid monthly, just like the regular monthly salaries.

In the COURSES table, three CATEGORY values are allowed:

- GEN (general), for introductory courses

- BLD (build), for building applications

- DSG (design), for system analysis and design

This means that these three values are the only values allowed for the CATEGORY column; this is an example of an *attribute constraint* (sometimes referred to as a *check constraint*). This would also have been an opportunity to design an additional entity (and thus another relational table) to implement course types. In that case, the CATEGORY column would have become a foreign key to this additional table. But again, simplicity is the main goal for this set of case tables.

In all database systems, you need procedures to describe how to handle *historical data* in an information system. This is a very important—and, in practice, far from trivial—component of system design. In our case tables, it is particularly interesting to consider course offerings and course registrations in this respect.

If a scheduled course offering is canceled at some point in time (for example, due to lack of registrations), the course offering is *not* removed from the OFFERINGS table, for statistical/historical reasons. Therefore, it is possible that the TRAINER and/or LOCATION columns are left empty; these two attributes are (of course) relevant only as soon as a scheduled course is going to happen. By the way, this brings up the valid question of whether scheduled course offerings and "real" course offerings might be two different entities. Again, this is an opportunity to end up with more tables; and again, simplicity is the main goal here.

Course *registrations* are considered synonymous with *course attendance* in our example database. This becomes obvious from the EVALUATION column in the REGISTRATIONS table, where the attendee's appreciation of the course is stored at the end of the course, expressed on a scale from 1 to 5; the meaning of these numbers ranges from bad (1) to excellent (5). In case a registration is canceled before a course takes place, we remove the corresponding row from the REGISTRATIONS table. In other words, if the BEGINDATE value of a course registration falls in the past, this means (by definition) that the corresponding course offering took place and was attended.

The HISTORY table maintains information about the working history of all employees. More specifically, it holds data about the departments they have been working for and the salaries they made over the years, starting from the day they were hired. Every change of department and/or monthly salary is recorded in this table. The current values for DEPTNO and MSAL can be stored in this table, too, by keeping the ENDDATE attribute empty until the next change. The COMMENTS column offers room for free text comments, for example, to justify or clarify certain changes.

CHAPTER 2

■ ■ ■

Introduction to SQL and SQL Developer

This chapter provides an introduction to the SQL language and one of two tools for working with it. Section 2.1 presents a high-level overview of the SQL language, which will give you an idea of the capabilities of this language. Then some important basic concepts of the SQL language are introduced in Section 2.2, such as constants, literals, variables, expressions, conditions, functions, operators, operands, and so on. Finally, in Section 2.3, this chapter provides a tour of SQL Developer, the main tool we recommend using to learn the SQL language. In order to maximize the benefits of any tool, you first must learn how to use it and to identify the main features available. In Chapter 11 the old, but still widely used SQL*Plus tool is explained in great detail. Even though many of the examples in this book are shown using SQL*Plus, feel free to use whichever tool you find most convenient.

This is the first chapter with real SQL statement examples. It thus would be beneficial for you to have access to an Oracle database and a schema with the seven case tables introduced in Chapter 1 and described in detail in Appendix A. You can find the scripts to create that schema in the download hosted from this book's catalog page or the Source Code page on the Apress website.

We assume that Oracle is running; database (instance) startup and shutdown are normally tasks of a system or database administrator. Specific startup and shutdown procedures might be in place in your environment. However, if you are working with a stand-alone Oracle environment, and you have enough privileges, you can try the SQL*Plus STARTUP command or use the GUI offered by Oracle Enterprise Manager to start up the database.

2.1 Overview of SQL

SQL (the abbreviation stands for Structured Query Language) is a language you can use in (at least) two different ways: *interactively* or *embedded*. Using SQL interactively means that you enter SQL commands via a keyboard, and you get the command results displayed on a terminal or computer screen. Using embedded SQL involves incorporating SQL commands within a program in a different programming language (such as Java or C). This book deals solely with interactive SQL usage.

Although SQL is called a *query language*, its possibilities go far beyond simply data retrieval. Normally, the SQL language is divided into the following four command categories:

- Data definition (Data Definition Language, or DDL)
- Data manipulation (Data Manipulation Language, or DML)
- Retrieval
- Security and authorization (Data Control Language, or DCL)

Data Definition

The SQL data definition commands allow you to create, modify, and remove components of a database structure. Typical database structure components are tables, views, indexes, constraints, synonyms, sequences, and so on. Chapter 1 introduced tables, columns, and constraints; other database object types (such as views, indexes, synonyms, and sequences) will be introduced in later chapters.

Almost all SQL data definition commands start with one of the following three keywords:

- CREATE, to create a new database object

- ALTER, to change an aspect of the structure of an existing database object

- DROP, to drop (remove) a database object

For example, with the CREATE VIEW command, you can create views. With the ALTER TABLE command, you can change the structure of a table (for example by adding, renaming, or dropping a column). With the DROP INDEX command, you can drop an index.

One of the strengths of an RDBMS is the fact that you can change the structure of a table without needing to change anything in your existing database application programs. For example, you can easily add a column or change its width with the ALTER TABLE command. In modern DBMSs such as Oracle, you can even do this while other database users or applications are connected and working on the database—like changing the wheels of a train at full speed. This property of an RDBMS is known as *logical data independence* (see Ted Codd's rules, discussed in Chapter 1).

Data definition is covered in more detail in Chapters 3 and 7.

Data Manipulation and Transactions

Just as SQL data definition commands allow you to change the *structure* of a database, SQL data manipulation commands allow you to change the *contents* of your database. For this purpose, SQL offers three basic data manipulation commands:

- INSERT, to add rows to a table

- UPDATE, to change column values of existing rows

- DELETE, to remove rows from a table

You can add rows to a table with the INSERT command in two ways. One way is to add rows one by one by specifying a list of column values in the VALUES clause of the INSERT statement. The other is to add one or more rows to a table based on a selection (and manipulation) of existing data in the database (called a *subquery*).

■ **Note**   You can also load data into an Oracle database with various tools specifically developed for this purpose—such as Data Pump since Oracle Database 10*g*, Export and Import in previous Oracle releases, and SQL*Loader. These tools are often used for high-volume data loads.

Data manipulation commands are always treated as being part of a *transaction*. This means (among other things) that all database changes caused by SQL data manipulation commands get a pending status until you confirm (commit) or cancel (roll back) the transaction. No one (except the transaction itself) can see the pending changes of a transaction before it is committed. That's why a transaction is often labeled *atomic*: it is impossible for other database users to see parts of a transaction in the database. It is "all or nothing," no matter how many DML operations the transaction comprises.

SQL offers two commands to control your transactions explicitly:

- COMMIT, to confirm all pending changes of the current transaction

- ROLLBACK, to cancel all pending changes and restore the original situation

Sometimes, transactions are committed implicitly; that is, without any explicit request from a user. For example, every data definition command (like CREATE, DROP, TRUNCATE etc.) implicitly commits your current transaction. Note the following important differences between data manipulation and data definition:

- DELETE *empties* a table; DROP *removes* a table. TRUNCATE allows you to delete all the rows in a table in an efficient (but irrevocable) way.

- UPDATE changes the *contents* of a table; ALTER changes its *structure*.

- You can undo the consequences of data manipulation with ROLLBACK; data definition commands are irrevocable.

Chapter 6 will revisit data manipulation in more detail. Chapter 7 discusses the TRUNCATE command, which is considered a data definition command.

Retrieval

The only SQL command used to query database data is SELECT. This command acts at the set (or table) level, and always produces a set (or table) as its result. If a certain query returns exactly one row, or no rows at all, the result is still a set: a table with one row or the empty table, respectively.

The SELECT command (as defined in the ANSI/ISO SQL standard) has six main components, which implement all SQL retrieval. Figure 2-1 shows a diagram with these six main components of the SELECT command.

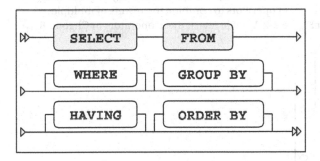

Figure 2-1. *The six main components of the SELECT command*

The lines in this diagram represent all possibilities of the SELECT command, like a railroad map. You can deduce the following three syntax rules from Figure 2-1:

- The order of these six command components is fixed.

- The SELECT and FROM components are mandatory.

- The remaining components (WHERE, GROUP BY, HAVING, and ORDER BY) are optional.

Table 2-1 gives a high-level description of the roles of these six components of the SELECT command.

Table 2-1. *The Six Main Components of the SELECT Command*

Component	Description
FROM	Which table(s) is (are) needed for retrieval?
WHERE	What is the condition to filter the rows?
GROUP BY	How should the rows be grouped/aggregated?
HAVING	What is the condition to filter the aggregated groups?
SELECT	Which columns do you want to see in the result?
ORDER BY	In which order do you want to see the resulting rows?

■ **Tip** The order of the SELECT command components as displayed in Table 2-1 is also a good order to think about them when writing SQL statements. Notice that the SELECT clause is almost the last one.

Components of the SELECT command implement three of the relational operators introduced in Chapter 1 (Section 1.6) as follows:

- The SELECT component acts as the *projection* operator.

- The FROM component implements the *join* operator.

- The *restriction* operator corresponds to the WHERE component.

Now that we are on the subject of relational operators, note that the *union*, *intersection*, and *difference* (*minus*) operators are also implemented in SQL. You can use these three set operators to combine the results of multiple SELECT commands into a single result table, as illustrated in Figure 2-2. We will revisit these operators in Chapter 8.

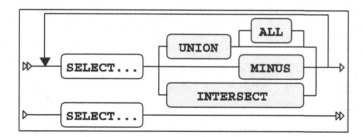

Figure 2-2. *A SQL set operators syntax diagram*

Security

SQL offers several commands to implement data security and to restrict data access.

First of all, access to the database must be defined. User authorization is implemented by providing database users a login name and a password, together with some database-wide privileges. These are the most important commands in this area:

- CREATE USER, to define new database users

- ALTER USER, to change properties (privileges and passwords) of existing database users

- DROP USER, to remove user definitions from the database

Privileges and Roles

If users are authorized to access the database, you can implement fine-grained data access by granting specific *privileges*. The Oracle DBMS offers two types of privileges: system privileges and object privileges.

System privileges pertain to the right to perform certain (nonobject-related) actions; for example, you can have the CREATE SESSION privilege (allows you to log on to the database) and the CREATE TABLE privilege. Oracle supports approximately 190 different system privileges.

Object privileges involve the right to access a specific database object in a specific way; for example, the right to issue SELECT, INSERT, and UPDATE commands against the EMPLOYEES table. Table 2-2 lists the most important Oracle object privileges.

Table 2-2. *Important Oracle Object Privileges*

Object Privilege	Allowable Action
ALTER	Change the table structure (with ALTER TABLE)
DELETE	Delete rows
EXECUTE	Execute stored functions or procedures
FLASHBACK	Go back in time (with FLASHBACK TABLE)
INDEX	Create indexes on the table
INSERT	Insert new rows
REFERENCES	Create foreign key constraints to the table
SELECT	Query the table (or view)
UPDATE	Change column values of existing rows

■ **Note**   Creating users, granting and revoking system privileges are typically tasks for database administrators. See *Oracle SQL Reference*, part of the official documentation set for the Oracle Database, for more details on user creation and system and object privileges.

The Oracle DBMS allows you to group privileges into *roles*. Roles make user management much easier, more flexible, and also more manageable. You will need to be given the 'create role' privilege by your DBA. The following are the corresponding SQL commands used to administer these privileges and roles:

- GRANT, to grant certain privileges or roles to users or roles

- REVOKE, to revoke certain privileges or roles from users or roles

A typical scenario is the following:

```
CREATE ROLE <role name>
GRANT privileges TO <role name>
GRANT <role name> TO user(s)
```

The first step creates a new (empty) role. The second step (which can be repeated as many times as you like) populates the role with a mix of object and system privileges. The third step grants the role (and thereby all its privileges) to a user in a single step.

Roles have several useful and powerful properties:

- Roles are dynamic; further changes to the role contents automatically affect all users previously granted that role.

- Roles can be enabled or disabled during a session.

- You can protect roles with a password. In that case, only users who know the role password can enable the role.

- The most important advantage of roles is their manageability.

GRANT and REVOKE

Each table has an owner, the user who created the table. Table owners are able to grant privileges on their tables to other database users using the GRANT command. As soon as you create a table, you implicitly get all object privileges on that table, WITH GRANT OPTION, as illustrated in Figure 2-3, which shows the syntax of the GRANT command.

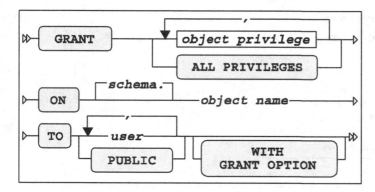

Figure 2-3. *The GRANT command syntax diagram*

■ **Note** System privileges and roles are not considered in Figure 2-3, so the syntax diagram is incomplete.

Here are some comments about the GRANT command:

- Table owners cannot grant the right to remove a table (DROP TABLE) to other database users. Note, however, that Oracle supports a (rather dangerous) DROP ANY TABLE system privilege.

- If you want to grant all object privileges to someone else, you can use the keyword ALL (see Figure 2-3). (Instead of ALL PRIVILEGES, the Oracle DBMS also allows you to specify ALL.)

- With a single GRANT command, you can grant privileges to a single user, a list of users, a role, or all database users. You can address all database users with the pseudo-user PUBLIC (see Figure 2-3).

- The UPDATE privilege supports an optional refinement: this privilege can also be granted for specific columns, by specifying column names between parentheses.

- In principle, there is no difference between tables and views when granting object privileges; however, the privileges ALTER, INDEX, and REFERENCES are meaningless in the context of views.

- The GRANT OPTION not only grants certain object privileges, but also grants the right to the grantee to spread these privileges further.

The counterpart of GRANT is the REVOKE command. Figure 2-4 shows the syntax diagram for REVOKE.

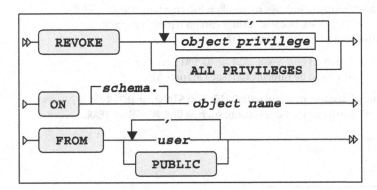

Figure 2-4. *The REVOKE command syntax diagram*

Besides the two standard SQL commands mentioned in this section (GRANT and REVOKE), Oracle supports several additional commands in the security and data access area; for example, to influence the locking behavior of the DBMS, to implement auditing, and to set up more detailed user authorization.

2.2 Basic SQL Concepts and Terminology

This section discusses the following topics:

- Constants (literals)

- Variables

- Operators, operands, conditions, and expressions

- Functions

- Database object names

- Comments

- Reserved words

Constants (Literals)

A *constant* (or *literal*) is something with a fixed value. We distinguish numbers (numeric constants) and text (alphanumeric constants). In database jargon, alphanumeric constants are also referred to as *strings*.

In the SQL language, alphanumeric constants (strings) must be placed between *single quotation marks* (quotes). Numbers are also relatively straightforward in SQL; however, don't put them between quotes or they will be interpreted as strings. If you like, you can explicitly indicate that you want SQL to interpret numeric values as *floating point* numbers by adding the suffixes f or d to indicate single (float) or double precision, respectively. Be careful with the decimal period and group separators (commas) in numbers, because the correct interpretation of these characters depends on the value of a session parameter (NLS_NUMERIC_CHARACTERS), and there are some cultural differences in this area.

In SQL, dates and time durations (intervals) are special cases. They are typically specified and represented as alphanumeric constants, but they need something else to distinguish them from regular strings. In other words, you must help the DBMS to interpret the strings correctly as date or time-interval constants. Probably the most straightforward (and elegant) method is to prefix the strings with a keyword (DATE, TIMESTAMP, or INTERVAL) and to adhere to a well-defined notation convention. (See the examples in Table 2-3 and the third option in the following list.) These are the three options to specify date and time-related constants in SQL:

- Specify them as alphanumeric constants (strings) and rely on implicit interpretation and conversion by the Oracle DBMS. This is dangerous, because things can go wrong if the actual format parameter for that session is different from the format of the string.

- Specify them as alphanumeric constants (strings) and use a CAST or TO_DATE conversion function to specify explicitly how the strings must be interpreted (see Chapter 5).

- Specify them as alphanumeric constants (strings), prefixed with DATE, TIMESTAMP, or INTERVAL. If you use INTERVAL, you also need a suffix to indicate a dimension, such as DAY, MONTH, or YEAR.

Table 2-3 shows examples of using SQL constants.

Table 2-3. *Examples of SQL Constants (Literals)*

Type	Example
Numeric	42 8.75 8.75F 132
Alphanumeric	'JOneS' 'GEN' '132'
Dates and intervals	DATE '2004-02-09' TIMESTAMP '2004-09-05 11.42.59.00000' INTERVAL '2' SECOND INTERVAL '1-3' YEAR TO MONTH

Note the subtle difference between 132 and '132'. The difference between numbers and strings becomes apparent when considering the operators they support. For example, numbers can be added or multiplied, but you cannot do that with strings. The only operator you can apply to strings is the concatenation operator.

In general, the SQL language is case-insensitive. However, there is one important exception: alphanumeric constants (strings) are case-sensitive. For example, 'JOneS' is not equal to 'Jones'. This is sometimes the explanation of getting the message "no rows selected" in cases where you were expecting to see rows in the result.

Variables

A *variable* is something that may have a varying value over time, or even an unknown value. A variable always has a name, so you can refer to it.

SQL supports two types of variables:

- **Column name variables:** The name of a column stays the same, but its value typically varies from row to row while scanning a table.

- **System variables:** These have nothing to do with tables; nevertheless, they can play an important role in SQL. They are commonly referred to as *pseudo columns*. See Table 2-4 for some examples of Oracle system variables.

Table 2-4. Examples of Oracle System Variables (Pseudo Columns)

Variable	Description
SYSDATE	The current system date in the database
CURRENT_DATE	The current date at the client application side
SYSTIMESTAMP	The system date and exact time, with time zone information
LOCALTIMESTAMP	The system date and exact time, with time zone information, at the client application side
USER	The name used to connect to the database

The difference between dates (and timestamps) at the *database* side and those at the *client application* side can be relevant if you are connected over a network connection with a database in a remote location.

Users commonly make mistakes by forgetting to include quotes in SQL statements. Consider the following SQL statement fragment:

```
...WHERE LOCATION = UTRECHT...
```

LOCATION and UTRECHT are both interpreted by Oracle as variable names (column names), although the following was probably the real intention:

```
...WHERE LOCATION = 'UTRECHT'...
```

Operators, Operands, Conditions, and Expressions

An *operator* does something. Operands are the "victims" of operations; that is, operands serve as input for operators. Sometimes, operators need only a single operand (in which case, they are also referred to as *monadic* operators), but most operators need two or more operands.

The SQL operators are divided in four categories, where the differentiating factor is the operand datatype:

- Arithmetic operators

- Alphanumeric operators

- Comparison operators

- Logical operators

Arithmetic Operators

The SQL language supports four arithmetic operators, as shown in Table 2-5.

Table 2-5. *SQL Arithmetic Operators*

Operator	Description
+	Addition
-	Subtraction
*	Multiplication
/	Division

You can apply arithmetic operators only on NUMBER values; however, there are some exceptions:

- If you subtract two DATE values, you get the difference between those two dates, expressed in days.

- You can add a DATE and an INTERVAL value, which results in another date.

- If you add a DATE and a NUMBER, the number is interpreted as an interval expressed in days.

The Alphanumeric Operator: Concatenation

SQL offers only one alphanumeric operator, allowing you to concatenate string expressions: ||. This modest number of operators is compensated for by the overwhelming number of alphanumeric *functions* in SQL, which are discussed in Chapter 5. For an example of the use of the concatenation operator, see Table 2-8, later in this chapter.

Comparison Operators

The comparison operators allow you to formulate conditions in SQL. Table 2-6 shows the comparison operators available in SQL.

Table 2-6. *SQL Comparison Operators*

Operator	Description
<	Less than
>	Greater than
=	Equal to
<=	Less than or equal to
>=	Greater than or equal to
<> or !=	Not equal to

Expressions with comparison operators are also referred to as *predicates* or *Boolean expressions*. These expressions evaluate to TRUE or FALSE. Sometimes, the outcome is UNKNOWN, such as when you have rows with missing information. We will revisit this topic in more detail in Chapter 4, when we discuss null values.

Logical Operators

SQL also offers three operators whose operands are conditions: the logical (or Boolean) operators. Table 2-7 lists these operators.

Table 2-7. *SQL Logical Operators*

Operator	Description
AND	Logical AND
OR	Logical OR (the *inclusive* OR)
NOT	Logical negation

Expressions

An *expression* is a well-formed string containing variables, constants, operators, or functions. Just like constants, expressions always have a certain datatype. See Table 2-8 for some examples of expressions.

Table 2-8. *SQL Expression Examples*

Expression	Datatype
3 + 4	Numeric
ENAME || ', ' || INIT	Alphanumeric
LOCATION = 'Utrecht'	Boolean
12*MSAL > 20000 AND COMM >= 100	Boolean
BDATE + INTERVAL '16' YEAR	Date
999	Numeric

The last example in Table 2-8 shows that the simplest expression is just a constant.

When SQL expressions get more complex, operator *precedence* can become an issue; in other words: what are the operator priority rules? Of course, SQL has some precedence rules. For example, arithmetic operators always have precedence over comparison operators, and comparison operators have precedence over logical operators. However, it is highly recommended that you use parentheses in your complex SQL expressions to force a certain expression evaluation order, just as you would do in regular mathematics.

Functions

Oracle has added a lot of functionality to the SQL standard in the area of *functions*. This is definitely one of the reasons why Oracle SQL is so powerful. You can recognize SQL functions by their signature: they have a name, followed by one or more arguments (between parentheses) in a comma-separated list. You can use functions in expressions, in the same way that you can use operators.

These are the six SQL function categories, based on their operand types:

- Numeric functions
- Alphanumeric functions
- Group functions
- Date functions
- Conversion functions
- Other functions

Table 2-9 shows some examples of SQL functions.

Table 2-9. *Examples of SQL Functions*

Function	Explanation
AVG(MSAL)	The average monthly salary
SQRT(16)	The square root of 16
LENGTH(INIT)	The number of characters in the INIT column value
LOWER(ENAME)	ENAME column value, in lowercase
SUBSTR(ENDDATE,4,3)	Three characters of the ENDDATE column value, from the fourth position

Oracle even allows you to create your own SQL functions by using the PL/SQL or Java languages. Chapter 5 will show a simple example of a user-defined function.

Database Object Naming

All objects in a database need *names*. This applies to tables, columns, views, indexes, synonyms, sequences, users, roles, constraints, functions, and so on. In general, to enhance the readability of your SQL code, it is highly recommended that you restrict yourself to using the characters A through Z, the digits 0 through 9, and optionally the underscore (_).

■ **Note**   In Oracle, object names are case-insensitive; that is, internally all database object names are converted to uppercase, regardless of how you enter those names.

You may use digits in database object names; however, database object names should always start with a letter. Oracle object names have a maximum length of 30 characters.

Database objects need *different* names to be able to distinguish them, obviously. To be more precise, database objects need unique names within their namespace. On the other hand, different database users may use the same names for their own objects if they like, because the owner/object name combination is used to uniquely identify an object in the database.

If you insist on creating your own object names in Oracle SQL using any characters you like (including, for example, spaces and other strange characters), and you also want your object names to be case-sensitive, you can include those names within double quotes. The only restriction that remains is the maximum name length: 30 characters. Using this "feature" is discouraged, because you will always need to include those names in double quotes again in every interactive SQL statement you want to execute against those objects. On the other hand, you can use this technique *in written applications* to prevent conflicts with reserved words, including reserved words of future DBMS versions not known to you at application development time. Actually, several Oracle database utilities use this technique under the hood for precisely this reason.

Comments

You can add *comments* to SQL commands in order to clarify their intent or to enhance their maintainability. In other words, you can add text that does not formally belong to the SQL statements themselves, and as such should be ignored by the Oracle DBMS. You can add such comments in two ways: between /* and */ or after two consecutive minus signs. Comments after two minus signs are implicitly ended by a newline character; comments between /* and */ can span multiple lines. See Listing 2-1 for two examples.

Listing 2-1. SQL Comments Examples

```
/* this text will be considered a comment,
   so the Oracle DBMS will ignore it ... */
-- and this text too, until the end of this line.
```

Listing 2-1 shows how you can add comments to *SQL commands*. Note that you can also add comments to *database objects* with the COMMENT command. See Chapter 7 for details.

Reserved Words

Just like any other language, SQL has a list of *reserved words*. These are words you are not allowed to use, for example, as database object names. If you insist on using a reserved word as an object name, you must enclose the name within double quotes, as explained earlier in the "Database Object Naming" section.

These are some examples of SQL reserved words: AND, CREATE, DROP, FROM, GRANT, HAVING, INDEX, INSERT, MODIFY, NOT, NULL, NUMBER, OR, ORDER, RENAME, REVOKE, SELECT, SYNONYM, SYSDATE, TABLE, UPDATE, USER, VALUES, VIEW, and WHERE.

■ **Tip** The Oracle data dictionary contains a V$RESERVED_WORDS view. You can check your object names against this view to avoid using reserved words.

See *Oracle SQL Reference* for more details about naming rules for database objects and a more complete listing of SQL reserved words.

2.3 Introduction to SQL Developer

SQL Developer is the graphical user interface (GUI) tool that Oracle supplies to query the database, explore objects, run reports, and run scripts. It runs on Windows, Linux, and Mac OSX. It can be used to access Oracle databases 9*i*, 10*g*, 11*g* and 12*c*, as well as other databases such as Times Ten, Microsoft Access, MySQL, and SQL Server.

Screenshots in the following pages come from SQL Developer 4.0.0.13.

SQL*Plus, which is the old, original tool for writing SQL and PL/SQL is explained in detail in Chapter 11.

Installing and Configuring SQL Developer

SQL Developer is included as part of Oracle Database 11*g* and 12*c*. You can also download it from the following URL—you need a free Oracle account to do the download.

```
http://www.oracle.com/technology/products/database/sql_developer/index.html
```

Once you save the downloaded zip file and extract it to a directory of your own choice, just double click sqldeveloper.exe to start SQL Developer.

■ **Note** SQL Developer for Windows does not create any menu shortcuts or icons on the desktop. You need to create these manually if you want them. Create a desktop shortcut by right clicking on the file and selecting Send To ➤ Desktop (create shortcut). SQL Developer also does not create any registry entries. Thus, uninstalling SQL Developer is as simple as deleting the SQL Developer directory that you created when you unpacked the archive.

One of the first tasks that you may be prompted to do when you start SQL Developer for the first time is to locate the Java Development Kit (JDK). If you selected the option to download SQL Developer with the JDK, then java.exe will be included. In this example, SQL Developer is installed in C:\oracle\product\sqldeveloper and the location of the JDK will be in the subdirectory structure show in Figure 2-5.

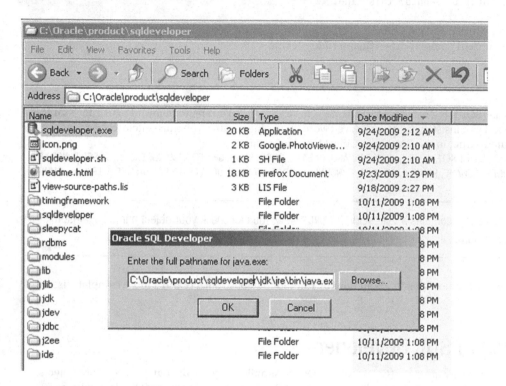

Figure 2-5. *SQL Developer java.exe location*

When SQL Developer first starts, the Start Page shown in Figure 2-6 opens. This page includes links to documentation, to tutorials, and to the SQL Developer Forum.

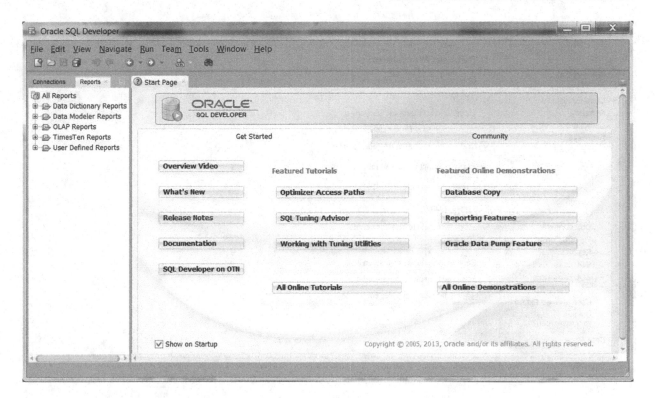

Figure 2-6. *The SQL Developer start page*

■ **Note** As SQL Developer is a non-licensed (free) product, support is not obtained through the MyOracleSupport site, formerly known as Metalink. The SQL Developer Forum on Oracle Technet (`http://sqldeveloper.oracle.com/`) is the location for support and questions. When you have questions or issues, look there for assistance.

There is not a great deal of basic configuration for SQL Developer that you need to do at this time. The "out of the box" settings are fairly good for most users, but there are a couple of items that are worth considering: setting the default script file location and enabling the zebra striped output.

It is usually a good idea to specify the default location for saving and running scripts. One minor annoyance with SQL Developer is that the settings for the file locations are spread among several different dialogs. Select Tools ➤ Preferences to bring up the Preferences dialog box, as shown in Figure 2-7. To set the Script location, select Databases ➤ Worksheet and enter the preferred location for scripts in the "Select default path to look for scripts" box.

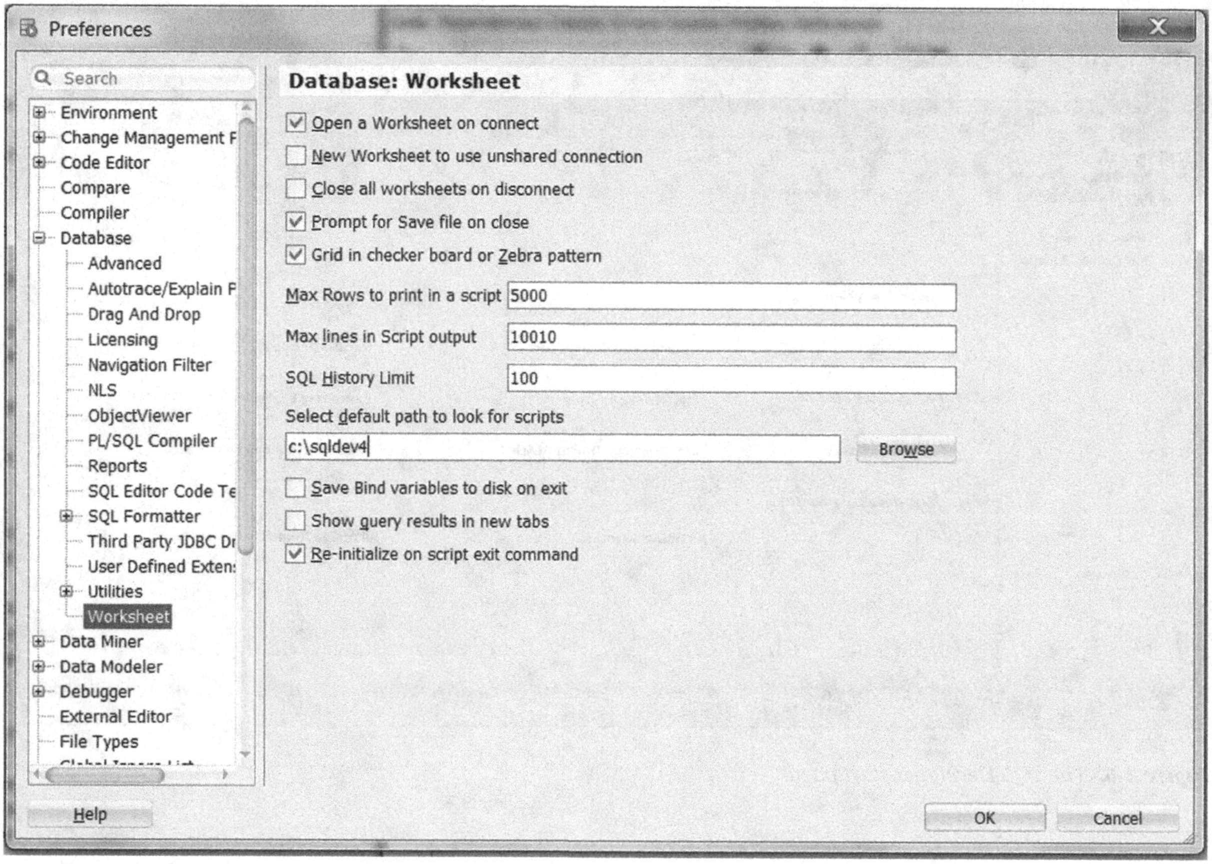

Figure 2-7. *Setting the default script location*

A second task might be to ensure readable output by turning on the option "Grid in checker board or Zebra pattern." Every second line will now appear in a slightly darker tone for better readability as shown here.

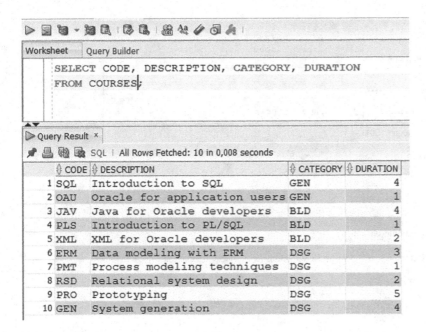

Figure 2-8. *Zebra striped output*

Connecting to a Database

Unlike SQL*Plus, you do not have to enter your username, password, and database name every time you connect. With SQL Developer you can have multiple connections that can be saved and organized. If you are using multiple accounts for a single database, you can have a connection created for each of those accounts.

■ **Note** You can have multiple connections open at one time, but be careful when one of those connections is to a production database. Two common problems leading to the need for database recovery are when a table is accidently dropped and when data is mistakenly modified in production. Hint: Change the background color of your production connections to an easily distinguishable color.

To create a new connection, click on the Connections tab to make it active and then click on the large green cross (+) in the upper left corner. You can also right click on the Connections icon and select New Connection. This will bring up the New / Select Database Connection dialog as seen in Figure 2-9. In this example, the connection is the book user to a local database.

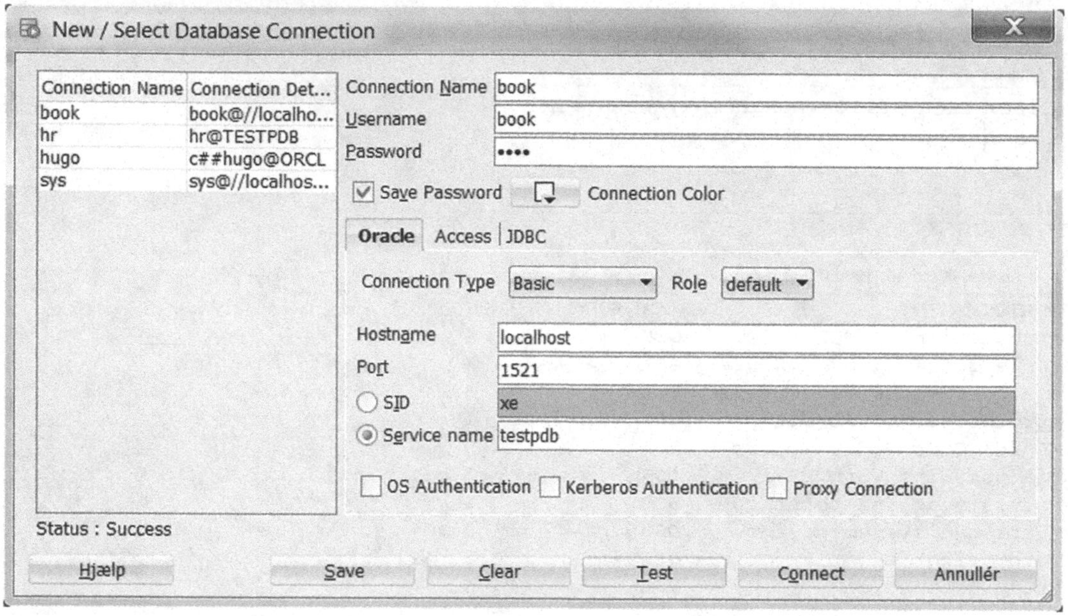

Figure 2-9. *Creating a database connection*

To organize your connections, you can create folders and add them to folders. You could organize by database name, type, and location, or any meaningful criteria. There is no option to create a new folder, so you add a connection to a new folder. Right click on the connection, select Add to Folder, and if there aren't any folders defined you will only have the New Folder option. Enter a folder name in the dialog box. If folders have already been defined, you have the option to add to an existing folder or create a new folder. For existing folders, you can drag and drop the connection onto a folder name to assign it to that folder.

Exploring Objects

SQL Developer includes an Object Browser, which enables you to see the tables, indexes, procedures, and so on that you own and have access to query or execute. You activate the object browser simply by clicking the object in the Navigator Pane on the left hand side.

The tabs on the table object window enable you to see additional details about the object. There are two tabs that deserve special mention, Data and SQL. The Data tab will display the actual data in the table, which is like doing a SELECT * from <table_name>. By default the result window will show the first 50 records from your table. The SQL tab, which is in every object window, displays the actual SQL calls to create the object. Figure 2-10 shows the data in the Employees table that is displayed by clicking the Data tab.

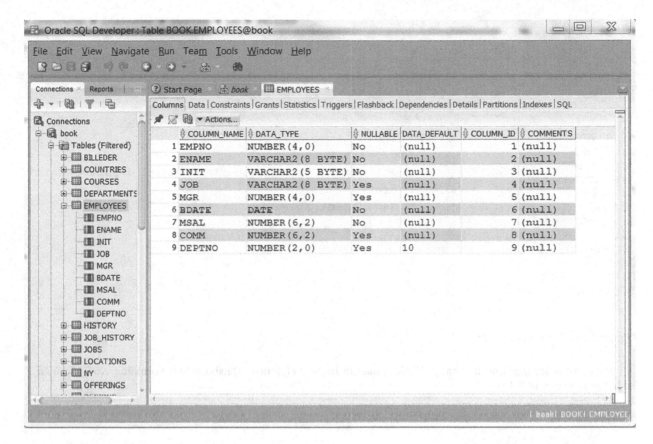

Figure 2-10. *Browsing a table*

You can also explore the objects owned by others that you are able to access. At the very bottom of the object list, the Other Users entry can be expanded to show all of the objects you can access. All the users in the database are displayed, even if you cannot see any of their objects.

Schema Browser

You may find it more convenient to browse your database objects using the Schema Browser, which you invoke by right clicking your connection in the left hand navigator panel and choosing Schema Browser. That looks like this:

The SQL in Figure 2-11 doesn't look too good. You might like Ctrl+F7 to beautify your code. This is very useful, especially with inherited code over many, many lines!

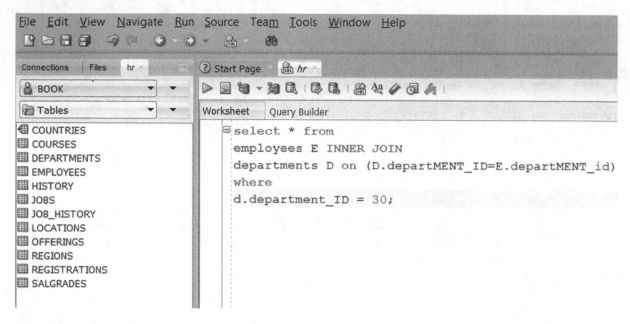

Figure 2-11. *Schema Browser*

Formatting settings may be changed to your likes in Tools/Preferences/Database/SQL Formatter. Now it looks a lot better (see Figure 2-12).

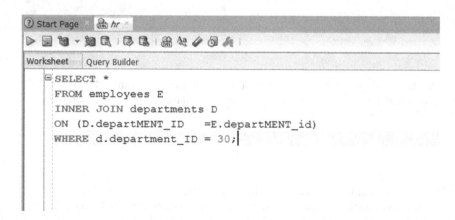

Figure 2-12. *Formatted*

Entering Commands

The SQL Worksheet is where you enter commands to query and modify data. Like SQL*Plus, you can enter SQL and PL/SQL commands. Some SQL*Plus commands are supported, such as COLUMN, DESCRIBE, and SPOOL. For a full list of supported and unsupported SQL*Plus commands, please refer to the online *Oracle SQL Developers User's Guide*.

The worksheet is automatically opened when you connect to a database. If you need to open another worksheet or have closed the only one open, click on the SQL Worksheet icon or select the Tools ➤ SQL Worksheet menu option.

■ **Note**   If the worksheet contains more than one statement, the statements must be terminated with a ; or / (on a separate line). If they are not properly terminated, the session will return an error message: ORA-00933: SQL command not properly ended.

Browsing table data

In Figure 2-13 the Data tab is shown when about to enter a new record. We pressed the 3rd icon, the green plus-sign, and now the Commit and Rollback icons are active. You may enter data in the fields, where it now says (null), and then press Commit. An automatic INSERT statement will be executed for you. But notice that SQL Developer does both the INSERT and the COMMIT when you press the icon.

	EMPNO	ENAME	INIT	JOB	MGR	BDATE	MSAL	COMM	DEPTNO
1	7369	SMITH	N	TRAINER	7902	17-DEC-65	800	(null)	20
2	7499	ALLEN	JAM	SALESREP	7698	20-FEB-61	1600	300	30
3	7521	WARD	TF	SALESREP	7698	22-FEB-62	1250	500	30
4	7566	JONES	JM	MANAGER	7839	02-APR-67	2975	(null)	20
5	7654	MARTIN	P	SALESREP	7698	28-SEP-56	1250	1400	30
6	7698	BLAKE	R	MANAGER	7839	01-NOV-63	2850	(null)	30
7	7782	CLARK	AB	MANAGER	7839	09-JUN-65	2450	(null)	10
8	7788	SCOTT	SCJ	TRAINER	7566	26-NOV-59	3000	(null)	20
9	7839	KING	CC	DIRECTOR	(null)	17-NOV-52	5000	(null)	10
10	7844	TURNER	JJ	SALESREP	7698	28-SEP-68	1500	0	30
11	7876	ADAMS	AA	TRAINER	7788	30-DEC-66	1100	(null)	20
12	7900	JONES	R	ADMIN	7698	03-DEC-69	800	(null)	30
13	7902	FORD	MG	TRAINER	7566	13-FEB-59	3000	(null)	20
14	7934	MILLER	TJA	ADMIN	7782	23-JAN-62	1300	(null)	10
+15	(n...	(null)	...	(null)	(null)	(null)	(...	(null)	(n...

Figure 2-13. *Browsing a table's data*

Run Statement

Unlike SQL*Plus, a statement is not automatically run when you enter a ; or /. The Run Statement (Ctrl+Enter) command or the large green triangle icon is used to run a single command. If the worksheet contains more than one command, Run Statement will run the command under the cursor, assuming that the previous statement(s) have been terminated with a ; or /.

Let's start by entering the following, simple statement:

```
SELECT * FROM EMPLOYEES;
```

There are two things worth noting: First, the SQL statement reserved words are highlighted; second, EMPLOYEES is suggested as the table after you type FROM E. The syntax highlighting is handy when you accidentally type FORM instead of FROM. The auto-complete feature is also a time saver as it can suggest table or view and column names. You can invoke Auto-complete/Completion Insight with Ctrl+Space if it doesn't appear or if you accidentally dismissed it with Esc.

Click on the Run Statement button or press Ctrl+Enter (or the old way: F9) to execute the query and display the data in the Query Result window, as seen in Figure 2-14.

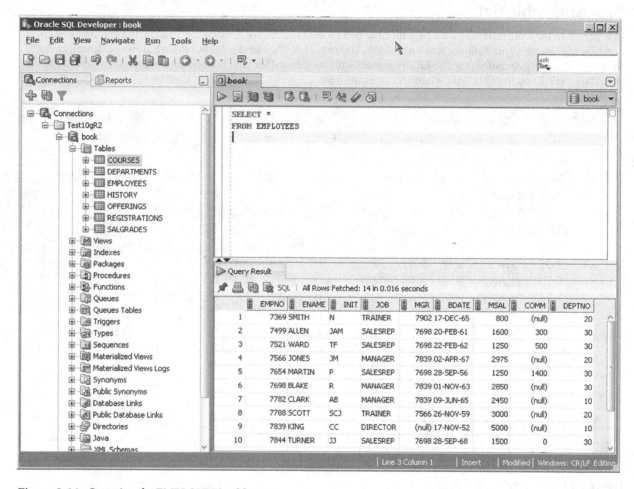

Figure 2-14. *Querying the EMPLOYEES table*

To change the sort order of the data, double click on a column heading in the Query Result window.

Run Script

The Run Script command will run all the statements and/or SQL*Plus commands in the worksheet. This is the command to use when you have multiple statements or want to format the output using supported SQL*Plus commands.

Below the SELECT * FROM EMPLOYEES; we entered in the worksheet, enter SELECT * FROM DEPARTMENTS; and then click the Run Script button or press F5. The output will be displayed in the Script Output window alongside the Query Result window. Notice that the output is almost identical to what you would see in SQL*Plus and is displayed below in Figure 2-15.

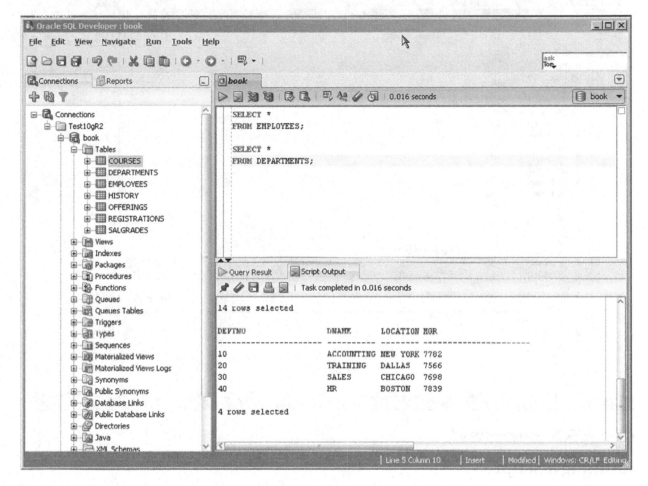

Figure 2-15. *Querying EMPLOYEES and DEPARTMENTS tables*

When running scripts, the output is appended to the Script Output window. To clear the window so that only new output is displayed, click on the Clear button (the picture of the pencil eraser).

■ **Note**   Not all supported SQL*Plus output formatting commands are properly interpreted for Run Script. For example, the COLUMN command does not change the column headings, but SET FEEDBACK OFF works as expected.

Saving Commands to a Script

After taking time to create a complex statement, it is wise to save that command to a script that you can run later. After entering the commands and statement(s), select File ➤ Save, press Ctl+S, or click on the disk button to bring up the File Save dialog box. The directory that it opens should be the same one you set in the Configuration section. The File Save dialog box is shown in Figure 2-16.

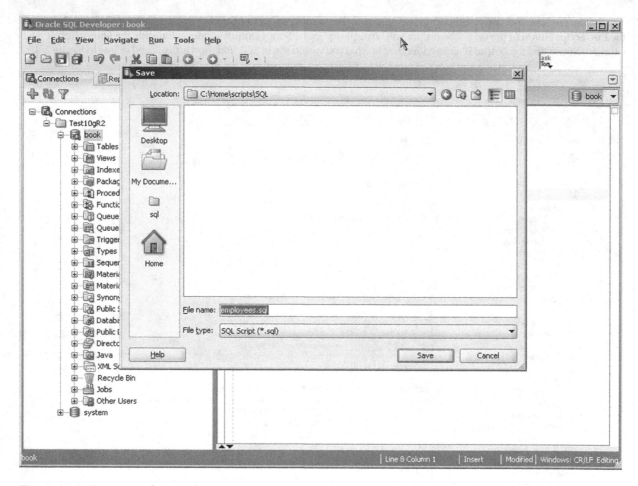

Figure 2-16. *Saving employees.sql*

Running a Script

To run the script we just saved, there are two ways to load and run. The SQL*Plus standard of using @ is supported. To use the @ command, type @employees.sql in the worksheet and select Run Script (F5). This is demonstrated in Figure 2-17.

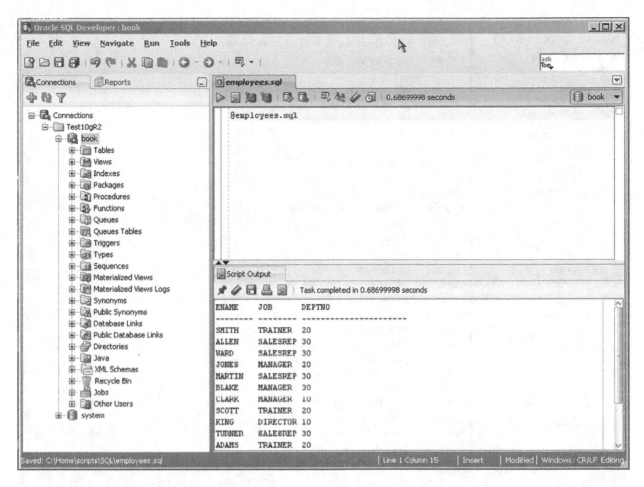

Figure 2-17. *Running employees.sql using @*

The second option is to select File ➤ Open and pick the employees.sql file you just saved. The commands contained in that file will be loaded into the worksheet. Select the database connection you want to use in the Choose db Connection drop down box in the upper right of the employees.sql window. Until you select the connection, the other buttons will remain grayed out. After you select the connection, press the Run Script button to see the output, as seen in Figure 2-18.

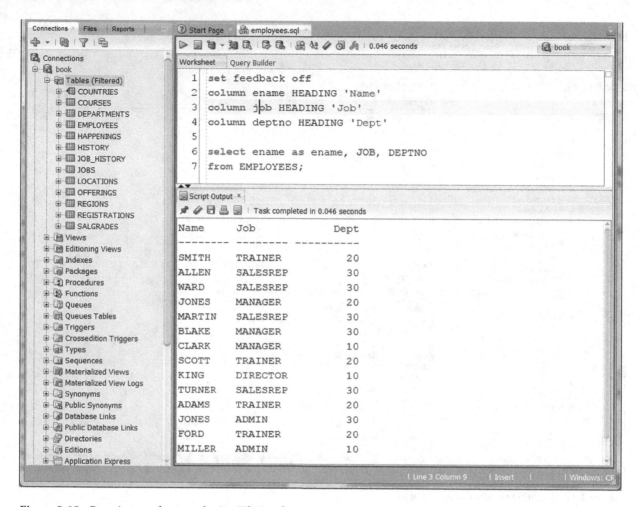

Figure 2-18. *Running employees.sql using File Load*

You may not like the Shortcut Keys predefined in SQL Developer, and you are free to change them. Go to Tools/Preferences/Shortcut Keys where you see them all and where you may change them to your liking. (see Figure 2-19)

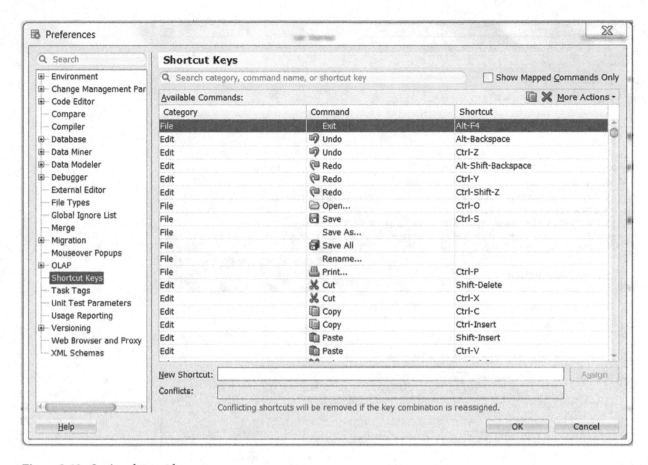

Figure 2-19. *Setting shortcut keys*

Exporting Your Data

After running your statement with Ctrl+Enter you might like to export your data to a file. SQL Developer provides many file formats such as csv, html, xml, excel, pdf, insert, sqlloader.

Right click your output in the Query Result window, choose Export, and set your choice. You can even predefine what choice should appear by default in Tools/Preferences/Database/Utilities/Export. (see Figure 2-20)

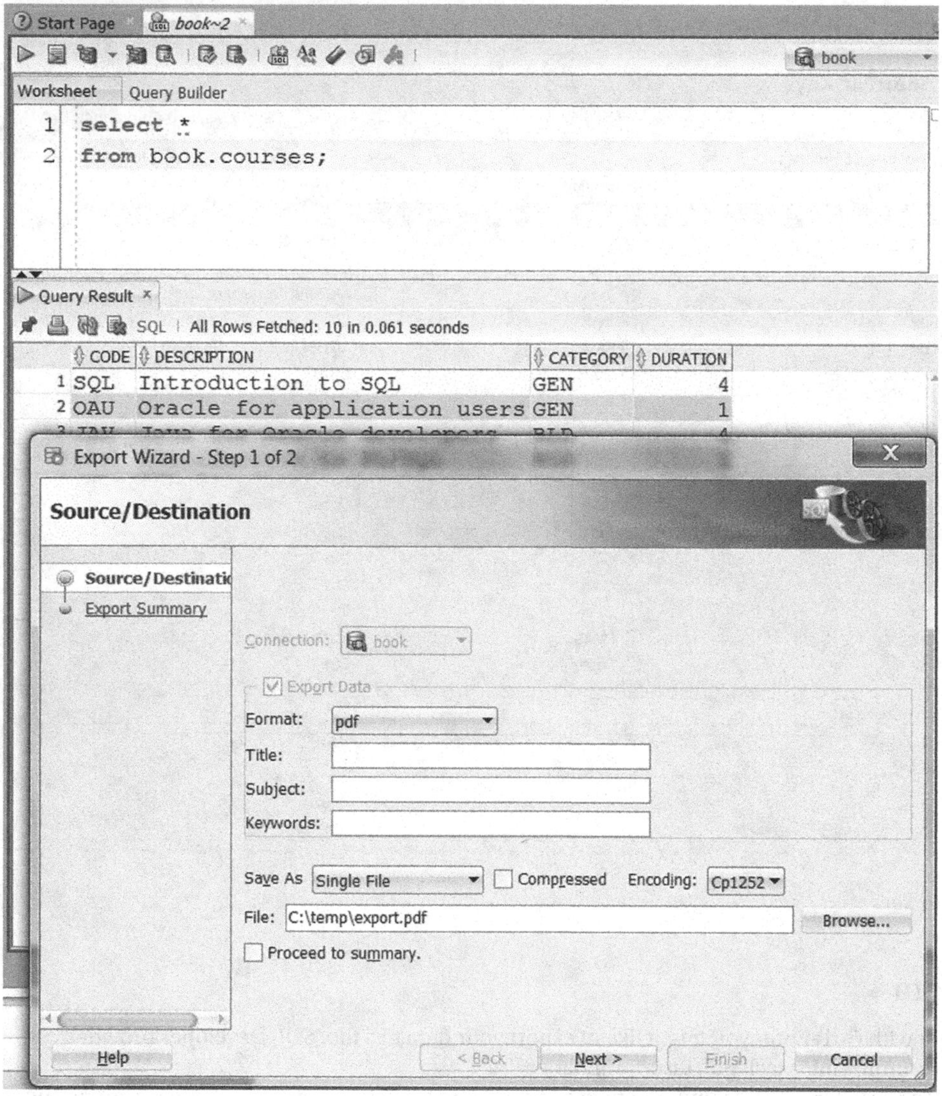

***Figure 2-20.** Exporting data*

User-Defined Reports

You may choose to include your statement as a user-defined report that you can run from the Report library. Right click your output in the Query Result window, and choose Save Grid as Report. (see Figure 2-21)

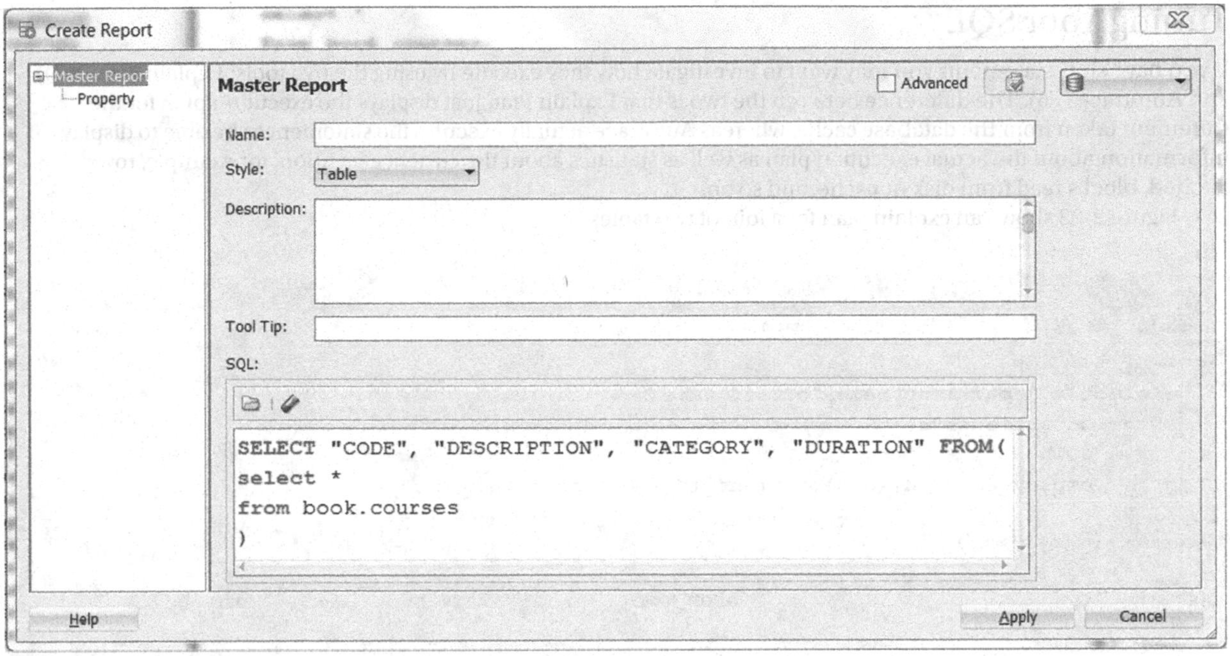

Figure 2-21. *Create Report*

Now that your statement is saved as a report you may run by just clicking the name of your report. Open the menu View/Reports—at the bottom of the list you have User Defined Reports. (see Figure 2-22) If you wish, you can also schedule your report to be run automatically using SQL Developer's GUI interface to the Oracle supplied package *dbms_scheduler*, which you find in the Navigator under your connection in the node Scheduler.

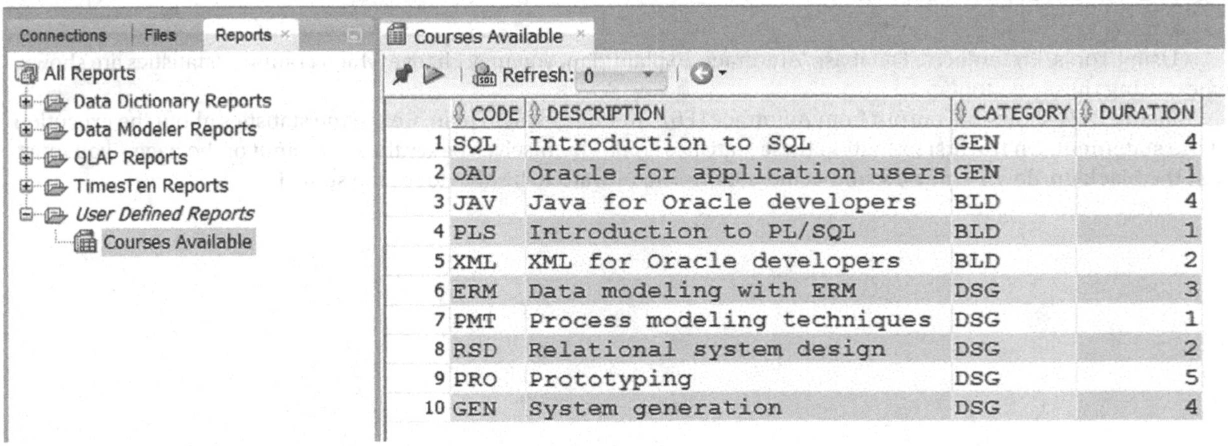

Figure 2-22. *User Defined Reports*

Tuning Your SQL

If you have slow statements you may want to investigate how they execute by using the two tools: Explain Plan (F10) and Autotrace (F6). The difference between the two is that Explain Plan just displays the execution plan for the statement taken from the database cache, whereas Autotrace actually executes the statement to be able to display information about the actual execution plan as well as statistics about the current execution, for example, rows fetched, blocks read from disk or cache, and so on.

Figure 2-23 shows an explain plan for a join of two tables.

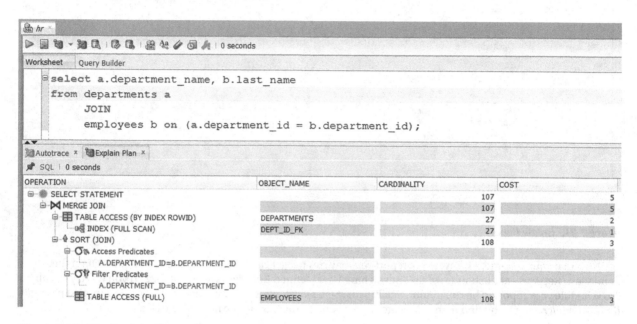

Figure 2-23. *The Explain Plan tool*

Using Tools/Preferences/Database/Autotrace-ExplainPlan, you may change which columns/statistics are shown when using these two tools.

Figure 2-24 shows the output from Autotrace (F6). After the explain plan, we see the statistics about the execution of the statement. On the first execution these statistics "hide" themselves below the lower limit of the page—you must pull the black up/down arrows, found at the bottom left, upward to be able to see the statistics.

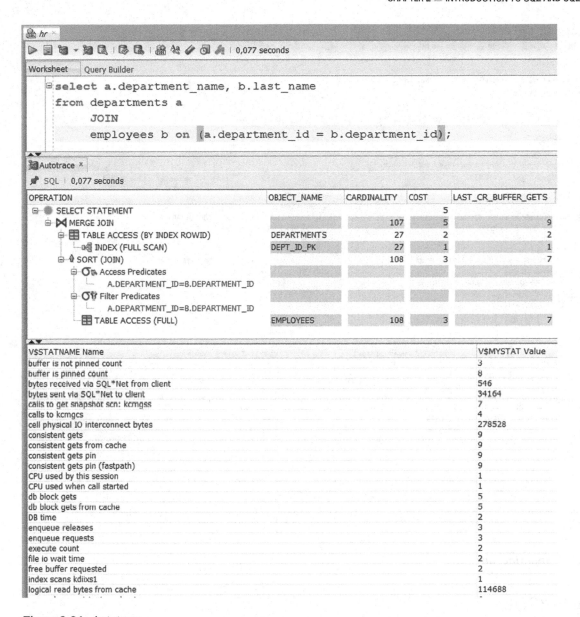

Figure 2-24. *Autotrace*

By pressing the little red pin you may keep this first autotrace output, change the SQL statement, and reuse Autotrace to get a second explain plan plus statistics, and those can then be compared by right clicking the second Autotrace tab and chosing Compare with Autotrace.

Then your output would look like what appears in Figure 2-25, with differences marked in red.

Figure 2-25. *Comparing Autotrace*

Writing PL/SQL

The SQL Developer tool is also intended for PL/SQL development, complete with wizards, editors, compilation, and debugging. The editor for writing a function or procedure looks like Figure 2-26 and is reacheable through the left hand navigator. Just right click the node for the object type; for example, for a function, choose New Function, fill in the wizard fields, and click OK. You are now in the PL/SQL editor where you can edit, compile, compile for debug, set breakpoints, and debug. As you see in Figure 2-26 the function is only started. You must fill in contents for the executable part of the function before the stub RETURN NULL, and, of course, you must change the return value.

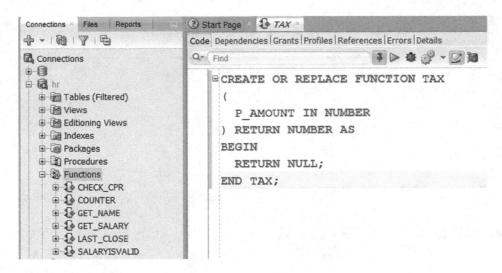

Figure 2-26. *PL/SQL Editor*

Running PL/SQL Code for Testing

When running your code with the green arrow, SQL Developer offers an anonymous block for executing the function. Fill in your chosen test value and click OK. (see Figure 2-27)

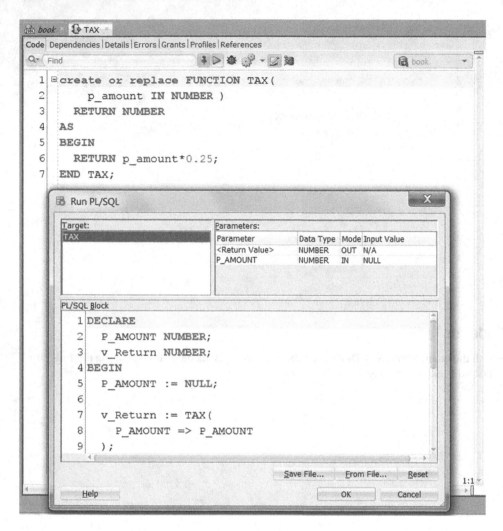

Figure 2-27. *Using the Run function*

Debugging Code to Find Errors

When your code compiles without errors, you may still experience that the code delivers wrong results. To find out why, we debug. By the way, in the childhood of programming, insects actually got stuck on the hot machine panels, and removing these moths became known as *debugging*. When debugging your code, you first compile for debug using the Compile option under the two small gray wheels. All references here are for Figure 2-28. The compiled version of your function now contains both the executable p-code and the source code for reference purposes while running.

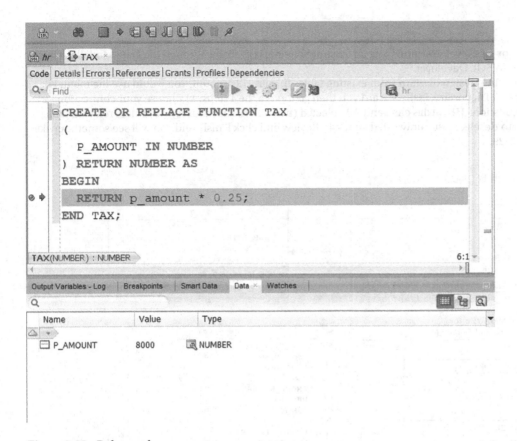

Figure 2-28. *Debug code*

Then you set stopping points, *breakpoints*, at different interesting places in your code, which show up as red points in the margin. Now run the code using the little red ladybug. Again you see the automatically provided anonymous block for running the code, input your chosen test values, and click OK.

The program now provides an extra debug bar at the top for navigating through your code while debugging. The bottom part shows several tabs for investigating the stack of variables and the breakpoints and for setting watches for especially interesting variables—these are very useful if you have many variables in your code.The fourth icon (the red arrow pointing into the code page) means Step Into; which is most useful for stepping one statement at a time through the code; the current statement is identifiable via the red arrow in the margin. When stepping this slowly, you have time to investigate all stages your variables go through; you are even able to see when they are NULL, that is, without value, a situation that is often the cause of wrong results.

The procedure is about the same for making and debugging stored procedures.

The wizards for stored packages and triggers are fairly easy to use. The online documentation can be found at:

Packages:

```
http://docs.oracle.com/cd/E16655_01/server.121/e17209/statements_6006.htm#SQLRF01306
```

Triggers:

```
http://docs.oracle.com/cd/E16655_01/server.121/e17209/statements_7004.htm#SQLRF01405
```

Data Modeller

Modelling the database, or else reverse engineering an existing schema, is available through the Data Modeller, which is now free and included in SQL Developer.

To produce the following Design diagram from existing tables in your HR account, you would use the menu File/ Data Modeler/Import/Data Dictionary. In the wizard you then go though the 4 steps: 1) Choose your connection - 2) Choose the schema in question: HR in this case and All Selected (two diffent checkboxes) - 3) Select relevant tables and go to the other tabs to deselect other unwanted stuff - 4) Review and click Finish and you will see something like what appears in Figure 2-29.

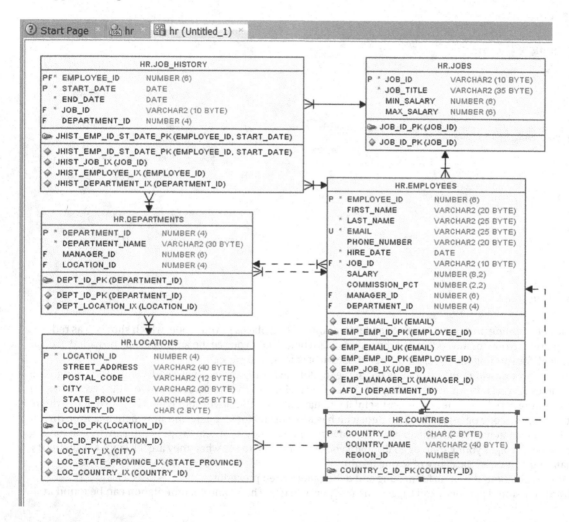

Figure 2-29. *Data Modeller—reverse engineering*

Here we have just touched upon the many many features of SQL Developer.

For further information, visit the SQL Developer home page at: http://www.oracle.com/technology/products/ database/sql_developer/index.html.

Since GUI interfaces like SQL Developer are not always available, it is also very useful to be able to work through the original SQL*Plus interface, which is explained in depth in Chapter 11.

■ ■ ■

Data Definition, Part I

This short chapter is the first one about data definition with SQL. It's intended to get you started using SQL for data retrieval as soon as possible. Therefore, this chapter covers only the data definition basics, such as how to create simple tables using standard datatypes. In Chapter 7, we will revisit data definition with SQL and explore topics such as indexes, synonyms, and constraints.

This chapter is mainly theoretical in nature in that it still offers no hands-on exercises and only a few examples. In the next chapter, you will start writing SQL commands yourself.

The first section introduces the concept of database schemas and database users. In an Oracle database, tables always belong to a schema, and, in general, a schema has a database user as its owner. The second section explains how you can create simple tables, and the most common Oracle datatypes are covered in the third section. To illustrate the contents of the first three sections, Section 3.4 shows the CREATE TABLE commands to create the sample tables used in the examples in this book (introduced in chapter 1) without bothering about constraints yet.

The last section of this chapter, Section 3.5, covers the Oracle data dictionary. It provides a global overview of the data dictionary, lists some typical examples of data dictionary tables, and shows how to execute some simple queries against some of those data dictionary tables.

3.1 Schemas and Users

Before you can start creating and populating tables with SQL, you need to understand how data stored in an Oracle database is organized internally. In the previous chapter, you learned that you cannot do anything in an Oracle database if you do not identify yourself first by specifying a *username* and a *password*. This process identifies you as a certain *database user*.

In an Oracle database there is, in general, a one-to-one relationship between database *users* and database *schemas* with the same name. Briefly, these are the differences between a database user and a database schema:

- A *database user* has a password and certain database privileges (privileges would allow viewing or manipulating data).

- A *database schema* is a logical collection of database objects (such as tables, indexes, views, and so on) that is usually owned by the user of the same name.

Normally, when you log on to an Oracle database, you are automatically connected with the corresponding database schema with the same name. However, it is also possible that certain database users don't have their own schema; in other words, they don't have any database objects of their own, and they don't have the privileges to create them either. These "schema-less" users are, for example, authorized only to retrieve or manipulate data in a different database schema.

For example, in SQL*Plus, you can use the CONNECT command to establish a new connection with a different schema, provided you are able to enter a valid combination of a database name and a corresponding password. With the ALTER SESSION SET CURRENT_SCHEMA command, you can "visit" a different schema in SQL*Plus without changing your identity as database user, and therefore without changing any of your privileges.

All of the examples and exercises in this book assume the presence of a database user BOOK, with the password BOOK, and a schema BOOK that contains the seven case tables introduced in the previous chapter. You can find all of the scripts to create the BOOK schema, to create the seven tables, and to insert the rows in the Book Resources section of this book's catalog page on the Apress website at http://apress.com/book/view/1430271970.

3.2 Table Creation

The SQL command to create tables is CREATE TABLE. If you create a table, you must specify a name for the new table, followed by a specification of all table columns. The columns must be specified as a comma-separated list between parentheses. You might also create a new table by inheriting properties from an existing one by running a CREATE TABLE ... AS SELECT (CTAS) statement

---

■ **Note**   The right to create tables in an Oracle database is not granted to everyone; you need some additional system privileges. If you get error messages when you try to create tables, contact your database administrator or check *Oracle Database Administrator's Guide* in the Oracle online documentation.

The basic syntax of the . CREATE TABLE command is shown in Figure 3-1.

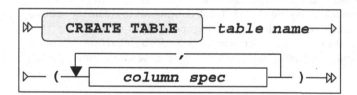

Figure 3-1. *A CREATE TABLE basic command syntax diagram*

■ **Note**   Figure 3-1 does *not* show the complete syntax of the . CREATE TABLE command. Just for fun, check out *Oracle SQL Reference* for the amount of documentation describing the CREATE TABLE command. Chapter 7 of this book will revisit this command with the full syntax and more details.

Column specifications normally consist of several components. Figure 3-2 shows the column specification syntax.

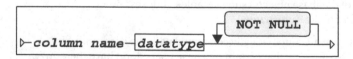

Figure 3-2. *Column specification syntax diagram*

Each column specification starts with a column name, followed by the datatype (discussed in the next section). If you add the optional expression NOT NULL to a column definition, each future row of the table you are creating *must* have a value specified for this column, and you will not be able to update future rows by removing a value for this column. In other words, you define the column to be a mandatory attribute.

The NOT NULL addition is an example of a constraint. You can specify many additional constraints in the CREATE TABLE command. The other types of constraints are UNIQUE, CHECK, PRIMARY KEY, and FOREIGN KEY. Chapter 7 will discuss these options of the CREATE TABLE command.

3.3 Datatypes

Oracle supports many standard datatypes, as you will see if you take a look at the Oracle documentation. Some Oracle datatypes look very similar; some are even synonyms for each other. These datatypes are supported for compatibility purposes of Oracle with other DBMSs or with the ANSI/ISO SQL standard. For example, INT and INTEGER are synonyms for NUMBER(38). Some datatypes are very specific in nature, making them irrelevant for us at this point in time. This section covers only the most common and widely used Oracle datatypes.

In general, there are three categories of column data: numbers (numeric data), text (alphanumeric data), and time-related data. The most important corresponding Oracle datatypes are NUMBER, VARCHAR or VARCHAR2, and DATE, respectively.

Number Datatype

The number datatype stores numbers that can be positive or negative and have defined maximum precision and scale; here is an example of how this looks: COLUMN_NAME(P,S) The precision of the numeric datatype is the number of significant digits that can be used. If you specify the column as: COLUMN_NAME NUMBER, this would allow up to Oracle's maximum of 38 significant digits.

Table 3-1 shows some examples of the NUMBER datatype.

Table 3-1. *NUMBER Datatype Examples*

Example	Description
NUMBER(4)	An integer with a maximum length of four digits
NUMBER(6,2)	A number with a maximum precision of six digits; at most two digits behind the decimal point
NUMBER(7,-3)	A multiple of thousand with at most seven digits
NUMBER	Identical to NUMBER(38,*)
NUMBER(*,5)	Identical to NUMBER(38,5)

Character Datatype

Character datatypes are used to store strings that contain character data. You decide which type to use based on the maximum length needed and possible use of Unicode character literals, where some characters consist of multiple bytes. Oracle offers a number of alphanumeric datatypes. Depending on the Oracle version you are using, there are some differences due to the evolution of the ANSI/ISO SQL standard over the years. For example, since Oracle7, the two datatypes VARCHAR and VARCHAR2 are identical, but this could change in a future Oracle release. If you create a table and you use the VARCHAR datatype, the Oracle DBMS translates VARCHAR to VARCHAR2 on the fly. Therefore, this book refers to only the VARCHAR2 datatype. In cases where the maximum size of the VARCHAR2 datatype (32767) is insufficient for a specific column, you can use the CLOB (Character Large Object) datatype.

Table 3-2 shows some simple examples of character datatypes.

Table 3-2. *Character Datatype Examples*

Example	Description
VARCHAR2(25)	Alphanumeric, *variable* length, up to 25 characters
CHAR(4)	Alphanumeric, *fixed* length, four characters
CLOB	Alphanumeric, larger than the maximum size of the VARCHAR2 datatype

Table 3-3 lists the maximum size values for the datatypes mentioned so far.

Table 3-3. *Maximum Datatype Sizes*

Datatype	Maximum Size
NUMBER	38 digits precision
CHAR	2000
VARCHAR2	4000 or 32767
CLOB	4GB

■ **Note** The actual units of measure used for the size of CHAR and VARCHAR2 datatypes depend on character semantics (bytes or characters). See Chapter 7 for details.

The indicated maximum CLOB size (4GB) is not completely correct. Depending on some configuration parameters, CLOB columns may contain much more than 4GB worth of data. Refer to *Oracle SQL Reference* for details.

VARCHAR2 length depends on the database parameter MAX_STRING_SIZE. 'STANDARD' allows a maximum of 4000 characters, 'EXTENDED' allows 32767 characters. 'STANDARD' is the default value of this new parameter in Oracle 12c.

Date Datatype

The basic datatype for time-related data is DATE. By default, date values are interpreted and displayed according to a standard date format, typically showing only the day, the month, and the last two digits of the year. You can change the default date format for your session or use conversion functions in your SQL commands to display dates in different ways. Oracle stores dates in such a way that DATE column values are allowed from the year 4712 BC until the year 9999. Oracle dates are internally stored with much more precision than you might expect on first consideration.

■ **Caution** DATE columns also contain a time indication (hours, minutes, and seconds), which may cause problems when comparing two dates. For example, seemingly equal dates could be different due to their invisible time components.

Apart from the DATE datatype, Oracle also supports the related datatypes TIMESTAMP (with or without TIME ZONE and INTERVAL to store other time-related data in table columns. Chapter 5provides more details on the time-related datatypes.

This book focuses on the usage of the three standard Oracle datatypes: NUMBER, VARCHAR2, and DATE.

3.4 Commands for Creating the Case Tables

This sectionlists the SQL commands to create the seven case tables, introduced in Chapter 1, as an illustration of the concepts covered in the previous three sections, without much additional explanation. Since the BOOK schema consists of seven tables, this section also shows seven CREATE TABLE commands, presented in Listings 3-1 through 3-7.

Listing 3-1. The EMPLOYEES Table

```
create table  EMPLOYEES
( empno        number(4)   not null
, ename        varchar2(8) not null
, init         varchar2(5) not null
, job          varchar2(8)
, mgr          number(4)
, bdate        date        not null
, msal         number(6,2) not null
, comm         number(6,2)
, deptno       number(2)              );
```

Listing 3-2. The DEPARTMENTS Table

```
create table  DEPARTMENTS
( deptno       number(2)    not null
, dname        varchar2(10) not null
, location     varchar2(8)  not null
, mgr          number(4)              );
```

Listing 3-3. The SALGRADES Table

```
create table  SALGRADES
( grade        number(2)   not null
, lowerlimit   number(6,2) not null
, upperlimit   number(6,2) not null
, bonus        number(6,2) not null );
```

Listing 3-4. The COURSES Table

```
create table  COURSES
( code         varchar2(6)  not null
, description  varchar2(30) not null
, category     char(3)      not null
, duration     number(2)    not null );
```

Listing 3-5. The OFFERINGS Table

```
create table  OFFERINGS
( course     varchar2(6)  not null
, begindate  date         not null
, trainer    number(4)
, location   varchar2(8)              );
```

Listing 3-6. The REGISTRATIONS Table

```
create table  REGISTRATIONS
( attendee    number(4)   not null
, course      varchar2(6) not null
, begindate   date        not null
, evaluation  number(1)               );
```

Listing 3-7. The HISTORY Table

```
create table  HISTORY
( empno      number(4)   not null
, beginyear  number(4)   not null
, begindate  date        not null
, enddate    date
, deptno     number(2)   not null
, msal       number(6,2) not null
, comments   varchar2(60)            );
```

■ **Note**   As mentioned earlier, constraint definition (and constraint checking) is not taken into consideration in this chapter; therefore, the following listings do *not* show the complete commands to create the case tables.

3.5 The Data Dictionary

If you are interested in knowing which tables are present in your database, which columns they have, whether or not those columns are indexed, which privileges are granted to you, and similar information, you should query the *data dictionary*. Another common term for data dictionary is *catalog*. By the way, when we used the SQL*Plus DESCRIBE command (see Chapter 11), this command queries the data dictionary under the hood.

The data dictionary is more orless the internal housekeeping administration of Oracle. The data dictionary stores information about the data, also referred to as *metadata*. The data dictionary is automatically maintained by Oracle; therefore, the data dictionary is always up-to-date.

DBMSs, like Oracle, store data dictionary data in precisely the same way as they store "regular" data: in tables. This is in compliance with Ted Codd's rules (see Chapter 1). The big advantage of this approach is that you can use the SQL language to query data dictionary data in the same way that you query ordinary data. In other words, if you master the SQL language, you need to know only the names of the data dictionary tables and the names of their columns.

Data dictionary access is a potential security risk. That's why the Oracle DBMS offers system privileges and roles to regulate and protect access to the data dictionary. For example, there is a role, SELECT_CATALOG_ROLE, which contains all privileges that you need to be able to access the data dictionary data. Listing 3-8 demonstrates how Oracle controls data dictionary access. The listing was generated from SQL*Plus.

Listing 3-8. Needing the SELECT_CATALOG_ROLE Role

```
SQL> describe dba_sys_privs
ERROR:
ORA-04043: object "SYS"."DBA_SYS_PRIVS" does not exist

SQL> connect / as sysdba
Connected.

SQL> grant select_catalog_role to book;
Grant succeeded.

SQL> connect book/book
Connected.

SQL> desc dba_sys_privs
 Name                              Null?    Type
 -------------------------------- -------- ----------------
 GRANTEE                          NOT NULL VARCHAR2(30)
 PRIVILEGE                        NOT NULL VARCHAR2(40)
 ADMIN_OPTION                              VARCHAR2(3)

SQL>
```

Although the information is stored in data dictionary *tables*, most of the time, you access data dictionary *views* instead. On the other hand, views are much like tables anyway. See Chapter 10 for details about views.

You can refer to *Oracle Database Reference* in the Oracle documentation to get a complete overview of the Oracle data dictionary. Fortunately, the Oracle data dictionary contains a view that lists all Oracle data dictionary views, with a short description of their contents. This view is called DICTIONARY; DICT is a shorter synonym for the same view. Listing 3-9 shows an abbreviated version of the query results. It's abbreviated for a practical reason: the DICT view contains more than 3000 rows!

Listing 3-9. Using the DICT View

```
select * from dict order by table_name;

TABLE_NAME           COMMENTS
-------------------- ----------------------------------------
ALL_ALL_TABLES       Description of all object and relational
                     tables accessible to the user
ALL_APPLY            Details about each apply process that
                     dequeues from the queue visible to the
                     current user
...
USER_COL_COMMENTS    Comments on columns of user's tables and
                     views
USER_COL_PRIVS       Grants on columns for which the user is
                     the owner, grantor or grantee
...
V$TIMEZONE_NAMES     Synonym for V_$TIMEZONE_NAMES
V$VERSION            Synonym for V_$VERSION

3124 rows selected.
```

Data dictionary view names typically have prefixes that suggest the existence of four main categories. In Listing 3-9, you can see the ALL, USER, and V$ prefixes. The fourth common prefix is DBA. The idea behind this is that, most of the time, you are interested in information about a certain subcategory of database objects. By using the appropriate views, you automatically suppress information that is not of interest to you. Also, depending on your database privileges, you will not be allowed to use certain categories of data dictionary views. Table 3-4 lists the most common data dictionary view name prefixes. (Note that not all data dictionary views have one of these prefixes.)

Table 3-4. *Common Data Dictionary View Prefixes*

Prefix	Description
USER_...	Information about your own objects
ALL_...	Information about all objects you can access
DBA_...	All information in the database; for database administrators only
[G]V$...	Dynamic performance views; for database administrators only

The *dynamic performance views* (those with a V$ or GV$ name prefix) are a special category. These views are not based on database tables, but rather on information from other sources such as internal memory structures. They are mainly relevant for, and accessible to, database administrators.

Most data dictionary view names give a clear indication of their contents; however, as a consequence, some of these names are very long. That's why some of the most popular data dictionary views also have alternative (shorter) synonyms, such as CAT, OBJ, IND, TABS, and COLS. The CAT view is an especially useful one, because it lists the objects in the current schema. Listing 3-10 shows an example of using the CAT view with our BOOK schema.

Listing 3-10. Using the CAT View

```
select * from cat;

TABLE_NAME                     TABLE_TYPE
------------------------------ -----------
EMPLOYEES                      TABLE
DEPARTMENTS                    TABLE
SALGRADES                      TABLE
COURSES                        TABLE
OFFERINGS                      TABLE
REGISTRATIONS                  TABLE
HISTORY                        TABLE
```

Suppose you want to query a specific data dictionary view, and you don't know the actual column names of that view. In that case, you can use the SQL*Plus command DESCRIBE, just as you would do for regular tables. As you can see in Listing 3-11, you can use the DESCRIBE command, or you can query the data dictionary view DICT_COLUMNS.

Listing 3-11. Using the DESCRIBE Command and the DICT_COLUMNS View

```
describe ALL_USERS
Name                   Null?     Type
USERNAME       NOT NULL VARCHAR2(30)
USER_ID        NOT NULL NUMBER
CREATED        NOT NULL DATE


select column_name, comments
from   dict_columns
where  table_name = 'ALL_USERS';

COLUMN_NAME                    COMMENTS
---------------------------    -------------------------
USERNAME                       Name of the user
USER_ID                        ID number of the user
CREATED                        User creation date
```

Listing 3-12 shows a query against the NLS_SESSION_PARAMETERS view (NLS stands for National Language Support). The result shows, for example, the NLS_DATE_FORMAT value used to display dates.

Listing 3-12. Using the NLS_SESSION_PARAMETERS View

```
select * from nls_session_parameters;

PARAMETER                 VALUE
----------------------    ----------------------
NLS_LANGUAGE              AMERICAN
NLS_TERRITORY            AMERICA
NLS_CURRENCY             $
NLS_ISO_CURRENCY         AMERICA
NLS_NUMERIC_CHARACTERS   .,
NLS_CALENDAR             GREGORIAN
NLS_DATE_FORMAT          DD-MON-YYYY
NLS_DATE_LANGUAGE        AMERICAN
NLS_SORT                 BINARY
NLS_TIME_FORMAT          HH.MI.SSXFF AM
NLS_TIMESTAMP_FORMAT     DD-MON-RR HH.MI.SSXFF AM
NLS_TIME_TZ_FORMAT       HH.MI.SSXFF AM TZR
NLS_TIMESTAMP_TZ_FORMAT DD-MON-RR HH.MI.SSXFF AM TZR
NLS_DUAL_CURRENCY        $
NLS_COMP                 BINARY
NLS_LENGTH_SEMANTICS     BYTE
NLS_NCHAR_CONV_EXCP      FALSE
```

The NLS features in Oracle are documented in great detail in the *Globalization Support Guide* in the Oracle documentation set.

Table 3-5 lists a selection of useful Oracle data dictionary tables.

Table 3-5. *Some Useful Oracle Data Dictionary Views*

View	Description
DICTIONARY	Description of the data dictionary itself
DICT_COLUMNS	Data dictionary column descriptions
ALL_USERS	Information about all database users
ALL_INDEXES[1]	All indexes
ALL_SEQUENCES[1]	All sequences
ALL_OBJECTS[1]	All objects
ALL_SYNONYMS[1]	All synonyms
ALL_TABLES[1]	All tables
ALL_VIEWS[1]	All views
USER_INDEXES[2]	Indexes
USER_SEQUENCES[2]	Sequences
USER_OBJECTS[2]	Objects
USER_SYNONYMS[2]	Synonyms
USER_TABLES[2]	Tables
USER_TAB_COLUMNS[2]	Columns
USER_VIEWS[2]	Views
USER_RECYCLEBIN	Dropped objects
CAT	Synonym for USER_CATALOG
COLS	Synonym for USER_TAB_COLUMNS
DICT	Synonym for DICTIONARY
DUAL	Dummy table, with one row and one column
IND	Synonym for USER_INDEXES
OBJ	Synonym for USER_OBJECTS
SYN	Synonym for USER_SYNONYMS
TABS	Synonym for USER_TABLES

[1]*Accessible to the user*
[2]*Owned by the user*

The Oracle online documentation, *Oracle Database Reference* provides all the details you need about the Oracle data dictionary.

CHAPTER 4

■ ■ ■

Retrieval: The Basics

In this chapter, you will start to access the seven case tables with SQL. To be more precise, you will learn how to *retrieve* data from your database. For data retrieval, the SQL language offers the SELECT command, introduced in Section 4.1. SQL statements that use the SELECT command are commonly referred to as *queries*.

An SQL statement has six main clauses. Three of them—SELECT, WHERE, and ORDER BY—are discussed in this chapter in Sections 4.2, 4.3 and 4.4, respectively. An introduction to the remaining three clauses—FROM, GROUP BY, and HAVING—is postponed until Chapter 8.

You can write queries as independent SQL statements, but queries can also occur inside other SQL statements. These are called *subqueries*. This chapter introduces subqueries, and then in Chapter 9, we will revisit subqueries to discuss some of their more advanced features.

Null values and their associated three-valued logic—SQL conditions have the three possible outcomes of TRUE, FALSE, or UNKNOWN—are also covered in this chapter in Section 4.9. A thorough understanding of null values and three-valued logic is critical for anyone using the SQL language. Finally, this chapter presents the truth tables of the AND, OR, and NOT operators in Section 4.10, showing how these operators handle three-valued logic.

4.1 Overview of the SELECT Command

We start this chapter with a short recap of what we already discussed in previous chapters. The six main clauses of the SELECT command are shown in Figure 4-1.

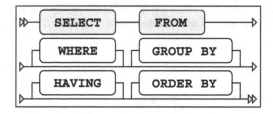

Figure 4-1. *The six main clauses of the SELECT command*

Figure 4-1 is identical to Figure 2-1, and it illustrates the following main syntax rules of the SELECT statement:

- There is a predefined mandatory order of these six clauses.

- The SELECT and FROM clauses are mandatory.

- WHERE, GROUP BY, HAVING, and ORDER BY are optional clauses.

Table 4-1 is identical to Table 2-1, and it shows high-level descriptions of the main SELECT command clauses.

Table 4-1. *The Six Main Clauses of the SELECT Command*

Component	Description
FROM	Which table(s) is (are) needed for retrieval?
WHERE	What is the condition to filter the rows?
GROUP BY	How should the rows be grouped/aggregated?
HAVING	What is the condition to filter the aggregated groups?
SELECT	Which columns do you want to see in the result?
ORDER BY	In which order do you want to see the resulting rows?

According to the ANSI/ISO SQL standard, these six clauses must be processed in the following order: FROM, WHERE, GROUP BY, HAVING, SELECT, ORDER BY. Note that this is *not* the order in which you must specify them in your queries.

As mentioned in the introduction to this chapter, SQL retrieval statements (using SELECT commands) are commonly referred to as *queries*. In this chapter, we will focus on queries using three SELECT command statement clauses:

- SELECT: With the SELECT clause of a SELECT command statement, you specify the columns that you want to be displayed in the query result and, optionally, which column headings you prefer to see above the result table. This clause implements the relational *projection* operator, explained in Chapter 1.

- WHERE: The WHERE clause allows you to formulate conditions that must be true in order for a row to be retrieved. In other words, this clause allows you to filter rows from the base tables; as such, it implements the relational *restriction* operator. You can use various operators in your WHERE clause conditions—such as BETWEEN, LIKE, IN, CASE, NOT, AND, and OR—and make them as complicated as you like.

- ORDER BY: With the ORDER BY clause, you specify the order in which you want to see the rows sorted in the result of your queries.

The FROM clause allows you to specify which tables you want to access. In this chapter, we will work with queries that access only a single table, so the FROM clause in the examples in this chapter simply specifies a single table name. The FROM clause becomes more interesting when you want to access multiple tables in a single query, as described in Chapter 8.

4.2 The SELECT Clause

Let's start with a straightforward example of a SELECT command statement, shown in Listing 4-1.

Listing 4-1. Issuing a Simple SELECT Command

```
select * from departments;

    DEPTNO DNAME      LOCATION      MGR
  -------- ---------- -------- --------
        10 ACCOUNTING NEW YORK     7782
        20 TRAINING   DALLAS       7566
        30 SALES      CHICAGO      7698
        40 HR         BOSTON       7839
```

The asterisk (*) symbol is used to specify that you would like *all* columns of the DEPARTMENTS table to be displayed in the column listing for the resultset. Listing 4-2 shows a slightly more complicated query that selects specific columns from the EMPLOYEES table and uses a WHERE clause to specify a condition for the rows retrieved.

Listing 4-2. Selecting Specific Columns

```
select  ename, init, job, msal
from    employees
where   deptno = 30;


ENAME     INIT  JOB           MSAL
--------  ----- --------  --------
ALLEN     JAM   SALESREP      1600
WARD      TF    SALESREP      1250
MARTIN    P     SALESREP      1250
BLAKE     R     MANAGER       2850
TURNER    JJ    SALESREP      1500
JONES     R     ADMIN          800
```

Let's look at the *syntax* (the statement construction rules of a language) of this statement more closely. You have a lot of freedom in this area. For example, you can enter an entire SQL command statement in a single line, spread a SQL command statement over several lines, and use as many spaces and tabs as you like. New lines, spaces, and tabs are commonly referred to as *white space*. The amount of white space in your SQL statements is meaningless to the Oracle DBMS.

■ **Tip** It is a good idea to define some SQL statement layout standards and stick to them. This increases both the readability and the maintainability of your SQL statements. At this point, our SQL statements are short and simple, but in real production database environments, SQL statements are sometimes several pages long. Recall from Chapter 2 that you may also use SQL Developer formatting techniques to help you organize the layout of your SQL statements.

In the SELECT clause, white space is mandatory after the keyword SELECT. The columns (or *column expressions*) are separated by commas; therefore, white space is not mandatory. However, as you can see in Listing 4-2, spaces after the commas enhance readability.

White space is also mandatory after the keywords FROM and WHERE. Again, any additional white space is not mandatory, but it might enhance readability. For example, you can use spaces around the equal sign in the WHERE clause.

Column Aliases

By default, the column names of the table are displayed above your query result. If you don't like those names—for example, because they do not adequately describe the meaning of the column in the specific context of your query—you can specify different result column headings. You include the heading you want to appear, called a *column alias*, in the SELECT clause of your query, as shown in the example in Listing 4-3.

Listing 4-3. Changing Column Headings

```
select ename, init, msal salary
from   employees
where  deptno = 30;
```

```
ENAME     INIT   SALARY
--------  -----  --------
ALLEN     JAM        1600
WARD      TF         1250
MARTIN    P          1250
BLAKE     R          2850
TURNER    JJ         1500
JONES     R           800
```

In this example, there is *no* comma between MSAL and SALARY. This small detail has a great effect, as the result in Listing 4-3 shows: SALARY is used instead of MSAL as a column heading (compare this with the result shown in Listing 4-2).

By the way, the ANSI/ISO SQL standard also supports the optional keyword AS between any column name and its corresponding column heading (column alias). Using this keyword enhances readability. In other words, you can also formulate the query in Listing 4-3 as follows:

```
select ename, init, msal AS salary
from   employees
where  deptno = 30;
```

The DISTINCT Keyword

Sometimes, your query results contain duplicate rows. You can eliminate such rows by adding the keyword DISTINCT immediately after the keyword SELECT, as demonstrated in Listing 4-4.

Listing 4-4. Using DISTINCT to Eliminate Duplicate Rows

```
select DISTINCT job, deptno
from   employees;
```

```
JOB        DEPTNO
--------  --------
ADMIN          10
ADMIN          30
DIRECTOR       10
MANAGER        10
MANAGER        20
MANAGER        30
SALESREP       30
TRAINER        20
```

```
8 rows selected.
```

Without the addition of the DISTINCT keyword, this query would produce 14 rows, because the EMPLOYEES table contains 14 rows. Remove the keyword DISTINCT from the first line of the query in Listing 4-4, and then execute the query again to see the difference.

■ **Note**   Using DISTINCT in the SELECT clause might incur some performance overhead, because the Oracle DBMS must sort the result in order to eliminate the duplicate rows.

Column Expressions

Instead of column names, you can also specify column expressions in the SELECT clause. For example, Listing 4-5 shows how you can derive the range of the salary grades in the SALGRADES table, by selecting the difference between upper limits and lower limits.

Listing 4-5. Using a Simple Expression in a SELECT Clause

```
select grade, upperlimit - lowerlimit
from   salgrades;

   GRADE UPPERLIMIT-LOWERLIMIT
-------- ---------------------
       1                   500
       2                   199
       3                   599
       4                   999
       5                  6998
```

In the next example, shown in Listing 4-6, we concatenate the employee names with their initials into a single column, and also calculate each employee's yearly salary by multiplying their monthly salary value by 12.

Listing 4-6. Another Example of Using Expressions in a SELECT Clause

```
select init||' '||ename name
,      12 * msal       yearsal
from   employees
where  deptno = 10;

NAME                             YEARSAL
-------------------------------- --------
AB CLARK                           29400
CC KING                            60000
TJA MILLER                         15600
```

Now take a look at the rather odd query shown in Listing 4-7.

Listing 4-7. Selecting an Expression with Literals

```
select 3 + 4 from departments;

     3+4
--------
       7
       7
       7
       7
```

The query result might look strange at first; however, it makes sense when you think about it. The outcome of the expression 3+4 is calculated for each row of the DEPARTMENTS table. This is done four times, because there are four departments and we did not specify a WHERE clause. Because the expression 3+4 does not contain any variables, the result (7) is obviously the same for every department row.

The DUAL Table

It makes more sense to execute queries (that do not refer to any particular schema object (table or view), such as the one shown in Listing 4-7, against a dummy table, with only one row and one column. You could create such a table yourself, but the Oracle DBMS supplies a standard dummy table for this purpose, named DUAL, which is stored in the data dictionary. Because the Oracle DBMS *knows* that the DUAL table contains only one single row, you usually get better performance results by using the DUAL table rather than a dummy table that you created yourself.

■ **Tip** In 10g and above, the Oracle DBMS treats the use of DUAL like a function call that simply evaluates the expression used in the column list. This provides even better performance results than directly accessing the DUAL table.

Listing 4-8 shows two examples of DUAL table usage. Note that the contents of this DUAL table are totally irrelevant; you use only the property that the DUAL table contains a single row.

Listing 4-8. Using the DUAL Table

```
select 123 * 456 from dual;

 123*456
--------
   56088


select sysdate from dual;

SYSDATE
-----------
21-JAN-2014
```

The second query in Listing 4-8 shows an example of using the system date. You can refer to the system date in Oracle with the keyword SYSDATE. Actually, to be more precise, SYSDATE is a *function* that returns the system date. These functions are also referred to as *pseudo columns*. See Appendix A of this book for examples of other such pseudo columns.

Listing 4-9 shows an example of using SYSDATE to derive the age of an employee, based on the date of birth stored in the BDATE column of the EMPLOYEES table.

Listing 4-9. Using the System Date

```
select ename, (sysdate-bdate)/365
from   employees
where  empno = 7839;

ENAME    (SYSDATE-BDATE)/365
-------- -------------------
KING                51.83758
```

■ **Note** The results of your queries using SYSDATE depend on the precise moment the command was run; therefore, when you execute the examples, the results will not be the same as those shown in Listings 4-8 and 4-9.

Null Values in Expressions

You should always consider the possibility of null values occurring in expressions. In case one or more variables in an expression evaluate to a null value, the result of the expression as a whole becomes unknown. We will discuss this area of concern in more detail later in this chapter, in Section 4.9. As a preview, please look at the result of the query in Listing 4-10.

Listing 4-10. The Effect of Null Values in Expressions

```
select  ename, msal, comm, 12*msal + comm
from    employees
where   empno < 7600;


ENAME       MSAL      COMM  12*MSAL+COMM
--------  --------  --------  ------------
SMITH        800
ALLEN       1600       300         19500
WARD        1250       500         15500
JONES       2975
```

As you can see, the total yearly salary (including commission) for two out of four employees is unknown, because the commission column of those employees contains a null value.

4.3 The WHERE Clause

With the WHERE clause, you can specify a *condition* to filter the rows for the result. We distinguish *simple* and *compound* conditions.

Simple conditions typically contain one of the SQL comparison operators listed in Table 4-2.

Table 4-2. *SQL Comparison Operators*

Operator	Description
<	Less than
<=	Less than or equal to
>	Greater than
>=	Greater than or equal to
=	Equal to
<>	Not equal to (alternative syntax: !=)

Expressions containing comparison operators constitute statements that can evaluate to TRUE or FALSE. At least, that's how things are in mathematics (logic), as well as in our intuition. (In Section 4.9, you will see that null values make things slightly more complicated in SQL, but for the moment, we won't worry about them.)

Listing 4-11 shows an example of a WHERE clause with a simple condition.

Listing 4-11. A WHERE Clause with a Simple Condition

```
select ename, init, msal
from   employees
where  msal >= 3000;
```

```
ENAME     INIT    MSAL
--------  -----  --------
SCOTT     SCJ      3000
KING      CC       5000
FORD      MG       3000
```

Listing 4-12 shows another example of a WHERE clause with a simple condition, this time using the <> (not equal to) operator.

Listing 4-12. Another Example of a WHERE Clause with a Simple Condition

```
select dname, location
from   departments
where  location <> 'CHICAGO';
```

```
DNAME       LOCATION
----------  --------
ACCOUNTING  NEW YORK
TRAINING    DALLAS
HR          BOSTON
```

Compound conditions consist of multiple subconditions, combined with logical operators. In Section 4.5 of this chapter, you will see how to construct compound conditions by using the logical operators AND, OR, and NOT.

4.4 The ORDER BY Clause

The result of a query is a table; that is, a set of rows. The order in which these rows appear in the result typically depends on two aspects:

- The strategy chosen by the optimizer to access the data

- The operations chosen by the optimizer to produce the desired result

This means that it is sometimes difficult to predict the order of the rows in the result. In any case, the order is *not* guaranteed to be the same under all circumstances.

If you insist on getting the resulting rows of your query back in a guaranteed order, you must use the ORDER BY clause in your SELECT command statements. Figure 4-2 shows the syntax of this clause.

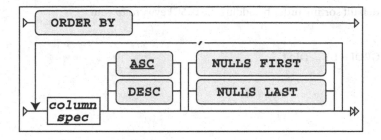

Figure 4-2. *ORDER BY clause syntax diagram*

As Figure 4-2 shows, you can specify multiple sort specifications, separated by commas. Each sort specification consists of a column specification (or column expression), optionally followed by the keyword DESC (descending), in case you want to sort in descending order. Without this addition, the default sorting order is ASC (ascending). ASC is underlined in Figure 4-2 to denote that it is the default.

The column specification may consist of a single column name or a column expression. To refer to columns in the ORDER BY clause, you can use any of the following:

- Regular column names

- Column aliases defined in the SELECT clause (especially useful in case of complex expressions in the SELECT clause)

- Column ordinal numbers

Column ordinal numbers in the ORDER BY clause have no relationship with the order of the columns in the database; they are dependent on only the SELECT clause of your query. Try to avoid using ordinal numbers in the ORDER BY clause. Using column aliases instead increases SQL statement readability, and ensures your ORDER BY clauses also become independent of the SELECT clauses of your queries.

Listing 4-13 shows how you can sort query results on column combinations. As you can see, the query result is sorted on department number, and then on employee name for each department.

Listing 4-13. Sorting Results with ORDER BY

```
select  deptno, ename, init, msal
from    employees
where   msal < 1500
order   by deptno, ename;
```

```
DEPTNO ENAME     INIT    MSAL
-------- -------- ---- --------
      10 MILLER   TJA     1300
      20 ADAMS    AA      1100
      20 SMITH    N        800
      30 JONES    R        800
      30 MARTIN   P       1250
      30 WARD     TF      1250
```

Listing 4-14 shows how you can reverse the default sorting order by adding the DESC keyword to your ORDER BY clause.

Listing 4-14. Sorting in Descending Order with ORDER BY ... DESC

```
select  ename, 12*msal+comm as yearsal
from    employees
where   job = 'SALESREP'
order   by yearsal desc;


ENAME     YEARSAL
--------  --------
ALLEN        19500
TURNER       18000
MARTIN       16400
WARD         15500
```

When sorting, null values cause trouble (when don't they, by the way?). How should columns with missing information be sorted? The rows need to go somewhere, so you need to decide. You have four options as to how to treat null values when sorting:

- Always as *first* values (regardless of the sorting order)

- Always as *last* values (regardless of the sorting order)

- As *low* values (lower than any existing value)

- As *high* values (higher than any existing value)

Figure 4-2 shows how you can explicitly indicate how to treat null values in the ORDER BY clause for each individual column expression.

Let's try to find out Oracle's default behavior for sorting null values. See Listing 4-15 for a first test.

Listing 4-15. Investigating the Ordering of Null Values

```
select  evaluation
from    registrations
where   attendee = 7788
order   by evaluation;


EVALUATION
----------
         4
         5
```

The null value in the result is tough to see; however, it is the third row. If you change the ORDER BY clause to specify a descending sort, the result becomes as shown in Listing 4-16.

Listing 4-16. Testing the Ordering of Null Values

```
select  evaluation
from    registrations
where   attendee = 7788
order   by evaluation DESC;
```

EVALUATION

     5

     4

Listings 4-15 and 4-16 show that Oracle treats null values, by default, as high values. In other words, the default behavior is as follows:

- NULLS LAST is the default for ASC.
- NULLS FIRST is the default for DESC.

4.5 AND, OR, and NOT

You can combine simple and compound conditions into more complicated compound conditions by using the logical operators AND and OR. If you use the AND operator, you indicate that each row should evaluate to TRUE for both conditions. If you use the OR operator, only one of the conditions needs to evaluate to TRUE. Sounds easy enough, doesn't it?

Well, the fact is that we use the words *and* and *or* in a rather sloppy way in spoken languages. The listener easily understands our precise intentions from the context, intonation, or body language. This is why there is a risk of making mistakes when translating questions from a natural language, such as English, into queries in a formal language, such as SQL.

■ **Tip** It is not uncommon to see discussions (mostly after the event) about misunderstandings in the precise wording of the original question in any natural language. Therefore, you should always try to sharpen your question in English as much as possible before trying to convert those questions into SQL statements. In cases of doubt, ask clarifying questions for this purpose.

Therefore, in SQL, the meaning of the two keywords AND and OR must be defined very precisely, without any chance for misinterpretation. You will see the formal truth tables of the AND, OR, and NOT operators in Section 4.10 of this chapter, after the discussion of null values. First, let's experiment with these three operators and look at some examples.

The OR Operator

Consider the operator OR. We can make a distinction between the *inclusive* and the *exclusive* meaning of the word. Is it alright if both conditions evaluate to TRUE, or would it be alright if only one of the two conditions evaluates to TRUE? In natural languages, this distinction is almost always implicit. For example, suppose that you want to know when someone can meet with you, and the answer you get is "next Thursday or Friday." In this case, you probably interpret the OR in its exclusive meaning.

What about SQL—is the OR operator inclusive or exclusive? Listing 4-17 shows the answer.

Listing 4-17. Combining Conditions with OR

```
select  code, category, duration
from    courses
where   category = 'BLD'
or      duration = 2;
```

```
CODE CAT DURATION
---- --- --------
JAV  BLD        4
PLS  BLD        1
XML  BLD        2
RSD  DSG        2
```

In this example, you can see that the OR operator in SQL is inclusive; otherwise, the third row wouldn't show up in the result. The XML course belongs to the BLD course category (so the first condition evaluates to TRUE) *and* its duration is two days (so the second condition also evaluates to TRUE).

Another point of note regarding the evaluation order for an OR operator is that conditions are evaluated in order until a TRUE condition is found. All subsequent conditions are ignored. This is due to the fact that for an OR operator to be satisfied, only one condition must evaluate to TRUE. So, even if you had many OR conditions, evaluation will stop as soon as the first TRUE condition is met.

In the upcoming discussion of the NOT operator, you will see how to construct an exclusive OR.

Figure 4-3 illustrates the differences between the AND and OR operators when represented pictorially with a Venn diagram. When the OR operator is used, satisfying either condition will result in a record being returned. However, when the AND operator is used, all conditions must be satisfied before a record is returned.

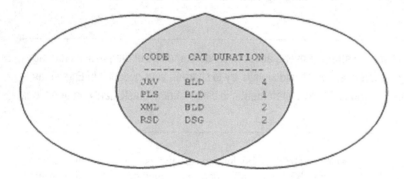

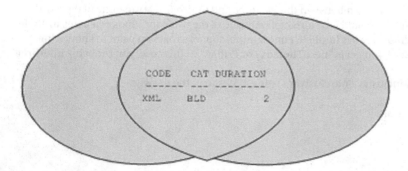

Figure 4-3. *OR and AND Venn Diagram*

The AND Operator and Operator Precedence Issues

There is a possible problem if your compound conditions contain a mixture of AND and OR operators. See Listing 4-18 for an experiment with a query against the DUAL table.

Listing 4-18. Combining Conditions with OR and AND

```
select 'is true  ' as condition
from   dual
where  1=1 or 1=0 and 0=1;

CONDITION
---------
is true
```

The compound condition in Listing 4-18 consists of three rather trivial, simple conditions, evaluating to TRUE, FALSE, and FALSE, respectively. But what is the outcome of the compound predicate as a whole, and why? Apparently, the compound predicate evaluates to TRUE; otherwise, Listing 4-18 would have returned the message "no rows selected."

In such cases, the result depends on the operator *precedence* rules. You can interpret the condition of Listing 4-18 in two ways, as follows:

1=1 OR ...	If one of the operands of OR is true, the overall result is TRUE.
... AND 0=1	If one of the operands of AND is false, the overall result is FALSE.

Listing 4-18 obviously shows an overall result of TRUE. The Oracle DBMS evaluates the expressions in the order that will require the fewest conditional checks. This decision is based on the demographics of your data and is an advanced topic not covered in this book.

With compound conditions, it is always better to use parentheses to indicate the order in which you want the operations to be performed, rather than relying on implicit language precedence rules. Listing 4-19 shows two variants of the query from Listing 4-18, using parentheses in the WHERE clause.

Listing 4-19. Using Parentheses to Force Operator Precedence

```
select 'is true  ' as condition
from   dual
where  (1=1 or 1=0) and 0=1;

no rows selected

select 'is true  ' as condition
from   dual
where  1=1 or (1=0 and 0=1);

CONDITION
---------
is true
```

■ **Caution**   Remember that you can use white space to beautify your SQL commands; however, *never* allow an attractive SQL command layout (for example, with suggestive indentations) to confuse you. Tabs, spaces, and new lines may increase statement readability, but they don't change the meaning of your SQL statements in any way.

The NOT Operator

You can apply the NOT operator to any arbitrary condition to negate that condition. Listing 4-20 shows an example.

Listing 4-20. Using the NOT Operator to Negate Conditions

```
select  ename, job, deptno
from    employees
where   NOT deptno > 10;

ENAME    JOB       DEPTNO
-------- --------- --------
CLARK    MANAGER       10
KING     DIRECTOR      10
MILLER   ADMIN         10
```

In this simple case, you could achieve the same effect by removing the NOT operator and changing the comparison operator > into <=, as shown in Listing 4-21.

Listing 4-21. Equivalent Query Without Using the NOT Operator

```
select  ename, job, deptno
from    employees
where   deptno <= 10;

ENAME    JOB       DEPTNO
-------- --------- --------
CLARK    MANAGER       10
KING     DIRECTOR      10
MILLER   ADMIN         10
```

The NOT operator becomes more interesting and useful in cases where you have complex compound predicates with AND, OR, and parentheses. In such cases, the NOT operator gives you more control over the correctness of your commands.

In general, the NOT operator should be placed in front of the condition. Listing 4-22 shows an example of illegal syntax and a typical error message when NOT is positioned incorrectly.

Listing 4-22. Using the NOT Operator in the Wrong Place

```
select  ename, job, deptno
from    employees
where   deptno NOT > 10;
where   deptno NOT > 10
                   *
ERROR at line 3:
ORA-00920: invalid relational operator
```

There are some exceptions to this rule. As you will see in Section 4.6, the SQL operators BETWEEN, IN, and LIKE have their own built-in negation option.

■ **Tip** Just as you should use parentheses to avoid confusion with AND and OR operators in complex compound conditions, it is also a good idea to use parentheses to specify the precise scope of the NOT operator explicitly. See Listing 4-23 for an example.

By the way, do you remember the discussion about inclusive and exclusive OR? Listing 4-23 shows how you can construct an exclusive OR condition in an SQL statement by explicitly excluding the possibility that both OR condition evaluations evaluate to TRUE (on the fourth line). That's why the XML course is now missing. Compare the result with Listing 4-17.

Listing 4-23. Constructing the Exclusive OR Operator

```
select   code, category, duration
from     courses
where    (category = 'BLD' or  duration = 2)
and not (category = 'BLD' and duration = 2);

CODE CAT DURATION
---- --- --------
JAV  BLD         4
PLS  BLD         1
RSD  DSG         2
```

Just as in mathematics, you can eliminate parentheses from SQL expressions. The following two queries are logically equivalent:

```
select * from employees where NOT (ename = 'BLAKE' AND init = 'R')
select * from employees where      ename <> 'BLAKE' OR init <> 'R'
```

In the second version, the NOT operator disappeared, the negation is applied to the two comparison operators, and last, but not least, the AND changes into an OR. You will look at this logical equivalence in more detail in one of the exercises at the end of this chapter.

4.6 BETWEEN, IN, and LIKE

Section 4.3 introduced the WHERE clause, and Section 4.5 explained how you can combine simple and compound conditions in the WHERE clause into more complicated compound conditions by using the logical operators AND, OR, and NOT. This section introduces three new operators you can use in simple conditions: BETWEEN, IN, and LIKE.

The BETWEEN Operator

The BETWEEN operator does not open up new possibilities; it only allows you to formulate certain conditions a bit more easily and more readably. See Listing 4-24 for an example.

Listing 4-24. Using the BETWEEN Operator

```
select ename, init, msal
from   employees
where  msal between 1300 and 1600;

ENAME     INIT    MSAL
--------  -----   --------
ALLEN     JAM       1600
TURNER    JJ        1500
MILLER    TJA       1300
```

This example shows that the BETWEEN operator includes both border values (1300 and 1600) of the interval.

The BETWEEN operator has its own built-in negation option. Therefore, the following three SQL expressions are logically equivalent:

```
where msal NOT between 1000 and 2000
where NOT msal between 1000 and 2000
where msal < 1000 OR msal > 2000
```

The IN Operator

With the IN operator, you can compare a column or the outcome of a column expression against a list of values. Using the IN operator is also a simpler way of writing a series of OR conditions. Instead of writing empno = 7499 OR empno = 7566 OR empno = 7788, you simply use an IN-list. See Listing 4-25 for an example.

Listing 4-25. Using the IN Operator

```
select empno, ename, init
from   employees
where  empno in (7499,7566,7788);

  EMPNO ENAME     INIT
-------- --------  -----
   7499 ALLEN     JAM
   7566 JONES     JM
   7788 SCOTT     SCJ
```

Just like BETWEEN, the IN operator also has its own built-in negation option. The example in Listing 4-26 produces all course registrations that do *not* have an evaluation value of 3, 4, or 5.

Listing 4-26. Using the NOT IN Operator

```
select * from registrations
where evaluation NOT IN (3,4,5);

ATTENDEE COUR BEGINDATE EVALUATION
-------- ---- --------- ----------
   7876 SQL  12-APR-99          2
   7499 JAV  13-DEC-99          2
```

Check for yourself that the following four expressions are logically equivalent:

```
where       evaluation NOT in (3,4,5)
where NOT   evaluation    in (3,4,5)
where NOT   (evaluation=3  OR evaluation=4   OR evaluation=5)
where       evaluation<>3 AND evaluation<>4 AND evaluation<>5
```

A rather obvious requirement for the IN operator is that all of the values you specify between the parentheses must have the same (relevant) datatype.

The LIKE Operator

You typically use the LIKE operator in the WHERE clause of your queries in combination with a *search pattern*. In the example shown in Listing 4-27, the query returns all courses that have something to do with SQL, using the search pattern %SQL%.

Listing 4-27. Using the LIKE Operator with the Percent Character

```
select * from courses
where description LIKE '%SQL%';

CODE DESCRIPTION                     TYP DURATION
---- ------------------------------- --- --------
SQL  Introduction to SQL             GEN        4
PLS  Introduction to PL/SQL          BLD        1
```

Two characters have special meaning when you use them in a string (the search pattern) after the LIKE operator. These two characters are commonly referred to as *wildcards*:

%: A percent sign after the LIKE operator means zero, one, or more arbitrary characters (see Listing 4-27).

_: An underscore after the LIKE operator means exactly *one* arbitrary character.

■ **Note** If the LIKE operator (with its two wildcard characters) provides insufficient search possibilities, you can use the REGEXP_LIKE function and regular expressions. See Chapter 5 for information about using regular expressions.

The query shown in Listing 4-28 returns all employees with an uppercase *A* as the second character in their name.

Listing 4-28. Using the LIKE Operator with the Percent and Underscore Characters

```
select empno, init, ename
from   employees
where  ename like '_A%';

 EMPNO INIT  ENAME
------- ----- --------
   7521 TF    WARD
   7654 P     MARTIN
```

Just like the BETWEEN and IN operators, the LIKE operator also features a built-in negation option; in other words, you can use WHERE ... NOT LIKE ....

The following queries show two special cases: one using LIKE without wildcards and one using the % character without the LIKE operator.

```
select * from employees where ename like 'BLAKE'
select * from employees where ename = 'BL%'
```

Both queries will be executed by Oracle, without any complaints or error messages. However, in the first example, we could have used the equal sign (=) instead of the LIKE operator to get the same results. In the second example, the percent sign (%) has no special meaning, since it doesn't follow the LIKE operator, so it is very likely we would get back the "no rows selected" message.

If you really want to search for actual percent sign or underscore characters with the LIKE operator, you need to suppress the special meaning of those characters. You can do this with the ESCAPE option of the LIKE operator, as demonstrated in Listing 4-29.

Listing 4-29. Using the ESCAPE Option of the LIKE Operator

```
select empno, begindate, comments
from   history
where  comments like '%0\%%' escape '\';

   EMPNO BEGINDATE   COMMENTS
-------- ----------- -----------------------------------------------------
    7566 01-JUN-1989 From accounting to human resources; 0% salary change
    7788 15-APR-1985 Transfer to human resources; 0% salary raise
```

The WHERE clause in Listing 4-29 is used to filter the result set to include only those comments that include a textual reference to 0% in the COMMENTS column of the HISTORY table. The backslash (\) suppresses the special meaning of the second percent sign in the search string. Note that you can pick a character other than the backslash to use as the ESCAPE character.

4.7 CASE Expressions

You can tackle complicated procedural problems with CASE expressions. Oracle supports two CASE expression types: *simple* CASE expressions and *searched* CASE expressions.

Figure 4-4 illustrates the syntax of the simple CASE expression. With this type of CASE expression, you specify an *input expression* to be compared with the *values* in the WHEN ... THEN loop. The implicit comparison operator is always the equal sign. The left operand is always the input expression, and the right operand is the value from the WHEN clause.

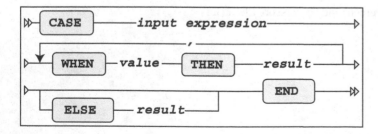

Figure 4-4. *Simple CASE expression syntax diagram*

Figure 4-5 shows the syntax of the searched CASE expression. The power of this type of CASE expression is that you don't specify an input expression, but instead specify complete conditions in the WHEN clause. Therefore, you have the freedom to use any logical operator in each individual WHEN clause.

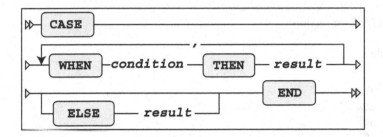

Figure 4-5. *Searched CASE expressions syntax diagram*

CASE expressions are evaluated as follows:

- Oracle evaluates the WHEN expressions in the order in which you specified them, and returns the THEN result of the *first* condition evaluating to TRUE. Note that Oracle does *not* evaluate the remaining WHEN clauses; therefore, the order of the WHEN expressions is important.

- If none of the WHEN expressions evaluates to TRUE, Oracle returns the ELSE expression.

- If you didn't specify an ELSE expression, Oracle returns a null value.

Obviously, you must handle datatypes in a consistent way. The input expressions and the THEN results in the simple CASE expression (Figure 4-4) must have the same datatype, and in both CASE expression types (Figures 4-4 and 4-5), the THEN results should have the same datatype, too.

Listing 4-30 shows a straightforward example of a simple CASE expression, which doesn't require any explanation.

Listing 4-30. Simple CASE Expression Example

```
select  attendee, begindate
,       case evaluation
             when 1 then 'bad'
             when 2 then 'mediocre'
             when 3 then 'ok'
             when 4 then 'good'
             when 5 then 'excellent'
                    else 'not filled in'
        end
from    registrations
where   course = 'SO2';

ATTENDEE BEGINDATE CASEEVALUATIO
-------- --------- -------------
    7499 12-APR-99 good
    7698 12-APR-99 good
    7698 13-DEC-99 not filled in
    7788 04-OCT-99 not filled in
    7839 04-OCT-99 ok
```

```
7876 12-APR-99 mediocre
7902 04-OCT-99 good
7902 13-DEC-99 not filled in
7934 12-APR-99 excellent
```

Listing 4-31 shows an example of a searched CASE expression.

Listing 4-31. Searched CASE Expression Example

```
select ename, job
,      case when job = 'TRAINER' then '  10%'
            when job = 'MANAGER' then '  20%'
            when ename = 'SMITH' then '  30%'
                             else '   0%'
       end  as raise
from   employees
order  by raise desc, ename;


ENAME    JOB       RAISE
-------- --------- -----
BLAKE    MANAGER   20%
CLARK    MANAGER   20%
JONES    MANAGER   20%
ADAMS    TRAINER   10%
FORD     TRAINER   10%
SCOTT    TRAINER   10%
SMITH    TRAINER   10%
ALLEN    SALESREP   0%
JONES    ADMIN      0%
KING     DIRECTOR   0%
MARTIN   SALESREP   0%
MILLER   ADMIN      0%
TURNER   SALESREP   0%
WARD     SALESREP   0%
```

In Listing 4-31, note that SMITH gets only a 10% raise, despite the fourth line of the query. This is because he is a trainer, which causes the second line to result in a match; therefore, the remaining WHEN expressions are not considered.

■ **Note** CASE expressions may contain other CASE expressions. The only limitation is that a single CASE may have a maximum of 255 conditional expressions. Even though you can create large CASE expressions, take care to not use so many embedded conditions that your logic is hard to follow.

CASE expressions are very powerful and flexible; however, they sometimes become rather long. That's why Oracle offers several functions that you could interpret as abbreviations (or shorthand notations) for CASE expressions, such as COALESCE and NULLIF (both of these functions are part of the ANSI/ISO SQL standard), NVL, NVL2, and DECODE. We will look at some of these functions in the next chapter.

4.8 Subqueries

Section 4.6 introduced the IN operator. This section introduces the concept of subqueries by starting with an example of the IN operator.

Suppose you want to launch a targeted e-mail campaign, because you have a brand-new course that you want to promote. The target audience for the new course is the developer community, so you want to know who attended one or more build (BLD category) courses in the past. You could execute the following query to get the desired result:

```
select attendee
from   registrations
where  course in ('JAV','PLS','XML')
```

This solution has at least two problems. To start with, you have looked at the COURSES table to check which courses belong to the BLD course category, apparently (evidenced by the JAV, PLS, and XML course listings in the WHERE clause). However, the original question was not referring to any specific courses; it referred to BLD courses. This lookup trick is easy in our demo database, which has a total of only ten courses, but it might be problematic, or even impossible, in real information systems. Another problem is that the solution is rather rigid. Suppose you want to repeat the e-mail promotion one year later for another new course. In that case, you may need to revise the query to reflect the current set of BLD courses.

A much better solution to this problem is to use a *subquery*. This way, you leave it up to the Oracle DBMS to query the COURSES table, by replacing the list of course codes between the parentheses (JAV, PLS, and XML) with a query that retrieves the desired course codes for you. Listing 4-32 shows the subquery for this example.

Listing 4-32. Using a Subquery to Retrieve All BLD Courses

```
select attendee
from   registrations
where  course in (select code
                  from   courses
                  where  category = 'BLD');
```

```
ATTENDEE
--------
    7499
    7566
    7698
    7788
    7839
    7876
    7788
    7782
    7499
    7876
    7566
    7499
    7900
```

This eliminates both problems with the initial solution with the hard-coded course codes. Oracle first substitutes the subquery between the parentheses with its result—a number of course codes—and then executes the main query. (Consider "first substitutes ... and then executes ..." conceptually; the Oracle optimizer could actually decide to execute the SQL statement in a different way.)

Apparently, 13 employees attended at least one build course in the past (see Listing 4-32). Is that really true? Upon closer investigation, you can see that some employees apparently attended several build courses, or maybe some employees even attended the same build course twice. In other words, the conclusion about the number of employees (13) was too hasty. To retrieve the correct number of employees, you should use SELECT DISTINCT in the main query to eliminate duplicates.

The Joining Condition

It is always your own responsibility to formulate subqueries in such a way that you are not comparing apples with oranges. For example, the next variant of the query shown in Listing 4-33 does not result in an error message; however, the result is erroneous.

Listing 4-33. Comparing Apples with Oranges

```
select  attendee
from    registrations
where   EVALUATION in (select  DURATION
                       from    courses
                       where   category = 'BLD');

ATTENDEE
--------
    7900
    7788
    7839
    7900
    7521
    7902
    7698
    7499
    7499
    7876
```

This example compares evaluation numbers (from the main query) with course durations from the subquery. Just try to translate this query into an English sentence....

Fortunately, the Oracle DBMS does not discriminate between meaningful and meaningless questions. You have only two constraints:

- The datatypes must match, or the Oracle DBMS must be able to make them match with implicit datatype conversion.

- The subquery should not select too many column values per row.

When a Subquery Returns Too Many Values

What happens when a subquery returns too many values? Look at the query in Listing 4-34 and the resulting error message.

Listing 4-34. Error: Subquery Returns Too Many Values

```
select attendee
from   registrations
where  course in
       (select course, begindate
        from   offerings
        where  location = 'CHICAGO');
       (select course, begindate
        *
ERROR at line 4:
ORA-00913: too many values
```

The subquery in Listing 4-34 returns (COURSE, BEGINDATE) value pairs, which cannot be compared with COURSE values. However, it is certainly possible to compare attribute combinations with subqueries in SQL. The query in Listing 4-34 was an attempt to find all employees who ever attended a course in Chicago.

In our data model, course offerings are uniquely identified by the combination of the course code and the begin date. Therefore, you can correct the query as shown in Listing 4-35.

Listing 4-35. Fixing the Error from Listing 4-34

```
select attendee
from   registrations
where (course, begindate) in
      (select course, begindate
       from   offerings
       where  location = 'CHICAGO');

ATTENDEE
--------
    7521
    7902
    7900
```

■ **Note**   Subqueries may, in turn, contain other subqueries. This principle is known as *subquery nesting*, and there is no practical limit to the number of subquery levels you might want to create in Oracle SQL. But be aware that at a certain level of nesting, you will probably lose the overview.

Comparison Operators in the Joining Condition

So far, we have explored subqueries with the IN operator. However, you can also establish a relationship between a main query and its subquery by using one of the comparison operators (=, <, >, <=, >=, <>), as demonstrated in Listing 4-36. In that case, there is one important difference: the subquery *must* return precisely one row. This additional constraint makes sense if you take into consideration how these comparison operators work: they are able to compare only a single left operand with a single right operand.

Listing 4-36. Using a Comparison Operator in the Joining Condition

```
select  ename, init, bdate
from    employees
where   bdate > (select bdate
                 from    employees
                 where   empno = 7876);
```

```
ENAME     INIT   BDATE
--------  -----  ---------
JONES     JM     02-APR-67
TURNER    JJ     28-SEP-68
JONES     R      03-DEC-69
```

The query in Listing 4-36 returns all employees who are younger than employee 7876. The subquery will never return more than one row, because `EMPNO` is the primary key of the `EMPLOYEES` table.

In case there is *no* employee with the employee number specified, you receive the "no rows selected" message. You might expect an error message like "single row subquery returns no rows" (actually, this error message once existed in Oracle, many releases ago), but apparently there is no error returned. See Listing 4-37 for an example.

Listing 4-37. When the Subquery Returns No Rows

```
select  ename, init, bdate
from    employees
where   bdate > (select bdate
                 from    employees
                 where   empno = 99999);
```

```
no rows selected
```

The subquery (returning *no* rows, or producing an empty set) is treated like a subquery returning one row instead, containing a null value. In other words, SQL treats this situation as if there *were* an employee 99999 with an unknown date of birth. This may sound strange; however, this behavior is fully compliant with the ANSI/ISO SQL standard.

When a Single-Row Subquery Returns More Than One Row

In case the subquery happens to produce *multiple* rows, the Oracle DBMS reacts with the error message shown in Listing 4-38.

Listing 4-38. Error: Single-Row Subquery Returns More Than One Row

```
select  ename, init, bdate
from    employees
where   bdate > (select bdate
                 from    employees
                 where   ename = 'JONES');
where   bdate > (select bdate
                 *
ERROR at line 3:
ORA-01427: single-row subquery returns more than one row
```

In this example, the problem is that we have two employees with the same name (Jones). Note that you always risk this outcome, unless you make sure to use an equality comparison against a unique column of the table accessed in the subquery, as in the example in Listing 4-36.

So far, we have investigated subqueries only in the WHERE clause of the SELECT statement. Oracle SQL also supports subqueries in other SELECT statement clauses, such as the FROM clause and the SELECT clause. Chapter 9 will revisit subqueries.

4.9 Null Values

If a column (in a specific row of a table) contains no value, we say that such a column contains a null value. The term *null value* is actually slightly misleading, because it is an indicator of missing information. Null *marker* would be a better term, because a null value is *not* a value.

There can be many different reasons for missing information. Sometimes, an attribute is *inapplicable*; for example, only sales representatives are eligible for commission. An attribute value can also be *unknown*; for example, the person entering data did not know certain values when the data was entered. And, sometimes, you don't know whether an attribute is applicable or inapplicable; for example, if you don't know the job of a specific employee, you don't know whether a commission value is applicable. The REGISTRATIONS table provides another good example. A null value in the EVALUATION column can mean several things: the course did not yet take place, the attendee had no opinion, the attendee refused to provide her opinion, the evaluation forms are not yet processed, and so on.

It would be nice if you could represent the *reason* why information is missing, but SQL supports only one null value, and according to Ted Codd's Rule 3: Systematic Treatment of Missing Information (see Chapter 1) null values can have only one *context-independent* meaning.

■ **Caution** Don't confuse null values with the number zero (0), a series of one or more spaces, or even an empty string. Although an empty string ('') is formally different from a null value, Oracle sometimes interprets empty strings as null values (see Chapter 6 for some examples). However, you should *never* rely on this (debatable) interpretation of empty strings. You should always use the reserved word NULL to refer to null values in your SQL commands. Furthermore, the Oracle documentation states that empty strings may no longer be interpreted as NULL at some point in the future.

Null Value Display

By default, null values are displayed on your computer screen as "nothing," as shown earlier in Listings 4-15 and 4-16. You can change this behavior in SQL Developer at the session level.

You can specify how null values appear at the session level by modifying the Display NULL Value AS environment setting, available in the SQL Developer Preferences dialog box, shown in Figure 4-6. Select the Tools ➤ Preferences menu option to open this dialog box.

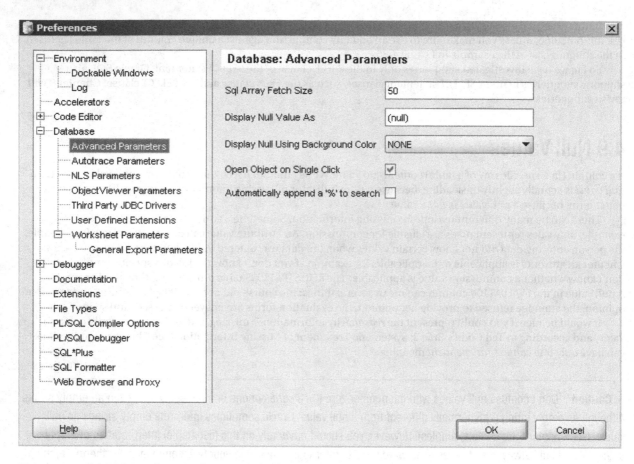

Figure 4-6. *The SQL Developer Preferences dialog box*

The Nature of Null Values

Null values sometimes behave counter-intuitively. Compare the results of the two queries in Listing 4-39.

Listing 4-39. Comparing Two "Complementary" Queries

```
select empno, ename, comm
from   employees
where  comm > 400;

  EMPNO ENAME        COMM
-------- -------- --------
   7521 WARD          500
   7654 MARTIN       1400

select empno, ename, comm
from   employees
where  comm <= 400;
```

```
EMPNO ENAME      COMM
-------- -------- --------
   7499 ALLEN      300
   7844 TURNER       0
```

The first query in Listing 4-39 returns 2 employees, so you might expect to see the other 12 employees in the result of the second query, because the two WHERE clauses complement each other. However, the two query results actually are *not* complementary.

If Oracle evaluates a condition, there are three possible outcomes: the result can be TRUE, FALSE, or UNKNOWN. In other words, the SQL language is using *three-valued logic*.

Only those rows for which the condition evaluates to TRUE will appear in the result—no problem. However, the EMPLOYEES table contains several rows for which *both* conditions in Listing 4-39 evaluate to UNKNOWN. Therefore, these rows (ten, in this case) will not appear in either result.

Just to stress the nonintuitive nature of null values in SQL, you could say the following:

In SQL, NOT is not "not"

The explanation of this (case-sensitive) statement is that in three-valued logic, the NOT operator is not the complement operator anymore:

```
NOT TRUE is equivalent with FALSE
not TRUE is equivalent with FALSE OR UNKNOWN
```

The IS NULL Operator

Suppose you are looking for all employees except the lucky ones with a commission greater than 400. In that case, the second query in Listing 4-39 does not give you the correct answer, because you would expect to see 12 employees instead of 2. To fix this query, you need the SQL IS NULL operator, as shown in Listing 4-40.

Listing 4-40. Using the IS NULL Operator

```
select empno, ename, comm
from   employees
where  comm <= 400
or     comm is null;
```

```
EMPNO ENAME      COMM
-------- -------- --------
   7369 SMITH
   7499 ALLEN      300
   7566 JONES
   7698 BLAKE
   7782 CLARK
   7788 SCOTT
   7839 KING
   7844 TURNER       0
   7876 ADAMS
   7900 JONES
   7902 FORD
   7934 MILLER
```

■ **Note**   Oracle SQL provides some functions with the specific purpose of handling null values in a flexible way (such as NVL and NVL2). These functions are covered in the next chapter.

The IS NULL operator—just like BETWEEN, IN, and LIKE—has its own built-in negation option. See Listing 4-41 for an example.

Listing 4-41. Using the IS NOT NULL Operator

```
select ename, job, msal, comm
from   employees
where  comm is not null;


ENAME     JOB        MSAL      COMM
--------  --------  --------  --------
ALLEN     SALESREP    1600      300
WARD      SALESREP    1250      500
MARTIN    SALESREP    1250     1400
TURNER    SALESREP    1500        0
```

■ **Note**   The IS NULL operator *always* evaluates to TRUE or FALSE. UNKNOWN is an impossible outcome.

Null Values and the Equality Operator

The IS NULL operator has only *one* operand: the preceding column name (or column expression). Actually, it is a pity that this operator is not written as IS_NULL (with an underscore instead of a space) to stress the fact that this operator has just a single operand. In contrast, the equality operator (=) has *two* operands: a left operand and a right operand.

Watch the rather subtle syntax difference between the following two queries:

```
select * from registrations where evaluation IS null
select * from registrations where evaluation  = null
```

If you were to read both queries aloud, you might not even hear any difference. However, the seemingly innocent syntax change has definite consequences for the query results. They don't produce error messages, because both queries are syntactically correct.

If one (or both) of the operands being compared by the equality comparison operator (=) evaluates to a null value, the result is UNKNOWN. In other words, you cannot say that a null value is equal to a null value. The following shows the conclusions:

Expression	Evaluates to
NULL = NULL	UNKNOWN
NULL IS NULL	TRUE

This explains why the query in Listing 4-42 doesn't return all 14 rows of the EMPLOYEES table.

Listing 4-42. Example of a Counterintuitive WHERE Clause

```
select ename, init
from   employees
where  comm = comm;


ENAME    INIT
-------- -----
ALLEN    JAM
WARD     TF
MARTIN   P
TURNER   JJ
```

In mathematical logic, we call expressions always evaluating to TRUE a *tautology*. The example in Listing 4-42 shows that certain trivial tautologies from two-valued logic (such as COMM = COMM) don't hold true in SQL.

Null Value Pitfalls

Null values in SQL often cause trouble. You must be aware of their existence in the database *and* their odds of being generated by Oracle in (intermediate) results, and you must continuously ask yourself how you want them to be treated in the processing of your SQL statements. Otherwise, the correctness of your queries will be debatable, to say the least.

You have already seen that null values in expressions generally cause those expressions to produce a null value. In the next chapter, you will learn how the various SQL functions handle null values.

It is obvious that there are many pitfalls in the area of missing information. It may be possible to circumvent at least some of these problems by properly designing your databases. In one of his books, Ted Codd, the "inventor" of the relational model, even proposed introducing *two* types of null values: *applicable* and *inapplicable*. This would imply the need for a four-valued logic (see *The Relational Model for Database Management: Version 2* by Ted Codd (Addison-Wesley, 1990)).

■ **Tip**   If you are interested in more details about null values (or other theoretical information about relational databases and pitfalls in SQL), the books written by Chris Date are the best starting point for further exploration. In particular, his *Relational Database: Selected Writings* series (Addison-Wesley, 1986) is brilliant. Chris Date's ability to write in an understandable, entertaining, and fascinating way about these topics far exceeds others in the field.

Here's a brain-twister to finish this section about null values: why does the query in Listing 4-43 produce "no rows selected"? There *are* registrations with evaluation values 4 and 5, for sure....

Listing 4-43. A Brain-Twister

```
select * from registrations
where evaluation not in (1,2,3,NULL);

no rows selected
```

The following WHERE clause:

```
where evaluation not in (1,2,3,NULL)
```

is logically equivalent with the following "iterated AND" condition:

```
where evaluation <> 1
AND    evaluation <> 2
AND    evaluation <> 3
AND    evaluation <> NULL
```

If you consider a row with an EVALUATION value of 1, 2, or 3, it is obvious that out of the first three conditions, one of them returns FALSE, and the other two return TRUE. Therefore, the complete WHERE clause returns FALSE.

If the EVALUATION value is NULL, all four conditions return UNKNOWN. Therefore, the end result is also UNKNOWN. So far, there are no surprises.

If the EVALUATION value is 4 or 5 (the remaining two allowed values), the first three conditions all return TRUE, but the last condition returns UNKNOWN. So you have the following expression:

```
(TRUE) and (TRUE) and (TRUE) and (UNKNOWN)
```

This is logically equivalent with UNKNOWN, so the complete WHERE clause returns UNKNOWN. However, if you were to change the WHERE clause to read:

```
where evaluation not in (1,2,3)
  and evaluation is not null
```

then the new result would return any rows with an evaluation value of 4 or 5, but no other rows.

4.10 Truth Tables

Section 4.5 of this chapter showed how to use the AND, OR, and NOT operators to build compound conditions. In that section, we didn't worry too much about missing information and null values, but we are now in a position to examine the combination of three-valued logic and compound conditions. This is often a challenging subject, because three-valued logic is not always intuitive. The most reliable way to investigate compound conditions is to use truth tables.

Table 4-3 shows the truth table of the NOT operator. In truth tables, UNK is commonly used as an abbreviation for UNKNOWN.

Table 4-3. *Truth Table of the NOT Operator*

Op1	NOT (Op1)
TRUE	FALSE
FALSE	TRUE
UNK	UNK

In Table 4-3, Op1 stands for the operand. Since the NOT operator works on a single operand, the truth table needs three rows to describe all possibilities. Note that the negation of UNK is UNK.

Table 4-4 shows the truth table of the AND and OR operators; Op1 and Op2 are the two operands, and the truth table shows all nine possible combinations.

Table 4-4. Truth Table of the AND and OR Operators

Op1	Op2	Op1 AND Op2	Op1 OR Op2
TRUE	TRUE	TRUE	TRUE
TRUE	FALSE	FALSE	TRUE
TRUE	UNK	UNK	TRUE
FALSE	TRUE	FALSE	TRUE
FALSE	FALSE	FALSE	FALSE
FALSE	UNK	FALSE	UNK
UNK	TRUE	UNK	TRUE
UNK	FALSE	FALSE	UNK
UNK	UNK	UNK	UNK

Note that the AND and OR operators are symmetric; that is, you can swap Op1 and Op2 without changing the operator outcome.

If you are facing complicated compound conditions, truth tables can be very useful to rewrite those conditions into simpler, logically equivalent, expressions.

4.11 Exercises

These exercises assume you have access to a database schema with the seven case tables (see Appendix A of this book). You can download the scripts to create this schema from this book's catalog page on the Apress website. The exact URL is http://www.apress.com/9781430271970. Look in the "Source Code/Downloads" section of the catalog page for a link to the download.

When you're done with the exercises, check your answers against ours. We give our answers in Appendix B.

1. Provide the code and description of all courses with an exact duration of four days.

2. List all employees, sorted by job, and per job by age (from young to old).

3. Which courses have been held in Chicago and/or in Seattle?

4. Which employees attended both the Java course and the XML course? (Provide their employee numbers.)

5. List the names and initials of all employees, except for R. Jones.

6. Find the number, job, and date of birth of all trainers and sales representatives born before 1960.

7. List the numbers of all employees who do not work for the training department.

8. List the numbers of all employees who did not attend the Java course.

9. Which employees have subordinates? Which employees *don't* have subordinates?

10. Produce an overview of all general course offerings (course category GEN) in 1999.

11. Provide the name and initials of all employees who have ever attended a course taught by N. Smith. Hint: Use subqueries, and work "inside out" toward the result; that is, retrieve the employee number of N. Smith, then search for the codes of all courses he ever taught, and so on.

12. How could you redesign the EMPLOYEES table to avoid the problem that the COMM column contains null values meaning *not applicable*?

13. In Section 4.9, you saw the following statement: In SQL, NOT is not "not." What is this statement trying to say?

14. At the end of Section 4.5, you saw the following statement.

    The following two queries are logically equivalent:

    ```
    select * from employees where NOT (ename = 'BLAKE' AND init = 'R')
    select * from employees where      ename <> 'BLAKE' OR init <> 'R'
    ```

    Prove this, using a truth table. Hint: Use P as an abbreviation for ename = 'BLAKE', and use Q as an abbreviation for init = 'R'.

CHAPTER 5

■ ■ ■

Retrieval: Functions

This chapter is a logical continuation of the previous chapter. The main topic is still retrieval. It introduces *functions* and *regular expressions*, which enable you to formulate more powerful and complicated queries in an easy way.

Oracle supports an abundance of functions. Apart from the various ANSI/ISO SQL standard functions, many Oracle-specific functions have been added to Oracle's SQL implementation over the years.

The chapter begins with an overview of the seven categories of functions: arithmetic, text, regular expression, date, general, conversion, and group. The remaining sections discuss each type, with the exception of group functions, which are introduced in Chapter 8. You will also learn about regular expressions, which are used with some text functions to search for certain patterns in text. The last section of this chapter briefly explains how you can define your own SQL functions in Oracle using the PL/SQL programming language.

5.1 Overview of Functions

In Chapter 2, you saw that SQL supports the following standard SQL operators:

- Arithmetic operators: +, -, *, and /

- Alphanumeric operator: || (concatenation)

Besides using these operators, you can also perform many operations on your data using *functions*. You can use functions virtually anywhere within queries: in the SELECT, WHERE, HAVING, and ORDER BY clauses.

You can recognize functions as follows: they each have a name, followed by one or more arguments (between parentheses). In general, function arguments can be constants, variables, or expressions, and sometimes function arguments contain functions themselves. Functions inside function arguments are referred to as *nested functions*. In some cases, function arguments are optional. This means that you can omit the optional argument and allow Oracle to use a standard (or default) value.

Functions are usually listed in two groups: single-row functions, which have one row as input, and multiple-row functions, which have many rows as their input. Multiple-row functions are also called group functions. When they are used as aggregate functions, they return one value for each group they look at—examples are SUM, AVG, COUNT, and so on. They may also be used as analytic functions, in which case they return one value for each row that they evaluate. All the other functions are single-row functions, taking one row value as input and returning one value. Examples are UPPER, LOWER, TRUNC, and TO_CHAR.

■ **Note** Online documentation *Oracle SQL Reference* uses different terms for two similar concepts: functions without arguments and pseudo columns. For example, SYSDATE and USER are listed as functions, and ROWNUM, LEVEL, and NEXTVAL are listed as pseudo columns. If you check older versions of the documentation, you will see that Oracle has changed terminology over the years. In version 5.1, both SYSDATE and USER were pseudo columns; in version 6.0, SYSDATE was promoted to a function, but USER was still a pseudo column; and in version 7.3, both SYSDATE and USER were documented as functions. You could argue that SYSDATE and USER return the same value for every row, while ROWNUM, LEVEL, and NEXTVAL normally return different values. According to the current *Oracle SQL Reference*, functions take *zero* or more arguments. This book sometimes refers to items as *pseudo columns* where *Oracle SQL Reference* refers to them as *functions*.

Obviously, the function arguments come with some constraints. For example, the datatype of the function arguments must make some logical sense. The Oracle DBMS always tries to perform implicit datatype conversion, and it will generate an error message only if such an attempt fails. In other words, if you specify a number as an argument for a function that expects a string instead, the number will be interpreted alphanumerically. However, if you ask for the square root of an employee name, you will get the error message ORA-01722: invalid number."

1. Here are some examples of calls to functions to illustrate the above. A number given to a string function (incorrect usage)—number interpreted as string:

   ```
   SQL> select upper(123) from dual;
   UPP
   ---
   123
   ```

2. A string given to a string function (correct usage):

   ```
   SQL> select upper('de haan') from dual;
   UPPER('
   -------
   DE HAAN
   ```

3. A string given to a number function (incorrect apostrophes). Implicit datatype conversion is done.

   ```
   SQL> select trunc('123.4555', 2) from dual;
   TRUNC('123.4555',2)
   -------------------
                123.45
   ```

4. A number given to a number function (correct usage):

   ```
   SQL> select trunc(123.4555 , 2) from dual;
   TRUNC(123.4555,2)
   -----------------
              123.45
   ```

5. Pseudo columns do not have arguments:

```
SQL> select sysdate, user from dual;
SYSDATE           USER
----------------- ----------
13 February  2014 BOOK
```

■ **Caution**   It is *not* a good idea to rely on implicit datatype conversion in your SQL statements. You should always use explicit conversion functions instead. This improves SQL readability, robustness, and possibly performance.

Testing against the public DUAL table, introduced in Chapter 4, is practical, since you get only one result because there is only one row in the table. It is present in all Oracle databases, is owned by the most privileged user SYS, and has one column and one row, containing an X.

```
SQL> select * from dual;
D
-
X
```

DUAL seems to indicate something to do with "two," and the original table did indeed have two rows. Now it has only one row, and that is the important thing about it, but the name remained unchanged.

As stated previously, Oracle supports many functions. You can categorize them based on the datatype they expect in their arguments, as shown in Table 5-1.

Table 5-1. *Function Types*

Function Type	Applicable To
Arithmetic functions	Numerical data
Text functions	Alphanumeric data
Regular expression functions	Alphanumeric data
Date functions	Date/time-related data
General functions	Any datatype
Conversion functions	Datatype conversion
Group functions	Sets of values

The last category in Table 5-1, group functions, is covered in Chapter 8, where we discuss the GROUP BY and HAVING clauses of the SELECT command, since that chapter is a more natural place to introduce them. The other function types are discussed in the following sections.

5.2 Arithmetic Functions

The most popular arithmetic functions of Oracle are listed in Table 5-2.

Table 5-2. *Common Oracle Arithmetic Functions*

Function	Description
ROUND(n[,m])	Round n on m decimal positions
TRUNC(n[,m])	Truncate n on m decimal positions
CEIL(n)	Round n upward to an integer
FLOOR(n)	Round n downward to an integer
ABS(n)	Absolute value of n
SIGN(n)	–1, 0, or 1 if n is negative, zero, or positive
SQRT(n)	Square root of n
EXP(n)	e (= 2,7182813...) raised to the nth power
LN(n), LOG(m,n)	Natural logarithm, and logarithm base m
POWER(n,m)	n raised to the mth power
MOD(n,m)	Remainder of n divided by m
SIN(n), COS(n), TAN(n)	Sine, cosine, and tangent of n (n expressed in radians)
ASIN(n), ACOS(n), ATAN(n)	Arcsine, arccosine, and arctangent of n
SINH(n), COSH(n), TANH(n)	Hyperbolic sine, hyperbolic cosine, and hyperbolic tangent of n

As Table 5-2 shows, the ROUND and TRUNC functions have an optional argument m; the default value for m is zero. Note that you can also use negative values for m, as you can see from the second example in Listing 5-1.

Listings 5-1 through 5-4 show some self-explanatory examples of using the following arithmetic functions: ROUND, CEIL, FLOOR, ABS, SIGN, POWER, and MOD.

Listing 5-1. Using the ROUND, CEIL, and FLOOR Functions

```
select round(345.678, 0), ceil(345.678), floor(345.678)
from   dual;

ROUND(345.678) CEIL(345.678) FLOOR(345.678)
-------------- ------------- --------------
           346           346            345

select round(345.678, 2)
,      round(345.678,-1)
,      round(345.678,-2)
from   dual;

ROUND(345.678,2) ROUND(345.678,-1) ROUND(345.678,-2)
---------------- ----------------- -----------------
          345.68               350               300
```

Listing 5-2. Using the ABS and SIGN Functions

```
select  abs(-123),  abs(0),  abs(456)
,       sign(-123), sign(0), sign(456)
from    dual;

ABS(-123)   ABS(0) ABS(456) SIGN(-123)  SIGN(0) SIGN(456)
--------- -------- -------- ---------- -------- ---------
      123        0      456         -1        0         1
```

Listing 5-3. Using the POWER and MOD Functions

```
select power(2,3), power(-2,3)
,        mod(8,3),    mod(13,0)
from    dual;

POWER(2,3) POWER(-2,3) MOD(8,3) MOD(13,0)
---------- ----------- -------- ---------
         8          -8        2        13
```

Listing 5-4. Using MOD in the WHERE Clause

```
select empno as odd_empno
,      ename
from    employees
where   mod(empno,2) = 1;
ODD_EMPNO ENAME
--------- --------
     7369 SMITH
     7499 ALLEN
     7521 WARD
     7839 KING
```

The example in Listing 5-5 calculates the age (expressed in weeks and additional days) of all employees working for department 10. In this example, we use the difference between the BDATE column and the pseudo column SYSDATE. Of course, your results will be different from the results in Listing 5-5, because they depend on the point in time that you execute the query.

Listing 5-5. Using the FLOOR and MOD Functions

```
select ename
,      floor((sysdate-bdate)/7)   as weeks
,      floor(mod(sysdate-bdate,7)) as days
from    employees
where   deptno = 10;

ENAME      WEEKS    DAYS
-------- -------- --------
CLARK      2032       5
KING       2688       0
MILLER     2208       6
```

Listing 5-6 shows an example using the arithmetic functions SIN, TANH, EXP, LOG, and LN. You probably recognize the number 3.14159265 as an approximation of π (pi), which is used in the SIN function example to convert degrees into radians.

Listing 5-6. Trigonometric, Exponential, and Logarithmic Functions

```
select sin(30*3.14159265/180), tanh(0.5)
,      exp(4), log(2,32), ln(32)
from   dual;

SIN(30*3.14159265/180) TANH(0.5)   EXP(4) LOG(2,32)   LN(32)
---------------------- --------- -------- --------- --------
                   .5  .4621172 54.59815         5 3.465736
```

5.3 Text Functions

The most important Oracle text functions are listed in Table 5-3.

Table 5-3. *Common Oracle Text Functions*

Function	Description
LENGTH(t)	Length (expressed in characters) of t
ASCII(t)	ASCII value of first character of t
CHR(n)	Character with ASCII value n
UPPER(t), LOWER(t)	t in uppercase/lowercase
INITCAP(t)	Each word in t with initial uppercase; remainder in lowercase
LTRIM(t[,k])	Remove characters from the left of t, until the first character not in k
RTRIM(t[,k])	Remove characters from the right of t, after the last character not in k
TRIM([[option][c FROM]]t)	Trim character c from t; option = LEADING, TRAILING, or BOTH
LPAD(t,n[,k])	Left-pad t with sequence of characters in k to length n
RPAD(t,n[,k])	Right-pad t with k to length n (the default k is a space)
SUBSTR(t,n[,m])	Substring of t from position n, m characters long (the default for m is until end)
INSTR(t,k)	Position of the first occurrence of k in t
INSTR(t,k,n)	Same as INSTR(t,k), but starting from position n in t
INSTR(t,k,n,m)	Same as INSTR(t,k,n), but now the mth occurrence of k
TRANSLATE(t,v,w)	Replace characters from v (occurring in t) by corresponding character in w
REPLACE(t,v)	Remove each occurrence of v from t
REPLACE(t,v,w)	Replace each occurrence of v in t by w
CONCAT(t1,t2)	Concatenate t1 and t2 (equivalent to the || operator)

■ **Note**   When counting positions in strings, always start with one, not with zero.

Several text functions have a corresponding function with a B suffix, such as SUBSTRB, INSTRB, and LENGTHB. These special functions express their results in bytes instead of characters. This distinction is relevant only if you are using multibyte character sets. See *Oracle SQL Reference* for more details.

Listing 5-7 shows some examples of the LOWER, UPPER, INITCAP, and LENGTH text functions; the results are self-explanatory.

Listing 5-7. Using the LOWER, UPPER, INITCAP, and LENGTH Functions

```
select  lower(job), initcap(ename)
from    employees
where   upper(job) = 'SALESREP'
order   by length(ename);

LOWER(JOB) INITCAP(ENAME)
---------- --------------
salesrep   Ward
salesrep   Allen
salesrep   Martin
salesrep   Turner
```

Listing 5-8 illustrates the text functions ASCII and CHR. If you compare the third and the fifth columns of the result, you can see that the ASCII function considers only the *first* character of its argument, regardless of the length of the input text (see Table 5-3 for the description of the ASCII text function).

Listing 5-8. Using the ASCII and CHR Functions

```
select ascii('a'), ascii('z')
,      ascii('A'), ascii('Z')
,      ascii('ABC'), chr(77)
from   dual;

ASCII('A') ASCII('Z') ASCII('A') ASCII('Z') ASCII('ABC') CHR(77)
---------- ---------- ---------- ---------- ------------ -------
        97        122         65         90           65 M
```

The first two column headings in Listing 5-8 are very confusing, because SQL*Plus converts all SELECT clause expressions to uppercase, including your function arguments. If you want lowercase characters in your column headings, you must add column aliases and specify them between double quotes. For example, the first line of Listing 5-8 would look like this:

```
select ascii('a') as "ASCII('a')", ascii('z') as "ASCII('z')"
```

Listings 5-9 and 5-10 show some examples of using the INSTR, SUBSTR, LTRIM, and RTRIM text functions. (The layout in Listing 5-9 is formatted to increase readability.)

Listing 5-9. Using the INSTR and SUBSTR Functions

```
select dname
,      substr(dname,4)      as substr1
,      substr(dname,4,3)    as substr2
,      instr(dname,'I')     as instr1
,      instr(dname,'I',5)   as instr2
,      instr(dname,'I',3,2) as instr3
from   departments;
```

DNAME	SUBSTR1	SUBSTR2	INSTR1	INSTR2	INSTR3
ACCOUNTING	OUNTING	OUN	8	8	0
HR			0	0	0
SALES	ES	ES	0	0	0
TRAINING	INING	INI	4	6	6

Listing 5-10. Using the LTRIM and RTRIM Functions

```
select ename
,      ltrim(ename,'S') as ltrim_s
,      rtrim(ename,'S') as rtrim_s
from   employees
where  deptno = 20;
```

ENAME	LTRIM_S	RTRIM_S
ADAMS	ADAMS	ADAM
FORD	FORD	FORD
JONES	JONES	JONE
SCOTT	COTT	SCOTT
SMITH	MITH	SMITH

As we can see, the SUBSTR function returns a fragment of the string cut from position n (remember, we start counting from 1). The length of this fragment is defined by parameter m. If m is unspecified, all characters will be returned from position n to the end of string. The INSTR function returns the starting position of the expression in the string. In a case where n parameter is given, we will start checking only from nth position, but we will still count from the beginning of the string. If the m parameter is not given, the first iteration of expression occurrence in the string will be returned, and the mth occurrence is returned if m is specified.

LTRIM and RTRIM functions in Listing 5-10 remove specified characters but only if they appear at the left or right end of the string. This is a very useful function for removing trailing blanks in a string.

Listing 5-11 demonstrates using the LPAD and RPAD functions. Note that they not only *lengthen* strings, as their names suggest, but sometimes they also *shorten* strings; for example, see what happens with ACCOUNTING and TRAINING in Listing 5-11.

Listing 5-11. Using the LPAD and RPAD Functions

```
select dname
,      lpad(dname,9,'>')
,      rpad(dname,6,'<')
from   departments;
```

```
DNAME      LPAD(DNAM RPAD(D
---------- --------- ------
ACCOUNTING ACCOUNTIN ACCOUN
HR         >>>>>>>HR HR<<<<
SALES      >>>>SALES SALES<
TRAINING   >TRAINING TRAINI
```

You can use the LPAD and RPAD functions to produce column-value histograms by providing variable expressions, instead of constant values, as their second argument. For an example, see Listing 5-12, which shows how to create a salary histogram with a granularity of 100.

Listing 5-12. Producing Histograms with the LPAD and RPAD Functions

```
select lpad(msal,4)||' '||
       rpad('o',msal/100,'o') as histogram
from   employees
where  deptno = 30;

HISTOGRAM
------------------------------------------------
1600 oooooooooooooooo
1250 oooooooooo000
1250 ooooooooooooo
2850 oooooooooooooooooooooooooooooo
1500 ooooooooooooooo
 800 oooooooo
```

Listing 5-13 shows the difference between the functions REPLACE and TRANSLATE. TRANSLATE replaces individual characters. REPLACE offers the option to replace words with other words. Note also what happens if you use the REPLACE function with only two arguments, instead of three: the function *removes* words instead of replacing them.

Listing 5-13. Using the TRANSLATE and REPLACE Functions

```
select translate('beer bucket','beer','milk') as translate
,      replace  ('beer bucket','beer','milk') as replace_1
,      replace  ('beer bucket','beer')        as replace_2
from   dual;

TRANSLATE   REPLACE_1   REPLACE_2
----------- ----------- ---------
miik muckit milk bucket  bucket
```

5.4 Regular Expressions

The previous chapter introduced the LIKE operator, and the previous section of this chapter introduced the INSTR, SUBSTR, and REPLACE functions. All of these SQL functions search for text. The LIKE operator offers the two wildcard characters % and _, which allow you to perform more advanced searches. The other three functions accept plain text searches only. This functionality is sometimes insufficient for complicated search operations. Therefore, Oracle SQL also supports four functions: REGEXP_LIKE, REGEXP_INSTR, REGEXP_SUBSTR, and REGEXP_REPLACE. These SQL functions support, as their names suggest, so-called *regular expressions*. Apart from that, they serve the same purpose as their non-REGEXP counterparts.

Regular expressions are well known in all UNIX operating system variants (such as Linux, Solaris, and HP/UX) and are part of the international POSIX standard. They are documented in great detail in *Oracle SQL Reference*, Appendix C. This section provides an introduction to regular expressions, focusing on their use with the Oracle SQL regular expression functions.

Regular Expression Operators and Metasymbols

Table 5-4 shows the most important regular expression metasymbols and their meanings. The Type column in Table 5-4 may contain the following:

- Postfix, which means that the operator *follows* its operand

- Prefix, which means that the operator *precedes* its operand

- Infix, which means that the operator *separates* its operands

- Nothing (empty), which means that the operator has no operands

Table 5-4. *Common Regular Expression Operators and Metasymbols*

Operator	Type	Description
*	Postfix	Zero or more occurrences
+	Postfix	One or more occurrences
?	Postfix	Zero or one occurrence
		Infix	Operator to separate alternative choices
^	Prefix	Beginning of a string, or position immediately following a newline character
$	Postfix	End of the line
.	--	Any single character
[[^]list]	--	One character out of a list; a circumflex (^) at the beginning works as a negation; a dash (-) between two characters works as a range indicator
( )	--	Groups a (sub)expression, allowing you to refer to it further down in the expression
{m}	Postfix	Precisely m times
{m,}	Postfix	At least m times
{m,n}	Postfix	At least m times, and at most n times
\n	--	Refers back to the nth subexpression between parentheses (n is a digit between 1 and 9)

If the square brackets notation does not give you enough precision or flexibility, you can use multicharacter collation elements, character classes, and equivalence classes, as follows:

- *Multicharacter collation elements* are relevant for certain languages. Valid values are predefined and depend on the NLS_SORT setting. Use [. and .] to enclose collation elements.

- *Character classes* give you more flexibility than the dash symbol between square brackets; for example, you can refer to alphabetic characters, numeric digits, alphanumeric characters, blank spaces, punctuation, and so on. Use [: and :] to enclose character classes.

- *Equivalence classes* allow you to match all accented and unaccented versions of a letter. Use [= and =] to enclose equivalence classes.

Before we look at some examples of how these regular expression operators work with the regular expression functions (in Listings 5-14 through 5-16), we need to discuss the syntax of the functions.

Regular Expression Function Syntax

The four regular expression functions have the following syntax. You can specify regular expressions in their `pattern` argument.

- `REGEXP_LIKE(text, pattern[, options])`

- `REGEXP_INSTR(text, pattern[, pos[, occurrence[, return[, options]]]])`

- `REGEXP_SUBSTR(text, pattern[, pos[, occurrence[, options]]])`

- `REGEXP_REPLACE(text, pattern[, replace [, pos[, occurrence[, options]]]])`

For all four functions, the first two arguments (`text` and `pattern`) are mandatory. These arguments provide the source text and the regular expression to search for, respectively. All of the remaining arguments are optional. However, function arguments can *only* be omitted from the right to the left. For example, if you want to specify a value for the `options` argument of the `REGEXP_INSTR` function, all six arguments are mandatory and must be specified.

In `REGEXP_INSTR`, `REGEXP_SUBSTR`, and `REGEXP_REPLACE`, you can use the `pos` argument to specify from which position in `text` you want the search to start (the default value is 1), and with `occurrence`, you can specify how often you want to find the search `pattern` (the default value is 1). The `options` argument of all four of the functions and the `return` argument of the `REGEXP_INSTR` function require a bit more explanation.

Influencing Matching Behavior

You can influence the matching behavior of the regular expression functions with their `options` argument. Table 5-5 shows the values you can specify in the `options` function argument.

Table 5-5. *Regular Expression Option Values*

Option	Description
i	Case-insensitive search (no distinction between uppercase and lowercase)
c	Case-sensitive search
n	Allows the period (`.`) to match the newline character
m	Treat `text` as multiple lines; `^` and `$` refer to the beginning and end of any of those lines

You can specify one or more of these values. If you specify conflicting combinations, such as `ic`, the Oracle DBMS uses the last value (`c`) and ignores the first one.

■ **Note** The default behavior for case-sensitivity depends on the `NLS_SORT` parameter value.

REGEXP_INSTR Return Value

The return option of the REGEXP_INSTR function allows you to influence the return value. By default, the position where the pattern was found is returned, but sometimes you want to know the position immediately *after* the found pattern. Of course, you can add the length of the pattern to the result of the function; however, using the return option is easier in that case. Table 5-6 shows the values you can specify in the return function argument.

Table 5-6. *Regular Expression Return Values*

Return	Description
0	Position of the first character of the pattern found (default)
1	Position of the first character after the pattern found

REGEXP_LIKE

Let's look at an example of the REGEXP_LIKE function, using a SQL*Plus trick that will be explained in a later chapter. The ampersand character (&) in the WHERE clause of the query in Listing 5-14 makes SQL*Plus prompt for a value for text; therefore, you can repeat this query in the SQL buffer with the / command as often as you like, specifying different source text values to explore the effect of the search pattern.

Listing 5-14. Using the REGEXP_LIKE Function

```
SQL> select 'found!' as result from dual
  2  where regexp_like('&text', '^.a{1,2}.+$', 'i');

Enter value for text: bar

RESULT
------
found!

SQL> /
Enter value for text: BAARF

RESULT
------
found!

SQL> /
Enter value for text: ba

no rows selected

SQL>
```

The results of Listing 5-14 show that the pattern means the following: the first character is arbitrary, followed by at least one and at most two a characters, followed by one or more arbitrary characters, while ignoring the differences between uppercase and lowercase. By the way, Listing 5-14 shows that REGEXP_LIKE is a Boolean function; its result is TRUE or FALSE.

CHAPTER 5 ■ RETRIEVAL: FUNCTIONS

REGEXP_INSTR

Listing 5-15 uses the REGEXP_INSTR function to search for history comments with nine or more words. It looks for at least nine nonempty (+) substrings that do not contain spaces ([^]).

Listing 5-15. Using the REGEXP_INSTR Function

```
select  comments
from    history
where   regexp_instr(comments, '[^ ]+', 1, 9) > 0;
```

```
COMMENTS
--------------------------------------------------------------
Not a great trainer; let's try the sales department!
Sales also turns out to be not a success...
Hired as the new manager for the accounting department
Junior sales rep -- has lots to learn... :-)
```

Notice that the last row of the result contains only seven actual words. It is found because the text strings -- and :-) are counted as "words."

REGEXP_SUBSTR

Listing 5-16 demonstrates searching for comments between parentheses, using the REGEXP_SUBSTR function. The search pattern looks for a left parenthesis, followed by at least one character not equal to a right parenthesis, followed by a right parenthesis. Note that you need the backslash character (\) to suppress the special meaning of the parentheses.

Listing 5-16. Using the REGEXP_SUBSTR Function

```
select  comments
,       regexp_substr(comments, '\([^\)]+\)') as substring
from    history
where   comments like '%(%';
```

```
COMMENTS
--------------------------------------------------------------
SUBSTRING
--------------------------------------------------------------
Project (half a month) for the ACCOUNTING department
(half a month)
```

REGEXP_REPLACE

Listing 5-17 shows how you can use the REGEXP_REPLACE function to replace all words starting with an f with a question mark.

Listing 5-17. Using the REGEXP_REPLACE Function

```
select  regexp_replace(comments, ' f[a-z]* ',' ? ',1,1,'i')
from    history
where   regexp_like(comments, ' f[a-z]* ','i');
```

```
REGEXP_REPLACE(COMMENTS,'F[A-Z]*','?',1,1,'I')
----------------------------------------------------------------
Hired as the new manager ? the accounting department
Founder and ? employee of the company
Project (half a month) ? the ACCOUNTING department
```

Notice that you must specify values for all function arguments if you want to make the replacement case-insensitive, including default values for pos and occurrence. The WHERE clause ensures that the query returns only the matching rows. Also notice that the word 'Founder' is not substituted, because there is no blank in front of it. See the blank at the beginning of the pattern.

5.5 Date Functions

Before discussing the various Oracle date functions, let's first review the syntax to specify date/time-related constants (or literals), using predefined ANSI/ISO SQL standard formats.

Table 5-7 shows the syntax for the literals and examples.

Table 5-7. *Syntax for Date/Time-Related Constants*

Literal	Example
DATE 'yyyy-mm-dd'	DATE '2014-09-25'
TIMESTAMP 'yyyy-mm-dd hh24:mi:ss.ffffff' [AT TIME ZONE '...']	TIMESTAMP '2014-09-25 23:59:59.99999' AT TIME ZONE 'CET'
TIMESTAMP 'yyyy-mm-dd hh24:mi:ss.ffffff {+|-}hh:mi'	TIMESTAMP '2014-09-25 23:59:59.99 -5:00'
INTERVAL 'expr' <qualifier>	INTERVAL '1' YEAR INTERVAL '1 2:3' DAY TO MINUTE

You can experiment with this syntax by entering the following query, using the SQL*Plus ampersand (&) substitution method (as in Listing 5-14):

```
select &input_date from dual;
```

If you simply enter an alphanumeric string, such as '21-JUN-04', you must rely on an implicit conversion by Oracle. This implicit conversion succeeds or fails depending on the NLS_DATE_FORMAT and NLS_TIMESTAMP_FORMAT parameter settings for your session. If you want to see an overview of all current NLS parameter settings for your session, you can use the following query:

```
select * from nls_session_parameters;
```

If you execute this query, you will see the current values for NLS_DATE_FORMAT and NLS_TIMESTAMP_FORMAT.
In SQL Developer you may see and change this information at session level using Tools/Preferences/Database/NLS.
In SQL*Plus (and of course also SQL Developer) you may set your preferred date format using for instance:

```
SQL> alter session set NLS_DATE_FORMAT = 'dd Month yyyy hh24:mi:ss';
SYSDATE
--------------------------
13 February  2014 10:33:42
```

Table 5-8 shows the most commonly used Oracle date functions.

Table 5-8. *Common Oracle Date Functions*

Function	Description
ADD_MONTHS(d, n)	Date d plus n months
MONTHS_BETWEEN(d, e)	Months between dates d and e
LAST_DAY(d)	Last day of the month containing date d
NEXT_DAY(d, weekday)	The first *weekday* (mon, tue, etc.) after d
NEW_TIME(d, z1, z2)	Convert date/time from time zone z1 to z2
ROUND(d[, fmt])	d rounded on fmt (the default for fmt is midnight)
TRUNC(d[, fmt])	d truncated on fmt (the default for fmt is midnight)
EXTRACT(c FROM d)	Extract date/time component c from expression d

We'll start with the last function listed in Table 5-8.

EXTRACT

You can extract various components of a date or timestamp expression with the ANSI/ISO standard EXTRACT function. Depending on the datatype of the argument d (DATE, TIMESTAMP, or INTERVAL) the following values for c are supported: YEAR, MONTH, DAY, HOUR, MINUTE, SECOND, TIMEZONE_ABBR, and so on. Listing 5-18 shows an example.

Listing 5-18. Using the EXTRACT Function

```
select bdate
,      extract(year  from bdate) as year_of_birth
,      extract(month from bdate) as month_of_birth
,      extract(day   from bdate) as day_of_birth
from   employees
where  ename = 'KING';

BDATE       YEAR_OF_BIRTH MONTH_OF_BIRTH DAY_OF_BIRTH
----------- ------------- -------------- ------------
17-NOV-1952          1952             11           17
```

ROUND and TRUNC

Table 5-9 lists the date formats (fmt) supported by the date functions ROUND and TRUNC. The default format is 'DD', resulting in rounding or truncating to midnight. For example, TRUNC(SYSDATE, 'DD') truncates the current system date and time to midnight.

Table 5-9. *ROUND and TRUNC Date Formats*

Format	Description
CC, SCC	Century, with or without minus sign (BC)
[S]YYYY, [S]YEAR, YYY, YY, Y	Year (in various appearances)
IYYY, IYY, IY, I	ISO year
Q	Quarter
MONTH, MON, MM, RM	Month (full name, abbreviated name, numeric, Roman numerals)
IW, WW	(ISO) week number
W	Day of the week
DDD, DD, J	Day (of the year/of the month/Julian day)
DAY, DY, D	Closest Sunday
HH, HH12, HH24	Hours
MI	Minutes

MONTHS_BETWEEN and ADD_MONTHS

Listings 5-19 and 5-20 show examples of using the date functions MONTHS_BETWEEN and ADD_MONTHS.

Listing 5-19. Using the MONTHS_BETWEEN Function

```
select ename, months_between(sysdate,bdate)
from    employees
where   deptno = 10;

ENAME    MONTHS_BETWEEN(SYSDATE,BDATE)
-------- -----------------------------
CLARK                         467.5042
KING                          618.2461
MILLER                        508.0525
```

Listing 5-20. Using the ADD_MONTHS Function

```
select add_months('29-JAN-1996', 1) add_months_1
,      add_months('29-JAN-1997', 1) add_months_2
,      add_months('11-AUG-1997',-3) add_months_3
from    dual;

ADD_MONTHS_1 ADD_MONTHS_2 ADD_MONTHS_3
------------ ------------ ------------
29-FEB-1996  28-FEB-1997  11-MAY-1997
```

Notice what happens in Listing 5-20 with a non-leap year. There is something else worth noting about the query in Listing 5-20. As explained earlier, you could get back an error message because you rely on implicit interpretation and conversion of the three strings by Oracle. It would have been preferable to specify the three date literals in Listing 5-20 using the keyword DATE (see the beginning of this section) or using the TO_DATE conversion function. (See Section 5.7 later in this chapter for details about conversion functions.)

NEXT_DAY and LAST_DAY

Listing 5-21 shows examples of using the date functions NEXT_DAY, LAST_DAY, ROUND, and TRUNC. Compare the various function results with the first column, showing the current SYSDATE value.

Listing 5-21. Using the NEXT_DAY, LAST_DAY, ROUND, and TRUNC Functions

```
select sysdate
,      next_day(sysdate,'SAT') as next_sat
,      last_day(sysdate)        as last_day
,      round(sysdate,'YY')      as round_yy
,      trunc(sysdate,'CC')      as trunc_cc
from   dual;


SYSDATE      NEXT_SAT     LAST_DAY     ROUND_YY     TRUNC_CC
-----------  -----------  -----------  -----------  -----------
13-feb-2014  15-feb-2014  28-feb-2014  01-jan-2014  01-jan-2001
```

5.6 General Functions

The most important general (datatype-independent) functions are shown in Table 5-10.

Table 5-10. *Common General Oracle Functions*

Function	Description
GREATEST(a, b, ...)	Greatest value of the function arguments
LEAST(a, b, ...)	Least value of the function arguments
NULLIF(a, b)	NULL if a = b; otherwise a
COALESCE(a, b, ...)	The first NOT NULL argument (and NULL if all arguments are NULL)
NVL(x, y)	y if x is NULL; otherwise x
NVL2(x, y, z)	y if x is not NULL; otherwise z
CASE x when a1 then b1 when a2 then b2 ... else y end	
DECODE(x, a1, b1, a2, b2, ..., an, bn [, y])	b1 if $x = $ a1, b2 if $x = $ a2, ... bn if $x = $ an, and otherwise y (or default: NULL)

You can express all of the other functions as CASE expressions, too, because they all share a procedural nature. In other words, you don't really need them. Nevertheless, these functions can be useful in your SQL code because, for example, they make your code more compact. Note also that only the CASE, NULLIF, and COALESCE functions are part of the ANSI/ISO standard. The remaining five functions (GREATEST, LEAST, NVL, NVL2, and DECODE) are Oracle-specific SQL extensions. In other words, if your goal is to write portable SQL code, you should use only CASE, NULLIF, and COALESCE.

GREATEST and LEAST

The GREATEST and LEAST functions can be useful in certain situations. Don't confuse them with the MAX and MIN group functions (which are covered in detail in Chapter 8). For now, remember the following differences:

- GREATEST and LEAST allow you to make *horizontal* comparisons; they operate at the *row* level, therefore listed as single-row functions.

- MAX and MIN allow you to make *vertical* comparisons; they operate at the *column* level - these are multi-row functions or group functions.

Listing 5-22 shows an example of the GREATEST and LEAST functions, selecting three constant expressions against the DUAL table.

Listing 5-22. Using the GREATEST and LEAST Functions

```
select greatest(12*6,148/2,73)
,      least   (12*6,148/2,73)
from   dual;

GREATEST(12*6,148/2,73) LEAST(12*6,148/2,73)
----------------------- --------------------
                     74                   72
```

NVL

The NVL function is useful if you want to prevent certain expressions, or expression components, from evaluating to a null value, as you can see in Listing 5-23.

Listing 5-23. Using the NVL Function

```
select ename, msal, comm
,      12*msal+nvl(comm,0) as yearsal
from   employees
where  ename like '%T%';

ENAME       MSAL     COMM  YEARSAL
--------  --------  -------- --------
SMITH        800              9600
MARTIN      1250      1400    16400
SCOTT       3000             36000
TURNER      1500         0    18000
```

DECODE

The DECODE function is a typical remnant from the days that Oracle SQL did not yet support CASE expressions. There are three good reasons *not* to use DECODE anymore:

- DECODE function expressions are quite difficult to read.

- DECODE is not part of the ANSI/ISO SQL standard.

- CASE expressions are much more powerful.

For completeness, and because you may encounter the DECODE function in legacy Oracle SQL programs, Listing 5-24 shows a query where the DECODE function is used in the SELECT clause (to get a certain output) and in the ORDER BY clause (to do a customized sorting of the records).

Listing 5-24. Using the DECODE Function

```
select job, ename
,      decode(greatest(msal,2500)
              ,2500,'cheap','expensive') as class
from   employees
where  bdate < date '1964-01-01'
order  by decode(job,'DIRECTOR',1,'MANAGER',2,3);
```

```
JOB       ENAME     CLASS
--------  --------  ---------
DIRECTOR  KING      expensive
MANAGER   BLAKE     expensive
SALESREP  ALLEN     cheap
SALESREP  WARD      cheap
ADMIN     MILLER    cheap
TRAINER   FORD      expensive
TRAINER   SCOTT     expensive
SALESREP  MARTIN    cheap
```

And then using CASE for the exact same result:

```
select job, ename
,      case greatest(msal,2500)
            when 2500 then 'cheap'
            else 'expensive'
            end as class
from   employees
where  bdate < date '1964-01-01'
order  by decode(job,'DIRECTOR',1,'MANAGER',2,3);
```

SAMPLE Function

You might have millions of records and want to do statistics on only 1% of randomly selected rows, so you want to sample, and you want it to be fast. Well, there is a function SAMPLE:

```
SQL> select * from orders sample (1);
```

When you are testing you may want the same sample each time you test. For that you need to add SEED, like this:

```
SQL> select * from orders sample (1) seed (1234);
```

5.7 Conversion Functions

Conversion functions allow you to convert expressions explicitly from one datatype into another datatype. Table 5-11 lists the most common conversion functions in Oracle SQL. See *Oracle SQL Reference* for more conversion functions.

Table 5-11. *Common Oracle Conversion Functions*

Function	Description
TO_CHAR(n[,fmt])	Convert number n to a string
TO_CHAR(d[,fmt])	Convert date/time expression d to a string
TO_NUMBER(t)	Convert string t to a number
TO_BINARY_FLOAT(e[,fmt])	Convert expression e to a floating-point number
TO_BINARY_DOUBLE(e[,fmt])	Convert expression e to a double-precision, floating-point number
TO_DATE(t[,fmt])	Convert string t to a date
TO_YMINTERVAL(t)	Convert string t to a YEAR TO MONTH interval
TO_DSINTERVAL(t)	Convert string t to a DAY TO SECOND interval
TO_TIMESTAMP (t[,fmt])	Convert string t to a timestamp
CAST(e AS t)	Convert expression e to datatype t

■ **Note**   The syntax in Table 5-11 is not complete. Most conversion functions allow you to specify additional NLS parameters after the format (fmt) argument. For example, you can influence the currency symbol, the numeric characters (period and comma), and the date language. See *Oracle SQL Reference* and *Globalization Support Guide* for more details.

TO_NUMBER and TO_CHAR

Listing 5-25 shows how you can use the TO_NUMBER and TO_CHAR functions (with or without a format argument) to convert strings to numbers and vice versa.

Listing 5-25. Using the TO_CHAR and TO_NUMBER Functions

```
select 123
,      to_char(123)
,      to_char(123,'$09999.99')
,      to_number('123')
from   dual;

    123 TO_ TO_CHAR(12 TO_NUMBER('123')
-------- --- ---------- ----------------
    123 123 $00123.00                123
```

Listing 5-26 shows how you can nest conversion functions. On the third line, you use the TO_DATE function to interpret the string '01/01/2006' as a date value; then, you use the TO_CHAR function to extract the day from the date value, as you can see in the third column of the query result.

Listing 5-26. Nesting the TO_CHAR and TO_DATE Functions

```
select sysdate                           as today
,      to_char(sysdate,'hh24:mi:ss') as time
,      to_char(to_date('01/01/2014','dd/mm/yyyy')
                  ,'"is on "Day') as new_year_2014
from dual;

TODAY       TIME     NEW_YEAR_2014
----------- -------- ---------------
13-feb-2014 11:39:09 is on Wednesday
```

In this example, the format Day results in Wednesday because the default language is English. You can set the NLS_LANGUAGE parameter to another language to influence this behavior. For example, if you set this session (or system) parameter to Dutch, the result becomes Woensdag. You could also override this default at the statement level, by setting the NLS_DATE_LANGUAGE parameter, as shown in Listing 5-27.

Listing 5-27. Influencing the Date Language at the Statement Level

```
select to_char(sysdate, 'Day')
,      to_char(sysdate, 'Day', 'nls_date_language=Dutch')
from   dual;

TO_CHAR(S TO_CHAR(S
--------- ---------
Tuesday   Dinsdag
```

Conversion Function Formats

Table 5-11 showed that several Oracle conversion functions support an optional format (fmt) argument. These format arguments allow you to deviate from the default conversion. Table 5-12 shows most of the possibilities.

Table 5-12. *Conversion Functions: Optional Format Components*

Format	Description
[S]CC	Century; S stands for the minus sign (BC)
[S]YYYY	Year, with or without minus sign
YYY, YY, Y	Last 3, 2, or 1 digits of the year
[S]YEAR	Year spelled out, with or without minus sign (S)
BC, AD	BC/AD indicator
Q	Quarter (1,2,3,4)
MM	Month (01-12)
MONTH	Month name, padded with spaces to length 9
MON	Month name, abbreviated (three characters)
WW, IW	(ISO) week number (01-53)

(continued)

121

Table 5-12. (*continued*)

Format	Description
W	Week number within the month (1–5)
DDD	Day number within the year (1–366)
DD	Day number within the month (1–31)
D	Day number within the week (1–7)
DAY	Day name, padded with spaces to length 9
DY	Day name abbreviation (three characters)
J	Julian date; day number since 01/01/4712 BC
AM, PM	AM/PM indicator
HH[12]	Hour within the day (01–12)
HH24	Hour within the day (00–23)
MI	Minutes within the hour (00–59)
SS	Seconds within the minute (00–59)
SSSSS	Seconds after midnight (0–86399)
/.,	Punctuation characters; displayed verbatim (between date fields)
"..."	String between double quotes displayed within the date expression

■ **Note** You can influence several date characteristics, such as the first day of the week, with the NLS_TERRITORY parameter.

Oracle supports some additions that you can use in conversion function format strings to further refine the results of those functions. Table 5-13 shows these additions.

Table 5-13. *Conversion Functions: Format Component Additions*

Addition	Description
FM	Fill mode toggle
TH	Ordinal number (e.g., 4th)
SP	Spelled-out number (e.g., four)
THSP, SPTH	Spelled-ordinal number (e.g., fourth)

In *fill mode*, Oracle does not perform padding with spaces, and numbers are not prefixed with leading zeros. You can enable and disable this fill mode mechanism within the same format string as many times as you like, by repeating FM (it is a *toggle*). Ordinal numbers indicate a relative position in a sequence.

The conversion function formats are case-sensitive, as demonstrated in Listing 5-28.

Listing 5-28. TO_CHAR Formats and Case-Sensitivity

```
select to_char(sysdate,'DAY dy Dy') as day
,      to_char(sysdate,'MONTH mon') as month
from dual;

DAY                MONTH
---------------- -------------
MONDAY    mon Mon MAY       may
```

Datatype Conversion

In the area of datatype conversion, you can leave many issues up to the Oracle DBMS. However, for reasons of syntax clarity, it is better to express the datatype conversions explicitly with the appropriate conversion functions. See the query in Listing 5-29 for an example.

Listing 5-29. Relying on Implicit Datatype Conversion

```
select ename, substr(bdate,8)+16
from   employees
where  deptno = 10;

ENAME     SUBSTR(BDATE,8)+16
--------  ------------------
CLARK                     81
KING                      68
MILLER                    78
```

This query is internally interpreted and executed by the Oracle DBMS as the following:

```
select ename, TO_NUMBER(substr(to_char(bdate,'...'),8))+16
from   employees
where  deptno = 10
```

You should have formulated the query that way in the first place.

CAST

The last function to discuss in this section about conversion functions is CAST. This function is part of the ANSI/ISO SQL standard, as opposed to all other conversion functions discussed so far in this section. The CAST function is a *generic* conversion function. It allows you to convert *any* expression to *any* specific datatype, including the option to specify a datatype precision. See Listing 5-30 for some examples.

Listing 5-30. CAST Function Examples

```
select  cast(12.98 as number(2)) example1
,       cast('oak' as char(10) ) example2
,       cast(null  as date     ) example3
from    dual;

EXAMPLE1 EXAMPLE2   EXAMPLE3
-------- ---------- ---------
      13 oak
```

5.8 Stored Functions

Although you might argue that Oracle already offers more than enough functions, you may find that you need a specific capability that isn't already provided. In that case, you can develop your own functions (using PL/SQL) and add them to the SQL language.

PL/SQL is the standard procedural programming language for Oracle databases. PL/SQL is a superset of SQL, adding several procedural capabilities to the nonprocedural SQL language. Here, we will investigate one simple example of PL/SQL language usage in relation to custom functions. For more information about PL/SQL, refer to *Oracle PL/SQL User's Guide and Reference*.

Listing 5-31 shows how to define a function to determine the number of employees for a given department.

Listing 5-31. Creating a Stored Function Using PL/SQL

```
create or replace function emp_count(p_deptno in number)
return number
is
       cnt number(2) := 0;
begin
       select count(*)
       into cnt
       from    employees e
       where   e.deptno = p_deptno;
       return (cnt);
end;
/

Function created.
```

Now it becomes relatively easy to produce an overview of all departments, with their (correct) number of employees, as you can see in Listing 5-32. This query would be more complicated without this function. In particular, department 40 (the well-known department without employees) would not show up in your query results without some extra work. Without the stored function, you would need a so-called OUTER JOIN (see Chapter 8) or you would need a subquery in the SELECT clause (see Chapter 9).

Listing 5-32. Using the Stored Function

```
select deptno, dname, location
,      emp_count(deptno)
from   departments;
```

```
  DEPTNO DNAME      LOCATION EMP_COUNT(DEPTNO)
-------- ---------- -------- -----------------
      10 ACCOUNTING NEW YORK                 3
      20 TRAINING   DALLAS                   5
      30 SALES      CHICAGO                  6
      40 HR         BOSTON                   0
```

Listing 5-33 shows how the SQL*Plus DESCRIBE command treats these stored functions.

Listing 5-33. Describing a Stored Function

```
SQL> describe emp_count

FUNCTION emp_count RETURNS NUMBER

Argument Name             Type             In/Out Default?
------------------------- ---------------- ------ --------
P_DEPTNO                  NUMBER           IN

SQL>
```

When the purpose of the function is to call it within a SQL statement, it should not have side effects, so you are not allowed to be doing things like commit/rollback, inserts, deletes or changing package variables.

You may read more about these restrictions here:

http://docs.oracle.com/cd/E16655_01/appdev.121/e17620/adfns_packages.htm#ADFNS00908

Function in WITH Clause of Query

It is now—in 12c onward—possible to define your own function as a local object directly within the WITH clause of a SELECT. Then you avoid storing all kinds of one-time-only functions to the Data Dictionary. It looks like this if you want to concatenate an e-mail based on the employee's first and last names:

```
with
function email
(p_first_name in varchar2, p_last_name in varchar2)
return varchar2
is
begin
return substr(p_first_name,1,1)||substr(p_last_name,1,7);
end;
select first_name, last_name, email(first_name,last_name)
from employees
order by first_name;
```

The result looks like Figure 5-1:

Query Result ×

SQL | Fetched 50 rows in 0,082 seconds

	FIRST_NAME	LAST_NAME	EMAIL(FIRST_NAME,LAST_NAME)
1	Adam	Fripp	AFripp
2	Alana	Walsh	AWalsh
3	Alberto	Errazuriz	AErrazur
4	Alexander	Hunold	AHunold
5	Alexander	Khoo	AKhoo
6	Alexis	Bull	ABull
7	Allan	McEwen	AMcEwen
8	Alyssa	Hutton	AHutton
9	Amit	Banda	ABanda
10	Anthony	Cabrio	ACabrio
11	Britney	Everett	BEverett
12	Bruce	Ernst	BErnst
13	Charles	Johnson	CJohnson
14	Christopher	Olsen	COlsen
15	Clara	Vishney	CVishney

***Figure 5-1.** Function in WITH*

In 12c you may improve the performance of an inline PL/SQL function by including the following compiler instruction in the `DECLARE` section of the function: `PRAGMA UDF`. UDF is the abbreviation for User Defined Function.

```
with
function email
(p_first_name in varchar2, p_last_name in varchar2)
return varchar2
is
pragma udf;
begin ...................
```

5.9 Exercises

Use a database schema with the seven case tables (see Appendix A of this book) to perform the following exercises. The answers are presented in Appendix B

1. For all employees, provide their last name, a comma, followed by their initials.
2. For all employees, list their last name and date of birth in a format such as April 2nd, 1967.
3. On which day are (or were) you exactly 10,000 days old? On which day of the week is (was) this?
4. Rewrite the example in Listing 5-23 using the `NVL2` function.

5. Rewrite the example in Listing 5-24 to remove the DECODE functions using CASE expressions, both in the SELECT clause and in the ORDER BY clause.

6. Rewrite the example in Listing 5-20 using DATE and INTERVAL constants, in such a way that they become independent of the NLS_DATE_FORMAT setting.

7. Investigate the difference between the date formats WW and IW (week number and ISO week number) using an arbitrary date and explain your findings.

8. Look at Listing 5-15, where we use the REGEXP_INSTR function to search for words. Rewrite this query using REGEXP_LIKE. Hint: You can use {n,} to express "at least *n* times."

9. If you have a 12c database, try out the local PL/SQL function in the WITH of a query. Use the code for Figure 5-1 as a template.

CHAPTER 6

∎∎∎

Data Manipulation

In this chapter, you will learn how to change the contents of an Oracle database. The SQL commands to change the database contents are commonly referred to as Data Manipulation Language (DML) commands.

The first four sections of this chapter cover the DML commands INSERT, UPDATE, DELETE, and MERGE. The first three commands have names that are self-explanatory. The fourth one, MERGE, allows you to perform a mixture of insertions, updates, and deletions in a single statement, which is especially useful in data warehousing environments without using a procedural language like PL/SQL.

∎ **Note**   Many of the commands in this chapter modify data that is used in later chapters. It is important to issue the ROLLBACK commands indicated in this chapter or to re-create the tables and data before continuing to Chapter 7.

In production environments, especially when dealing with high-volume transactions, data manipulation is mostly performed via database applications. In general, these database applications are built (or generated) with application development tools such as Application Express (APEX) and Oracle JDeveloper. Such applications offer a pleasant user-friendly interface to the database; however, they still use the basic INSERT, UPDATE, and DELETE commands under the hood to communicate with the database, so you should understand how these commands work. Additionally, sometimes "manual" data manipulation via SQL Developer and SQL*Plus can be very efficient. For example, you may want to perform global updates (such as to change a certain column for all rows of a table at the same time) or to remove all rows of a table.

Following are some of what we'll cover in this chapter:

- In the first section (Section 6.1) we will introduce the INSERT command, which is used to populate tables with data.

- The second section (Section 6.2) introduces the UPDATE command that modifies data that is already in a table.

- Section 6.3 explains how to remove data from tables using DELETE.

- Section 6.4 introduces the MERGE statement, which is used to either INSERT, UPDATE, or DELETE data depending on the rules you define.

- Section 6.5 explains the concept of *transactions* and introduces three transaction-related SQL commands: COMMIT, SAVEPOINT, and ROLLBACK.This chapter is also the most obvious place in this book to pay some attention to *read consistency* and *locking*. So, the last section (Section 6.6) discusses how the Oracle RDBMS guarantees transaction isolation in a multiuser environment. It provides an introduction to the concepts involved, without going into too many technical details.

6.1 The INSERT Command

You use the INSERT command to add rows to a table. Along with the standard INSERT command, Oracle SQL also supports a multitable insert, which adds rows into several tables at one time. Multitable inserts are an advanced topic and are not covered in this book.

Standard INSERT Commands

The standard INSERT command supports the following two ways to insert rows:

- Use the VALUES clause, followed by a list of column values (between parentheses). This method allows you to insert only *one* row at a time per execution of the INSERT command.

- Formulate a subquery, thus using existing data to generate new rows.

Both alternatives are shown in the syntax diagram in Figure 6-1.

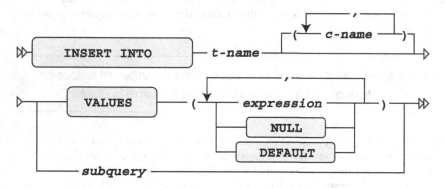

Figure 6-1. *INSERT command syntax diagram*

If you know all of the table columns, including the internal physical order in which they are presented by the SQL*Plus DESCRIBE command, you don't need to specify column names after the table name in the INSERT command. If you omit column names, you must provide *precisely enough* values and specify them in the correct order.

■ **Caution**   Leaving out column names is rather dangerous, because your INSERT statement may become invalid after nondestructive table modifications, such as adding columns. Column names also improve the readability of your SQL statements.

In the VALUES clause, you can specify a comma-separated list of literals or an expression. You can use the reserved word NULL to specify a null value for a specific column. You can also specify the reserved word DEFAULT to instruct the Oracle DBMS to insert the default value associated with the corresponding column. These default values are part of the table definition, stored in the data dictionary. If you don't specify a value for a specific column in your INSERT statement, there are two possibilities:

- If the column has an associated DEFAULT value, the Oracle DBMS will insert that value.

- If you did not define a DEFAULT value for the column, the Oracle DBMS inserts a null value (provided, of course, that the column allows null values).

■ **Note**   Because the Oracle DBMS will automatically insert the DEFAULT value when another value isn't specified, the DEFAULT keyword isn't really necessary for INSERT statements. However, the DEFAULT keyword can be quite useful when writing UPDATE statements, which are discussed in Section 6.2.

The second way of using the INSERT command fills a table with a subquery. There are no special constraints for these subqueries, as long as you make sure they produce the right number of values of the right datatype. You can even use a subquery against the table into which you are inserting rows. This sounds like a strange approach; however, insert into X select * from x is one of the fastest methods to fill a table, provided you don't have unique or primary key constraints.

■ **Note**   The fact that you are able to query and insert into the same table at the same time is due to Oracle's read consistency implementation. See Section 6.6 for details.

Listing 6-1 shows four INSERT statement examples: three using the VALUES clause and one using the subquery method.

Listing 6-1. Four INSERT Command Examples

```
insert into departments                          -- Example 1
values (90,'SUPPORT','SEATTLE', NULL);

1 row created.

insert into employees(empno,ename,init,bdate,msal,deptno)  -- Example 2
values (7001,'ZOMBIE','ZZ',trunc(sysdate), 0, DEFAULT);

1 row created.

select * from employees where empno = 7001;

EMPNO ENAME  INIT JOB MGR BDATE       MSAL COMM DEPTNO
----- ------ ---- --- --- ----------- ---- ---- ------
 7001 ZOMBIE ZZ           15-SEP-2004    0        10

insert into departments(dname,location,deptno)   -- Example 3
values('CATERING','ORLANDO', 10);
insert into departments(dname,location,deptno)
*
ERROR at line 1:
ORA-00001: unique constraint (BOOK.D_PK) violated
```

```
insert into salgrades                              -- Example 4
select grade + 5
,       lowerlimit + 2300
,       least(9999, upperlimit + 2300)
,       500
from    salgrades;

5 rows created.

rollback;
Rollback complete.
```

The examples work as follows:

- The first example inserts a new department 90 without specifying column names. It also shows how you can insert a null value with the reserved word NULL.

- The second example shows how you can use DEFAULT to assign the default department number to a new employee. (Chapter 7 explains how to assign such default values.) The default value for the DEPTNO column of the EMPLOYEES table is 10, as you can see in Listing 6-1.

- The third example shows a violation of a primary key constraint; department 10 already exists.

- The fourth example shows how you can use a subquery to insert rows with the INSERT command. It uses the LEAST function (introduced in Chapter 5) to avoid constraint violations. The first argument (9999) ensures that the upper limit will never become greater than 9999.

At the end of Listing 6-1, we use ROLLBACK to undo our changes. The ROLLBACK command is explained in Section 6-5.

■ **Note**   After this chapter, we need all tables again in their unmodified state. Make sure to undo all changes you apply in this chapter, or re-create the tables before proceeding with Chapter 7.

INSERT Using Subqueries

If existing data should be used as the source for a new table, using a subquery can speed up the process. Another, longer way for the same task, would be running a set of INSERT statements the same way as explained above. Listing 6-2 creates a table that we'll insert some new data into. Listing 6-2 also shows the query that we'll use to generate the data that we'll be inserting. Listing 6-2 just gets everything ready; Listing 6-3 is where we'll do the actual INSERT statement.

Listing 6-2. Preparation for the INSERT Using a Subquery Example

```
CREATE TABLE dept_emp_names   -- create a table to populate
( deptname   VARCHAR2(10),
  location   VARCHAR2(8),
  empname    VARCHAR2(8),
  job        VARCHAR2(8)
);

Table created.
```

```
SELECT d.dname, d.location, e.ename, e.job
FROM   departments d, employees e
WHERE  e.deptno = d.deptno;
```

```
DNAME         LOCATION     ENAME     JOB
-----------   ----------   -------   ---------
TRAINING      DALLAS       SMITH     TRAINER
SALES         CHICAGO      ALLEN     SALESREP
SALES         CHICAGO      WARD      SALESREP
TRAINING      DALLAS       JONES     MANAGER
SALES         CHICAGO      MARTIN    SALESREP
SALES         CHICAGO      BLAKE     MANAGER
ACCOUNTING    NEW YORK     CLARK     MANAGER
TRAINING      DALLAS       SCOTT     TRAINER
ACCOUNTING    NEW YORK     KING      DIRECTOR
SALES         CHICAGO      TURNER    SALESREP
TRAINING      DALLAS       ADAMS     TRAINER
SALES         CHICAGO      JONES     ADMIN
TRAINING      DALLAS       FORD      TRAINER
ACCOUNTING    NEW YORK     MILLER    ADMIN

14 rows selected.
```

When performing DML, it is always a good idea to test it, where possible, by running a query or the subquery first and verifying the results. Not only does this help you create the query before actually modifying data, but it can also catch mistakes that might result in loss of data or the need to perform a recovery. In Listing 6-2, the subquery that is used as the source for our intended INSERT is run and the output displayed. Because the target table is empty before the INSERT, a query of the table after the INSERT will display exactly the same data if the INSERT was executed properly.

Having confirmed from the output in Listing 6-2 that our query to generate data is correct, we can use that query as a subquery to an INSERT statement. Listing 6-3 shows the results. The INSERT statement in Listing 6-3 executes our query and inserts the resulting rows into the target table named dept_emp_names.

Listing 6-3. Using Subqueries to Rapidly Populate a Table

```
INSERT INTO dept_emp_names            -- Example 1
  ( deptname, location, empname, job)
  ( SELECT d.dname, d.location, e.ename, e.job
    FROM   departments d, employees e
    WHERE  e.deptno = d.deptno
  );

14 rows created.

SELECT *   -- Verify that the data is the same as Listing 6-2
FROM dept_emp_names;

DEPTNAME      LOCATION      EMPNAME      JOB
-----------   -----------   ----------   ------
TRAINING      DALLAS        SMITH        TRAINER
SALES         CHICAGO       ALLEN        SALESREP
SALES         CHICAGO       WARD         SALESREP
TRAINING      DALLAS        JONES        MANAGER
```

```
SALES         CHICAGO      MARTIN     SALESREP
SALES         CHICAGO      BLAKE      MANAGER
ACCOUNTING    NEW YORK     CLARK      MANAGER
TRAINING      DALLAS       SCOTT      TRAINER
ACCOUNTING    NEW YORK     KING       DIRECTOR
SALES         CHICAGO      TURNER     SALESREP
TRAINING      DALLAS       ADAMS      TRAINER
SALES         CHICAGO      JONES      ADMIN
TRAINING      DALLAS       FORD       TRAINER
ACCOUNTING    NEW YORK     MILLER     ADMIN
```

14 rows selected.

```
INSERT INTO dept_emp_names - Example 2
(SELECT *
 FROM dept_emp_names
);
```

14 rows created.

```
/
```

28 rows created.

```
/
```

56 rows created.

```
COMMIT;
```

Commit complete.

```
SELECT COUNT(1)
FROM dept_emp_names;

  COUNT(1)
----------
       112
```

1 row selected.

The examples work as follows:

- In the first example, the subquery joining employees and departments creates a set that is inserted into the table. As the subquery was properly formed and executed, the rows in the table are the same as the rows from the query executed in Listing 6-2.

- The second example reads rows from the table and then inserts the same rows, effectively doubling the number of rows in the table every time the INSERT statement is executed. In this case, you do not need to specify the columns as the source and target of the insert is the same table and columns cannot be changed during the query and insert.

6.2 The UPDATE Command

You can change column values of existing rows in your tables with the UPDATE command. As shown in the syntax diagram in Figure 6-2, the UPDATE command has three main components:

- UPDATE ...: The table you want to update
- SET ...: The change you want to apply
- WHERE ...: The rows to which you want to apply the change

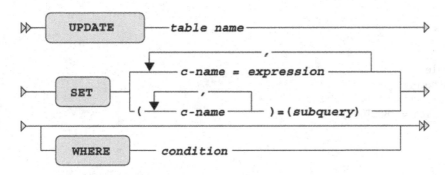

Figure 6-2. *UPDATE command syntax diagram*

If you omit the optional WHERE clause, the change is applied to all rows of the table. This illustrates the fact that the UPDATE command operates at the table level, so you need the WHERE clause as the relational restriction operator to limit the scope of the UPDATE command to a subset of the table.

As you can see from Figure 6-2, the SET clause offers two alternatives:

- You can specify a comma-separated list of single column changes. With this approach, you can use the DEFAULT keyword as an expression. This allows you to change column default values in the data dictionary at any point in time without the need to change the UPDATE commands in your applications.

- You can drive the change with a subquery. The subquery must provide the right number of values for the list of column names specified between the parentheses. Of course, the datatypes should also match, or the Oracle DBMS should at least be able to convert values to the appropriate datatypes on the fly.

The first approach is illustrated in Example 1 in Listing 6-4, and the second approach is shown in Examples 2 and 3.

Listing 6-4. UPDATE Command Examples

```
update employees            -- Example 1
set    job   = 'SALESREP'
,      msal  = msal - 500
,      comm  = 0
,      deptno = 30
where  empno = 7876;

1 row updated.

rollback;
```

```
Rollback complete.

UPDATE employees        -- Example 2
SET deptno = (SELECT deptno
              FROM    departments
              WHERE   location = 'BOSTON')
WHERE empno = 7900;

1 row updated.

rollback;

Rollback complete.

UPDATE employees        -- Example 3
SET (deptno,mgr) = (SELECT deptno,mgr
                    FROM    departments
                    WHERE   location = 'BOSTON')
WHERE empno = 7900;

1 row updated.

rollback;

Rollback complete.
```

The examples work as follows:

- In the first example, the employee with empno of 7876 has their job, msal, comm, and deptno updated with new values. In the case of msal, the new value is based on the current (pre-UPDATE) value of the column.

- The second example uses a subquery to determine the value of deptno. For an UPDATE, this subquery can return one and only one row. This type of subquery is called a *scalar subquery* and is addressed in more detail in Chapter 9.

- The third example also uses a subquery to determine the value of deptno and mgr. Instead of having two different subqueries for deptno and mgr, you can use a scalar subquery that returns multiple columns. The number, datatypes, and order of the subquery columns must match the columns that are being updated.

As with the INSERT examples in Listing 6-1, in both of these listings, we use the ROLLBACK command to undo any changes made.

A subquery can also be used to filter the records being updated. Instead of using a literal value, such as DEPTNO = 20, a subquery can be used so that the update can be driven by data in a table. Listing 6-5 applies a subquery to the task of determining the department number.

Listing 6-5. UPDATE Command Examples Using WHERE Subquery

```
UPDATE employees e        -- Example 2
SET e.msal = e.msal * 1.1
WHERE e.deptno IN (SELECT  d.deptno
                   FROM    departments d
                   WHERE   d.location = 'DALLAS'
                   );
```

```
5 rows updated.
```

```
rollback;
```

```
Rollback complete.
```

6.3 The DELETE Command

The simplest data manipulation command is DELETE, as shown in the syntax diagram in Figure 6-3. This command also operates at the table level, and you use the WHERE clause to restrict the set of rows you want to delete from the table. If you omit the WHERE clause, the DELETE command results in an empty table.

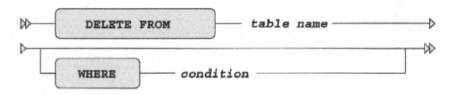

Figure 6-3. *DELETE command syntax diagram*

Note the difference between, but do not actually run, the following two commands:

```
drop  table departments
delete from departments
```

The DROP TABLE command not only removes the contents of the table, but also the table itself, including all dependent objects/structures such as indexes and privileges. DROP TABLE is a *data definition* (DDL) command. The DELETE command does not change the database structure, but only the contents—it is a *data manipulation* (DML) command. Moreover, the effects of a DROP TABLE command cannot be undone with a ROLLBACK command, as opposed to the effects of a DELETE command, which can. (The ROLLBACK command is introduced in Section 6.5.)

■ **Note** In Chapter 7, you will see that there is a different way to get a table back after a DROP TABLE statement.

Listing 6-6 shows how you can delete a salary grade.

Listing 6-6. Example of a DELETE Command

```
select *
from salgrades;

GRADE LOWERLIMIT UPPERLIMIT     BONUS
----- ---------- ---------- ----------
    1        700       1200          0
    2       1201       1400         50
    3       1401       2000        100
    4       2001       3000        200
    5       3001       9999        500


delete from salgrades
where  grade = 5;

1 row deleted.
select *
from salgrades;

GRADE LOWERLIMIT UPPERLIMIT     BONUS
----- ---------- ---------- ----------
    1        700       1200          0
    2       1201       1400         50
    3       1401       2000        100
    4       2001       3000        200


rollback;
Rollback complete.
```

To illustrate the fact that you can also use subqueries in the FROM clause of the DELETE statement, Listing 6-7 shows an alternative formulation for the same DELETE statement. Again, we use the ROLLBACK command to undo our changes.

Listing 6-7. Alternative DELETE Command, Using a Subquery

```
select *
from salgrades;

GRADE LOWERLIMIT UPPERLIMIT     BONUS
----- ---------- ---------- ----------
    1        700       1200          0
    2       1201       1400         50
    3       1401       2000        100
    4       2001       3000        200
    5       3001       9999        500


delete from (select *
             from   salgrades
             where  grade = 5);

1 row deleted.
```

```
select *
from salgrades;

GRADE LOWERLIMIT UPPERLIMIT    BONUS
----- ---------- ---------- ----------
    1        700       1200          0
    2       1201       1400         50
    3       1401       2000        100
    4       2001       3000        200

rollback;

Rollback complete.
```

In this case, there are no obvious advantages to using a subquery over using a regular DELETE statement.

You can use subqueries in the WHERE clause of the DELETE statement. Listing 6-8 shows how you can use a subquery to filter the rows for the DELETE statement. In this case, the deptname 'TRAINING' is returned from the subquery and used to filter out the deptname for the dept_emp_names table. Again, we use the ROLLBACK command to undo our changes.

Listing 6-8. Alternative DELETE Command, Using a Subquery in the WHERE Clause

```
DELETE FROM dept_emp_names
  WHERE deptname = (SELECT dname
                      FROM departments
                     WHERE location = 'DALLAS');

40 rows deleted.

rollback;

Rollback complete.
```

Deleting rows may seem rather straightforward, but you might encounter complications due to constraint violations. In Listing 6-9, the DELETE fails because rows exist in a child table.

Listing 6-9. Unable to Delete Due to a Constraint Violation

```
DELETE FROM employees
    WHERE deptno IN (SELECT deptno
                     FROM   departments
                     WHERE  location = 'NEW YORK')
    /
DELETE FROM employees
*
ERROR at line 1:
ORA-02292: integrity constraint (BOOK.D_MGR_FK) violated - child record found
```

The same is true for the UPDATE and INSERT commands, by the way. Constraints are discussed in the next chapter.

Because this section is about deleting rows, there is another SQL command that deserves mention here: TRUNCATE. The TRUNCATE command allows you to delete *all rows* of a table in a more efficient way than with the DELETE command. The TRUNCATE command belongs to the category of the data definition (DDL) commands, and so it is covered in the next chapter.

6.4 The MERGE Command

The MERGE command is a rather strange and complex one. It is able to perform insertions, updates, and deletions in a single statement. This makes the MERGE command very efficient in data warehouse environments, where the tables are often populated/updated in bulk from external sources. The MERGE command is able to react appropriately to the existence (or nonexistence) of certain rows in the tables you are updating.

This book is not about data warehousing, so we will look at only a rather simple example of the MERGE command to see how it operates. For more details, see the *Oracle SQL Reference* and *Oracle Data Warehousing Guide*.

Listing 6-10 shows the first step of our example, where we create and populate two small tables. Both tables have three columns: a product ID, a cumulative quantity sold, and a product status.

Listing 6-10. Preparation for the MERGE Example

```
create table delta_tab
(pid number, sales number, status varchar2(6));
Table created.

create table master_tab
(pid number, sales number, status varchar2(6));
Table created.

insert into master_tab values(1,12,'CURR');
1 row created.

insert into master_tab values(2,13,'NEW' );
1 row created.

insert into master_tab values(3,15,'CURR');
1 row created.

insert into delta_tab  values(2,24,'CURR');
1 row created.

insert into delta_tab  values(3, 0,'OBS' );
1 row created.

insert into delta_tab  values(4,42,'CURR');
1 row created.

commit;
Commit complete.
```

Listing 6-11 shows the starting point of our example, before we execute a MERGE command. In the master table, we have three rows, for products 1, 2, and 3. In the delta table, we also have three rows, for products 2, 3, and 4.

Listing 6-11. Situation Before Executing the MERGE Command

```
select * from master_tab;

   PID    SALES STATUS
-------- -------- ------
      1       12 CURR
      2       13 NEW
      3       15 CURR


select * from delta_tab;

   PID    SALES STATUS
-------- -------- ------
      2       24 CURR
      3        0 OBS
      4       42 CURR
```

Now we use the MERGE command, as shown in Listing 6-12.

Listing 6-12. The MERGE Command and Its Effect on the MASTER_TAB Table

```
merge into master_tab m
        using delta_tab d
      on (m.pid = d.pid)
  when  matched
  then  update set  m.sales  = m.sales+d.sales
                ,   m.status = d.status
        delete where m.status = 'OBS'
  when  not matched
  then  insert values (d.pid,d.sales,'NEW');

3 rows merged.

select * from master_tab;

   PID   SALES STATUS
-------- -------- ------
      1       12 CURR
      2       37 CURR
      4       42 NEW
```

In Listing 6-12, the first three command lines specify the roles of the two tables involved and the joining condition between the two tables. Lines 5, 6, and 7 specify what must be done when processing a row from the DELTA_TAB table if there is a matching row in the MASTER_TAB table. Line 9 specifies what must be done when such a matching row does not exist.

Do you see what happened with the contents of the MASTER_TAB table?

- The first row is not touched, because the DELTA_TAB contains no row for product 1.

- The second row is updated: the SALES value is incremented with 24, and the STATUS is set to CURR.

- The third (original) row is deleted, because after applying the UPDATE clause, the DELETE condition became TRUE.

- The fourth row is inserted, because there was no row for product 4.

6.5 Transaction Processing

All DML changes (INSERT, UPDATE, DELETE, and MERGE) that you apply to the contents of the database initially get a "pending" status. This means (among other things) that your session can see the changed rows, but other database users will see *the original data* when they query the same table rows. Moreover, as long as your changes are in this pending state, other database users will not be able to change those rows, until you confirm or abandon your pending changes. The SQL command to confirm pending changes to the database is COMMIT, and the command to abandon them is ROLLBACK. This allows you to perform a number of changes, then confirm them with a COMMIT or abandon them with ROLLBACK, then perform another number of changes, and so on.

COMMIT and ROLLBACK end the current *transaction* and start a new one. A transaction is considered to be a *logical unit of work*. In other words, a transaction is a set of changes that will succeed or fail as a whole.

■ **Note**　The Oracle DBMS also allows you to define *autonomous transactions* using PL/SQL. These are subtransactions that you can COMMIT or ROLLBACK independently from their main transactions. Among other things, autonomous transactions can be useful for logging information to tables while a program is running, without affecting that program, for debugging purposes. So, even if the main program fails and must be rolled back, the logged information has still been committed and is visible for understanding what may have gone wrong. See *PL/SQL User's Guide and Reference* for details.

For example, account transfer transactions in a banking system normally consist of (at least) two updates: a debit to account A and a credit to account B. In such situations, it makes a lot of sense to COMMIT after each debit/credit combination, and *not* in between each update. What if something went wrong (for example, the system crashed) after the debit update was committed but the credit update had not been processed yet? You would end up with corrupted administration records. Moreover, even in the absence of any disasters, a different database user could start a reporting application precisely at the "wrong" moment in between the two updates, which would result in inconsistent financial reports.

On the other hand, if you wait too long before committing your changes, you risk losing your work when the system crashes. During system recovery, all pending transactions will be rolled back to guarantee database consistency. This may be annoying, but it's necessary.

However, the examples we've discussed so far involve very simple logic: if everything succeeds, then COMMIT, but if something fails, then ROLLBACK. Simple.

But, what if a transaction is long and very complex, with lots of steps and lots of conditional logic?. If a failure occurs, then perhaps it should not be necessary to roll everything back all the way to the beginning.

For this situation, the SAVEPOINT command is provided, to provide the ability to only roll back part of a long transaction. Here is a simple illustration:

Listing 6-13. Using SAVEPOINT commands

```
begin
        insert into table_a values (...);  /* operation #1 */
        savepoint sp_1;
        if var_d = TRUE then
                begin   insert into table_b select ... from table_c where ...;  /* operation #2 */
                exception
                        when others then rollback to sp_1;
                end;
```

```
        else
                begin   insert into table_b select ... from table_d where ...;   /* operation #3 */
                exception when others then rollback to sp_1;
                end;
        end if;
        savepoint sp_2;
        if var_e = TRUE then
                begin   update table_a set ... where ...;   /* operation #4 */
                exception
                        when others then rollback to sp_2;
                end;
        else
                begin   update table_b set ... where ...;   /* operation #5 */
                exception when others then rollback to sp_2;
                end;
        end if;
        insert into table_b select ... from table_e where...;   /* operation #6 */
        commit;
end;
```

The pseudo-code in Figure 6-13 above shows a series of six (6) DML operations. The first INSERT statement, labeled as "operation #1" succeeds and we then proceed to set a savepoint named SP_1. Then, depending on the boolean value in the variable named VAR_D, we execute either the INSERT statement labeled as "operation #2" or "operation #3". If either of these operations fails, then we don't rollback all the way to the beginning, but instead just to the savepoint named SP_1. And we proceed onward.

Then, we proceed to set another savepoint, named SP_2. Depending on the boolean value in the variable named VAR_E, we will either execute the UPDATE statement labeled as "operation #4" or the one labeled "operation #5". If any errors occur during those operations, then again we don't rollback all the way to the beginning, but instead just to the savepoint named SP_2, preserving all of the changes made previous to that.

And we proceed onward, executing one more large INSERT statement labeled "operation #6". If that operation fails, we will rollback all the way to beginning, because we haven't trapped any exceptions. But if it succeeds, then we finally COMMIT and we're done.

By the way, all of these examples illustrate the fact that not only database users are able to issue *explicit* COMMIT and ROLLBACK commands. Oracle tools can also issue those commands *implicitly*. For example, if you leave SQL*Plus in a normal way with the EXIT or QUIT command, or if you create a new session with the SQL*Plus CONNECT command, SQL*Plus first sends a COMMIT command to the database.

Another consequence of a delayed committing of your changes is that you block other database users who want to update or delete the same rows. Section 6.6 discusses this locking behavior in a little more detail.

All DDL commands (such as CREATE, ALTER, DROP, GRANT, and REVOKE) always imply an *implicit* COMMIT. To put it another way, each single DDL command is executed as a transaction in itself, consisting of a single command, and is committed immediately.

■ **Note**   For this reason, it is important that DDL commands not be accidentally interspersed with transactions involving INSERT, UPDATE, DELETE, and MERGE commands, due to the chance of inadvertently committing changes.

6.6 Locking and Read Consistency

Normally, many users and applications access database systems at the same time. This is known as *concurrency*. The RDBMS must make sure that concurrency is handled properly. The most drastic approach for a RDBMS would be to handle all user transactions one by one, blocking all data exclusively until the end of each transaction. Such a transaction serialization approach would result in unnecessary and unacceptable wait times; the overall system *throughput* would be very poor.

RDBMSs like Oracle control concurrent data access with *locking* to prevent database users from updating rows with pending (uncommitted) changes from other database users. This section gives some information about how the Oracle RDBMS handles locking and concurrency.

Locking

To understand how the Oracle RDBMS handles locking, we need to identify a difference between two categories of database users:

- **Readers:** Users *retrieving* data (issuing SELECT statements)

- **Writers:** Users *changing* data (issuing INSERT, UPDATE, DELETE, and MERGE commands)

The Oracle RDBMS does not lock any data for retrieval. This means that *readers* never block *readers*. Moreover, this also means that *writers* never need to wait for *readers*, and vice versa.

■ **Note** The Oracle RDBMS's handling of data locking does *not* mean that readers and writers do not hinder each other in any way. Readers and writers can cause delays for each other by contending for certain system resources, such as CPU.

Multiple database users trying to change the same rows need to wait for each other, so *writers* may block other *writers*. Each attempt to change a row tries to acquire the corresponding *row-level lock* first. If the lock cannot be acquired, you must wait until the pending change is committed or rolled back. All row-level locks are released upon a COMMIT (explicit or implicit) or ROLLBACK. This means that the Oracle DBMS tries to minimize locking overhead and tries to maximize throughput and concurrency.

■ **Note** Only those rows that are actually being modified are locked. Many separate users and sessions can simultaneously lock rows in a single table.

Read Consistency

In a database environment, *read consistency* is an important concept. Read consistency is a first requirement to guarantee correct query results, regardless of how long it runs *and* regardless what else happens simultaneously in the database. The Oracle RDBMS must make sure that each SQL query creates a *snapshot* of the data at the point in time when the query started. It needs this snapshot because a query should *never* see any uncommitted changes nor any changes that were committed *after* the query started. Imagine the problems that would occur if one person was updating salaries (even making mistakes that had to be rolled back) while another person was running a payroll report. Without read consistency, the payroll report might include old salaries, new salaries and salary mistakes and there would be no way to know which person was being paid incorrectly.

This means that the Oracle RDBMS must be able to reconstruct previous versions of the data in order to process queries. We will not go into technical details here, but the Oracle RDBMS accomplishes this by using information stored in undo segments. One way to think about undo segments is that they contain the "before image" of the data before any modification, though this is not technically precise.

Believe it or not, read consistency is even important in a *single-user* environment. Suppose that upper management has decided to grant a salary raise of 50% to all employees who currently earn less than the average salary of their department. You might want your salary to be checked last by the UPDATE statement, hoping that earlier salary raises have influenced your department's average salary in such a way that you became entitled to a raise, too. In an Oracle environment, this hope is in vain, because the read consistency mechanism will ensure that the subquery in the UPDATE statement (to derive the average salary of your department) returns the same result, regardless of how often the subquery is re-executed for the same department, within the scope of that single UPDATE command.

But note that because the Oracle RDBMS does *not* use any locking or other obstructive techniques when you do this, you incur the risk that, at a point in time, the Oracle RDBMS will not be able to reconstruct the desired original data anymore, especially if your query is running a long time. You get the following error message in such situations:

```
ORA-01555: Snapshot too old
```

Oracle will never return data to a query that is inconsistent with the point in time at which the query began. (You could term such data as being *read inconsistent*). Instead, Oracle terminates the query with the "Snapshot too old" error. This error simply means that the query is unable to create the before image of the data as of the time the query started. Read consistency and the Oracle mechanisms used to enforce it also insure the integrity of the data in the query.

This completes your introduction to data manipulation commands and concepts.

Terms Review

You learned about the four DML commands of the SQL language: INSERT, UPDATE, DELETE, and MERGE. Then we discussed transaction processing, using the commands COMMIT, SAVEPOINT, and ROLLBACK. Finally, we briefly discussed read consistency and locking, and introduced the SET TRANSACTION command, which you can use to influence the default read consistency behavior of the Oracle DBMS.

Before continuing with Chapter 7, which returns to the topic of data definition, make sure that all of your case tables are in their unmodified state. You should have rolled back all of the changes you applied in this chapter. Alternatively, you can drop and re-create the tables before proceeding.

■■■

Data Definition, Part II

Chapter 3 introduced just enough data definition (DDL) syntax to enable you to create the seven case tables for this book, using simple CREATE TABLE commands without any constraint specifications. This second DDL chapter goes into more detail about some data definition aspects, although it is still not intended as a complete reference on the topic. (Discussion of the CREATE TABLE command alone covers more than 100 pages in the Oracle Database documentation.)

The first two sections revisit the CREATE TABLE command and the datatypes supported by Oracle Database 12*c*. Section 7.3 introduces the ALTER TABLE command, which allows you to change the structure of an existing table (such as to add columns or change datatypes), and the RENAME command, which allows you to rename a table or view. You will learn how to define and handle constraints in Section 7.4.

Section 7.5 covers indexes. The main purpose of indexes is to improve performance (response time) by providing more efficient access paths to table data. Thus, Section 7.6 provides a brief introduction to performance, mainly in the context of checking if the optimizer is using your indexes.

The most efficient method to generate sequence numbers (for example, for order numbers) in an Oracle environment is by using sequence objects, which are introduced in Section 7.7.

We continue with synonyms, in Section 7.8. By creating synonyms you can work with abbreviations for table names, hide the schema name prefix of table names, or even hide the remote database where the table resides. Section 7.9 explains the CURRENT_SCHEMA session parameter.

Section 7.10 discusses the DROP TABLE command and the recycle bin, a concept introduced back in Oracle Database 10*g*. By default, all dropped tables go to the recycle bin, allowing you to recover from human errors.

The last two sections of the chapter cover some other SQL commands related to data definition: TRUNCATE and COMMENT.

7.1 The CREATE TABLE Command

Chapter 3 introduced the CREATE TABLE command and showed a basic command syntax diagram. This section explores the CREATE TABLE command in a little more detail. Figure 7-1 shows a more complete syntax diagram, but please be aware that even this is far from complete.

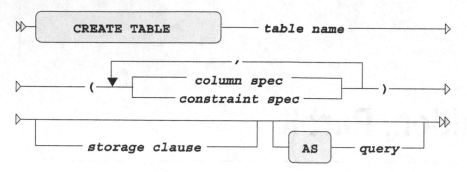

Figure 7-1. *A CREATE TABLE command syntax diagram*

Figure 7-1 shows that the CREATE TABLE command supports two component types: *column* specifications and *constraint* specifications.

You can provide an optional STORAGE clause, with various physical storage specifications for the table you are creating. This is an important means to optimizing and spreading the physical storage of your data on disk. For more information about the STORAGE clause and handling physical storage, see *Oracle SQL Reference.*

According to the syntax diagram in Figure 7-1, you can also create new tables based on a subquery with the AS clause. The CREATE TABLE ... AS SELECT ... command (also known as CTAS) is comparable to one of the possibilities of the INSERT command shown in Figure 6-1 (in Chapter 6), where you insert rows into an existing table using a subquery. The only difference is that with CTAS you create *and* populate the table in a single SQL command. In this case, you can omit the column specifications between the parentheses. If you want to use column specifications anyway, you are not allowed to specify datatypes. In CTAS commands, the new table always inherits the datatypes from the results of the subquery.

The syntax for column specifications in a CREATE TABLE command is detailed in Figure 7-2.

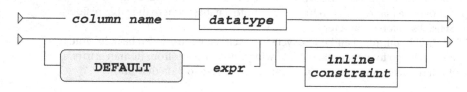

Figure 7-2. *A CREATE TABLE column specification syntax*

Figure 7-2 shows that you can specify constraints in two ways:

- As independent (*out-of-line*) components of the CREATE TABLE command (see Figure 7-1)

- As *inline constraints* inside a column specification (see Figure 7-2)

We will discuss both types of constraints in Section 7.4.

You can use the DEFAULT option to specify a value (or a SQL expression or a reference to the CURRVAL or NEXTVAL of a sequence object[1]) to be used for INSERT commands that don't contain an explicit value for the corresponding column.

---

[1]Sequence objects and their CURRVAL and NEXTVAL expressions are described later in the chapter, in Section 7.7.

7.2 More on Datatypes

Datatypes were introduced in Chapter 3. Table 7-1 provides a more complete overview of the most important Oracle datatypes.

Table 7-1. *Important Oracle Datatypes*

Datatype	Description
CHAR[(n)]	Character string with fixed length n (default 1) using the database characterset
VARCHAR|VARCHAR2(n)	Variable-length string; maximum n characters using the database characterset
NCHAR[(n)]	Character string with fixed length n (default 1) using the national characterset
NVARCHAR|NVARCHAR2(n)	Variable-length string; maximum n characters using the national characterset
DATE	Date (between 4712 BC and 9999 AD)
TIMESTAMP	Timestamp, with or without time zone information
INTERVAL	Date/time interval
BLOB	Unstructured binary data (Binary Large Object)
CLOB	Large text (Character Large Object) using the database characterset
NCLOB	Large text (Character Large Object) using the national characterset
RAW(n)	Binary data; maximum n bytes
NUMBER	Can store any number, maximum precision and scale 38 digits
NUMBER(n)	Integer; maximum n digits
NUMBER(n,m)	Total of n digits; maximum m digits right of the decimal point
BINARY_FLOAT	32-bit floating-point number
BINARY_DOUBLE	64-bit floating-point number

■ **Note** If you insert values into a NUMBER(n,m) column and you exceed precision n, you get an error message. If you exceed scale m, the Oracle DBMS rounds the value.

The Oracle DBMS supports many datatype synonyms for portability with other DBMS implementations and for compliance with the ANSI/ISO standard. For example, CHARACTER is identical to CHAR; DECIMAL(n,m) is identical to NUMBER(n,m); and NUMBER even has multiple synonyms, such as INTEGER, REAL, and SMALLINT.

Each Oracle datatype has its own precision or length limits, as shown in Table 7-2.

Table 7-2. *Oracle Datatype Limits*

Datatype	Limit
NUMBER	38 digits
CHAR	2000 bytes
VARCHAR	4000 bytes
VARCHAR2	4000 bytes or 32,767 bytes[2]
RAW	2000 bytes or 32,767 bytes[3]
BLOB	(4GB – 1) × (database block size)
CLOB	(4GB – 1) × (database block size)

Character Datatypes

You may have noticed that Table 7-2 shows 2000 and 4000 for the CHAR and VARCHAR2 datatype limits, respectively. You might wonder in which unit these numbers are expressed. That depends on the value of the NLS_LENGTH_SEMANTICS parameter. The default for the Oracle DBMS is to use BYTE length semantics. If you want to make your SQL code independent of this parameter, you can override its value by using explicit BYTE and CHAR suffixes in your datatype specifications. With single-byte characterset encodings, BYTE and CHAR are equivalent. However, if either your database characterset or your national characterset are using variable-length or multibyte characterset codes, then you may want to be aware that a column specified as VARCHAR2(20) or VARCHAR2(20 BYTE) can store only 10 multibyte characters. Here are a couple examples:

- CHAR(42 BYTE): Fixed string, 42 bytes maximum in database characterset

- VARCHAR2(2000 CHAR): Variable-length string, maximum of 2000 characters in database characterset

- NVARCHAR2(150 BYTE): Variable-length string, maximum of 150 bytes in the national characterset

- NVARCHAR2(150 CHAR): Variable-length string, maximum of 150 characters in the national characterset

Comparison Semantics

The difference between VARCHAR2 and CHAR datatypes is the treatment of comparisons involving strings of different lengths. There are two different semantics to compare strings of different lengths: padded comparison (padding with spaces) and nonpadded comparison.

If you compare two strings, character by character, and all of the characters are identical until the point where the shortest string is processed, nonpadded comparison semantics automatically "declares" the longest string as being greater than the shorter string. On the other hand, padded comparison semantics extends the shortest string with spaces until the length of the longest string and continues comparing characters. This means that trailing spaces in strings don't influence padded comparison results. Here are examples of the comparison types:

- Padded comparison: 'RAID5' = 'RAID5   '

- Nonpadded comparison: ' RAID5' < ' RAID5   '

---

[2]When the database initialization parameter MAX_STRING_SIZE has the value of STANDARD, then the VARCHAR2 datatype has a maximum size of 4,000 bytes. When the parameter is set to EXTENDED in Oracle12c or above, then the maximum is 32,767 bytes.
[3]When MAX_STRING_SIZE has the value of STANDARD, then the RAW datatype has a maximum size of 2,000 bytes; when the parameter is set to EXTENDED in Oracle 12c or above, then the maximum is 32.767 bytes.

By using the VARCHAR2 datatype, especially in all your SQL script files, you are guaranteed to get *nonpadded* comparison semantics.

Column Data Interpretation

There is an important difference between the RAW and VARCHAR2 datatypes. RAW column data (like BLOB data) is never interpreted by the DBMS in any way. For example, VARCHAR2 column data is converted automatically during transport from an ASCII to an EBCDIC environment. You typically use the RAW and BLOB datatypes for columns containing binary data, such as scanned documents, sound tracks, and movie fragments.

Numbers Revisited

Before we move on to the ALTER TABLE command in the next section, let's briefly revisit numbers. The Oracle DBMS has always stored NUMBER values in a proprietary internal format, to maintain maximum *portability* to the impressive list of different platforms (operating systems) that it supports. The NUMBER datatype is still the best choice for most columns containing numeric data. However, the internal storage of this datatype implies some processing overhead, especially when you are performing many nontrivial numerical computations in your SQL statements.

Since Oracle Database 10g you can also store *floating-point* numbers in your table columns. Floating-point numbers don't offer the same precision as NUMBER values, but they may result in better response times for numerical computations. You can choose between two floating-point datatypes:

- BINARY_FLOAT: 32-bit, single precision

- BINARY_DOUBLE: 64-bit, double precision

You can also specify floating-point constants (literals) in your SQL statements with a suffix f (single precision) or d (double precision), as shown in Listing 7-1.

Listing 7-1. Floating-Point Literals

```
SQL> select 5.1d, 42f from dual;

      5.1D       42F
---------- ----------
 5.1E+000   4.2E+001

SQL>
```

We won't use these two floating-point datatypes in this book. See *Oracle SQL Reference* for more details.

7.3 The ALTER TABLE and RENAME Commands

Sometimes, it is necessary to change the structure of existing tables. For example, you may find that the maximum width of a certain column is defined too low, you may want to add an extra column to an existing table, or you may need to modify a constraint. In these situations, you can use the ALTER TABLE command. Figure 7-3 shows the syntax diagram for this command.

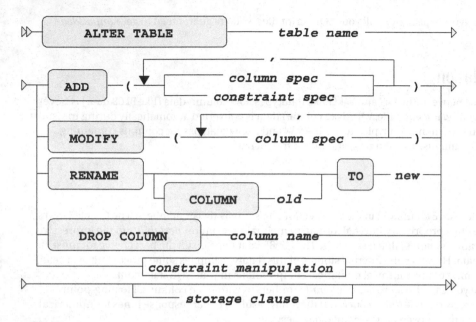

Figure 7-3. *An ALTER TABLE command syntax diagram*

■ **Note** The ALTER TABLE command is much more complicated and extended than Figure 7-3 suggests. See *Oracle SQL Reference* for more details.

You can add columns or constraint definitions to an existing table with the ADD option. The MODIFY option allows you to change definitions of existing columns. For example, you can widen a column, allow null values with NULL, or prohibit null values with NOT NULL.

You can drop columns from tables with the DROP COLUMN option. This will remove the column physically from the table structure. You can also set columns to "unused" with the ALTER TABLE ... SET UNUSED command, and physically remove them from the database later with the ALTER TABLE ... DROP UNUSED COLUMNS command. This may be useful when you want to drop multiple columns in a single scan (accessing the rows only once). The RENAME COLUMN option allows you to change the name of a column.

■ **Caution** You should be careful with the "destructive" DROP COLUMN option. Some database applications may depend on the existence of the column you are dropping.

Dropping columns in very big tables could be a very time and resource consuming operation. To avoid exhaustion of undo space (used for rollback purposes), we can use a CHECKPOINT option, such as "ALTER TABLE...DROP UNUSED COLUMNS CHECKPOINT 300", which would will checkpoint or save changes permanently every 300 rows changed.

With the constraint manipulation option, you can remove, enable, or disable constraints. Figure 7-4 shows the syntax details of this ALTER TABLE command option. For more details about constraint handling, see the next section.

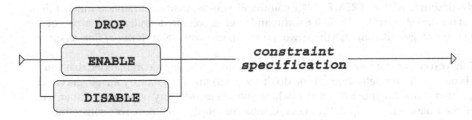

Figure 7-4. *ALTER TABLE constraint manipulation syntax*

Just like the CREATE TABLE command, the ALTER TABLE command also allows you to influence various physical table storage attributes.

In general, you can apply any structure change to existing tables, even when they contain rows. However, there are some exceptions. For example, for obvious reasons you cannot add a NOT NULL column to a nonempty table, unless you immediately specify a DEFAULT value in the same ALTER TABLE command. Listing 7-2 shows an example

Listing 7-2. ALTER TABLE Command Example

```
SQL> alter table registrations
  2  add  (entered_by number(4) default 7839 not null);

Table altered.

SQL> alter table registrations
  2  drop  column entered_by;

Table altered.

SQL>
```

■ **Note** The ALTER TABLE statement is probably the best illustration of the power of the relational model. Think about this: you can change a table definition while the table contains data and applications are running.

The RENAME command is rather straightforward. It allows you to change the name of a table or view (views are discussed in Chapter 10). Figure 7-5 shows the syntax diagram for the RENAME command.

Figure 7-5. *RENAME command syntax diagram*

7.4 Constraints

As you saw in the previous sections, you can specify constraint definitions in the CREATE TABLE and ALTER TABLE commands. As noted earlier in the description of the CREATE TABLE command, you can treat constraints as independent table components (for example, at the end of your CREATE TABLE command after all column definitions) or as part of a column definition. A common terminology to distinguish these two ways to specify constraints is *out-of-line* versus *inline* constraints.

For each constraint definition, you can optionally specify a constraint name. It is highly recommended that you assign a meaningful name for all your constraint definitions. If you don't specify a constraint name yourself, the Oracle DBMS generates a far from informative name for you: SYS_Cnnnnn, where nnnnn is an arbitrary sequence number. Once constraints are created, you need their names to manipulate (enable, disable, or drop) them. Moreover, constraint names show up in constraint violation error messages. Therefore, well-chosen constraint names make error messages more informative. See Listing 7-3 later in this section for an example, showing a foreign key constraint violation.

Out-of-Line Constraints

Figure 7-6 shows the syntax details for out-of-line constraints. This syntax is slightly different from the inline constraint syntax.

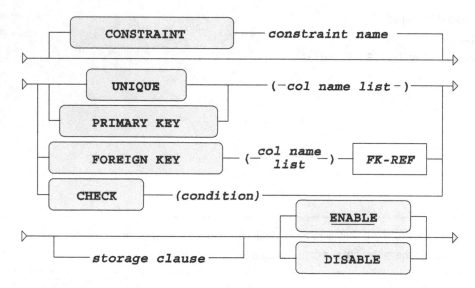

Figure 7-6. *Out-of-line constraint syntax diagram*

In the syntax diagram, col name list refers to a comma-separated list of one or more column names. The type of constraint can be UNIQUE, PRIMARY KEY, FOREIGN KEY, and CHECK. By default, constraints become active immediately, unless you specify the DISABLE option; in other words, the default option is ENABLE.

The four types of constraints work as follows:

- UNIQUE allows you to prevent duplicate values in a column or a column combination.

- PRIMARY KEY and FOREIGN KEY allow you to implement *entity integrity* and *referential integrity*. See Chapter 1 for a detailed discussion of these concepts.

- CHECK allows you to specify any arbitrary condition as a constraint.

Figure 7-7 shows the syntax details of a foreign key constraint reference (FK-REF in Figure 7-6).

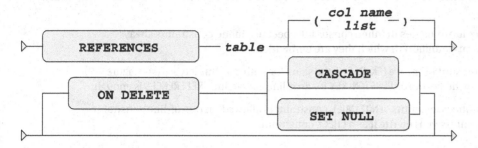

Figure 7-7. *Foreign key reference syntax diagram*

You can omit the comma-separated list of column names (col name list in Figure 7-7) in the foreign key reference. In that case, the foreign key constraint automatically refers to the primary key of the referenced table.

■ **Tip**   In general, it is considered good practice to have foreign keys always refer to primary keys, although foreign keys may also reference unique keys.

To understand the ON DELETE option of the foreign key reference, consider the example of a foreign key constraint violation shown in Listing 7-3. Normally, it is impossible to remove parent (master) rows if the database still contains child (detail) rows. In Listing 7-3, we try to remove the XML course while the database still apparently contains XML course offerings.

Listing 7-3. Example of a Foreign Key Constraint Violation

```
SQL> delete from courses
  2  where  code = 'XML';

delete from courses
*
ERROR at line 1:
ORA-02292: integrity constraint (BOOK.O_COURSE_FK) violated -
          child record found

SQL>
```

■ **Note**   Listing 7-10 shows the definition of the O_COURSE_FK constraint.

The ON DELETE CASCADE option (see Figure 7-7) changes the behavior in such situations. The master/detail problems are solved by a cascading effect, in which, apart from the parent row, all child rows are implicitly deleted, too. The ON DELETE SET NULL option solves the same problem in a different way: the child rows are updated, rather than deleted. This approach is applicable only if the foreign key columns involved may contain null values, of course.

Inline Constraints

The *inline* constraint syntax is shown in Figure 7-8. There are some subtle differences from the syntax for out-of-line constraints:

- You don't specify column names in inline constraints, because inline constraints always belong to the column definition in which they are embedded.

- The foreign key constraint reference (FK-REF) is the same for both constraint types (see Figure 7-7), but you don't specify the keywords FOREIGN KEY for an inline constraint—REFERENCES is enough.

- In the context of inline constraints, a NOT NULL constraint is allowed. In out-of-line constraints, this is impossible, unless you rewrite it as a CHECK constraint.

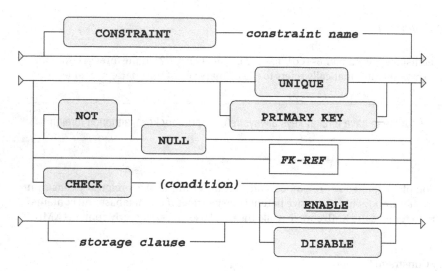

Figure 7-8. *Inline constraint syntax diagram*

Constraint Definitions in the Data Dictionary

Constraint definitions are stored in the data dictionary. The two most important views are USER_CONSTRAINTS and USER_CONS_COLUMNS. Listing 7-4 shows how you can produce an overview of all referential integrity constraints for the current user.

Listing 7-4. Foreign Key Constraints in the Data Dictionary

```
SQL> select table_name
  2  ,      constraint_name
  3  ,      status
  4  ,      r_constraint_name as references
  5  from   user_constraints
  6  where  constraint_type = 'R';
```

TABLE_NAME	CONSTRAINT_NAME	STATUS	REFERENCES
EMPLOYEES	E_MGR_FK	ENABLED	E_PK
DEPARTMENTS	D_MGR_FK	ENABLED	E_PK
EMPLOYEES	E_DEPT_FK	ENABLED	D_PK
OFFERINGS	O_TRAIN_FK	ENABLED	E_PK
OFFERINGS	O_COURSE_FK	ENABLED	C_PK
REGISTRATIONS	R_OFF_FK	ENABLED	O_PK
REGISTRATIONS	R_ATT_FK	ENABLED	E_PK
HISTORY	H_DEPT_FK	ENABLED	D_PK
HISTORY	H_EMPNO_FK	ENABLED	E_PK

SQL>

Tools like Oracle Forms can use constraint definitions from the data dictionary—for example, to generate code for constraint checking in database applications.

Last but not least, the Oracle optimizer uses knowledge about constraint information from the data dictionary to decide about efficient execution plans for SQL statements. To reiterate what we discussed in Chapter 1, constraints are very important, and they *must* be defined in the database.

Case Table Definitions with Constraints

Listings 7-5 through 7-12 show the CREATE TABLE commands for the seven case tables of this book. The constraints in these CREATE TABLE commands are meant to be self-explanatory, showing various examples of PRIMARY KEY, FOREIGN KEY, UNIQUE, CHECK, and NOT NULL constraints.

■ **Note**   For more details about the seven case tables, refer to Appendix C of this book.

Listing 7-5. The EMPLOYEES Table

```
create table  employees
( empno       NUMBER(4)    constraint E_PK        primary key
                           constraint E_EMPNO_CHK check (empno > 7000)
, ename       VARCHAR2(8)  constraint E_NAME_NN   not null
, init        VARCHAR2(5)  constraint E_INIT_NN   not null
, job         VARCHAR2(8)
, mgr         NUMBER(4)    constraint E_MGR_FK    references employees
, bdate       DATE         constraint E_BDAT_NN   not null
, msal        NUMBER(6,2)  constraint E_MSAL_NN   not null
, comm        NUMBER(6,2)
, deptno      NUMBER(2)    default 10
,                          constraint E_SALES_CHK check
                                    (decode(job,'SALESREP',0,1)
                                     + nvl2(comm,        1,0) = 1)
) ;
```

Listing 7-6. The DEPARTMENTS Table

```
create table departments
( deptno NUMBER(2)      constraint D_PK           primary key
                        constraint D_DEPTNO_CHK   check (mod(deptno,10) = 0)
, dname   VARCHAR2(10)  constraint D_DNAME_NN     not null
                        constraint D_DNAME_UN     unique
                        constraint D_DNAME_CHK    check (dname = upper(dname))
, location VARCHAR2(8)  constraint D_LOC_NN       not null
                        constraint D_LOC_CHK      check (location = upper(location))
, mgr     NUMBER(4)     constraint D_MGR_FK       references employees
) ;
```

Listing 7-7. Adding a Foreign Key Constraint

```
alter table employees add
(constraint E_DEPT_FK foreign key (deptno) references departments);
```

Listing 7-8. The SALGRADES Table

```
create table salgrades
( grade        NUMBER(2)   constraint S_PK        primary key
, lowerlimit NUMBER(6,2) constraint S_LOWER_NN  not null
                         constraint S_LOWER_CHK check (lowerlimit >= 0)
, upperlimit NUMBER(6,2) constraint S_UPPER_NN  not null
, bonus      NUMBER(6,2) constraint S_BONUS_NN  not null
,                        constraint S_LO_UP_CHK check
                                                (lowerlimit <= upperlimit)
) ;
```

Listing 7-9. The COURSES Table

```
create table courses
( code         VARCHAR2(6)  constraint C_PK        primary key
, description VARCHAR2(30) constraint C_DESC_NN  not null
, category    CHAR(3)      constraint C_CAT_NN   not null
, duration    NUMBER(2)    constraint C_DUR_NN   not null
,                          constraint C_CODE_CHK check
                                                 (code = upper(code))
,                          constraint C_CAT_CHK check
                                                 (category in ('GEN','BLD','DSG'))
) ;
```

Listing 7-10. The OFFERINGS Table

```
create table offerings
( course      VARCHAR2(6)  constraint O_COURSE_NN not null
                           constraint O_COURSE_FK references courses
, begindate  DATE         constraint O_BEGIN_NN  not null
, trainer    NUMBER(4)    constraint O_TRAIN_FK  references employees
, location   VARCHAR2(8)
,                          constraint O_PK        primary key
                                                  (course,begindate)
) ;
```

Listing 7-11. The REGISTRATIONS Table

```
create table registrations
( attendee    NUMBER(4)    constraint R_ATT_NN     not null
                           constraint R_ATT_FK     references employees
, course      VARCHAR2(6)  constraint R_COURSE_NN  not null
, begindate   DATE         constraint R_BEGIN_NN   not null
, evaluation  NUMBER(1)    constraint R_EVAL_CHK   check (evaluation in (1,2,3,4,5))
,                          constraint R_PK         primary key
                                                   (attendee,course,begindate)
,                          constraint R_OFF_FK     foreign key (course,begindate)
                                                   references offerings
) ;
```

Listing 7-12. The HISTORY Table

```
create table history
( empno       NUMBER(4)    constraint H_EMPNO_NN   not null
                           constraint H_EMPNO_FK   references employees
                                                   on delete cascade
, beginyear   NUMBER(4)    constraint H_BYEAR_NN   not null
, begindate   DATE         constraint H_BDATE_NN   not null
, enddate     DATE
, deptno      NUMBER(2)    constraint H_DEPT_NN    not null
                           constraint H_DEPT_FK    references departments
, msal        NUMBER(6,2)  constraint H_MSAL_NN    not null
, comments    VARCHAR2(60)
,                          constraint H_PK         primary key (empno,begindate)
,                          constraint H_BEG_END    check (begindate < enddate)
) ;
```

A Solution for Foreign Key References: CREATE SCHEMA

While we are on the topic of creating multiple tables, Oracle SQL also supports the ANSI/ISO standard CREATE SCHEMA command. This command allows you to create a complete schema (consisting of tables, views, and grants) with a single DDL command/transaction. One advantage of the CREATE SCHEMA command is that it succeeds or fails as an atomic transaction. It also solves the problem of two tables having foreign key references to each other (see Listings 7-5, 7-6, and 7-7), where you normally need at least one ALTER TABLE command, because foreign keys can reference only existing tables.

Listing 7-13 shows how you could have created the case tables with the CREATE SCHEMA command.

Listing 7-13. The CREATE SCHEMA Command

```
SQL> create schema authorization BOOK
  2         create table employees     (...)
  3         create table departments   (...)
  4         create table salgrades     (...)
  5         create table courses       (...)
  6         create table offerings     (...)
  7         create table registrations (...)
  8         create table history       (...)
  9         create view ... as select ... from ...
 10         grant select on ... to public;
```

■ **Note**   The name of this command (as implemented by Oracle) is confusing, because it does not actually create a schema. Oracle schemas are created with the CREATE USER command. The command succeeds only if the schema name is the same as your Oracle database username.

You can specify the CREATE SCHEMA command components in any order. Within each component definition, you can refer to other (earlier or later) schema components.

Deferrable Constraints

The Oracle DBMS also supports *deferrable constraints,* allowing you to specify *when* you want the constraints to be checked. These are the two possibilities:

- IMMEDIATE checks at the statement level.

- DEFERRED checks at the end of the transaction.

Before you can use this distinction, you must first allow a constraint to be deferrable. The default option for all constraints that you create is NOT DEFERRABLE. If you want your constraints to be deferrable, add the DEFERRABLE option in the constraint definition, as shown in Figure 7-9, just before the storage clause specification (see Figures 7-6 and 7-8).

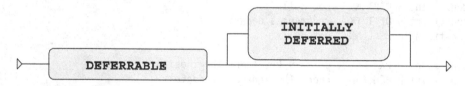

Figure 7-9. *DEFERRABLE option for constraint definitions*

If you allow constraints to be deferrable using the DEFERRABLE option, they still have a default behavior of INITIALLY IMMEDIATE. The INITIALLY option allows you to specify the desired default constraint checking behavior, using IMMEDIATE or DEFERRED.

You can dynamically change or override the default behavior of deferrable constraints at the transaction level with the SET CONSTRAINTS command, as shown in Figure 7-10.

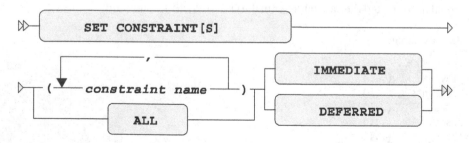

Figure 7-10. *SET CONSTRAINTS command syntax diagram*

At first sight, the complexity of all this constraint-checking syntax may look overwhelming. The following summary may help clarify how it works:

- By default, the Oracle DBMS *always* uses immediate constraint checking.

- You must explicitly allow a constraint to be deferrable. By default, constraints are *not* deferrable.

- If constraints are deferrable, you can choose how they should be checked *by default*: immediate or deferred.

- If constraints are deferrable, you can influence their behavior with the SET CONSTRAINTS command.

7.5 Indexes

In general, rows within a regular table are unordered. Although the Oracle DBMS offers many different ways to physically organize tables on disk (heap tables, index clusters, hash clusters, index-organized tables, and sorted hash clusters), you should never expect the rows to be physically stored in a certain order. Even if a particular order exists today, there is no guarantee that it will be the same tomorrow. This is a fundamental property of relational databases (see Ted Codd's rule 8 in Chapter 1 about physical data independence).

Suppose the EMPLOYEES table contains 50,000 rows (instead of the 14 rows we have), and suppose you want to know which employees have a name starting with a Q. Normally, the Oracle DBMS can use only one method to produce the results for this query: by accessing all 50,000 rows (with a full table scan) and checking the name for each of those rows. This could take quite some time, and perhaps there would be no employees at all with such a name.

An *index* on employee names would be very useful in this situation. When you create an index, the Oracle DBMS creates, and starts to maintain, a separate database object containing a sorted list of column values (or column combination values) with row identifiers referring to the corresponding rows in the table. To further optimize access, indexes are internally organized in a tree structure. (See *Oracle Concepts* for more details on physical index structures.) If there were such an index on employee names, the optimizer could decide to abandon the full table scan approach and perform an index search instead. The index offers a very efficient access path to all names, returning all row identifiers of employees with a name starting with a Q. This probably would result in a huge performance improvement, because there are only a few database blocks to be visited to produce the query result.

For some of your other queries, indexes on department numbers or birth dates could be useful. You can create as many indexes per table as you like.

In summary, the performance of your SQL statements can often be improved significantly by creating indexes. Sometimes, it is obvious that an index will help, such as when your tables contain a lot of rows and your queries are very selective (only retrieving a few rows). On the other hand, though, you may find that your application benefits from an index on a single-row, single-column table.

Indexes may speed up queries, but the other side of the index picture is the maintenance overhead. Every additional index slows down data manipulation further, because every INSERT/UPDATE/DELETE statement against a table must immediately be processed against all corresponding indexes to keep the indexes synchronized with the table. Also, indexes occupy additional space in your database. This means that you should carefully consider which columns should be indexed and which ones should not be indexed.

These are some suggestions for index candidates:

- Foreign key columns

- Columns often used in WHERE clauses

- Columns often used in ORDER BY and GROUP BY clauses

Here, we'll look at the commands for index creation and management.

Index Creation

Figure 7-11 shows the (simplified) syntax of the CREATE INDEX command.

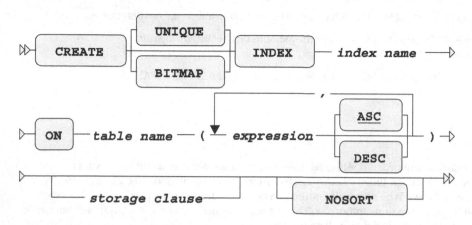

Figure 7-11. *CREATE INDEX command syntax diagram*

The storage clause allows you to influence various physical index storage attributes, such as the storage location and the space allocation behavior. See the *Oracle SQL Reference* for more details. If the table rows happen to be inserted and stored in index order, you can specify the NOSORT option to speed up index creation. The Oracle DBMS will skip the sort phase (normally needed during index creation), but if the rows turn out to be in the wrong order, the CREATE INDEX command will fail with an error message.

Unique Indexes

Unique indexes serve two purposes: they provide additional access paths to improve response times (like nonunique indexes), and they also prevent duplicate values. You create unique indexes by specifying the UNIQUE option of the CREATE INDEX command (see Figure 7-11).

Note, however, that it is recommended to ensure uniqueness in your tables using the PRIMARY KEY and UNIQUE constraints, leaving it up to the Oracle DBMS to choose an appropriate physical implementation of those constraints.

Bitmap Indexes

Regular indexes work the best if the corresponding columns contain many different values, resulting in better selectivity. Unique indexes offer the best selectivity, because they contain only different values. This means that every equality search (... WHERE COL = ...) results in at most one row. At the other side of the spectrum, if a column contains only a few values (typical examples are gender, status, and yes/no columns), a regular index is not very useful, because the average selectivity of equality searches will be poor.

For such low-cardinality columns, the Oracle DBMS supports *bitmap indexes*. Bitmap indexes may also outperform regular indexes if your WHERE clause is complicated, using many AND, OR, and NOT connectives. You create bitmap indexes by specifying the BITMAP option (see Figure 7-11).

■ **Caution**   Indexes slow down data manipulation, and bitmap indexes are the most expensive index type in terms of maintenance. Don't create bitmap indexes on tables with a lot of DML activity.

Function-Based Indexes

As Figure 7-11 shows, you can specify an expression between the parentheses when defining the table columns to be indexed. That means that instead of simply specifying a single column or a comma-separated list of columns, you can choose to specify a more complicated expression in an index definition. Indexes containing such expressions are referred to as *function-based indexes*. See Listing 7-14 for an example, where we create an index on an expression for the yearly salary.

Listing 7-14. Creating a Function-Based Index

```
SQL> create index year_sal_idx
  2  on employees (12*msal + coalesce(comm,0));
Index created.

SQL>
```

The index we created in Listing 7-14 can provide an efficient access path for the Oracle DBMS to produce the result of the following query:

```
SQL> select * from employees where 12*msal+coalesce(comm,0) > 18000;
```

Function-based indexes can be used in combination with various NLS features to enable linguistic sorting and searching. See *Oracle SQL Reference* and *Oracle Globalization Support Guide* for more details.

Index Management

Since indexes are maintained by the Oracle DBMS, each table change is immediately propagated to the indexes. In other words, indexes are always up-to-date. However, if your tables incur continuous and heavy DML activity, you might want to consider rebuilding your indexes. Of course, you could simply drop them and then re-create them. However, using the ALTER INDEX ... REBUILD or ALTER INDEX ... COALESCE command is more efficient. Figure 7-12 shows the (partial) syntax diagram for the ALTER INDEX command.

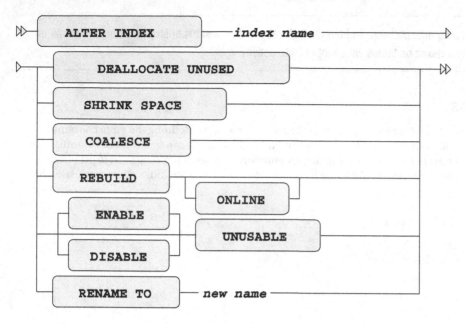

Figure 7-12. *ALTER INDEX command syntax diagram*

The various ALTER INDEX command options in Figure 7-12 (which is far from complete) show that this command belongs to the purview of database administrators, so we will not discuss them here.

■ **Note** The ENABLE and DISABLE options of the ALTER INDEX command (see Figure 7-12) apply only to function-based indexes. If you set indexes to UNUSABLE, you must REBUILD (or DROP and CREATE) them before they can be used again.

You can remove indexes with the DROP INDEX command. Figure 7-13 shows the syntax diagram for DROP INDEX.

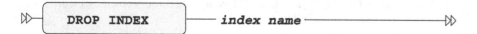

Figure 7-13. *DROP INDEX command syntax diagram*

Here is an example of removing an index:

```
SQL> drop index year_sal_idx;
Index dropped.

SQL>
```

■ **Tip**   In periods of heavy data-manipulation activity, without a lot of reporting (retrieval) activity, you may consider dropping indexes temporarily, and re-creating them later.

When you're working with indexes, keep in mind that although you can decide about index *existence* with the CREATE INDEX and DROP INDEX commands, the Oracle optimizer decides about index *usage*. The optimizer chooses the execution plan for each SQL statement. The next section explains how you can see if the optimizer is using your indexes.

7.6 Performance Monitoring with SQL Developer AUTOTRACE

This is *not* a book about SQL performance tuning. However, in a chapter where we talk about creating indexes, it makes sense to at least show how you can see whether the indexes you create are actually used. What you need for that purpose is a way to see SQL execution plans.

Oracle provides many *diagnostic tools* (such as the SQL trace facility, TKPROF, and EXPLAIN PLAN) to help you with your performance-tuning efforts. However, discussion of these useful Oracle tools is not appropriate here; see *Oracle Performance Tuning Guide* for more details. Fortunately, SQL Developer offers a limited but user-friendly alternative for those diagnostic tools: the AUTOTRACE facility.

If you want to use all of the options of the AUTOTRACE setting, you may need to prepare your Oracle environment:

- SQL Developer assumes the existence of a PLAN_TABLE table to store execution plans. If necessary, you can create a local copy in your own schema with the utlxplan.sql script. Oracle Database 10g and above has a public synonym PLAN_TABLE, pointing to a global temporary table. Creating a local PLAN_TABLE is necessary only in earlier releases.

- You must have sufficient privileges for certain AUTOTRACE features. You need the SELECT_CATALOG_ROLE and SELECT ANY DICTIONARY privileges. These grants must be executed from the SYSTEM database user account. If you don't have access to that privileged account, contact your local database administrator.

Your display preferences for AUTOTRACE output can be modified by selecting Tools ➤ Preferences ➤ Database ➤ Autotrace ➤ Explain Plan. By clicking the checkboxes for the values you wish to display, you can customize your Autotrace output to your needs. Figure 7-14 shows the preferences I typically use and recommend.

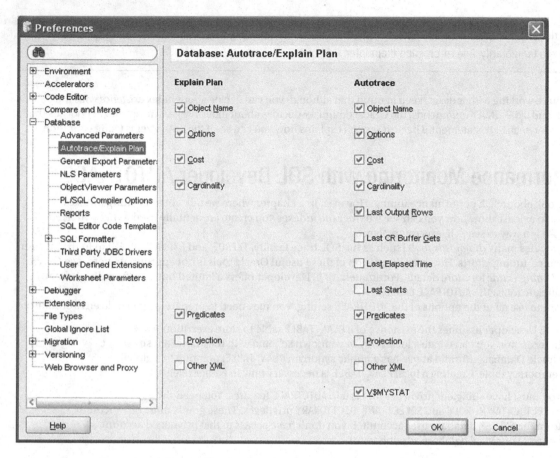

Figure 7-14. *SQL Developer AUTOTRACE Preferences settings*

After you have verified your privileges and set your display preferences, you can use AUTOTRACE. You may use either the F10 key, the AUTOTRACE toolbar button, or simply execute the query and click on the Autotrace tab to view the output. SQL Developer will execute the query, then show the execution plan and resource statistics that you chose in your Preferences settings. Figure 7-15 shows an example of using AUTOTRACE.

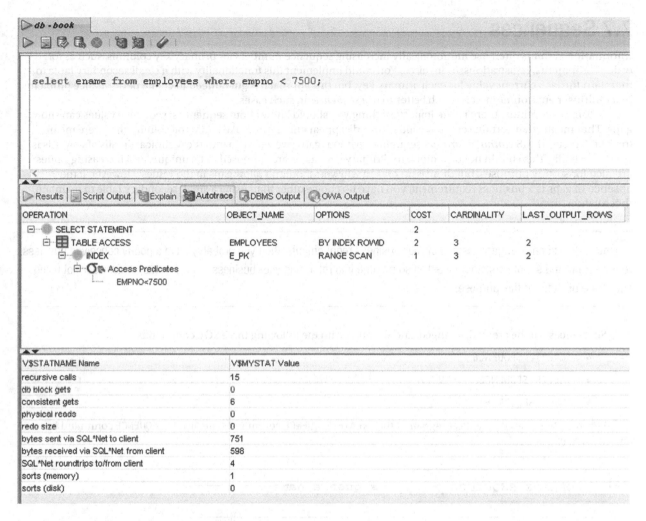

Figure 7-15. *SQL Developer AUTOTRACE output*

From Figure 7-15, you can see that the optimizer decided to use the unique index E_PK for a range scan, and it chose to access the EMPLOYEES table using the row identifiers resulting from the index range scan.

By choosing the Display Preference for V$MYSTAT, a list of performance-related statement execution statistics is captured and displayed beneath the execution plan. A detailed discussion of these statistics is not appropriate here, but you can see (for example) that no data was read from disk (physical reads) and six buffer cache block visits (consistent gets and db block gets) were needed.

■ **Note**   If you use EXPLAIN, the SQL statement is *not* executed. This is because you ask for only an execution plan, *not* for statement results and *not* for execution statistics.

7.7 Sequences

Information systems often use monotonically increasing sequence numbers for primary key columns, such as for orders, shipments, registrations, or invoices. You could implement this functionality with a small secondary table to maintain the last/current value for each primary key, but this approach is guaranteed to create performance problems in a multiuser environment. It is much better to use *sequences* in such cases.

Before we continue, there is one important thing you should know about sequences: sequence values can show gaps. That means that certain sequence values may disappear and never make it into the column they were meant for. The Oracle DBMS *cannot guarantee* sequences without gaps (we won't go into the technical details of why this is true). Normally, this should not be a problem. Primary key values are supposed to be unique, and increasing values are nice for sorting purposes, but there is no reason why you shouldn't allow gaps in the values. However, if the absence of gaps is a business requirement, you have no choice other than using a small secondary table to maintain these values.

■ **Note** If "absence of gaps" is one of your business requirements, then you probably have a poorly conceived business requirement. You should consider investing some time into reforming your business requirements, or consider not using sequence objects for this purpose.

Sequences can be created, changed, and dropped with the following three SQL commands:

- CREATE SEQUENCE

- ALTER SEQUENCE

- DROP SEQUENCE

Figure 7-16 shows the syntax diagram of the CREATE SEQUENCE command. The ALTER SEQUENCE command has a similar syntax.

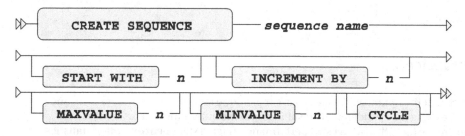

Figure 7-16. *A CREATE SEQUENCE command syntax diagram*

A sequence definition may consist of a start value, increment value, minimum value, and maximum value. You can also specify whether the sequence generator should stop when reaching a boundary value, or CYCLE the sequence numbers within the minimum/maximum range. All sequence attributes are optional, as Figure 7-16 shows; they all have default values.

Each sequence has two pseudo columns: NEXTVAL and CURRVAL. The meaning of each of these columns is self-explanatory. Listing 7-15 shows how you can create and use a sequence DEPTNO_SEQ to generate department numbers, using the DUAL table. (Note that normally you would use sequence values in INSERT statements.)

Listing 7-15. Creating and Using a Sequence

```
SQL> create sequence deptno_seq
  2  start with 50 increment by 10;

Sequence created.

SQL> select deptno_seq.nextval, deptno_seq.currval from dual;

  NEXTVAL   CURRVAL
--------- ---------
       50        50

SQL> select deptno_seq.currval from dual;

  CURRVAL
---------
       50

SQL> select deptno_seq.currval, deptno_seq.nextval from dual;

  CURRVAL   NEXTVAL
--------- ---------
       60        60

SQL>
```

You can use CURRVAL multiple times, in different SQL statements, once you have selected NEXTVAL in an earlier statement, as shown in Listing 7-15. For example, in an order-entry system, you might select a sequence value with NEXTVAL to insert a new order, and then use the same value (CURRVAL) several times to insert multiple line items for that order.

Note the result of the last query in Listing 7-15. Since you select CURRVAL *before* NEXTVAL in the SELECT clause, you might expect to see the current value (50), followed by the next value (60), but apparently that is not the case. This behavior is based on the consistency principle that it doesn't matter in which order you specify the expressions in the SELECT clause of your queries, because you actually select those expressions *at the same time*. Try selecting NEXTVAL multiple times in the same SELECT clause and see what happens (the explanation is the same).

One of the most eagerly-awaited new features of Oracle12c was the ability to use the CURRVAL and NEXTVAL of a sequence in the DEFAULT clause for a column. Now, instead of having to code an AFTER INSERT FOR EACH ROW database trigger on the table to populate a column with a value from a sequence, it can simply be specificied declaratively using a CREATE TABLE or ALTER TABLE command.

7.8 Synonyms

You can use the CREATE SYNONYM command to create synonyms for tables or views. Once created, you can use synonyms in all your SQL commands instead of "real" table (and view) names. For example, you can use synonyms for tables with very long table names.

Synonyms are especially useful if you are accessing tables from different schemas, not owned by yourself. Without synonyms, you must explicitly prefix those object names with the schema name and a period. The Oracle data dictionary is a perfect example of synonym usage. You can simply specify the data dictionary view names in your queries, without any prefix, although you obviously don't own those data dictionary objects.

Synonyms are a "convenience" feature. They don't provide any additional privileges, and they don't create security risks. They just save you some typing, and they also allow you to make your applications schema-independent.

Schema-independence is important. By using synonyms, your applications don't need to contain explicit schema names. This makes your applications more flexible and easier to maintain, because the mapping to physical schema and object names is in the synonym definitions, separated from the application code.

Figure 7-17 shows the syntax diagram for the CREATE SYNONYM command.

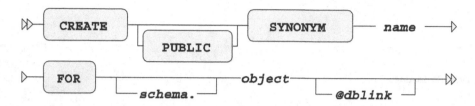

Figure 7-17. *A CREATE SYNONYM command syntax diagram*

Oracle supports public and private synonyms, as you can see in Figure 7-17. By default, synonyms are private. You need to specify the PUBLIC keyword to create public synonyms. All database users can *use* public synonyms, but you need DBA privileges to be able to *create* them. The synonyms for the data dictionary objects are examples of public synonyms. Anyone can create private synonyms, but only their owners can use them.

■ **Caution**   Although synonyms are useful, they can also cause performance problems. In particular, public synonyms are known to cause such problems. For further details, go to Steve Adams's web site (http://www.ixora.com.au) and search for "avoiding public synonyms."

Listing 7-16 shows how you can create a synonym, how the synonym shows up in the data dictionary views CAT and USER_SYNONYMS, and how you can drop a synonym.

Listing 7-16. Creating and Dropping a Synonym

```
SQL> create synonym e for employees;
Synonym created.

SQL> describe e
Name                    Null?    Type
----------------------- -------- ------------
EMPNO                   NOT NULL NUMBER(4)
ENAME                   NOT NULL VARCHAR2(8)
INIT                    NOT NULL VARCHAR2(5)
JOB                              VARCHAR2(8)
MGR                              NUMBER(4)
BDATE                   NOT NULL DATE
MSAL                    NOT NULL NUMBER(6,2)
COMM                             NUMBER(6,2)
DEPTNO                           NUMBER(2)

SQL> select * from cat;
```

```
TABLE_NAME           TABLE_TYPE
-------------------- -----------
EMPLOYEES            TABLE
DEPARTMENTS          TABLE
SALGRADES            TABLE
COURSES              TABLE
OFFERINGS            TABLE
REGISTRATIONS        TABLE
HISTORY              TABLE
DEPTNO_SEQ           SEQUENCE
E                    SYNONYM

SQL> select synonym_name, table_owner, table_name
  2  from   user_synonyms;

SYNONYM_NAME         TABLE_OWNER TABLE_NAME
-------------------- ----------- ----------------
E                    BOOK        EMPLOYEES

SQL> drop synonym e;
Synonym dropped.

SQL>
```

Synonyms are often used in distributed database environments to implement full data independence. The user (or database application) does not need to know where (in which database) tables or views are located. Normally, you need to specify explicit database links using the at sign (@) in the object name, but synonyms can hide those database link references.

7.9 The CURRENT_SCHEMA Setting

The ALTER SESSION command provides another convenient way to save you the effort of prefixing object names with their schema name, but without using synonyms. This is another "convenience" feature, just like synonyms.

Suppose the demo schema SCOTT (with the EMP and DEPT tables) is present in your database, and suppose you are currently connected as database user BOOK. In that situation, you can use the ALTER SESSION command as shown in Listing 7-17.

Listing 7-17. The CURRENT_SCHEMA Setting

```
SQL> alter session set current_schema=scott;
Session altered.

SQL> show user
USER is "BOOK"

SQL> select * from dept;
```

```
DEPTNO DNAME          LOC
-------- -------------- -------------
      10 ACCOUNTING     NEW YORK
      20 RESEARCH       DALLAS
      30 SALES          CHICAGO
      40 OPERATIONS     BOSTON

SQL> alter session set current_schema=book;
Session altered.

SQL>
```

You can compare the CURRENT_SCHEMA setting in the database with the change directory (cd) command at the operating system level. In a similar way, it allows you to address all objects locally.

Again, this does not change anything with regard to security and privileges. If you really want to assume the identity of a schema owner, you must use the SQL*Plus CONNECT command, and provide the username/schema name and the corresponding password.

7.10 The DROP TABLE Command

You can drop your tables with the DROP TABLE command. Figure 7-18 shows the syntax diagram for the DROP TABLE command.

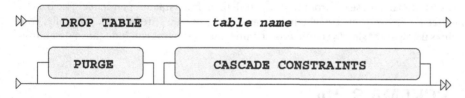

Figure 7-18. *A DROP TABLE command syntax diagram*

Unless you have specific system privileges, you cannot drop tables owned by other database users. Also, you cannot roll back a DROP TABLE command. As you've learned in previous chapters, this is true for all DDL statements (CREATE, ALTER, and DROP).

"*Errare humanum est*," as the Romans said. Because human errors occur occasionally, Oracle Database 10*g* introduced the concept of the database *recycle bin*. By default, all dropped tables (and their dependent objects) initially end up in the recycle bin. You can query the recycle bin using the [USER_]RECYCLEBIN view, as shown in Listing 7-18. To make sure we start with an empty recycle bin, we begin the experiment with a PURGE command.

Listing 7-18. Dropping Tables and Querying the Recycle Bin

```
SQL> purge recyclebin;
Recyclebin purged.

SQL> drop table history;
Table dropped.

SQL> select object_name, original_name, droptime
  2  from    recyclebin;
```

```
OBJECT_NAME                      ORIGINAL_NAME         DROPTIME
------------------------------   ------------------    -------------------
BIN$mlRH1je9TBOeVEUhukIpCw==$0   H_PK                  2004-07-01:20:22:23
BIN$EETkZCYORSKCR3BhtF9cJw==$0   HISTORY               2004-07-01:20:22:23

SQL>
```

As you can see, the objects are renamed, but the original names are kept as well. There is one entry for the HISTORY table and one entry for the primary key index. You can recover tables (and optionally rename them) from the recycle bin by using the FLASHBACK TABLE command:

```
SQL> flashback table history to before drop
  2  [rename to <new name>];
Flashback complete.

SQL>
```

■ **Caution**   There is no guarantee the FLASHBACK TABLE command always succeeds. The recycle bin can be purged explicitly (by a database administrator) or implicitly (by the Oracle DBMS).

If you want to drop a table and bypass the recycle bin, you can use the PURGE option of the DROP TABLE command, as shown in Figure 7-18. For example, if the command DROP TABLE HISTORY in Listing 7-18 had instead specified DROP TABLE HISTORY PURGE, then the HISTORY table would not have been moved to the recycle bin, the SELECT from the recycle bin would not have shown the new entry, and of course the command FLASHBACK TABLE HISTORY TO BEFORE DROP command would have failed.

If you drop a table, you implicitly drop certain dependent database objects, such as indexes, triggers, and table privileges granted to other database users. You also invalidate certain other database objects, such as views and packages. Keep this in mind during database reorganizations. To re-create a table, it is *not* enough to simply issue a CREATE TABLE command after a DROP TABLE command. You need to reestablish the full environment around the dropped table.

If you issue a DROP TABLE command, you may get the following error message if other tables contain foreign key constraints referencing the table that you are trying to drop:

```
ORA-02449: unique/primary keys in table referenced by foreign keys
```

Try to drop the EMPLOYEES table, and see what happens. You can solve this problem by using the CASCADE CONSTRAINTS option, as shown in Figure 7-18. Note, however, that this means that all offending foreign key constraints are dropped, too.

7.11 The TRUNCATE Command

The TRUNCATE command allows you to delete all rows from a table. Figure 7-19 shows the syntax diagram for the TRUNCATE command.

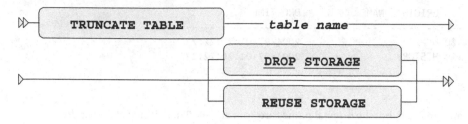

Figure 7-19. *A TRUNCATE command syntax diagram*

The default behavior is DROP STORAGE, as indicated by the underlining in Figure 7-19.

Compared with DROP TABLE (followed by a CREATE TABLE), the big advantage of TRUNCATE is that all related indexes and privileges survive the TRUNCATE operation.

This command has two possible advantages over the DELETE command: the performance (response time) is typically better for large tables, and you can optionally reclaim the allocated space. However, there is a price to pay for these two advantages: you cannot perform a ROLLBACK to undo a TRUNCATE, because TRUNCATE is a DDL command. The Oracle DBMS treats DDL commands as single-statement transactions and commits them immediately.

7.12 The COMMENT Command

The COMMENT command allows you to add clarifying (semantic) explanations about tables and table columns to the data dictionary. Figure 7-20 shows the syntax diagram for this command.

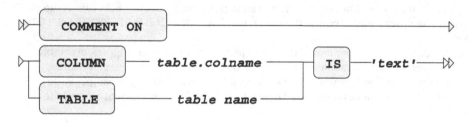

Figure 7-20. *A COMMENT command syntax diagram*

Listing 7-19 shows how you can use the COMMENT command to add comments to the data dictionary for a table (SALGRADES) and a column (EMPLOYEES.COMM) and how you can retrieve that information from the data dictionary.

Listing 7-19. Adding Comments to Columns and Tables

```
SQL> comment on table salgrades
  2  is      'Salary grades and net bonuses';
Comment created.

SQL> comment on column employees.comm
  2  is      'For sales reps only';
Comment created.

SQL> select comments
  2  from    user_tab_comments
  3  where   table_name = 'SALGRADES';
```

```
COMMENTS
-------------------------------------------
Salary grades and net bonuses

SQL> select comments
  2  from    user_col_comments
  3  where   table_name  = 'EMPLOYEES'
  4  and     column_name = 'COMM';

COMMENTS
-------------------------------------------
For sales reps only

SQL>
```

Think of adding comments like documentation. The little extra effort to document your columns and tables will help define and clarify your objects if questions arise in the future.

7.13 Exercises

The following exercises will help you to better understand the concepts described in this chapter. The answers are presented in Appendix D.

1. Listing 7-5 defines the constraint E_SALES_CHK in a rather cryptic way. Formulate the same constraint without using DECODE and NVL2.

2. Why do you think the constraint E_DEPT_FK (in Listing 7-7) is created with a separate ALTER TABLE command?

3. Although this is not covered in this chapter, try to come up with an explanation of the following phenomenon: when using sequences, you cannot use the pseudo column CURRVAL in your session without first calling the pseudo column NEXTVAL:

```
SQL> select deptno_seq.currval from dual;
select deptno_seq.currval from dual
       *
ERROR at line 1:
ORA-08002: sequence DEPTNO_SEQ.CURRVAL is not yet defined in this session

SQL>
```

4. Why is it better to use sequences in a multiuser environment, as opposed to maintaining a secondary table with the last/current sequence values?

5. How is it possible that the EVALUATION column of the REGISTRATIONS table accepts null values, in spite of the constraint R_EVAL_CHK (see Listing 7-11)?

6. If you define a PRIMARY KEY or UNIQUE constraint, the Oracle DBMS normally creates a unique index under the covers (if none of the existing indexes can be used) to check the constraint. Investigate and explain what happens if you define such a constraint as DEFERRABLE.

7. You can use function-based indexes to implement "conditional uniqueness" constraints. Create a unique function-based index on the REGISTRATIONS table to check the following constraint: employees are allowed to attend the OAU course only once. They may attend other courses as many times as they like. Test your solution with the following command (it should fail):

```
SQL> insert into registrations values (7900,'OAU',trunc(sysdate),null);
```

Hint: You can use a CASE expression in the index expression.

CHAPTER 8

■ ■ ■

Retrieval: Multiple Tables and Aggregation

This chapter resumes the **discussion** of the retrieval possibilities of the SQL language. It is a logical continuation of Chapters 4 and 5.

Section 8.1 introduces the concept of *row* or *tuple variables*. We did not discuss them so far, because we haven't needed them up to now. By the way, most SQL textbooks don't mention tuple variables at all—at least not the way this book does. When you start specifying multiple tables in the FROM clause of your SELECT statements, it is a good idea to start using tuple variables (also referred to as *table aliases* in Oracle) in a consistent way.

Section 8.2 explains *joins*, which specify a comma-separated list of table names in the FROM clause and filter the desired row combinations with the WHERE clause. Section 8.3 shows the ANSI/ISO standard syntax to produce joins, and Section 8.4 goes into more details about *outer joins*.

In large information systems (containing huge amounts of detailed information), it is quite common to be interested in *aggregated* (or *summarized* or *condensed*) information. For example, you may want to get a course overview for a specific year, showing the number of attendees per course, with the average evaluation scores. You can formulate the underlying queries you need for such reports by using the GROUP BY clause of the SELECT command. *Group functions* (such as COUNT, AVG, MIN, and MAX) play an important role in such queries. If you have aggregated your data with a GROUP BY clause, you can optionally use the HAVING clause to filter query results at the group level. Topics surrounding basic aggregation are covered in Sections 8.5, 8.6, and 8.7. Section 8.8 continues the discussion of aggregation to introduce some more advanced features of the GROUP BY clause, such as CUBE and ROLLUP. Section 8.9 introduces the concept of *partitioned outer joins*. Section 8.10 finishes with the three set operators of the SQL language: UNION, MINUS, and INTERSECT.

8.1 Tuple Variables

Until now, we have formulated our SQL statements as follows:

```
select ename, init, job
from   employees
where  deptno = 20;
```

Actually, this statement is rather incomplete. In this chapter, we must be a little more precise, because the SQL commands are getting slightly more complicated. To be complete and accurate, we should have written this statement as shown in Listing 8-1.

Listing 8-1. Using Tuple Variables in a Query

```
select  e.ename, e.init, e.job
from    employees e
where   e.deptno = 20;
```

In this example, e is a *tuple variable*. *Tuple* is just a "dignified" term for row, derived from the relational theory. In Oracle, tuple variables are referred to as *table aliases* (which is actually rather confusing), and the ANSI/ISO standard talks about *correlation names*.

Note the syntax in Listing 8-1: You "declare" the tuple variable in the FROM clause, immediately following the table name, separated by white space only.

A tuple variable always ranges over a table, or a table expression. In other words, in the example in Listing 8-1, e is a variable representing one row from the EMPLOYEES table at any time. Within the context of a specific row, you can refer to specific column (or attribute) values, as shown in the SELECT and WHERE clauses of the example in Listing 8-1. The tuple variable precedes the column name, separated by a period. Figure 8-1 shows the column reference e.JOB and its value ADMIN for employee 7900.

	EMPNO	ENAME	INIT	JOB	. . .	DEPTNO
	. . .					
	7876	ADAMS	AA			
e	7900	JONES	R	ADMIN	. . .	30
	7902	FORD	. . .			
	7934	. . .				
	. . .					

Figure 8-1. *The EMPLOYEES table with a tuple variable*

Do you remember those old-fashioned calendars with one page per month, with a transparent strip that could move up and down to select a certain week, and a little window that could move on that strip from the left to the right to select a specific day of the month? If not, Figure 8-2 shows an example of such a calendar. The transparent strip would be the tuple variable in this metaphor.

Figure 8-2. *Calendar with sliding day indicator window*

Using the concept of tuple variables, we can describe the execution of the SQL command in Listing 8-1 as follows:

1. The tuple variable e ranges (row by row) over the EMPLOYEES table (the row order is irrelevant).

2. Each row e is checked against the WHERE clause, and it is passed to an intermediate result set if the WHERE clause evaluates to TRUE.

3. For each row in the intermediate result set, the expressions in the SELECT clause are evaluated to produce the final query result.

As long as you are writing simple queries (as we have done so far in this book); you don't need to worry about tuple variables. The Oracle DBMS understands your SQL intentions anyway. However, as soon as your SQL statements become more complicated, it might be wise (or even mandatory) to start using tuple variables. Tuple variables always have at least one advantage: they enhance the readability and maintainability of your SQL code.

8.2 Joins

You can specify multiple tables in the FROM component of a query. We start this section with an intended mistake, to evoke an Oracle error message. See what happens in Listing 8-2 where our intention is to discover which employees belong to which departments.

Listing 8-2. Ambiguously Defined Columns

```
select deptno, location, ename, init
from   employees, departments;

select deptno, location, ename, init
          *
ERROR at line 1:
ORA-00918: column ambiguously defined
```

The message, including the asterisk (*), reveals the problem here. The Oracle DBMS cannot figure out which DEPTNO column we are referring to. Both tables mentioned in the FROM clause have a DEPTNO column, and that's why we get an error message.

Cartesian Products

See Listing 8-3 for a second attempt to find which employees belong to which departments. Because we fixed the ambiguity issue, we get query results, but these results don't meet our expectations. The tuple variables e and d range *freely* over both tables, because there is no constraining the WHERE clause; therefore, the query result we get is the *Cartesian product* of both tables, resulting in 56 rows. We have 14 employees and 4 departments, and 14 times 4 results in 56 possible combinations of all rows of employees and all rows of departments.

Listing 8-3. The Cartesian Product of Two Tables

```
select  d.deptno, d.location, e.ename, e.init
from    employees e, departments d;

  DEPTNO LOCATION ENAME      INIT
-------- -------- -------- -----
      10 NEW YORK SMITH      N
      10 NEW YORK ALLEN      JAM
      10 NEW YORK WARD       TF
      10 NEW YORK JONES      JM
      10 NEW YORK MARTIN     P
      10 NEW YORK BLAKE      R
      10 NEW YORK CLARK      AB
      10 NEW YORK SCOTT      SCJ
...
      40 BOSTON   ADAMS      AA
      40 BOSTON   JONES      R
      40 BOSTON   FORD       MG
      40 BOSTON   MILLER     TJA
```

Equijoins

The results in Listing 8-3 reveal the remaining problem: the query lacks a WHERE clause. In Listing 8-4, we fix the problem by adding a WHERE clause, and we also add an ORDER BY clause to get the results ordered by department, and within each department, by employee name.

Listing 8-4. Joining Two Tables

```
select  d.deptno, d.location, e.ename, e.init
from    employees e, departments d
where   e.deptno = d.deptno
order   by d.deptno, e.ename;
```

```
DEPTNO LOCATION ENAME      INIT
-------- -------- -------- -----
     10 NEW YORK CLARK     AB
     10 NEW YORK KING      CC
     10 NEW YORK MILLER    TJA
     20 DALLAS   ADAMS     AA
     20 DALLAS   FORD      MG
     20 DALLAS   JONES     JM
     20 DALLAS   SCOTT     SCJ
     20 DALLAS   SMITH     N
     30 CHICAGO  ALLEN     JAM
     30 CHICAGO  BLAKE     R
     30 CHICAGO  JONES     R
     30 CHICAGO  MARTIN    P
     30 CHICAGO  TURNER    JJ
     30 CHICAGO  WARD      TF
```

Listing 8-4 shows a *join* or, to be more precise, an *equijoin*. This is the most common join type in SQL.

SQL LAYOUT CONVENTIONS

Your SQL statements should be correct in the first place, of course. As soon as SQL statements get longer and more complicated, it becomes more and more important to adopt a certain layout style. Additional white space (spaces, tabs, and new lines) has no meaning in the SQL language, but it certainly enhances code readability and maintainability. You could have spread the query in Listing 8-4 over multiple lines, as follows:

```
select    d.deptno
,         d.location
,         e.ename
,         e.init
from      employees   e
,         departments d
where     e.deptno = d.deptno
order by  d.deptno
,         e.ename;
```

This SQL layout convention has proved itself to be very useful in practice. Note the placement of the commas at the beginning of the next line as opposed to the end of the current line. This makes adding and removing lines easier, resulting in fewer unintended errors. Any other standard is fine, too. This is mostly a matter of taste. Just make sure to adopt a style and use it consistently.

Non-equijoins

If you use a comparison operator other than an equal sign in the WHERE clause in a join, it is called a *non-equijoin* or *thetajoin*. For an example of a thetajoin, see Listing 8-5, which calculates the total annual salary for each employee.

Listing 8-5. Thetajoin Example

```
select  e.ename            employee
,       12*e.msal+s.bonus  total_salary
from    employees e
,       salgrades s
where   e.msal between s.lowerlimit
                  and s.upperlimit;
```

```
EMPLOYEE TOTAL_SALARY
-------- ------------
SMITH            9600
JONES            9600
ADAMS           13200
WARD            15050
MARTIN          15050
MILLER          15650
TURNER          18100
ALLEN           19300
CLARK           29600
BLAKE           34400
JONES           35900
SCOTT           36200
FORD            36200
KING            60500
```

By the way, you can choose any name you like for your tuple variables. Listing 8-5 uses e and s, but any other names would work, including longer names consisting of any combination of letters and digits. Enhanced readability is the only reason why this book uses (as much as possible) the first characters of table names as tuple variables in SQL statements.

Joins of Three or More Tables

Let's try to enhance the query of Listing 8-5. In a third column, we also want to see the name of the department that the employee works for. Department names are stored in the DEPARTMENTS table, so we add three more lines to the query, as shown in Listing 8-6.

Listing 8-6. Joining Three Tables

```
select  e.ename            employee
,       12*e.msal+s.bonus  total_salary
,       d.dname            department
from    employees   e
,       salgrades   s
,       departments d
where   e.msal between s.lowerlimit
                  and s.upperlimit
and     e.deptno = d.deptno;
```

```
EMPLOYEE TOTAL_SALARY DEPARTMENT
-------- ------------ ----------
SMITH           9600  TRAINING
JONES           9600  SALES
ADAMS          13200  TRAINING
WARD           15050  SALES
MARTIN         15050  SALES
MILLER         15650  ACCOUNTING
TURNER         18100  SALES
ALLEN          19300  SALES
CLARK          29600  ACCOUNTING
BLAKE          34400  SALES
JONES          35900  TRAINING
SCOTT          36200  TRAINING
FORD           36200  TRAINING
KING           60500  ACCOUNTING
```

The main principle is simple. We now have three free tuple variables (e, s, and d) ranging over three tables. Therefore, we need (at least) two conditions in the WHERE clause to get the correct row combinations in the query result.

For the sake of completeness, you should note that the SQL language supports table names as default tuple variables, without the need to declare them explicitly in the FROM clause. Look at the following example:

```
select employees.ename, departments.location
from   employees, departments
where  employees.deptno = departments.deptno;
```

This SQL statement is syntactically correct. However, we will avoid using this SQL "feature" in this book. It is rather confusing to refer to a table in one place and to refer to a specific row from a table in another place with the same name, without making a clear distinction between row and table references. Moreover, the names of the tables used in this book are long enough to justify declaring explicit tuple variables in the FROM clause and using them everywhere else in the SQL statement, thus reducing the number of keystrokes.

Self-Joins

In SQL, you can also join a table to itself. Although this join type is essentially the same as a regular join, it has its own name: *autojoin* or *self-join*. In other words, autojoins contain tables being referenced more than once in the FROM clause. This provides another good reason why you should use explicit tuple variables (as opposed to relying on table names as implicit tuple variables) in your SQL statements. In autojoins, the table names result in ambiguity issues. So why not use tuple variables consistently in all your SQL statements?

Listing 8-7 shows an example of an autojoin. The query produces an overview of all employees born after January 1, 1965, with a second column showing the name of their managers. (You may want to refer to Figure C-3 in Appendix C, which shows a diagram of the hierarchy of the EMPLOYEES table.)

Listing 8-7. Autojoin (Self-Join) Example

```
select e.ename as employee
,      m.ename as manager
from   employees m
,      employees e
where  e.mgr = m.empno
and    e.bdate > date '1965-01-01';
```

```
EMPLOYEE MANAGER
-------- --------
TURNER   BLAKE
JONES    BLAKE
ADAMS    SCOTT
JONES    KING
CLARK    KING
SMITH    FORD
```

Because we have two tuple variables e and m, both ranging freely over the same table, we get 14 × 14 = 196 possible row combinations. The WHERE clause filters out the correct combinations, where row m reflects the manager of row e.

8.3 The JOIN Clause

The join examples shown in the previous section use the Cartesian product operator (the comma in the FROM clause) as a starting point, and then filter the rows using an appropriate WHERE clause. There's absolutely nothing wrong with that approach, and the syntax is fully compliant with the ANSI/ISO SQL standard, but the ANSI/ISO SQL standard also supports alternative syntax to specify joins. This alternative join syntax is covered in this section.

First, let's look again at the join statement in Listing 8-7. You could argue that the WHERE clause of that query contains two different condition types: line 5 contains the *join condition* to make sure you combine the right rows, and line 6 is a "real" (non-join) condition to filter the employees based on their birth dates.

Listing 8-8 shows an equivalent query, producing the same results, using a different syntax. Note the keywords JOIN and ON. Also note that this join syntax doesn't use any commas in the FROM clause.

Listing 8-8. JOIN ... ON Example

```
select e.ename as employee
,      m.ename as manager
from   employees m
       JOIN
       employees e
       ON e.mgr = m.empno
where  e.bdate > date '1965-01-01'
order  by employee;


EMPLOYEE MANAGER
-------- --------
ADAMS    SCOTT
CLARK    KING
JONES    BLAKE
JONES    KING
SMITH    FORD
TURNER   BLAKE
```

The syntax of Listing 8-8 is more elegant than the syntax in Listing 8-7, because the join is fully specified in the FROM clause and the WHERE clause contains only the filtering (i.e., the non-join) condition.

Natural Joins

You can also use the NATURAL JOIN operator in the FROM clause. Listing 8-9 shows an example that joins the EMPLOYEES table with the HISTORY table.

Question: Before reading on, please try to answer, how is it possible that Listing 8-9 produces 15 rows in the result, instead of 14?

Listing 8-9. Natural Join Example

```
select ename, beginyear, msal, deptno
from    employees
        natural join
        history;
```

ENAME	BEGINYEAR	MSAL	DEPTNO
SMITH	2000	800	20
ALLEN	1999	1600	30
WARD	1992	1250	30
WARD	2000	1250	30
JONES	1999	2975	20
MARTIN	1999	1250	30
BLAKE	1989	2850	30
CLARK	1988	2450	10
SCOTT	2000	3000	20
KING	2000	5000	10
TURNER	2000	1500	30
ADAMS	2000	1100	20
JONES	2000	800	30
FORD	2000	3000	20
MILLER	2000	1300	10

Explanation: To understand what's happening in Listing 8-9, you must know how the NATURAL JOIN operator is defined in the SQL language. Listing 8-9 illustrates the behavior of the NATURAL JOIN operator:

1. The NATURAL JOIN operator determines which columns the two tables (EMPLOYEES and HISTORY) have in common. In this case, these are the three columns EMPNO, MSAL, and DEPTNO.

2. It joins the two tables (using an equijoin) over all columns they have in common.

3. It suppresses the duplicate columns resulting from the join operation in the previous step. This is why you don't get an error message about MSAL and DEPTNO in the SELECT clause being ambiguously defined.

4. Finally, the NATURAL JOIN operator evaluates the remaining query clauses. In Listing 8-9, the only remaining clause is the SELECT clause. The final result shows the desired four columns.

Apparently, every employee occurs only once in the result, except WARD. This means that this employee has been employed by the same department (30) for the same salary (1250) during two distinct periods of his career. This is a pure coincidence. If the query had returned 14 rows instead of 15, we would probably not have been triggered to investigate the query for correctness. Remember that some *wrong* queries may give "correct" results by accident.

This example shows that you should be very careful when using the NATURAL JOIN operator. Probably the biggest danger is that a natural join may "suddenly" start producing strange and undesirable results if you add new columns to your tables, or you rename existing columns, thus accidentally creating matching column names.

■ **Caution**   Natural joins are safe only if you practice a very strict column-naming standard in your database designs.

Equijoins on Columns with the Same Name

SQL offers an alternative way to specify equijoins, allowing you to explicitly specify the columns you want to participate in the equijoin operation. As you saw in Listing 8-8, you can use the ON clause followed by fully specified join predicates. You can also use the USING clause, specifying column names instead of full predicates. See Listing 8-10 for an example.

Listing 8-10. JOIN ... USING Example

```
select  e.ename, e.bdate
,       h.deptno, h.msal
from    employees e
        join
        history h
        using (empno)
where   e.job = 'ADMIN';
```

ENAME	BDATE	DEPTNO	MSAL
JONES	03-DEC-1969	30	800
MILLER	23-JAN-1962	10	1275
MILLER	23-JAN-1962	10	1280
MILLER	23-JAN-1962	10	1290
MILLER	23-JAN-1962	10	1300

Note that you need tuple variables again, because you join over only the EMPNO column; the columns h.DEPTNO and e.DEPTNO are now different.

Figure 8-3 shows the syntax diagram of the ANSI/ISO join syntax, including the NATURAL JOIN operator, the ON clause, and the USING clause.

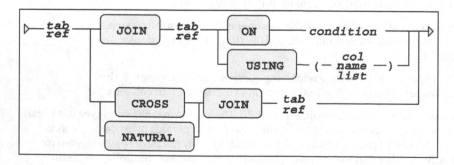

Figure 8-3. *ANSI/ISO join syntax diagram*

Note that you can also use a CROSS JOIN syntax. The result is identical to the effect of the comma operator in the FROM clause: the Cartesian product. The CROSS JOIN syntax prevents the use of the ON or USING clauses, but permits the use of WHERE clause predicates, which is how the Oracle SQL language syntax worked prior to the introduction of the ANSI/ISO SQL syntax. To put it another way, think of CROSS JOIN as the name for the "old-fashioned" join syntax in the context of the newer ANSI/ISO SQL join syntax.

The examples in the remainder of this book will show a mixture of "old-fashioned" joins (as introduced in Section 8.2) and the alternative ANSI/ISO SQL join syntax explained in this section.

8.4 Outer Joins

Earlier in the chapter, in Listing 8-4, we executed a regular join (an equijoin) similar to the one shown in Listing 8-11.

Listing 8-11. Regular Join

```
select d.deptno, d.location
,      e.ename, e.init
from   employees e, departments d
where  e.deptno = d.deptno
order  by d.deptno, e.ename;
```

DEPTNO	LOCATION	ENAME	INIT
10	NEW YORK	CLARK	AB
10	NEW YORK	KING	CC
10	NEW YORK	MILLER	TJA
20	DALLAS	ADAMS	AA
20	DALLAS	FORD	MG
20	DALLAS	JONES	JM
20	DALLAS	SCOTT	SCJ
20	DALLAS	SMITH	N
30	CHICAGO	ALLEN	JAM
30	CHICAGO	BLAKE	R
30	CHICAGO	JONES	R
30	CHICAGO	MARTIN	P
30	CHICAGO	TURNER	JJ
30	CHICAGO	WARD	TF

The result in Listing 8-11 shows no rows for department 40, for an obvious reason: that department does exist in the DEPARTMENTS table, but it has no corresponding employees. In other words, if tuple variable d refers to department 40, there is not a single row e in the EMPLOYEES table to make the WHERE clause evaluate to TRUE.

If you want the fact that department 40 exists to be reflected in your join results, you can make that happen with an *outer join*. For outer joins in Oracle, you can choose between two syntax options:

- The "old" outer join syntax, supported by Oracle since many releases, and implemented many years before the ANSI/ISO standard defined a more elegant outer join syntax

- The ANSI/ISO standard outer join syntax

We will discuss an example of both outer join syntax variants, based on the regular join in Listing 8-11.

Old Oracle-Specific Outer Join Syntax

First, change the fourth line of the command in Listing 8-11 and add a plus sign between parentheses, as shown in Listing 8-12.

Listing 8-12. The (+) Outer Join Syntax

```
select  d.deptno, d.location
,       e.ename, e.init
from    employees e, departments d
where   e.deptno(+) = d.deptno
order   by d.deptno, e.ename;
```

```
  DEPTNO LOCATION ENAME      INIT
-------- -------- --------   -----
      10 NEW YORK CLARK      AB
      10 NEW YORK KING       CC
      10 NEW YORK MILLER     TJA
      20 DALLAS   ADAMS      AA
      20 DALLAS   FORD       MG
      20 DALLAS   JONES      JM
      20 DALLAS   SCOTT      SCJ
      20 DALLAS   SMITH      N
      30 CHICAGO  ALLEN      JAM
      30 CHICAGO  BLAKE      R
      30 CHICAGO  JONES      R
      30 CHICAGO  MARTIN     P
      30 CHICAGO  TURNER     JJ
      30 CHICAGO  WARD       TF
      40 BOSTON
```

As you can see, department 40 now also appears in the result. The effect of the addition (+) in the WHERE clause has combined department 40 with two null values for the employee data. The main disadvantage of this outer join syntax is that you must make sure to add the (+) operator in the right places in your SQL command, namely on the "outer" or optional side of the join condition. Failing to do so normally results in disabling the outer join effect. Another disadvantage of this outer join syntax is its lack of readability.

New Outer Join Syntax

The new ANSI/ISO outer join syntax is much more elegant and readable. Listing 8-13 shows the version to get the same results as in Listing 8-12.

Listing 8-13. ANSI/ISO Outer Join Example

```
select  deptno, d.location
,       e.ename, e.init
from    employees e
        right outer join
        departments d
        using (deptno)
order   by deptno, e.ename;
```

```
DEPTNO LOCATION ENAME    INIT
-------- -------- -------- -----
     10 NEW YORK CLARK    AB
     10 NEW YORK KING     CC
     10 NEW YORK MILLER   TJA
     20 DALLAS   ADAMS    AA
     20 DALLAS   FORD     MG
     20 DALLAS   JONES    JM
     20 DALLAS   SCOTT    SCJ
     20 DALLAS   SMITH    N
     30 CHICAGO  ALLEN    JAM
     30 CHICAGO  BLAKE    R
     30 CHICAGO  JONES    R
     30 CHICAGO  MARTIN   P
     30 CHICAGO  TURNER   JJ
     30 CHICAGO  WARD     TF
     40 BOSTON
```

In Listing 8-13 we used a RIGHT OUTER JOIN, because we suspect the presence of rows at the right-hand side (the DEPARTMENTS table) without corresponding rows at the left-hand side (the EMPLOYEES table). If you switched the two table names in the FROM clause, you would need the LEFT OUTER JOIN operator. Oracle also supports the FULL OUTER JOIN syntax, where both tables participating in the join operation handle rows without corresponding rows on the other side in a special way. Figure 8-4 shows all three outer join syntax possibilities.

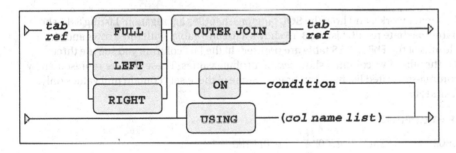

Figure 8-4. ANSI/ISO outer join syntax diagram

The outer join operator is especially useful if you want to aggregate (summarize) data; for example, when you want to produce a course overview showing the number of attendees for each scheduled course. In such an overview, you obviously also want to see all scheduled courses for which no registrations are entered yet, so you might consider cancelling or postponing those courses. This type of query (with aggregation) is the topic of Section 8.5.

Outer Joins and Performance

Although outer joins obviously imply some additional processing for the DBMS, there is no reason to avoid outer joins for performance reasons. The Oracle optimizer knows how to handle outer joins efficiently. Moreover, given a certain data model, you sometimes *need* outer joins. Don't try to invent your own workarounds in such cases, and don't believe unfounded statements like "outer joins are bad." As always, seek ways to empirically prove or disprove such theories, using SQL traces and utilities such as SQL*Plus AUTOTRACE, rather than blindly accepting someone's unfounded assertion.

In Section 8.9, we will revisit outer joins to discuss *partitioned* outer joins.

8.5 The GROUP BY Component

Until now, we have considered queries showing information about only individual rows. Each row in our query results so far had a one-to-one correspondence with some row in the database. However, in real life, you often want to produce aggregated information from a database, where the rows in the query results represent information about a set of database rows. For example, you might want to produce an overview showing the number of employees (the head count) per department. For this type of query, you need the GROUP BY clause of the SELECT command, as shown in Listing 8-14.

Listing 8-14. The GROUP BY Clause

```
select e.deptno      as "department"
,      count(e.empno) as "number of employees"
from   employees e
group  by e.deptno;

department number of employees
---------- -------------------
        10                   3
        20                   5
        30                   6
```

Listing 8-14 shows the COUNT function at work, to count the number of employees per department. COUNT is an example of a *group function*, and we'll look at it and the other group functions in Section 8.6.

The result of this query is a table, of course—just like any result of a query. However, there is no one-to-one mapping anymore between the rows of the EMPLOYEES table and the three rows of the result. Instead, you aggregate employee data per department.

To explain how the GROUP BY operator works, and how the SQL language handles aggregation, Listing 8-15 shows an imaginary representation of an intermediate result. Listing 8-15 shows a pseudo-table, with three rows and six columns. For readability, some columns of the EMPLOYEES table are omitted. In the last column, you see the three different department numbers, and the other five columns show *sets* of attribute values. These sets are represented by enumerating their elements in a comma-separated list between braces. Some of these sets contain null values only, such as e.COMM for departments 10 and 20.

Listing 8-15. The Effect of GROUP BY e.DEPTNO

```
e.EMPNO    e.JOB          e.MGR      e.MSAL     e.COMM     e.DEPTNO
=======    ============   ======     ======     ======     ========
{7782      {'MANAGER'     {7839      {2450      {NULL          10
,7839      ,'DIRECTOR'    ,NULL      ,5000      ,NULL
,7934}     ,'ADMIN'  }    ,7782}     ,1300}     ,NULL}
--------------------------------------------------------------------
{7369      {'TRAINER'     {7902      {  800     {NULL          20
,7566      ,'MANAGER'     ,7839      ,2975      ,NULL
,7788      ,'TRAINER'     ,7566      ,3000      ,NULL
,7876      ,'TRAINER'     ,7788      ,1100      ,NULL
,7902}     ,'TRAINER'}    ,7566}     ,3000}     ,NULL}
--------------------------------------------------------------------
{7499      {'SALESREP'    {7698      {1600      {  300         30
,7521      ,'SALESREP'    ,7698      ,1250      ,  500
,7654      ,'SALESREP'    ,7698      ,1250      ,1400
,7698      ,'MANAGER'     ,7839      ,2850      ,NULL
,7844      ,'SALESREP'    ,7698      ,1500      ,   0
,7900}     ,'ADMIN'  }    ,7698}     ,  800}    ,NULL}
--------------------------------------------------------------------
```

> ■ **Note** The representation in Listing 8-15 is purely fictitious and only serves educational purposes. Data structures as shown in Listing 8-15 do not occur in reality.

Going back to Listing 8-14, it now becomes clear what the COUNT(e.EMPNO) function does: it returns the number of elements of each e.EMPNO set.

You could argue that (as an effect of the GROUP BY e.DEPTNO clause) the last column in Listing 8-15 (e.DEPTNO) contains "regular" values, and the other five columns become "set-valued" attributes. You can use only e.DEPTNO in the SELECT clause. If you want to see data from the other columns in your query result, you must use group functions (such as COUNT) to aggregate those sets into a single value. See the next section for a discussion of group functions.

> ■ **Note** To be more precise, we should refer to multisets instead of sets in this context. Duplicate values are maintained, as you can see in Listing 8-15. We will discuss multisets in Chapter 12.

Multiple-Column Grouping

You can also group on multiple-column expressions, separated by commas. For example, the query in Listing 8-16 produces an overview of the number of registrations per course.

Listing 8-16. Grouping on Two Columns

```
select    r.course, r.begindate
,         count(r.attendee) as attendees
from      registrations r
group by r.course, r.begindate;
```

COURSE	BEGINDATE	ATTENDEES
JAV	13-DEC-1999	5
JAV	01-FEB-2000	3
OAU	10-AUG-1999	3
OAU	27-SEP-2000	1
PLS	11-SEP-2000	3
SQL	12-APR-1999	4
SQL	04-OCT-1999	3
SQL	13-DEC-1999	2
XML	03-FEB-2000	2

This result shows one row for each different (COURSE, BEGINDATE) combination found in the REGISTRATIONS table.

> ■ **Note** As you can see, the rows in Listing 8-16 are ordered on the columns of the GROUP BY clause. However, if you want a certain ordering of your query results, you should never rely on implicit DBMS behavior and always specify an ORDER BY clause.

GROUP BY and Null Values

If a column expression on which you apply the GROUP BY clause contains null values, these null values end up together in a separate group. See Listing 8-17 for an example.

Listing 8-17. GROUP BY and Null Values

```
select e.comm, count(e.empno)
from   employees e
group  by e.comm;

    COMM COUNT(E.EMPNO)
-------- --------------
       0              1
     300              1
     500              1
    1400              1
                     10
```

Apparently, we have ten employees without commission.

8.6 Group Functions

In the previous section, we used the COUNT function to count the number of employees per department and the number of registrations per course. COUNT is an example of a *group function*. All group functions have two important properties in common:

- They can be applied only to *sets* of values.

- They return a single aggregated value, derived from that set of values.

That's why group functions often occur in combination with GROUP BY (and optionally the HAVING clause, covered in Section 8.7) in SQL commands. The most important Oracle group functions are listed in Table 8-1.

Table 8-1. *Common Oracle Group Functions*

Function	Description	Applicable To
COUNT()	Number of values	All datatypes
SUM()	Sum of all values	Numeric data
MIN()	Minimum value	All datatypes
MAX()	Maximum value	All datatypes
AVG()	Average value	Numeric data
MEDIAN()	Median (middle value)	Numeric or date (time) data
STATS_MODE()	Modus (most frequent value)	All datatypes
STDDEV()	Standard deviation	Numeric data
VARIANCE()	Statistical variance	Numeric data

The last column in Table 8-1 shows the applicable datatypes for all group functions. The functions MIN and MAX are applicable to any datatype, including dates and alphanumeric strings. MIN and MAX need only an ordering (sorting) criterion for the set of values. Note also that you can apply the AVG function only to numbers, because the average is defined as the SUM divided by the COUNT, and the SUM function accepts only numeric data.

Let's look at some group function examples in Listing 8-18.

Listing 8-18. Some Examples of Group Functions

```
select e.deptno
,      count(e.job)
,      sum(e.comm)
,      avg(e.msal)
,      median(e.msal)
from   employees e
group  by e.deptno;
```

```
DEPTNO COUNT(E.JOB) SUM(E.COMM) AVG(E.MSAL) MEDIAN(E.MSAL)
------ ------------ ----------- ----------- --------------
    10            3              2916.667            2450
    20            5                  2175            2975
    30            6        2200     1541.667            1375
```

Group Functions and Duplicate Values

If you apply a group function to a set of column values, that set of values may contain duplicate values. By default, these duplicate values are all treated as individual values, contributing to the end result of all group functions applied to the set of values. For example, we have five employees in department 20, but we have only two different jobs in that department. Nevertheless, Listing 8-18 shows 5 as the result of COUNT(e.JOB) for department 20.

If you want SQL group functions to ignore duplicate values (except one, of course), you must specify the keyword DISTINCT immediately after the first parenthesis. Although it is syntactically correct, the addition of DISTINCT is meaningless for the MIN and MAX functions. Look at Listing 8-19 for some examples.

Listing 8-19. Using the DISTINCT Option for Group Functions

```
select count(deptno), count(distinct deptno)
,      avg(comm),  avg(coalesce(comm,0))
from   employees;
COUNT(DEPTNO) COUNT(DISTINCTDEPTNO) AVG(COMM) AVG(COALESCE(COMM,0))
------------- --------------------- --------- ---------------------
           14                     3       550              157.1429
```

Note that Listing 8-19 also shows that you can use group functions in the SELECT clause of a query *without* a GROUP BY clause. The absence of a GROUP BY clause in combination with the presence of group functions in the SELECT clause always results in a single-row result. In other words, the full table is aggregated into a single row. You can achieve precisely the same result by grouping on a constant expression. Try this yourself; for example, see what happens if you add GROUP BY 'x' to the query in Listing 8-19.

Group Functions and Null Values

The ANSI/ISO SQL standard postulates group functions to ignore null values completely. There is only one exception to this rule: the COUNT(*) function. This special case is discussed later in this section. This is a reasonable compromise. The only other consistent behavior for group functions would be to return a null value as soon as the input contains a null value. This would imply that all your SQL statements (containing group functions) should contain additional code to handle null values explicitly. So, ignoring null values completely is not a bad idea. Just make sure that you understand the consequences of this behavior. See Table 8-2 for some typical examples.

Table 8-2. Behavior of Group Functions and Null Values

Set X	SUM(X)	MIN(X)	AVG(X)	MAX(X)
{1,2,3,NULL}	6	1	2	3
{1,2,3,0}	6	0	1.5	3
{1,2,3,2}	8	1	2	3

The SUM function does not make any distinction between {1,2,3,NULL} and {1,2,3,0}. The MIN and AVG functions don't make any distinction between {1,2,3,NULL} and {1,2,3,2}. The MAX function gives the same result on all three sets.

Looking back at Listing 8-19, you see an example of function *nesting*: the AVG function operates on the result of the COALESCE function. This is a typical method to handle null values explicitly. As you can see from Listing 8-19, the results of AVG(COMM) and AVG(COALESCE(COMM,0)) are obviously different. In this case, the Oracle DBMS replaces all null values by zeros before applying the AVG function, because the null values in the COMM column actually mean "not applicable."

The next query, shown in Listing 8-20, tells us how many *different* courses are scheduled for each trainer and the total number of scheduled courses.

Listing 8-20. GROUP BY and DISTINCT

```
select  trainer
,       count(distinct course)
,       count(*)
from    offerings
group   by trainer;
```

```
 TRAINER COUNT(DISTINCTCOURSE) COUNT(*)
-------- --------------------- --------
    7369                     2        3
    7566                     2        2
    7788                     2        2
    7876                     1        1
    7902                     2        2
                             3        3
```

Apparently, we have three course offerings without a trainer being assigned.

Grouping the Results of a Join

The query in Listing 8-21 shows the average evaluation ratings for each trainer, over all courses delivered.

Listing 8-21. GROUP BY on a Join

```
select  o.trainer, avg(r.evaluation)
from    offerings o
        join
        registrations r
        using (course,begindate)
group   by o.trainer;
```

```
TRAINER AVG(R.EVALUATION)
-------- -----------------
   7369                 4
   7566              4.25
   7788
   7876                 4
   7902                 4
```

Notice the USING clause in line 5, with the COURSE and BEGINDATE columns. This USING clause with two columns is needed to get the correct join results.

The COUNT(*) Function

As mentioned earlier, group functions operate on a set of values, with one important exception. Besides column names, you can specify the asterisk (*) as an argument to the COUNT function. This widens the scope of the COUNT function from a specific column to the full row level. COUNT(*) returns the number of rows in the entire group.

■ **Note**   If you think that SELECT COUNT(1) is faster than SELECT COUNT(*), try a little experiment and prepare to be surprised—you will find out that there is no difference. Don't trust opinions, look for ways to prove using facts...

Listing 8-20 already showed an example of using the COUNT(*) function, to get the total number of scheduled courses for each trainer from the OFFERINGS table. Listing 8-22 shows another example of using the COUNT(*) function, this time applied against the EMPLOYEES table.

Listing 8-22. Count Employees Per Department (First Attempt)

```
select  e.deptno, count(*)
from    employees e
group   by e.deptno;
```

```
DEPTNO COUNT(*)
-------- --------
    10        3
    20        5
    30        6
```

Obviously, department 40 is missing in this result. If you want to change the query into an outer join in order to show department 40 as well, you must be careful. What's wrong with the query in Listing 8-23? Apparently, we suddenly have one employee working for department 40.

Listing 8-23. Count Employees Per Department (Second Attempt)

```
select deptno, count(*)
from    employees e
        right outer join
        departments d
        using (deptno)
group  by deptno;

  DEPTNO COUNT(*)
-------- --------
      10        3
      20        5
      30        6
      40        1
```

Compare the results in Listing 8-23 with the results in Listing 8-24. The only difference is the argument of the COUNT function. Listing 8-24 obviously shows the correct result, because department 40 has no employees. By counting over the primary key e.EMPNO, you are sure that all "real" employees are counted, while the null value introduced by the outer join is correctly ignored. You could have used any other NOT NULL column as well.

Listing 8-24. Count Employees Per Department (Third Attempt)

```
select deptno, count(e.empno)
from    employees e
        right outer join
        departments d
        using (deptno)
group  by deptno;

  DEPTNO COUNT(E.EMPNO)
-------- --------------
      10             3
      20             5
      30             6
      40             0
```

At the end of Chapter 5, you saw an example of a PL/SQL stored function to count all employees per department (Section 5.8, Listing 5-31). In that chapter, I mentioned that this counting problem is not trivial to solve in standard SQL. In Listings 8-22, 8-23, and 8-24, you see that you should indeed be careful. You need an outer join, and you should make sure to specify the correct argument for the COUNT function to get correct results.

■ **Caution**   You should be careful with the COUNT function, especially if null values might cause problems (since group functions ignore them) and you want to count row occurrences.

Valid SELECT and GROUP BY Clause Combinations

If your queries contain a GROUP BY clause, some syntax combinations are invalid and result in Oracle error messages, such as the following:

```
ORA-00937: not a single-group group function.
```

This always means that there is a mismatch between your SELECT clause and your GROUP BY clause.

To demonstrate valid versus invalid syntax, Table 8-3 shows one invalid and three valid syntax examples. Table 8-3 assumes you have a table T with four columns A, B, C, and D.

Table 8-3. *Valid and Invalid GROUP BY Syntax Examples*

Syntax	Valid?
select a, b, max(c) from t ... group by a	No
select a, b, max(c) from t ... group by a,b	Yes
select a, count(b), min(c) from t ... group by a	Yes
select count(c) from t ... group by a	Yes

The examples in Table 8-3 illustrate the following two general rules:

- You do not *need* to select the column expression you group on (see the last example).

- Any column expression that is *not* part of the GROUP BY clause can occur *only* in the SELECT clause as an argument to a group function. That's why the first example is invalid.

By the way, all GROUP BY examples so far showed only column names, but you can also group on column expressions, such as in the example shown in Listing 8-25.

Listing 8-25. Grouping on Column Expressions

```
select case mod(empno,2)
            when 0 then 'EVEN '
                   else 'ODD '
            end  as empno
        sum(msal)
from    employees
group  by mod(empno,2);

EMPNO SUM(MSAL)
----- ----------
EVEN     20225
ODD       8650
```

This query shows the salary sums for employees with even and odd employee numbers.

8.7 The HAVING Clause

If you aggregate rows into groups with GROUP BY, you might also want to filter your query result further by allowing only certain groups into the final query result. You can achieve this with the HAVING clause. Normally, you use the HAVING clause only following a GROUP BY clause. For example, Listing 8-26 shows information about departments with more than four employees.

Listing 8-26. HAVING Clause Example

```
select deptno, count(empno)
from   employees
group  by deptno
having count(empno) >= 4;

  DEPTNO COUNT(EMPNO)
-------- ------------
      20            5
      30            6
```

The Difference Between WHERE and HAVING

It is important to distinguish the WHERE clause from the HAVING clause. To illustrate this difference, Listing 8-27 shows a WHERE clause added to the previous query.

Listing 8-27. HAVING vs. WHERE

```
select    deptno, count(empno)
from      employees
where     bdate > date '1960-01-01'
group by  deptno
having    count(empno) >= 4;

  DEPTNO COUNT(EMPNO)
-------- ------------
      30            5
```

The WHERE condition regarding the day of birth (line 3) can be checked against *individual rows* of the EMPLOYEES table. On the other hand, the HAVING COUNT(EMPNO) condition (line 5) makes sense only at the *group* level. That's why group functions should never occur in a WHERE clause. They typically result in the following Oracle error message:

```
ORA-00934: group function is not allowed here.
```

You'll see this error message in Listing 8-29, caused by a classic SQL mistake, as discussed shortly.

HAVING Clauses Without Group Functions

The SQL language allows you to write queries with a HAVING clause without a preceding GROUP BY clause. In that case, Oracle assumes an implicit GROUP BY on a constant expression, just as when you use group functions in the SELECT clause without specifying a GROUP BY clause; that is, the full table is treated as a single group.

On the other hand, valid HAVING clauses without group functions are very rare, and they should be rewritten. In Listing 8-28, the second query is much more efficient than the first one, because it is more efficient to filter out rows using the WHERE clause before aggregation rather than afterward using the HAVING clause. It is a general rule to filter as early as possible in a multi-step operation like an aggregated SQL query, because filtering earlier passes less data along to subsequent operations, saving both processing and memory resources.

Listing 8-28. HAVING Clause Without a Group Function

```
select deptno, count(*)
from   employees
group  by deptno
having deptno <= 20;

  DEPTNO COUNT(*)
-------- --------
      10        3
      20        5

select deptno, count(*)
from   employees
where  deptno <= 20
group  by deptno;

  DEPTNO COUNT(*)
-------- --------
      10        3
      20        5
```

A Classic SQL Mistake

Take a look at the query in Listing 8-29. It looks very logical, doesn't it? Who earns more than the average salary?

Listing 8-29. Error Message: Group Function Is Not Allowed Here

```
select empno
from   employees
where  msal > avg(msal);

where  msal > avg(msal)
                    *
ERROR at line 3:
ORA-00934: group function is not allowed here
```

However, if you think in terms of tuple variables, the problem becomes obvious: the WHERE clause has only a *single row* as its context, turning the AVG function into something impossible to derive.

You can solve this problem in many ways. Listings 8-30 and 8-31 show two suggestions. In Listing 8-30, we use a sub-query to calculate average value.

Listing 8-30. One Way to Find Who Earns More Than the Average Salary

```
select e.empno
from   employees e
where  e.msal > (select avg(x.msal)
                 from   employees x );
```

```
   EMPNO
--------
    7566
    7698
    7782
    7788
    7839
    7902
```

Listing 8-31. Another Way to Find Who Earns More Than the Average Salary

```
select    e1.empno
from      employees e1
,         employees e2
group by  e1.empno
,         e1.msal
having    e1.msal > avg(e2.msal);
```

```
   EMPNO
--------
    7566
    7698
    7782
    7788
    7839
    7902
```

The solution in Listing 8-31 would probably not win an SQL beauty contest, but it is certainly worth further examination. This solution is based on the Cartesian product of the EMPLOYEES table with itself. Notice that it doesn't have a WHERE clause. Notice also that you group on e1.EMPNO and e1.MSAL, which allows you to refer to this column in the HAVING clause.

Grouping on Additional Columns

You sometimes need this (apparently) superfluous grouping on additional columns. For example, suppose you want to see the employee number and the employee name, followed by the total number of course registrations. The query in Listing 8-32, which could be a first attempt to solve this problem, produces an Oracle error message.

Listing 8-32. Error Message: Not a GROUP BY Expression

```
select    e.empno, e.ename, count(*)
from      employees e
          join
          registrations r
          on (e.empno = r.attendee)
group by  e.empno;
select    e.empno, e.ename, count(*)
                    *
ERROR at line 1:
ORA-00979: not a GROUP BY expression
```

The pseudo-intermediate result in Listing 8-33 explains what went wrong here and why you must also group on e.ENAME.

Listing 8-33. Pseudo-Intermediate GROUP BY Result

```
GROUP BY e.EMPNO                   GROUP BY e.EMPNO,e.ENAME

e.EMPNO     e.ENAME   e.INIT ...    e.EMPNO     e.ENAME   e.INIT ...
=======   =========  ======        =======   ========  ======
   7369   {'SMITH'}  {'N'}            7369   'SMITH'   {'N'}
   7499   {'ALLEN'}  {'JAM'}          7499   'ALLEN'   {'JAM'}
   7521   {'WARD' }   ...             7521    ...       ...
   7566    ...                         ...
```

The two results look similar; however, there is an important difference between sets consisting of a single element, such as {'SMITH'}, and a literal value, such as 'SMITH'. In mathematics, sets with a single element are commonly referred to as singleton sets, or just *singletons*.

Listing 8-34 shows another instructive mistake.

Listing 8-34. Error Message: Not a Single-Group Group Function

```
select  deptno
,       sum(msal)
from    employees;

select deptno
       *
ERROR at line 1:
ORA-00937: not a single-group group function
```

In the absence of a GROUP BY clause, the SUM function would return a single row, while DEPTNO would produce 14 department numbers. Two columns with different row counts cannot be presented side-by-side in a single result. After the correction in Listing 8-35, the error message disappears, and you get the desired results.

Listing 8-35. Correction of the Error Message in Listing 8-34

```
select    deptno
,         sum(msal)
from      employees
group by  deptno;

  DEPTNO    SUM(MSAL)
--------  -------------
      10         8750
      20        10875
      30         9250
```

In summary, if your query contains a GROUP BY clause), the SELECT clause is allowed to contain only group expressions. A *group expression* is a column name that is part of the GROUP BY clause, or a group function applied to any other column expression. See also Table 8-3 at the end of Section 8.6.

8.8 Advanced GROUP BY Features

The previous sections showed examples of using "standard" GROUP BY clauses. You can also use some more advanced features of the GROUP BY clause. Here, we will look at GROUP BY CUBE and GROUP BY ROLLUP.

Let's start with a regular GROUP BY example, shown in Listing 8-36.

Listing 8-36. Regular GROUP BY Example

```
select    deptno, job
,         count(empno) headcount
from      employees
group by deptno, job;
```

```
  DEPTNO JOB          HEADCOUNT
-------- ---------- ---------
      10 MANAGER            1
      10 DIRECTOR           1
      10 ADMIN              1
      20 MANAGER            1
      20 TRAINER            4
      30 MANAGER            1
      30 SALESREP           4
      30 ADMIN              1
```

You get an overview with the number of employees per department and within each department per job. To keep things simple, let's forget about department 40, the department without employees.

GROUP BY ROLLUP

Notice what happens if you change the GROUP BY clause and add the keyword ROLLUP, as shown in Listing 8-37.

Listing 8-37. GROUP BY ROLLUP Example

```
select    deptno, job
,         count(empno) headcount
from      employees
group by ROLLUP(deptno, job);
```

```
  DEPTNO JOB        HEADCOUNT
-------- -------- ---------
         10 ADMIN            1
         10 MANAGER          1
         10 DIRECTOR         1
>>>      10                  3  <<<
         20 MANAGER          1
         20 TRAINER          4
>>>      20                  5  <<<
         30 ADMIN            1
         30 MANAGER          1
         30 SALESREP         4
>>>      30                  6  <<<
>>>                         14  <<<
```

The ROLLUP addition results in four additional rows, marked with >>> and <<< in Listing 8-37 for readability. Three of these four additional rows show the head count per department over all jobs, and the last row shows the total number of employees.

GROUP BY CUBE

You can also use the CUBE keyword in the GROUP BY clause. Listing 8-38 shows an example.

Listing 8-38. GROUP BY CUBE Example

```
select    deptno, job
,         count(empno) headcount
from      employees
group by CUBE(deptno, job);

    DEPTNO JOB       HEADCOUNT
    -------- --------- ---------
                          14
>>>          ADMIN        2 <<<
>>>          MANAGER      3 <<<
>>>          TRAINER      4 <<<
>>>          DIRECTOR     1 <<<
>>>          SALESREP     4 <<<
        10               3
        10 MANAGER       1
        10 DIRECTOR      1
        10 ADMIN         1
        20               5
        20 MANAGER       1
        20 TRAINER       4
        30               6
        30 MANAGER       1
        30 SALESREP      4
        30 ADMIN         1
```

This time, you get five more rows in the query result, marked in the same way with >>> and <<<, showing the number of employees per job, regardless of which department employs them.

■ Tip Both GROUP BY CUBE and GROUP BY ROLLUP are special cases of the GROUP BY GROUPING SETS syntax, offering more flexibility. You can also merge the results of different grouping operations into a single GROUP BY clause by specifying them in a comma-separated list. For more details, see *Oracle SQL Reference*.

CUBE, ROLLUP, and Null Values

The CUBE and ROLLUP keywords generate many null values in query results, as you can see in Listings 8-37 and 8-38. You can distinguish these system-generated null values from other null values, for example, to replace them with some explanatory text. You can use the GROUPING and GROUPING_ID functions for that purpose.

The GROUPING Function

Listing 8-39 shows an example of the GROUPING function.

Listing 8-39. GROUPING Function Example

```
select    deptno
,         case GROUPING(job)
               when 0 then job
               when 1 then '**total**'
          end job
,         count(empno) headcount
from      employees
group by rollup(deptno, job);
```

```
 DEPTNO JOB        HEADCOUNT
-------- --------- ---------
     10 ADMIN             1
     10 MANAGER           1
     10 DIRECTOR          1
     10 **total**         3
     20 MANAGER           1
     20 TRAINER           4
     20 **total**         5
     30 ADMIN             1
     30 MANAGER           1
     30 SALESREP          4
     30 **total**         6
        **total**        14
```

Unfortunately, the GROUPING function can return only two results: 0 or 1. That's why the last two lines both show '**total**'.

The GROUPING_ID Function

The GROUPING_ID function is more flexible than the GROUPING function, because it can return several different results, as you can see in Listing 8-40.

Listing 8-40. GROUPING_ID Function Example with ROLLUP

```
select    deptno
,         case GROUPING_ID(deptno, job)
               when 0 then job
               when 1 then '**dept **'
               when 3 then '**total**'
          end   job
,         count(empno) headcount
from      employees
group by rollup(deptno, job);
```

```
DEPTNO JOB         HEADCOUNT
------ ---------   ---------
    10 ADMIN              1
    10 MANAGER            1
    10 DIRECTOR           1
    10 **dept **          3
    20 MANAGER            1
    20 TRAINER            4
    20 **dept **          5
    30 ADMIN              1
    30 MANAGER            1
    30 SALESREP           4
    30 **dept **          6
       **total**         14
```

You may be puzzled by the value 3 being used on the fifth line in Listing 8-40. Things become clear when you convert 3 to a binary representation, which results in the binary number 11. The two ones in this number act as a flag to trap the situation in which both columns contain a null value. GROUP BY ROLLUP can produce only 1 (binary 01) and 3 (binary 11), but GROUP BY CUBE can also generate 2 (binary 10). Look at the results in Listing 8-41. Obviously, GROUPING_ID produces a 0 (zero) for all "regular" rows in the result.

Listing 8-41. GROUPING_ID Function Example with CUBE

```
select    deptno, job
,         GROUPING_ID(deptno, job) gid
from      employees
group by  cube(deptno, job);

DEPTNO JOB         GID
------ ---------   --------
                     3
       ADMIN         2
       MANAGER       2
       TRAINER       2
       DIRECTOR      2
       SALESREP      2
    10               1
    10 ADMIN         0
    10 MANAGER       0
    10 DIRECTOR      0
    20               1
    20 MANAGER       0
    20 TRAINER       0
    30               1
    30 ADMIN         0
    30 MANAGER       0
    30 SALESREP      0
```

8.9 Partitioned Outer Joins

We discussed outer joins in Section 8.4. This section introduces *partitioned outer joins*. To explain what partitioned outer joins are, let's start with a regular (right) outer join in Listing 8-42.

Listing 8-42. Regular Right Outer Join Example

```
break on department skip 1 on job

select  d.dname as department
,       e.job   as job
,       e.ename as employee
from    employees e
        right outer join
        departments d
        using (deptno)
order   by department, job;

DEPARTMENT JOB      EMPLOYEE
---------- -------- --------
ACCOUNTING ADMIN    MILLER
           DIRECTOR KING
           MANAGER  CLARK

HR                           <<<

SALES      ADMIN    JONES
           MANAGER  BLAKE
           SALESREP ALLEN
                    WARD
                    TURNER
                    MARTIN

TRAINING   MANAGER  JONES
           TRAINER  SMITH
                    FORD
                    ADAMS
                    SCOTT

15 rows selected.
```

The SQL*Plus BREAK command allows you to enhance the readability of query results. In Listing 8-42, we use the BREAK command to suppress repeating values in the DEPARTMENT and JOB columns, and to insert an empty line between the departments. (See Chapter 11 for details about BREAK.) The result shows 15 rows, as expected. We have 14 employees, and the additional row (marked with <<<) is added by the outer join for the HR department without employees.

Look at Listing 8-43 to see what happens if we add one extra clause, just before the RIGHT OUTER JOIN operator.

Listing 8-43. Partitioned Outer Join Example

```
select  d.dname as department
,       e.job   as job
,       e.ename as employee
from    employees e
        PARTITION BY (JOB)
        right outer join
        departments d
        using (deptno)
order   by department, job;

DEPARTMENT JOB      EMPLOYEE
---------- -------- --------
ACCOUNTING ADMIN    MILLER
           DIRECTOR KING
           MANAGER  CLARK
           SALESREP          <<<
           TRAINER           <<<

HR         ADMIN             <<<
           DIRECTOR          <<<
           MANAGER           <<<
           SALESREP          <<<
           TRAINER           <<<

SALES      ADMIN    JONES
           DIRECTOR          <<<
           MANAGER  BLAKE
           SALESREP ALLEN
                    WARD
                    TURNER
                    MARTIN
           TRAINER           <<<

TRAINING   ADMIN             <<<
           DIRECTOR          <<<
           MANAGER  JONES
           SALESREP          <<<
           TRAINER  SMITH
                    FORD
                    ADAMS
                    SCOTT
```

Listing 8-43 shows at least one row for each combination of a department and a job. Compared with Listing 8-42, the single row for the HR department is replaced with 12 additional rows, highlighting all nonexisting department/ job combinations. A *regular* outer join considers full tables when searching for matching rows in the other table. The *partitioned* outer join works as follows:

1. Split the driving table in partitions based on a column expression (in Listing 8-43, this column expression is JOB).

2. Produce separate outer join results for each partition with the other table.

3. Merge the results of the previous step into a single result.

Partitioned outer joins are especially useful when you want to aggregate information over the time dimension, a typical requirement for data warehouse reporting. See *Oracle SQL Reference* for more details and examples.

8.10 Set Operators

You can use the SQL set operators UNION, MINUS, and INTERSECT to combine the results of two independent query blocks into a single result. As you saw in Chapter 2, the set operators have the syntax shown in Figure 8-5.

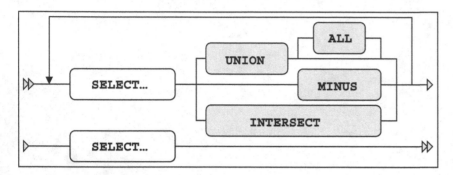

Figure 8-5. *Set operators syntax diagram*

These SQL operators correspond with the UNION, MINUS, and INTERSECT operators you know from mathematics. Don't we all have fond memories of our teachers drawing those Venn diagrams on the whiteboard (or blackboard, for you older readers)? See also Figure 1-3 (in Chapter 1). The meanings of these set operators in SQL are listed in Table 8-4.

Table 8-4. *Set Operators*

Operator	Result
Q1 UNION Q2	All rows occurring in Q1 *or* in Q2 (or in both)
Q1 UNION ALL Q2	As UNION, retaining duplicate rows
Q1 MINUS Q2	The rows from Q1, *without* the rows from Q2
Q1 INTERSECT Q2	The rows occurring in Q1 *and* in Q2

By default, all three set operators suppress duplicate rows in the query result. The only exception to this rule is the UNION ALL operator, which does *not* eliminate duplicate rows. One important advantage of the UNION ALL operator is that the Oracle DBMS does not need to sort the rows. Sorting is needed for all other set operators to trace duplicate rows.

The UNION, MINUS, and INTERSECT operators cannot be applied to any arbitrary set of two queries. The intermediate (separate) results of queries Q1 and Q2 must be "compatible" in order to use them as arguments to a set operator. In this context, compatibility means the following:

- Q1 and Q2 must select the same number of column expressions.

- The datatypes of those column expressions must match.

Some other rules and guidelines for SQL set operators are the following:

- The result table inherits the column names (or aliases) from Q1.

- Q1 cannot contain an ORDER BY clause.

- If you specify an ORDER BY clause at the end of the Q2 query, it doesn't refer to Q2, but rather to the total result of the set operator.

Set operators are very convenient when building new queries by combining the multiple query blocks you wrote (and tested) before, without writing completely new SQL code. This simplifies testing, because you have more control over correctness.

Listing 8-44 answers the following question: "Which locations host course offerings without having a department?"

Listing 8-44. MINUS Set Operator Example

```
select o.location from offerings o
MINUS
select d.location from departments d;


LOCATION
--------
SEATTLE
```

You can also try to solve this problem without using the MINUS operator. See Listing 8-45 for a suggestion.

Listing 8-45. Alternative Solution Without Using the MINUS Operator

```
select DISTINCT o.location
from    offerings o
where   o.location not in
        (select d.location
         from    departments d)
```

Note that you must add a DISTINCT operator to handle situations where you have multiple course offerings in the same location. As explained before, the MINUS operator automatically removes duplicate rows.

Are the two queries in Listing 8-44 and 8-45 logically equivalent? They appear to be logically the same, but they are not quite as identical logically as they first appear. The first query will return two rows. One is for Seattle. The other is a null, representing the one course offering with an unknown location. The MINUS operator does not remove the null value, whereas that same null value fails to pass the WHERE condition in Listing 8-45. This is just one more example of the subtle pitfalls inherent in dealing with nulls in your data. You can also produce outer join results by using the UNION operator. You will see how to do this in Listings 8-46 and 8-47.

Listing 8-46. Regular Join

```
select    d.deptno
,         d.dname
,         count(e.empno) as headcount
from      employees e
,         departments d
where     e.deptno = d.deptno
group by  d.deptno
,         d.dname;
```

```
DEPTNO DNAME      HEADCOUNT
-------- ---------- ---------
      10 ACCOUNTING         3
      20 TRAINING           5
      30 SALES              6
```

We start with a regular join in Listing 8-46. In Listing 8-47 you add the additional department(s) needed for the outer join with a UNION operator, while assigning the right number of employees for those departments: zero.

Listing 8-47. Expansion to an Outer Join with a UNION Operator

```
select    d.deptno
,         d.dname
,         count(e.empno) as headcount
from      employees e
,         departments d
where     e.deptno = d.deptno
group by  d.deptno
,         d.dname
union
select    x.deptno
,         x.dname
,         0          as headcount
from      departments x
where     x.deptno not in (select y.deptno
                           from    employees y);
```

```
DEPTNO DNAME      HEADCOUNT
-------- ---------- ---------
      10 ACCOUNTING         3
      20 TRAINING           5
      30 SALES              6
      40 HR                 0
```

8.11 Exercises

The following exercises will help you to better understand the topics covered in this chapter. The answers are presented in Appendix B

1. Produce an overview of all course offerings. Provide the course code, begin date, course duration, and name of the trainer.

2. Provide an overview, in two columns, showing the names of all employees who ever attended an SQL course, with the name of the trainer.

3. For all employees, list their name, initials, and yearly salary (including bonus and commission).

4. For all course offerings, list the course code, begin date, and number of registrations. Sort your results on the number of registrations, from high to low.

5. List the course code, begin date, and number of registrations for all course offerings in 1999 with at least three registrations.

6. Provide the employee numbers of all employees who ever taught a course as a trainer, but never attended a course as an attendee.

7. Which employees attended a specific course more than once?

8. For all trainers, provide their name and initials, the number of courses they taught, the total number of students they had in their classes, and the average evaluation rating. Round the evaluation ratings to one decimal.

9. List the name and initials of all trainers who ever had their own manager as a student in a general course (category GEN).

10. Did we ever use two classrooms at the same time in the same course location?

11. Produce a matrix report (one column per department, one row for each job) where each cell shows the number of employees for a specific department and a specific job. In a single SQL statement, it is impossible to dynamically derive the number of columns needed, so you may assume you have three departments only: 10, 20, and 30.

12. Listing 8-26 produces information about all departments with *more* than four employees. How can you change the query to show information about all departments with *fewer* than four employees?

13. Look at Listings 8-44 and 8-45. Are those two queries logically equivalent? Investigate the two queries and explain the differences, if any.

CHAPTER 9

■ ■ ■

Retrieval: Some Advanced Features

This is the fourth chapter in a series about retrieval features of SQL. It is a logical continuation of Chapters 4, 5, and 8.

First, in Section 9.1, we revisit subqueries, beginning with an introduction to the three operators ANY, ALL, and EXISTS. These operators allow you to create a special relationship between main queries and subqueries, as opposed to using the IN operator or standard comparison operators. You will also learn about *correlated subqueries*, which are subqueries where some subquery clauses refer to column expressions in the main query.

In Sections 9.2 and 9.3, we will look at subqueries in query components other than the WHERE clause: namely, the SELECT and the FROM clauses. In Section 9.4 we will discuss the WITH clause, also referred to as *subquery factoring*, which allows you to define one or more subqueries in the beginning of your SQL statement commands, and then to reference them by name in the remainder of your SQL statement command.

We continue with *hierarchical queries* in Section 9.5. Relational tables are essentially flat structures, but they can represent hierarchical data structures; for example, by using foreign key constraints referring to the primary key of the same table. The MGR column of the EMPLOYEES table is a classic example of such a hierarchical relationship (a foreign key is defined from the MGR column to the EMPLOYEE_ID primary key column of the EMPLOYEES table). Oracle SQL supports explicit syntax to simplify retrieval of hierarchical data structures.

The next subject we investigate is *analytic functions* (Section 9.6). Within the context of a single row (or tuple variable), you can reference data in other rows and use it for comparisons and calculations. Comparatively, Section 9.7 illustrates the *row limiting clause* you can employ to limit the rows returned by a query and to use simpler syntax that provides you with the ability to page through an ordered set.

Finally, Section 9.8 discusses a helpful Oracle SQL feature allowing you to travel back in time: *flashback queries*.

9.1 Subqueries Continued

Chapter 4 discussed various examples of subqueries, using the IN operator or standard logical comparison operators. As a refresher, let's start with two standard subquery examples.

The subquery in Listing 9-1 displays all 13 registrations we have for build courses; that is, for course category 'BLD'.

Listing 9-1. Subquery Using the IN Operator

```
select  r.attendee, r.course, r.begindate
from    registrations r
where   r.course in (select c.code
                     from    courses c
                     where   c.category='BLD');
```

```
ATTENDEE COURSE BEGINDATE
-------- ------ -----------
    7499 JAV    13-DEC-1999
    7566 JAV    01-FEB-2000
    7698 JAV    01-FEB-2000
    7788 JAV    13-DEC-1999
    7839 JAV    13-DEC-1999
    7876 JAV    13-DEC-1999
    7788 JAV    01-FEB-2000
    7782 JAV    13-DEC-1999
    7499 PLS    11-SEP-2000
    7876 PLS    11-SEP-2000
    7566 PLS    11-SEP-2000
    7499 XML    03-FEB-2000
    7900 XML    03-FEB-2000
```

Listing 9-2 shows how you can retrieve all employees who are younger than colleague 7566.

Listing 9-2. Single-Row Subquery Using a Comparison Operator

```
select e.empno, e.ename, e.init, e.bdate
from   employees e
where  e.bdate > (select x.bdate
                  from   employees x
                  where  x.empno = 7566);


  EMPNO ENAME    INIT  BDATE
-------- -------- ----- -----------
    7844 TURNER   JJ    28-SEP-1968
    7900 JONES    R     03-DEC-1969
```

Listing 9-2 shows an example of a *single-row subquery*. The subquery *must* return a single row, because the comparison operator (>) in the third line of the outer query would fail otherwise. If subqueries of this type nevertheless return more than a single row, you receive an Oracle error message, as you discovered in Chapter 4 (see Listing 4-38).

The following section continues the discussion of subqueries by explaining the possibilities of the ANY, ALL, and EXISTS operators. You'll also learn about correlated subqueries.

The ANY and ALL Operators

SQL allows you to combine standard comparison operators (<, >, =, and so on) with subqueries returning any number of rows. You can do that by specifying ANY or ALL between the comparison operator and the subquery. Listing 9-3 illustrates an example of using the ANY operator, showing all employees with a monthly salary that is higher than *at least one* manager.

Listing 9-3. ANY Operator Example

```
select e.empno, e.ename, e.job, e.msal
from   employees e
where  e.msal > ANY (select x.msal
                     from   employees x
                     where  x.job = 'MANAGER');
```

```
EMPNO ENAME     JOB        MSAL
-------- -------- -------- --------
   7839 KING     DIRECTOR   5000
   7788 SCOTT    TRAINER    3000
   7902 FORD     TRAINER    3000
   7566 JONES    MANAGER    2975
   7698 BLAKE    MANAGER    2850
```

Listing 9-4 shows an example of using the ALL operator, showing the "happy few" with a higher salary than *all* managers.

Listing 9-4. ALL Operator Example

```
select  e.empno, e.ename, e.job, e.msal
from    employees e
where   e.msal > ALL (select x.msal
                      from    employees x
                      where   x.job = 'MANAGER');
```

```
EMPNO ENAME     JOB        MSAL
-------- -------- -------- --------
   7788 SCOTT    TRAINER    3000
   7839 KING     DIRECTOR   5000
   7902 FORD     TRAINER    3000
```

Defining ANY and ALL

As the examples illustrate, the ANY and ALL operators work as follows:

- ANY: ... means the result is true for *at least one value* returned by the subquery.

- ALL: ... means the result is true *for all values* returned by the subquery.

Table 9-1 formulates the definitions of ANY and ALL a bit more formally, using iterated OR and AND constructs. In the table, the symbol, #, represents any standard comparison operator: <, >, =, >=, <=, or <>. Also, V1, V2, V3, and so on represent the values returned by the subquery.

Table 9-1. *Definition of ANY and ALL*

X # ANY(*subquery*)	X # ALL(*subquery*)
(X # V1) OR	(X # V1) AND
(X # V2) OR	(X # V2) AND
(X # V3) OR	(X # V3) AND

Rewriting SQL Statements Containing ANY and ALL

In most cases, you can rewrite your SQL statements in such a way that you don't need the ANY and ALL operators. For example, we could have used a group function in Listing 9-4 to rebuild the subquery into a single-row subquery, as shown in Listing 9-5.

Listing 9-5. Using the MAX Function in the Subquery, Instead of ALL

```
select e.ename, e.job, e.msal
from    employees e
where   e.msal > (select max(x.msal)
                  from    employees x
                  where   x.job = 'MANAGER');
```

```
ENAME     JOB       MSAL
--------  --------  --------
SCOTT     TRAINER    3000
KING      DIRECTOR   5000
FORD      TRAINER    3000
```

Note that the following SQL constructs are logically equivalent:

- X = ANY(*subquery*) <=> X IN (*subquery*)

- X <> ALL(*subquery*) <=> X NOT IN (*subquery*)

Look at the following two rather special cases of ANY and ALL:

- X = ALL(*subquery*)

- X <> ANY(*subquery*)

If the *subquery* returns two or more different values, the first expression is *always* FALSE, because X can never be equal to two different values at the same time. Likewise, if the *subquery* returns two or more different values, the second expression is *always* TRUE, because any X will be different from at least one of those two values from the *subquery*.

Correlated Subqueries

SQL also supports *correlated subqueries*. Look at the example in Listing 9-6, and you will find out why these subqueries are referred to as being correlated.

Listing 9-6. Correlated Subquery Example

```
select e.ename, e.init, e.msal
from    employees e
where   e.msal > (select avg(x.msal)
                  from    employees x
                  where   x.deptno = e.deptno  -- Note the reference to e
                  );
```

```
ENAME     INIT    MSAL
--------  -----  --------
ALLEN     JAM     1600
JONES     JM      2975
BLAKE     R       2850
SCOTT     SCJ     3000
KING      CC      5000
FORD      MG      3000
```

You may want to compare this query with Listing 8-30 in the previous chapter, because they are similar. This query displays all employees who earn a higher salary than the average salary of their own department. There is one thing that makes this subquery special: it contains a reference to the tuple variable e (see e.DEPTNO in the fifth line) from the main query. This means that you cannot execute this subquery independently, in isolation, because that would result in an Oracle error message. You must interpret this subquery within the context of a specific row from the main query. The subquery is related to the main query, thus it is referred to as being *correlated*.

The Oracle DBMS processes the query in Listing 9-6 as follows:

- The tuple variable e ranges over the EMPLOYEES table, thus assuming 14 different values.

- For *each* row e, the subquery is executed after replacing e.DEPTNO with the literal department value of row e.

■ **Caution**　Re-executing a subquery for every single row of the main query may have a significant performance impact. The Oracle optimizer will try to produce an efficient execution plan, and there are some smart optimization algorithms for correlated subqueries; nevertheless, it is always a good idea to consider and test performance while writing SQL statements for production systems. With many queries, performance with small data sets (such as you would find in a development database) can be considered to be quite good, but they do not perform well when large, near-production size data sets are queried.

In mathematics, a distinction is made between *free* and *bound* variables. In the subquery of Listing 9-6, x is the free variable and e is bound by the main query.

Let's look at another example in Listing 9-7. This query returns the fourth youngest employee of the company or, to be more precise, all employees for which there are three younger colleagues. Note that the result isn't necessarily a set containing a single employee.

Listing 9-7. Another Example of a Correlated Subquery

```
select e.*
from    employees e
where (select count(*)
       from    employees x
       where  x.bdate > e.bdate) = 3;
```

EMPNO	ENAME	INIT	JOB	MGR	BDATE	MSAL	COMM	DEPTNO
7876	ADAMS	AA	TRAINER	7788	30-DEC-1966	1100		20

You can also formulate these types of queries using analytic functions, as described in Section 9.6 of this chapter.

■ **Note**　Analytic functions can sometimes help in obtaining certain answers to SQL questions by providing simpler syntax and better performance. However, since an incorrect use of analytic functions can also degrade performance and SQL statement readability, any statement written using an analytic function should be carefully tested and code reviewed.

The EXISTS Operator

Correlated subqueries often occur in combination with the EXISTS operator. Again, let's start with an example. The query in Listing 9-8 returns all course offerings without registrations.

Listing 9-8. Correlated Subquery with EXISTS Operator

```
select o.*
from   offerings o
where  not exists
       (select r.*
        from   registrations r
        where  r.course    = o.course
        and    r.begindate = o.begindate);
```

```
COURSE BEGINDATE    TRAINER LOCATION
------ ----------- -------- --------
ERM    15-JAN-2001
PRO    19-FEB-2001          DALLAS
RSD    24-FEB-2001     7788 CHICAGO
XML    18-SEP-2000          BOSTON
```

The EXISTS operator is not interested in the actual rows (and column values) resulting from the subquery, if any. This operator checks for only the *existence* of subquery results. If the subquery returns at least one resulting row, the EXISTS operator evaluates to TRUE. If the subquery returns no rows at all, the result is FALSE.

Subqueries Following an EXISTS Operator

You could say that the EXISTS and NOT EXISTS operators are kind of empty set checkers. This implies that it doesn't matter which expressions you specify in the SELECT clause of the subquery. For example, you could also have written the query of Listing 9-8 as follows:

```
select o.*
from   offerings o
where   not exists
        (select 'x'
         from   registrations r ...
```

■ **Note**   The ANSI/ISO SQL standard defines * as being an arbitrary literal in this case.

Subqueries that follow an EXISTS operator are often *correlated*. Think about this for a moment. If they are *uncorrelated*, their result is precisely the same for each row from the main query. There are only two possible outcomes: the EXISTS operator results in TRUE for all rows or FALSE for all rows. In other words, EXISTS followed by an uncorrelated subquery becomes an "all or nothing" operator.

■ **Caution** A subquery returning a null value is *not* the same as a subquery returning nothing (that is, the empty set). This will be demonstrated later in this section.

EXISTS, IN, or JOIN?

See Listing 9-9 for another EXISTS example to finish this section. The query is intended to provide the personal details of all employees who ever taught an SQL course.

Listing 9-9. Another Correlated Subquery with EXISTS Operator

```
select  e.*
from    employees e
where   exists (select o.*
                from    offerings o
                where   o.course = 'SQL'
                and     o.trainer = e.empno);
```

EMPNO	ENAME	INIT	JOB	MGR	BDATE	MSAL	COMM	DEPTNO
7369	SMITH	N	TRAINER	7902	17-DEC-1965	800		20
7902	FORD	MG	TRAINER	7566	13-FEB-1959	3000		20

This problem can also be solved with an IN operator, as shown in Listing 9-10. The query results are omitted.

Listing 9-10. Alternative Formulation for Listing 9-9

```
select  e.*
from    employees e
where   e.empno in (select o.trainer
                    from    offerings o
                    where   o.course = 'SQL')
```

You can also use a join to solve the problem, as shown in Listing 9-11. This is probably the most obvious approach, although the choice between writing joins or subqueries is highly subjective. Some people think "bottom up" and prefer subqueries; others think "top down" and prefer to write joins.

Listing 9-11. Another Alternative Formulation for Listing 9-9

```
select  DISTINCT e.*
from    employees e
        join
        offerings o
        on e.empno = o.trainer
where   o.course = 'SQL'
```

Notice the DISTINCT option in the SELECT clause. Investigate what happens if you remove the DISTINCT option in Listing 9-11. You'll find that the query result will consist of *three* rows, instead of two. The query in Listing 9-11 can return multiple instances of the same employee if an employee is teaching more than one offering of the course, "SQL." Since the query in Listing 9-9 employs a correlated subquery, only two rows are returned. Since an employee is added to the result set once, and only once, it matches a trainer value selected from the correlated subquery.

So far, we have considered only subqueries in the WHERE clause. However, you can use subqueries in other SQL statement components, such as the SELECT and FROM clauses. In the next sections, we will look at subqueries in these other clauses.

NULLs with EXISTS and IN in subquery results often cause problems for people writing SQL for Oracle database systems, especially for those used to writing SQL for other database systems. Not only can NULLs in subquery results cause confusion, but they can lead to incorrect results.

There are several key concepts to keep in mind:

- NULL is not data, but rather a condition of data being unknown.

- Null = Null, NULL != NULL or NULL IN (NULL) always evaluates to UNKNOWN, which is neither TRUE nor FALSE.

- It is not possible to join two rows with NULLs in the join column.

We illustrate our point about the trouble NULLs cause with EXISTS and IN queries with the reports in Listing 9-12. The queries behind the reports show two different ways to generate a list of managers. One approach uses IN; the other uses EXISTS. At face value, either approach works, and there seems to be no difference between them.

Listing 9-12. Selecting All Managers Using IN or EXISTS

```
select ename
from employees
where empno in (select mgr from employees);

ENAME
--------
JONES
BLAKE
CLARK
SCOTT
KING
FORD

select e1.ename
from employees e1
where exists (select e2.mgr
              from    employees e2
              where e1.empno = e2.mgr);

ENAME
--------
JONES
BLAKE
CLARK
SCOTT
KING
FORD
```

As you see from Listing 9-12, the use of IN or EXISTS are equivalent in terms of results, though the actual operations are different. IN builds a list of values that are used for comparison with EMPNO. EXISTS executes the subquery for each EMPNO and returns TRUE if the join finds a matching EMPNO. However, the two queries return the same results only because NULLs are not involved in the EMPNO to MGR values evaluation. If there were a NULL EMPNO, the EXISTS subquery would not return a record for that employee number, because a NULL EMPNO value would not join with the NULL MGR value (NULL = NULL does not evaluate to TRUE).

EXISTS answers the question, "Is this value present in the specified table column?" If that value is present (as indicated by at least one row being returned from the subquery), the answer is yes and the EXISTS expression evaluates to TRUE. As NULLs cannot be equated, joining a NULL MGR to a NULL EMPNO does not return TRUE. Essentially, the query joins the inner and outer tables and returns the rows that match, one at a time. If the main query value does not have a match in the subquery (i.e., the join does not return at least one row), then the EXISTS evaluates to FALSE.

IN answers the question, "Does the value exist anywhere in this list?" If one list value matches the external value, then the expression evaluates to TRUE. One way to think of an IN list expression is to rephrase it as a series of OR expressions. For example, the following

```
1234 IN (1234, NULL)
```

is equivalent to

```
1234 = 1234 OR 1234 = NULL
```

Each equality check can be evaluated separately and the result would be TRUE or UNKNOWN. Reference the truth table in Section 4.10 (in Chapter 4). TRUE or UNKNOWN is TRUE. Essentially, once you find a match, you can stop looking and ignore any previous NOT TRUE (FALSE or UNKNOWN) results. If the value does not match at least one value in the list, then the expression returns FALSE.

NULLS with NOT EXISTS and NOT IN

Intuitively, NOT EXISTS and NOT IN should return the rows in a table that are not returned by EXISTS and IN, respectively. This is true for NOT EXISTS, but when NULLs are encountered, NOT IN will not return the rows not returned by IN. In the previous section, we reported the employees who were also managers. In this section, we want to report on the employees who are not managers, so NOT EXISTS and NOT IN are the expressions we can use. Listing 9-13 displays the results from using NOT EXISTS.

Listing 9-13. Selecting Employees Who Are Not Managers Using NOT EXISTS

```
select e1.ename
from employees e1
where not exists (select e2.mgr
                  from    employees e2
                  where e1.empno = e2.mgr);


ENAME
--------
SMITH
ALLEN
WARD
MARTIN
TURNER
ADAMS
JONES
MILLER
```

There are 14 employees, 6 who are managers (see Listing 9-12) and 8 who are not managers (see Listing 9-13). Using EXISTS and NOT EXISTS, all of the employees are listed, regardless of the presence of a NULL MGR state for one of the rows (employee KING, see Listing 9-12).

Now look at the results in Listing 9-14, showing the use of NOT IN. (The SET FEEDBACK ON command in the listing is specific to SQL*Plus). No rows are returned at all! Apparently we have all management and no workers. Why is that? The reason lies in the question that NOT IN answers, and in how it goes about answering that question.

Listing 9-14. Selecting Employees Who Are Not Managers Using NOT IN

```
set feedback on
select ename
from employees
where empno not in (select mgr from employees);


no rows selected
```

NOT IN also answers the question, "Does the value exist anywhere in this list?" As long as no list value matches the external value, then the expression evaluates to TRUE. One way to think of a NOT IN list expression is to rephrase it as a series of AND expressions. For example, 1234 NOT IN (1234, NULL) is equivalent to 1234 != 1234 AND 1234 != NULL. Each equality check can be evaluated separately and the result would be TRUE AND UNKNOWN. Reference the truth table in Section 4.10 in Chapter 4. TRUE AND UNKNOWN is UNKNOWN. In order for a row to be returned, the NOT IN expression must evaluate to TRUE, something it can never do as long as one of the values in the NOT IN list has the state of NULL.

9.2 Subqueries in the SELECT Clause

Check out Listings 5-31 and 5-32 in Chapter 5, which demonstrate how to determine the number of employees in each department. The ANSI/ISO SQL standard offers an alternative approach for that problem, using a subquery in the SELECT clause, as shown in Listing 9-15.

Listing 9-15. Example of a Subquery in the SELECT Clause

```
select d.deptno, d.dname, d.location,
    (select count(*)
       from    employees e
       where   e.deptno = d.deptno) as emp_count
from    departments d;
```

```
DEPTNO DNAME      LOCATION EMP_COUNT
-------- ---------- -------- ---------
    10 ACCOUNTING NEW YORK         3
    20 TRAINING   DALLAS           5
    30 SALES      CHICAGO          6
    40 HR         BOSTON           0
```

You could argue that this is not only a *correct* solution, but it also is a very *elegant* solution. It's elegant, because the driving table for this query (see the FROM clause) is the DEPARTMENTS table. After all, we are looking for information about departments, so the DEPARTMENTS table is the most intuitive and obvious table to start our search for the result. The first three attributes (DEPTNO, DNAME, and LOCATION) are "regular" attributes that can be found from the corresponding columns of the DEPARTMENTS table; however, the fourth attribute (the number of employees) is not stored as a column value in the database. See Chapter 1 for a discussion of database design and normalization as a technique to reduce redundancy.

Because the department head count is not physically stored in a column of the DEPARTMENTS table, we derive it by using a subquery in the SELECT clause. This is precisely how you can read this query: in the FROM clause you visit the DEPARTMENTS table, and in the SELECT clause you select four expressions. Without using an outer join, regular join, or GROUP BY, you still get the correct number of employees (zero) for Department 40.

■ **Note**   You could argue that the GROUP BY clause of the SQL language is redundant. You can solve most (if not all) aggregation problems using a correlated subquery in the SELECT clause without using GROUP BY at all.

As noted, the subquery in Listing 9-15 is correlated. d.DEPTNO has a different value for each row d of the DEPARTMENTS table, and the subquery is executed four times for those different values: 10, 20, 30, and 40. Although it is not strictly necessary, it is a good idea to assign a column alias (EMP_COUNT in Listing 9-15) to the subquery expression, because it enhances readability for both the query itself and for its results.

■ **Note**   As with any feature or method of query construction, performance can be better or worse than another method. Always test on production-like configurations and data sets to avoid the surprise of a solution that performs well in development but is utterly unable to scale.

So far, we have distinguished only single-row queries and subqueries returning any number of rows. At this point, it makes sense to identify a third subquery type, which is a subtype of the single-row subquery type: *scalar subqueries*. The name indicates an important property of this type of subqueries: the result not only consists of precisely one row, but also with precisely one column value. You can use scalar subqueries almost everywhere in your SQL commands in places where a column expression or literal value is allowed and makes sense. The scalar subquery generates a literal value.

In summary, you can say that SQL supports the following subquery hierarchy:

- Multirow subqueries: No restrictions

- Single-row subqueries: Result must contain a single row

- Scalar subqueries: Result must be a single row and a single column

9.3 Subqueries in the FROM Clause

The next clause we investigate is the FROM clause. Actually, the FROM clause is one of the most obvious places to allow subqueries in SQL. Instead of specifying "real" table names, you simply provide subqueries (or table expressions) to take their place as a derived table.

Listing 9-16 illustrates an example of a subquery in the FROM clause. The Oracle documentation refers to these subqueries as *inline views*, as does this book. The name *inline view* will become clearer in Chapter 10, when we discuss views in general.

Listing 9-16. Inline View Example

```
select  e.ename, e.init, e.msal
from    employees e
        join
        (select  x.deptno
        ,        avg(x.msal) avg_sal
        from     employees x
        group by x.deptno          ) g
        using (deptno)
where   e.msal > g.avg_sal;
```

```
ENAME     INIT    MSAL
--------  -----   --------
ALLEN     JAM      1600
JONES     JM       2975
BLAKE     R        2850
SCOTT     SCJ      3000
KING      CC       5000
FORD      MG       3000
```

A big difference between a "real" table and a subquery is that the real table has a name. Therefore, if you use subqueries in the FROM clause, you must define a tuple variable (or *table alias*, in Oracle terminology) over the result of the subquery. At the end of line 7 in Listing 9-16, we define tuple variable g. This tuple variable allows us to refer to column expressions from the subquery, as shown by g.AVG_SAL in the last line of the example. By the way, the query in Listing 9-16 is an alternative solution for the query in Listing 9-6. One requirement is that the subquery must be independent of the outer query, it cannot be correlated.

9.4 The WITH Clause

As stated earlier, Listing 9-16 illustrates an example of using a subquery in a FROM clause. We could have written the same query with a slightly different syntax, as shown in Listing 9-17. This construct is called a factored subquery (or subquery factoring).

Listing 9-17. WITH Clause Example

```
WITH g AS
      (select    x.deptno
      ,          avg(x.msal) avg_sal
      from       employees x
      group by x.deptno)
select e.ename, e.init, e.msal
from    employees e
        join      g
        using (deptno)
where   e.msal > g.avg_sal;
```

```
ENAME     INIT    MSAL
--------  -----   --------
ALLEN     JAM      1600
JONES     JM       2975
BLAKE     R        2850
SCOTT     SCJ      3000
KING      CC       5000
FORD      MG       3000
```

As you can see, we have isolated the subquery definition, in lines 1 through 5, from the actual query in lines 6 through 10. This makes the structure of the main query clearer. Using the WITH clause syntax becomes even more attractive if you refer multiple times to the same subquery from the main query. You can define as many subqueries as you like in a single WITH clause, separated by commas.

```
WITH   v1 AS (select ... from ...)
,      v2 AS (select ... from ...)
,      v3 AS ...
```

```
select ...
from   ...
```

There are several advantages to using factored subqueries. First, they can make development easier by isolating each query (as we demonstrate in Listing 9-18). Second, they make the code clearer. Using the previous example would look as follows:

```
select ...
from   (select ...
       from  (select ...
             from (select ... from ...) v3
             ) v2
       ) v1
```

When there is a problem with the query, it can be difficult to locate the actual problem. By using subquery factoring, you can create the subquery as a standalone query, then make it a factored subquery using WITH, SELECT * from it to check for completeness, and add in additional predicates, data transformations, exclude columns, and so on.. Listing 9-18 shows how a statement using a factored subquery can be developed using a three step process. Each step in Listing 9-18 is executed separately.

Listing 9-18. WITH Clause Development Example

```
select    x.deptno
,         avg(x.msal) avg_sal
from      employees x
group by x.deptno;

WITH g AS
      (select    x.deptno
      ,          avg(x.msal) avg_sal
       from      employees x
       group by x.deptno)
select *
from   g;

WITH g AS
     (select    x.deptno
     ,          avg(x.msal) avg_sal
      from      employees x
      group by x.deptno)
select e.ename, e.init, e.msal
from   employees e
       join    g
       using (deptno)
where  e.msal > g.avg_sal;
```

If you define multiple subqueries in the WITH clause, you are allowed to refer to any subquery name that you defined earlier in the same WITH clause; that is, the definition of subquery V2 can refer to V1 in its FROM clause, and the definition of V3 can refer to both V1 and V2, as in the following example:

```
WITH   v1 AS (select ... from ...)
,        v2 AS (select ... from V1)
```

```
,       v3 AS (select ... from V2 join V1)
select ...
from  ...
```

Under the hood, the Oracle DBMS has two ways to execute queries with a WITH clause:

- Merge the subquery definitions into the main query. This makes the subqueries behave just like inline views.

- Execute the subqueries, store the results in a temporary structure, and access the temporary structures from the main query.

See the *Oracle SQL Language Reference* (http://docs.oracle.com/cd/E16655_01/server.121/e17209/toc.htm) for more details and examples of the WITH clause and subquery factoring.

9.5 Hierarchical Queries

Relational tables are flat structures. All rows of a table are equally important, and the order in which the rows are stored is irrelevant. However, some data structures have hierarchical relationships. A famous example in most books about relational database design is the "bill of materials" (BOM) problem, where you are supposed to design an efficient relational database structure to store facts about which (sub)components are needed to build more complicated components to be used for highly complicated objects such as cars and airplanes. Figure 9-1 shows an ERM diagram with a typical solution. On the left, you see the most generic solution with a many-to-many relationship, and on the right you see a typical solution using two entities.

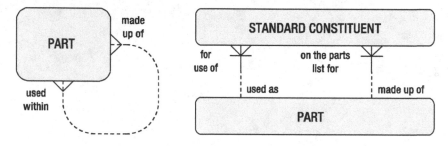

Figure 9-1. *A solution for the "bill of materials" problem*

Notice that for the solution on the left-hand side, if you replaced the entity name PART with THING, and you replaced the two relationship descriptions with "related to," then you would have the ultimate in generic data models! Although this book is not about database design, consider this joke as a serious warning: don't make your data models overly generic.

Even if hierarchical data structures are correctly translated into relational tables, the retrieval of such structures can still be quite challenging. We have an example of a simple hierarchical relationship in our sample tables: the management structure in the EMPLOYEES table is implemented with the MGR column and its foreign key constraint to the EMPNO column of the same table.

■ **Note** In hierarchical structures, it is common practice to refer to *parent* rows and *children* rows. Another common (and self-explanatory) terminology is using a tree metaphor by referring to *root*, *branch*, and *leaf* rows.

START WITH and CONNECT BY

Oracle SQL supports a number of operators—and pseudo columns populated by those operators—to facilitate queries against hierarchical data. Let's look at a simple example first, shown in Listing 9-19.

Listing 9-19. Hierarchical Query Example

```
select   ename, LEVEL
from     employees
START    WITH mgr is null
CONNECT BY NOCYCLE PRIOR empno = mgr;


ENAME        LEVEL
--------  --------
KING             1
JONES            2
SCOTT            3
ADAMS            4
FORD             3
SMITH            4
BLAKE            2
ALLEN            3
WARD             3
MARTIN           3
TURNER           3
JONES            3
CLARK            2
MILLER           3
```

The START WITH and CONNECT BY clauses allow you to do the following:

- Identify a starting point (root) for the tree structure.

- Specify how you can walk up or down the tree structure from any row.

The START WITH and CONNECT BY clauses must be specified *after* the WHERE clause (if any) and *before* the GROUP BY clause (if any).

■ **Note** It is your own responsibility to indicate the correct starting point (or root) for the hierarchy. Listing 9-19 uses the predicate, MGR is null, as a condition, because we know that the null value in the MGR column has a special meaning. The Oracle DBMS treats *each* row for which the START WITH condition evaluates to TRUE as root for a separate tree structure; that is, you can define multiple tree structures within the context of a single query.

The NOCYCLE keyword in the CONNECT BY clause is optional; however, if you omit NOCYCLE, you risk ending up in a loop. If that happens, the Oracle DBMS returns the following error message:

```
ORA-01436: CONNECT BY loop in user data
```

Conversely, one example of a looping condition that could take place is the scenario where the employee with an EMPNO value of 1 has a MGR value of 2. And the employee with an EMPNO value of 2 has a MGR value of 1. This could very well represent a logical data error. However, using the NOCYCLE keyword in such a situation would mask the error. You would not receive the Oracle DBMS error ORA-01436, but you could receive unexpected results in your query output.

Our EMPLOYEES table doesn't contain any cyclic references, but specifying NOCYCLE never hurts.

Pay special attention to the placement of the PRIOR operator. The PRIOR operator always points to the parent row. In Listing 9-19, PRIOR is placed before EMPNO, so we are able to find parent rows by starting from the MGR column value of the current row and then searching the EMPNO column values in all other rows for a match. If you put PRIOR in the wrong place, you define hierarchical relationships in the opposite direction. Just see what happens in Listing 9-19 if you change the fourth line to CONNECT BY PRIOR MGR = EMPNO or to CONNECT BY EMPNO = PRIOR MGR.

At first sight, the result in Listing 9-19 is not very impressive, since you just get a list of employee names, followed by a number. And if we had omitted LEVEL from the SELECT clause, the result would have been completely trivial. However, many things happened behind the scenes. We just have not exploited the full benefits yet.

LEVEL, CONNECT_BY_ISCYCLE, and CONNECT_BY_ISLEAF

As a consequence of using START WITH and CONNECT BY, the Oracle DBMS assigns several pseudo column values to every row. Listing 9-19 showed a first example of such a pseudo column: LEVEL. You can use these pseudo column values for many purposes, for example, to filter specific rows in the WHERE clause or to enhance the readability of your results in the SELECT clause.

The following are the hierarchical pseudo columns:

- LEVEL : The level of the row in the tree structure.

- CONNECT_BY_ISCYCLE: The value is 1 for each row with a *child* that is also a *parent* of the same row (that is, you have a cyclic reference); otherwise, the value is 0.

- CONNECT_BY_ISLEAF: The value is 1 if the row is a *leaf*; otherwise, the value is 0. Since a leaf is the last or lowest member of the hierarchy it does not have any children.

Listing 9-20 illustrates an example using the LEVEL pseudo column combined with the LPAD function, adding indentation to highlight the hierarchical query results.

Listing 9-20. Enhancing Readability with the LPAD Function

```
select   lpad(' ',2*level-1)||ename as ename
from     employees
start    with mgr is null
connect by nocycle prior empno = mgr;

ENAME
-----------------
 KING
   JONES
     SCOTT
       ADAMS
     FORD
       SMITH
   BLAKE
     ALLEN
     WARD
     MARTIN
     TURNER
     JONES
   CLARK
     MILLER
```

CONNECT_BY_ROOT and SYS_CONNECT_BY_PATH

If you use START WITH and CONNECT BY to define a hierarchical query, you can use two interesting hierarchical operators in the SELECT clause:

- CONNECT_BY_ROOT: Thisperator allows you to connect each row (regardless of its level in the tree structure) with its own root.

- SYS_CONNECT_BY_PATH : This function allows you to display the full path from the current row to its root.

See Listing 9-21 for an example of using both operators. Note that the START WITH clause in Listing 9-21 creates three separate tree structures: one for each manager.

Listing 9-21. Using CONNECT_BY_ROOT and SYS_CONNECT_BY_PATH

```
select  ename
,       connect_by_root ename            as manager
,       sys_connect_by_path(ename,' > ') as full_path
from    employees
start   with job = 'MANAGER'
connect by prior empno = mgr;


ENAME    MANAGER  FULL_PATH
-------- -------- ------------------------
JONES    JONES     > JONES
SCOTT    JONES     > JONES > SCOTT
ADAMS    JONES     > JONES > SCOTT > ADAMS
FORD     JONES     > JONES > FORD
SMITH    JONES     > JONES > FORD > SMITH
BLAKE    BLAKE     > BLAKE
ALLEN    BLAKE     > BLAKE > ALLEN
WARD     BLAKE     > BLAKE > WARD
MARTIN   BLAKE     > BLAKE > MARTIN
TURNER   BLAKE     > BLAKE > TURNER
JONES    BLAKE     > BLAKE > JONES
CLARK    CLARK     > CLARK
MILLER   CLARK     > CLARK > MILLER
```

You can specify additional conditions in the CONNECT BY clause, thus eliminating entire subtree structures. Note the important difference with conditions in the WHERE clause: those conditions filter only individual rows. See the *Oracle SQL Language Reference* (http://docs.oracle.com/cd/E16655_01/server.121/e17209/toc.htm) for more details and examples.

Hierarchical Query Result Sorting

If you want to sort the results of hierarchical queries, and you use a regular ORDER BY clause, the carefully constructed hierarchical tree gets disturbed in most cases. In such cases, you can use the SIBLINGS option of the ORDER BY clause. This option doesn't destroy the hierarchy of the rows in the result. See Listings 9-22 and 9-23 for an example, and watch what happens with the query result if we remove the SIBLINGS option. Listing 9-22 displays the use of siblings. Listing 9-23 shows the results without that keyword.

Listing 9-22. Results When Ordering By Siblings

```
select   ename
,        sys_connect_by_path(ename,'|') as path
from     employees
start    with mgr is null
connect  by prior empno = mgr
order    SIBLINGS by ename;
```

```
ENAME     PATH
--------  ------------------------------
KING      |KING
BLAKE     |KING|BLAKE
ALLEN     |KING|BLAKE|ALLEN
JONES     |KING|BLAKE|JONES
MARTIN    |KING|BLAKE|MARTIN
TURNER    |KING|BLAKE|TURNER
WARD      |KING|BLAKE|WARD
CLARK     |KING|CLARK
MILLER    |KING|CLARK|MILLER
JONES     |KING|JONES
FORD      |KING|JONES|FORD
SMITH     |KING|JONES|FORD|SMITH
SCOTT     |KING|JONES|SCOTT
ADAMS     |KING|JONES|SCOTT|ADAMS
```

Listing 9-23. Results from a Standard ORDER BY Clause

```
select   ename
,        sys_connect_by_path(ename,'|') as path
from     employees
start    with mgr is null
connect  by prior empno = mgr
order    by ename;
```

```
ENAME     PATH
--------  ------------------------------
ADAMS     |KING|JONES|SCOTT|ADAMS
ALLEN     |KING|BLAKE|ALLEN
BLAKE     |KING|BLAKE
CLARK     |KING|CLARK
FORD      |KING|JONES|FORD
JONES     |KING|JONES
JONES     |KING|BLAKE|JONES
KING      |KING
MARTIN    |KING|BLAKE|MARTIN
MILLER    |KING|CLARK|MILLER
SCOTT     |KING|JONES|SCOTT
SMITH     |KING|JONES|FORD|SMITH
TURNER    |KING|BLAKE|TURNER
WARD      |KING|BLAKE|WARD
```

9.6 Analytic Functions

This section introduces the concept of *analytic functions*, which are a very powerful part of the ANSI/ISO SQL standard syntax. Analytic functions enable you to produce derived attributes that would otherwise be very complicated to achieve in SQL. Rankings, Top N reports, and running totals are all possible using analytical SQL. In fact they are not just possible, but the resulting statement is clearer and performance is usually better than with multiple-pass statements.

Earlier in this chapter, in Section 9.2, you saw how subqueries in the SELECT clause allow you to add derived attributes to the SELECT clause of your queries. Analytic functions provide similar functionality, though with enhanced statement clarity and improved performance.

■ **Note** You should always test the performance of any analytic functions on production-like data sets. These functions are designed for use with large data sets and are optimized accordingly. When these functions are used with small data sets, as you might find in development, they may not perform as well as other statements. Do not conclude that the performance is unacceptable until you test with appropriately sized data sets.

Let's take a look at a simple query, reporting the salary ranking by department for all employees. Listing 9-24 displays the query and the results.

Listing 9-24. Ranking Employee Salary Using Multiple Table Access

```
SELECT e1.deptno, e1.ename, e1.msal,
       (SELECT COUNT(1)
         FROM employees e2
        WHERE  e2.msal > e1.msal)+1 sal_rank
FROM employees e1
ORDER BY e1.msal DESC;
```

DEPTNO	ENAME	MSAL	SAL_RANK
10	KING	5000	1
20	FORD	3000	2
20	SCOTT	3000	2
20	JONES	2975	4
30	BLAKE	2850	5
10	CLARK	2450	6
30	ALLEN	1600	7
30	TURNER	1500	8
10	MILLER	1300	9
30	WARD	1250	10
30	MARTIN	1250	10
20	ADAMS	1100	12
30	JONES	800	13
20	SMITH	800	13

This version of the query doesn't use an analytic function. It uses a more traditional, subquery-based approach to the problem of ranking. The problem is that the subquery essentially represents an additional query to the employees table for each row that is being ranked. If the employees table is large, this can result in a large number of data reads and consume minutes, perhaps hours, of response time. Listing 9-25 generates the same report using the analytic function RANK.

Listing 9-25. Ranking Employee Salary Using Analytic Funcions

```
SELECT e1.deptno, e1.ename, e1.msal,
       RANK() OVER (ORDER BY e1.msal DESC) sal_rank
FROM employees e1
ORDER BY e1.msal DESC;
```

DEPTNO	ENAME	MSAL	SAL_RANK
10	KING	5000	1
20	FORD	3000	2
20	SCOTT	3000	2
20	JONES	2975	4
30	BLAKE	2850	5
10	CLARK	2450	6
30	ALLEN	1600	7
30	TURNER	1500	8
10	MILLER	1300	9
30	WARD	1250	10
30	MARTIN	1250	10
20	ADAMS	1100	12
30	JONES	800	13
20	SMITH	800	13

Using the analytic function creates a statement that is simpler and self documenting. Figure 9-2 illustrates the basic format of the analytic function.

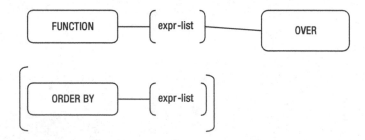

Figure 9-2. *Basic syntax for analytic functions*

The use of the term OVER indicates an analytic function, something you need to keep in mind as there are analytic functions with the same names as regular functions. For example, the analytic functions SUM and AVG have the same names as their non-analytic counterparts.

A key clause is ORDER BY. This indicates the order in which the functions are applied. In the preceding example, RANK is applied according to the employee salary. Remember that the default for ORDER BY is ascending, smallest to largest, so you have to specify the keyword DESC, for descending, to sort from largest to smallest. The ORDER BY clause must come last in the analytic function.

ORDER BY VERSUS ORDER BY

Do take care to remember that the statement ORDER BY and the function ORDER BY are independent of each other. If you place another clause after the ORDER BY in a function call, you receive the following rather cryptic error message:

```
            PARTITION BY empno) prev_sal
            *
ERROR at line 6:
ORA-00907: missing right parenthesis
```

The ORDER BY in a function call applies only to the evaluation of that function and has nothing to do with sorting the rows to be returned by the statement.

Partitions

A partition is a set of rows defined by data values in the result set. The default partition for any function is the entire result set. You can have one partition clause per function, though it may be a composite partition, including more than one data value. The PARTITION BY clause must come before the ORDER BY clause. Figure 9-3 illustrates the basic format of the analytic function using a PARTITION.

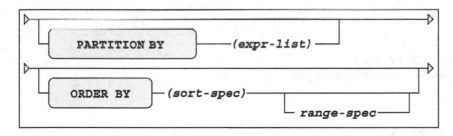

Figure 9-3. *Analytic function partitioning syntax*

When a partition is defined, the rows belonging to each partition are grouped together and the function is applied within each group. In Listing 9-26, one RANK is for the entire company and the second RANK is within each department.

Listing 9-26. Ranking Employee Salary Within the Company and Department

```
SELECT e1.deptno, e1.ename, e1.msal,
       RANK() OVER (ORDER BY e1.msal DESC) sal_rank,
       RANK() OVER (PARTITION BY e1.deptno
                    ORDER BY e1.msal DESC) dept_sal_rank
FROM employees e1
ORDER BY e1.deptno ASC, e1.msal DESC;
```

DEPTNO	ENAME	MSAL	SAL_RANK	DEPT_SAL_RANK
10	KING	5000	1	1
10	CLARK	2450	6	2
10	MILLER	1300	9	3
20	FORD	3000	2	1
20	SCOTT	3000	2	1
20	JONES	2975	4	3
20	ADAMS	1100	12	4
20	SMITH	800	13	5
30	BLAKE	2850	5	1
30	ALLEN	1600	7	2
30	TURNER	1500	8	3
30	MARTIN	1250	10	4
30	WARD	1250	10	4
30	JONES	800	13	6

Functions cannot span a partition boundary, which is the condition where the partition value changes. When the DEPTNO changes value, the RANK() with the PARTITION BY E1.DEPTNO resets to 1. Other functions, such as LAG or LEAD, cannot reference rows outside the current row's partition. Listing 9-27 shows how to reference data in rows other than the current row.

Listing 9-27. Listing Employee Current and Previous Salaries

```
SELECT     empno
     ,     begindate
     ,     enddate
     ,     msal
     ,     LAG(msal) OVER (PARTITION BY empno
                          ORDER BY begindate) prev_sal
FROM       history
ORDER BY   empno, begindate;
```

EMPNO	BEGINDATE	ENDDATE	MSAL	PREV_SAL
7369	01-JAN-00	01-FEB-00	950	
7369	01-FEB-00		800	950
7499	01-JUN-88	01-JUL-89	1000	
7499	01-JUL-89	01-DEC-93	1300	1000
7499	01-DEC-93	01-OCT-95	1500	1300
7499	01-OCT-95	01-NOV-99	1700	1500
7499	01-NOV-99		1600	1700

Here is an example of using the LAG function to calculate the raise someone received. The LAG function returns the same datatype as the expression, in this case a number, so it can be used in an expression itself. Listing 9-28 illustrates how to use the current and previous salaries to calculate the raise in pay.

Listing 9-28. Using LAG to Calculate a Raise

```
SELECT     empno
     ,     begindate
     ,     enddate
     ,     msal
```

```
,       LAG(msal) OVER (PARTITION BY empno
                          ORDER BY begindate) prev_sal
,       msal - LAG(msal) OVER (PARTITION BY empno
                          ORDER BY begindate) raise
FROM        history
ORDER BY    empno, begindate;

EMPNO BEGINDATE ENDDATE     MSAL PREV_SAL  RAISE
----- --------- ---------  ------ -------- ------
 7369 01-JAN-00 01-FEB-00    950
 7369 01-FEB-00              800      950   -150
 7499 01-JUN-88 01-JUL-89   1000
 7499 01-JUL-89 01-DEC-93   1300     1000    300
 7499 01-DEC-93 01-OCT-95   1500     1300    200
 7499 01-OCT-95 01-NOV-99   1700     1500    200
 7499 01-NOV-99             1600     1700   -100
```

Notice that the LAG(msal) does not look backward when the EMPNO changes from 7369 to 7499. A common mistake is to not specify the correct PARTITION BY and the function returns data that you did not intend. It is always a good practice to manually and visually validate the data as you are writing the query.

Function Processing

There are three distinct phases in which statements containing analytic functions are processed. They are shown in the following list. The list also shows the steps within each phase.

It is *very important* to keep in mind that all of the data retrieval for the query occurs before the analytic functions are executed. It is important to keep this in mind as it restricts what you can do with analytic functions in a single query.

1. Execute the query clauses, except

   ```
   ORDER BY
      SELECT
      WHERE/joins
      GROUP BY/HAVING
   ```

2. Execute the analytic function. This phase occurs once for every function in the statement.

   ```
       Define the partition(s)
   Order the data within each partition
   Define the window
       Apply function
   ```

3. Sort query results per the statement's ORDER BY clause.

Since analytic functions are not processed until after the WHERE clause has been evaluated, the use of analytic functions in the WHERE clause is not supported. (Similarly, you cannot apply analytic functions in a HAVING clause). If you try to use one in the WHERE clause, you receive a somewhat cryptic error, as shown in Listing 9-29.

Listing 9-29. Error Resulting from Analytic Function Placed in a WHERE Clause

```
SELECT      ename
,       job
,       mgr
,       msal
,       DENSE_RANK() OVER (ORDER BY msal DESC) sal_rank
```

```
FROM        employees
WHERE       (DENSE_RANK() OVER (ORDER BY msal DESC)) <= 3
ORDER BY    msal DESC;


WHERE       (DENSE_RANK() OVER (ORDER BY msal DESC)) <= 3
                *
ERROR at line 7:
ORA-30483: window  functions are not allowed here
```

If you want to filter records based on an analytic function, you will need to create a subquery that uses the function and then use the resulting value to filter on as shown in Listing 9-30.

Listing 9-30. Using a Factored Subquery to Filter on an Analytic Function

```
WITH ranked_salaries AS
( SELECT      ename
     ,        job
     ,        mgr
     ,        msal
     ,        DENSE_RANK() OVER (ORDER BY msal DESC) sal_rank
  FROM        employees
)
SELECT      ename
     ,      job
     ,      mgr
     ,      msal
     ,      sal_rank
FROM        ranked_salaries
WHERE       sal_rank <= 3
ORDER BY    msal DESC;


ENAME     JOB        MGR    MSAL SAL_RANK
--------  --------  -----  ------ --------
KING      DIRECTOR          5000         1
SCOTT     TRAINER    7566   3000         2
FORD      TRAINER    7566   3000         2
JONES     MANAGER    7839   2975         3
```

Analytic functions enable you to reference other rows and group data in different ways. This will require that you begin to look at your data and query requirements in a more complex way, which will be your biggest challenge in leveraging analytic functions. Begin to look for opportunities to use these functions as you get more familiar with them. When you find yourself accessing the same table several times in a query, this might indicate that the information you desire can be derived using analytic functions.

While the specific functions are documented in the *Oracle SQL Language Reference* (http://docs.oracle.com/cd/E16655_01/server.121/e17209/toc.htm), a more thorough treatment of the functions, partitions, and windows is given in the *Oracle Data Warehousing and Business Intelligence Reference* (http://docs.oracle.com/cd/E16655_01/nav/portal_6.htm).

9.7 Row Limiting

Oracle Database version 12c allows Top-N queries to employ simpler syntax with the use of the *row limiting clause*, which allows you to limit the rows returned by a query. This can greatly simplify the syntax required for providing you with the ability to page through an ordered set. Listing 9-31 displays two queries for comparison purposes: one that queries from the EMPLOYEES table with no row limiting applied, and one that queries the EMPLOYEES table with the row limiting FETCH FIRST and ROWS ONLY clauses employed.

Listing 9-31. A Comparison of Two Queries: One Without Row Limiting Applied and One with Row Limiting Applied

```
SQL> select empno, ename||','||init name, job, msal
  2    from employees
  3   order by msal desc, name;

EMPNO NAME            JOB        MSAL
----- --------------- --------  ------
 7839 KING,CC         DIRECTOR   5000
 7902 FORD,MG         TRAINER    3000
 7788 SCOTT,SCJ       TRAINER    3000
 7566 JONES,JM        MANAGER    2975
 7698 BLAKE,R         MANAGER    2850
 7782 CLARK,AB        MANAGER    2450
 7499 ALLEN,JAM       SALESREP   1600
 7844 TURNER,JJ       SALESREP   1500
 7934 MILLER,TJA      ADMIN      1300
 7654 MARTIN,P        SALESREP   1250
 7521 WARD,TF         SALESREP   1250
 7876 ADAMS,AA        TRAINER    1100
 7900 JONES,R         ADMIN       800
 7369 SMITH,N         TRAINER     800

14 rows selected.

SQL> select empno, ename||','||init name, job, msal
  2    from employees
  3   order by msal desc, name
  4  FETCH FIRST 5 ROWS ONLY;

EMPNO NAME            JOB        MSAL
----- --------------- --------  ------
 7839 KING,CC         DIRECTOR   5000
 7902 FORD,MG         TRAINER    3000
 7788 SCOTT,SCJ       TRAINER    3000
 7566 JONES,JM        MANAGER    2975
 7698 BLAKE,R         MANAGER    2850

5 rows selected.
```

Notice how with just a few extra keywords, FETCH FIRST 5 ROWS ONLY, the query is limited to the Top-N records we are interested in. This is a syntactical simplification over, for example, the RANK and DENSE_RANK analytic functions illustrated in Section 9.6. This is not to say that RANK and DENSE_RANK should not be used. (I am a huge fan of analytic functions.) This is simply a statement that many Top-N queries that are interested in, say, fetching the first five rows, and maybe the next five rows, for example, could make good use of the row limiting clause syntax available in Oracle Database version 12c.

The FETCH clause specifies the number of rows or percentage of rows to return. Comparing the second query with the first query, you can see that the omission of this clause results in all rows being returned. The second query fetches only the top five salary earners from the EMPLOYEES table. To then fetch the next top five salary earners, consider the query in Listing 9-32.

Listing 9-32. A Query That Uses the OFFSET and FETCH NEXT Options of the Row Limiting Clause

```
SQL> select empno, ename||','||init name, job, msal
  2    from employees
  3  order by msal desc, name
  4  OFFSET 5 ROWS FETCH NEXT 5 ROWS ONLY;
```

EMPNO	NAME	JOB	MSAL
7782	CLARK,AB	MANAGER	2450
7499	ALLEN,JAM	SALESREP	1600
7844	TURNER,JJ	SALESREP	1500
7934	MILLER,TJA	ADMIN	1300
7654	MARTIN,P	SALESREP	1250

```
5 rows selected.
```

The differences between the query in Listing 9-32 and the second query in Listing 9-31 are the OFFSET and FETCH NEXT clauses. The OFFSET clause specifies the number of rows to skip before the row limiting begins. The way to look at this is to read it as "skip the first five salary earners, and return the next five salary earners only." Notice how there are actually two employees who earn a salary value of 1250 (first query in Listing 9-31). What if it were important to you to keep such records for employees with the same salary value together (similar to the concept of widows and orphans control in typesetting)? Listing 9-33 provides an example of the type of query you could write to keep similar values together while employing row limiting syntax.

Listing 9-33. A Query That Uses the WITH TIES Option of the Row Limiting Clause

```
SQL> select empno, ename||','||init name, job, msal
  2    from employees
  3  order by msal desc
  4  OFFSET 5 ROWS FETCH NEXT 5 ROWS WITH TIES;
```

EMPNO	NAME	JOB	MSAL
7782	CLARK,AB	MANAGER	2450
7499	ALLEN,JAM	SALESREP	1600
7844	TURNER,JJ	SALESREP	1500
7934	MILLER,TJA	ADMIN	1300
7521	WARD,TF	SALESREP	1250
7654	MARTIN,P	SALESREP	1250

```
6 rows selected.
```

Note that even though the query in Listing 9-33 requested five rows, because it employed the WITH TIES option (NEXT 5 ROWS WITH TIES), instead of the ONLY option (NEXT 5 ROWS ONLY), six rows are actually returned. This is because the row limiting clause sorts the data according to the ORDER BY clause, and then sifts through the records to return only those records you've requested. Now we requested that the sort criteria be the MSAL value in descending order. We also requested that the first five records be skipped and not be returned as part of our data set. Then we stated that if five records are included in our result set but the last record actually has the same value for MSAL as another record(s) that is not currently part of our result set, then that record(s) should be included as well.

Note that if this query had used the same ORDER BY clause as that which we used in Listing 9-32, then only five records would have been returned as the entirety of the ORDER BY clause, both the MSAL and NAME values, would be evaluated. Only if the Oracle DBMS found other records with the same combination of MSAL and NAME values would it return extra records (beyond the specified limit of five).

9.8 Flashback Features

This section covers some Oracle-specific extensions to the SQL language. Although they might appear slightly off topic, the flashback features are simply too valuable to remain uncovered in this book.

In Chapter 6, we talked about the concept of *read consistency*. Read consistency means that your SQL statements always get a consistent view of the data, regardless of what other database users or applications do with the same data at the same time. The Oracle DBMS provides a *snapshot* of the data at the point in time when the statement execution began. In the same chapter, you also saw that you can change your session to be READ ONLY so that your query results depend on the data as it was at the beginning of your session.

The Oracle DBMS has its methods to achieve this, without using any locking techniques affecting other database users or applications. How this is done is irrelevant for this book. This section shows some interesting ways to use the same technique, by stating explicitly in your queries that you want to go back in time.

■ **Note** The flashback query feature may need some configuration efforts before you can use it. This is the task of a database administrator. Therefore, it is not covered in this book. See the Oracle documentation for more details.

Before we begin our flashback query experiments, we first create a temporary copy of the EMPLOYEES table, as shown in Listing 9-34. (The listing is generated using SQL*Plus). This allows us to perform various experiments without destroying the contents of the real EMPLOYEES table. We also change the NLS_TIMESTAMP_FORMAT parameter with the ALTER SESSION command to influence how timestamp values are displayed on the screen.

Listing 9-34. Preparing for the Flashback Examples

```
SQL> create table e as select * from employees;
Table created.

SQL> alter session set nls_timestamp_format='DD-MON-YYYY HH24:MI:SS.FF3';
Session altered.

SQL> select localtimestamp as table_created from dual;
TABLE_CREATED
--------------------------------------------------------
01-OCT-2004 10:53:42.746

SQL> update e set msal = msal + 10;
14 rows updated.
SQL> commit;
Commit complete.
```

```
SQL> select localtimestamp as after_update_1 from dual;
AFTER_UPDATE_1
----------------------------------------------------------
01-OCT-2004 10:54:26.138

SQL> update e set msal = msal - 20 where  deptno = 10;
3 rows updated.
SQL> commit;
Commit complete.

SQL> select localtimestamp as after_update_2 from dual;
AFTER_UPDATE_2
----------------------------------------------------------
01-OCT-2004 10:54:42.602

SQL> delete from e where  deptno <= 20;
8 rows deleted.
SQL> commit;
Commit complete.

SQL> select localtimestamp as now          from dual;
NOW
----------------------------------------------------------
01-OCT-2004 10:55:25.623

SQL>
```

■ **Tip**   Don't execute these four steps too quickly in a row. You should take some time in between the steps. This makes it much easier during your experiments to go back to a specific point in time.

AS OF

Listings 9-35 to 9-37 show a first example of a flashback query. First, we select the current situation with a regular query (Listing 9-35). Then we use the AS OF TIMESTAMP option in the FROM clause to go back in time (Listing 9-36). Finally, we look at what happens when you try to go back in time beyond the amount of historical data that Oracle maintains (Listing 9-37). As illustrated in examples in earlier chapters, we use the SQL*Plus ampersand (&) substitution trick, which allows us to repeat the query conveniently with different timestamp values.

Listing 9-35. Evaluating the Current Situation

```
select empno, ename, deptno, msal
from   e;

   EMPNO ENAME    DEPTNO      MSAL
-------- -------- -------- --------
    7499 ALLEN         30      1610
    7521 WARD          30      1260
    7654 MARTIN        30      1260
    7698 BLAKE         30      2860
    7844 TURNER        30      1510
    7900 JONES         30       810
```

Listing 9-36. Querying as of Some Point in the Past

```
select empno, ename, deptno, msal
from   e
       AS OF TIMESTAMP to_timestamp('01-OCT-2004 10:53:47.000');
```

EMPNO	ENAME	DEPTNO	MSAL
7369	SMITH	20	800
7499	ALLEN	30	1600
7521	WARD	30	1250
7566	JONES	20	2975
7654	MARTIN	30	1250
7698	BLAKE	30	2850
7782	CLARK	10	2450
7788	SCOTT	20	3000
7839	KING	10	5000
7844	TURNER	30	1500
7876	ADAMS	20	1100
7900	JONES	30	800
7902	FORD	20	3000
7934	MILLER	10	1300

Listing 9-37. Querying for a Point Too Far Back in Time

```
select empno, ename, deptno, msal
from   e
       AS OF TIMESTAMP to_timestamp('01-OCT-2004 10:53:42.000');
       *
ERROR at line 2:
ORA-01466: unable to read data - table definition has changed
```

Of course, the timestamps to be used in Listing 9-35 depend on the timing of your experiments. Choose appropriate timestamps if you want to test these statements yourself. If you executed the steps of Listing 9-34 with some decent time intervals (as suggested), you have enough appropriate candidate values to play with.

The Oracle error message at the bottom of Listing 9-37 indicates that this query is trying to go back too far in time. In this case, table E didn't even exist. Data definition changes (ALTER TABLE E ...) may also prohibit flashback queries, as suggested by the error message text.

VERSIONS BETWEEN

In Listing 9-38, we go one step further, using the VERSIONS BETWEEN operator. Now we get the complete history of the rows—that is, as far as the Oracle DBMS is able to reconstruct them.

Listing 9-38. Flashback Example: VERSIONS BETWEEN Syntax

```
break on empno

select empno, msal
,      versions_starttime
,      versions_endtime
from   e
       versions between timestamp minvalue and maxvalue
where  deptno = 10
order  by empno, versions_starttime nulls first;
```

```
  EMPNO     MSAL VERSIONS_STARTTIME        VERSIONS_ENDTIME
-------- -------- ------------------------- -------------------------
   7782     2450                            01-OCT-2004 10:54:23.000
            2460 01-OCT-2004 10:54:23.000   01-OCT-2004 10:54:41.000
            2440 01-OCT-2004 10:54:41.000   01-OCT-2004 10:55:24.000
            2440 01-OCT-2004 10:55:24.000
   7839     5000                            01-OCT-2004 10:54:23.000
            5010 01-OCT-2004 10:54:23.000   01-OCT-2004 10:54:41.000
            4990 01-OCT-2004 10:54:41.000   01-OCT-2004 10:55:24.000
            4990 01-OCT-2004 10:55:24.000
   7934     1300                            01-OCT-2004 10:54:23.000
            1310 01-OCT-2004 10:54:23.000   01-OCT-2004 10:54:41.000
            1290 01-OCT-2004 10:54:41.000   01-OCT-2004 10:55:24.000
            1290 01-OCT-2004 10:55:24.000
```

By using the VERSIONS BETWEEN operator in the FROM clause, you introduce several additional pseudo columns, such as VERSIONS_STARTTIME and VERSIONS_ENDTIME. You can use these pseudo columns in your queries.

By using the correct ORDER BY clause (watch the NULLS FIRST clause in Listing 9-38), you get a complete historical overview. You don't see a start time for the three oldest salary values because you created the rows too long ago, and you don't see an end time for the last value because it is the current salary value.

FLASHBACK TABLE

In Chapter 7, you learned that you can rescue an inadvertently dropped table from the recycle bin with the FLASHBACK TABLE command. Listing 9-39 shows another example of this usage.

Listing 9-39. Using FLASHBACK TABLE ... TO BEFORE DROP

```
drop table e;
Table dropped.

SQL> show recyclebin;
ORIGINAL NAME RECYCLEBIN NAME                 OBJECT TYPE  DROP TIME
------------- ------------------------------  ------------ -------------------
E             BIN$8lO2OsyQeOngRQAAAAAAAQ==$0 TABLE        2014-02-13:19:16:05

flashback table e to before drop;
Flashback complete.
```

```
select * from e;
```

EMPNO	ENAME	INIT	JOB	MGR	BDATE	MSAL	COMM	DEPTNO
7499	ALLEN	JAM	SALESREP	7698	20-FEB-1961	1610	300	30
7521	WARD	TF	SALESREP	7698	22-FEB-1962	1260	500	30
7654	MARTIN	P	SALESREP	7698	28-SEP-1956	1260	1400	30
7698	BLAKE	R	MANAGER	7839	01-NOV-1963	2860		30
7844	TURNER	JJ	SALESREP	7698	28-SEP-1968	1510	0	30
7900	JONES	R	ADMIN	7698	03-DEC-1969	810		30

You can go back to any point in time with the FLASHBACK TABLE command, as you can see in Listing 9-40. Note the following important difference: Listings 9-36 and 9-38 show *queries* against table E where you go back in time, but the FLASHBACK TABLE example in Listing 9-40 *changes* the database and restores table E to a given point in time.

Listing 9-40. Another FLASHBACK TABLE Example

```
select count(*) from e;

COUNT(*)
--------
       6

flashback table e to timestamp to_timestamp('&timestamp');
Enter value for timestamp: 01-OCT-2004 10:54:00.000

Flashback complete.

select count(*) from e;

COUNT(*)
--------
      14
```

It is not always possible to go back in time with one table using the FLASHBACK TABLE command. For example, you could have constraints referring to other tables prohibiting such a change. See the *Oracle SQL Language Reference* (http://docs.oracle.com/cd/E16655_01/server.121/e17209/toc.htm) for more details about the FLASHBACK TABLE command.

9.9 Exercises

You can practice applying the advanced retrieval functions covered in this chapter in the following exercises. The answers are presented in Appendix B.

1. It is normal practice that (junior) trainers always attend a course taught by a senior colleague before teaching that course themselves. For which trainer/course combinations did this happen?

2. Actually, if the junior trainer teaches a course for the first time, that senior colleague (see the previous exercise) sits in the back of the classroom in a supporting role. Try to find these course/junior/senior combinations.

3. Which employees never taught a course?

4. Which employees attended all build courses (category BLD)? They are entitled to get a discount on the next course they attend.

5. Provide a list of all employees having the same monthly salary and commission as (at least) one employee of Department 30. You are interested in only employees from other departments.

6. Look again at Listings 9-3 and 9-4. Are they really logically equivalent? Just for testing purposes, search on a nonexisting job and execute both queries again. Explain the results.

7. You saw a series of examples in this chapter about all employees that ever taught an SQL course (in Listings 9-9 through 9-11). How can you adapt these queries in such a way that they answer the negation of the same question (... all employees that *never* ...)?

8. Check out your solution for Exercise 4 in Chapter 8: "For all course offerings, list the course code, begin date, and number of registrations. Sort your results on the number of registrations, from high to low." Can you come up with a more elegant solution now, without using an outer join?

9. Who attended (at least) the same courses as employee 7788?

10. Give the name and initials of all employees at the bottom of the management hierarchy, with a third column showing the number of management levels above them.

CHAPTER 10

■ ■ ■

Views

This chapter covers views, a very important component of the relational model (see Ted Codd's rules in Chapter 1). The first section explains the concept of views. The second section discusses how to use the CREATE VIEW command to create views. In the next section, you'll learn about the various ways you can use views in SQL, in the areas of retrieval, logical data independency, and security.

Then, in Section 10.4, we explore the (im) possibilities of data manipulation via views. How does it work, which are the constraints, and what should we consider? You'll learn about updatable views, nonupdatable views, and the WITH CHECK OPTION clause of the CREATE VIEW command.

Section 10.5 discusses data manipulation via inline views. This name is slightly confusing, because inline views are not "real" views. Rather, they are subqueries in the FROM clause, as discussed in the previous chapter. Data manipulation via inline views allows you to perform various complicated and creative data manipulation operations, which would otherwise be very complex (or impossible) via the underlying base tables.

Section 10.6 covers views and performance. Following that is a section about materialized views. Materialized views are very popular in data warehousing environments, which have relatively high data volumes with mainly read-only access. Materialized views allow you to improve query response times with some form of controlled redundancy.

We then mention global temporary tables briefly, which are used for performance gains in batch jobs, and end by discussing invisible columns. Views that can see the invisible columns come in handy during development.

10.1 What Are Views?

The result of a query is always a table, or more precisely, a *derived* table. Compared with "real" tables in the database, the result of a query is volatile, but nevertheless, the result *is* a table. The only thing that is missing for the query result is a name. Essentially, a view is nothing more than a query with a given name. A more precise definition is as follows:

> *A view is a virtual table with the result of a stored query as its "contents," which are derived each time you access the view.*

The first part of this definition states two things:

- **A view is a virtual *table*:** That is, you can treat a view (in almost all circumstances) as a table in your SQL statements. Every view has a name, and that's why views are also referred to as *named queries*. Views have columns, each with a name and a datatype, so you can execute queries against views, and you can manipulate the "contents" of views (with some restrictions) with INSERT, UPDATE, DELETE, and MERGE commands.

- **A view is a *virtual* table:** In reality, when you access a view, it only *behaves* like a table. Views don't have any rows; that's why the view definition says "contents" (within quotation marks). You define views as named queries, which are stored in the data dictionary; that's why another common term for views is *stored queries*. Each time you access the "contents" of a view, Oracle DBMS retrieves the view query from the data dictionary and uses that query to produce the virtual table.

Data manipulation on a view sounds counterintuitive; after all, views don't have any rows. Therefore you cannot create indexes on views either. Nevertheless, views are supposed to behave like tables as much as possible. If you issue data manipulation commands against a view, the DBMS is supposed to translate those commands into corresponding actions against the underlying base tables. Note that some views are not updatable; that's why Ted Codd's rule (see Chapter 1) explicitly refers to views being *theoretically updatable*. We'll discuss data manipulation via views in Section 10.4 of this chapter.

Views are not only dependent on changes in the *contents* of the underlying base tables, but also on certain changes in the *structure* of those tables. For example, a view doesn't work anymore if you drop or rename columns of the underlying tables that are referenced in the view definition. On the other hand, if you define an index on a column in the underlying table, it may be used by queries against the column via the view.

10.2 View Creation

You can create views with the CREATE VIEW command. Figure 10-1 shows the corresponding syntax diagram.

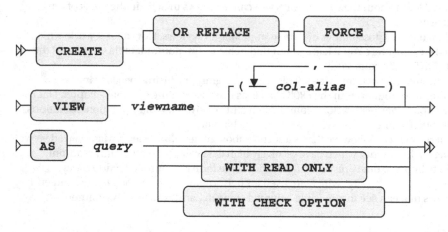

Figure 10-1. *A CREATE VIEW syntax diagram*

The OR REPLACE option allows you to replace an existing view definition. This is especially useful if you have granted various privileges on your views. View privileges are not retained when you use the DROP VIEW / CREATE VIEW command sequence (as explained later in this section), but a CREATE OR REPLACE VIEW command does preserve them. The FORCE option doesn't check whether the underlying base tables (used in the view definition) exist or whether you have sufficient privileges to access those base tables. Obviously, these conditions must eventually be met at the time you start using your view definition.

Normally, views inherit their column names from the defining query. However, you should be aware of some possible complications. For example, you might have a query result on your screen showing multiple columns with the same name, and you may have column headings showing functions or other arbitrary column expressions. Obviously, you cannot use query results with these problems as the basis for a view definition. Views have the same column naming rules and constraints as regular tables: column names must be different, and they cannot contain characters such as brackets and arithmetic operators. You can solve such problems in two ways:

- You can specify column aliases in the SELECT clause of the defining query, in such a way that the column headings adhere to all column naming rules and conventions. In this book's examples, we use this method as much as possible.

- You can specify explicit column aliases in the CREATE VIEW command between the view name and the AS clause (see Figure 10-1).

The WITH CHECK OPTION and WITH READ ONLY options influence view behavior under data manipulation activity, as described later in this chapter, in Section 10-4.

Listing 10-1 shows two very similar SQL statements. However, note the main difference; the first statement creates a *view*, and the second statement creates a *table*.

Listing 10-1. Views vs. Tables

```
SQL> create view dept20_v as
  2  select * from employees where deptno = 20;

View created.

SQL> create table dept20_t as
  2  select * from employees where deptno = 20;

Table created.

SQL>
```

The "contents" of the view DEPT20_V will always be fully dependent on the EMPLOYEES table. The table DEPT20_T uses the current EMPLOYEES table as only a starting point. Once created, it is a fully independent table with its own contents.

Creating a View from a Query

Listing 10-2 shows an example of a regular query with its result. The query is a join over three tables, providing information about all employees and their departments. Note that we use an alias in the SELECT clause (see line 6) to make sure that all columns in the query result have different names. See line 2, where you select the ENAME column, too.

Listing 10-2. A Regular Query, Joining Three Tables

```
SQL> select e.empno
  2  ,       e.ENAME
  3  ,       e.init
  4  ,       d.dname
  5  ,       d.location
  6  ,       m.ENAME      as MANAGER
  7  from    employees   e
  8          join
  9          departments d using (deptno)
 10          join
 11          employees   m on (e.empno = d.mgr);
```

EMPNO	ENAME	INIT	DNAME	LOCATION	MANAGER
7369	SMITH	N	TRAINING	DALLAS	JONES
7499	ALLEN	JAM	SALES	CHICAGO	BLAKE
7521	WARD	TF	SALES	CHICAGO	BLAKE
7566	JONES	JM	TRAINING	DALLAS	JONES
7654	MARTIN	P	SALES	CHICAGO	BLAKE
7698	BLAKE	R	SALES	CHICAGO	BLAKE

```
7782 CLARK    AB    ACCOUNTING NEW YORK CLARK
7788 SCOTT    SCJ   TRAINING   DALLAS   JONES
7839 KING     CC    ACCOUNTING NEW YORK CLARK
7844 TURNER   JJ    SALES      CHICAGO  BLAKE
7876 ADAMS    AA    TRAINING   DALLAS   JONES
7900 JONES    R     SALES      CHICAGO  BLAKE
7902 FORD     MG    TRAINING   DALLAS   JONES
7934 MILLER   TJA   ACCOUNTING NEW YORK CLARK
```

14 rows selected.

SQL>

Listing 10-3 shows how you can transform this query into a view definition, by inserting one additional line at the beginning of the command.

Listing 10-3. Creating a View from the Query in Listing 10-2

```
SQL> create view empdept_v as       -- This line is added
  2  select e.empno
  3  ,      e.ENAME
  4  ,      e.init
  5  ,      d.dname
  6  ,      d.location
  7  ,      m.ENAME    as MANAGER
  8  from   employees   e
  9         join
 10         departments d using (deptno)
 11         join
 12         employees   m on (m.empno = d.mgr);
```

View created.

SQL>

This view is now a permanent part of your collection of database objects. However, note that if we had not used an alias for m.ENAME in line 7, Listing 10-3 would give the following Oracle error message:
ORA-00957: duplicate column name

Getting Information about Views from the Data Dictionary

Listing 10-4 queries the USER_OBJECTS data dictionary view. As you can see, you now have two views in your schema: DEPT20_V and EMPDEPT_V.

Listing 10-4. Querying the Data Dictionary to See Your Views

```
SQL> select object_name, object_type
  2  from   user_objects
  3  where  object_type in ('TABLE','VIEW')
  4  order  by object_type, object_name;
```

```
OBJECT_NAME                      OBJECT_TYPE
-------------------------------  -----------
COURSES                          TABLE
DEPARTMENTS                      TABLE
DEPT20_T                         TABLE
E                                TABLE
EMPLOYEES                        TABLE
HISTORY                          TABLE
OFFERINGS                        TABLE
REGISTRATIONS                    TABLE
SALGRADES                        TABLE
DEPT20_V                         VIEW
EMPDEPT_V                        VIEW

11 rows selected.

SQL>
```

Listing 10-5 shows that you can use the SQL*Plus DESCRIBE command on a view, just as you can on regular tables, and it also shows an example of a query against a view.

Listing 10-5. Using DESCRIBE and Writing Queries Against Views

```
SQL> describe empdept_v
Name                             Null?     Type
-------------------------------  --------  -------------
EMPNO                            NOT NULL  NUMBER(4)
ENAME                            NOT NULL  VARCHAR2(8)
INIT                             NOT NULL  VARCHAR2(5)
DNAME                            NOT NULL  VARCHAR2(10)
LOCATION                         NOT NULL  VARCHAR2(8)
MANAGER                          NOT NULL  VARCHAR2(8)

SQL> select * from empdept_v where manager = 'CLARK';

    EMPNO ENAME    INIT  DNAME      LOCATION MANAGER
--------- -------- ----- ---------- -------- --------
     7934 MILLER   TJA   ACCOUNTING NEW YORK CLARK
     7839 KING     CC    ACCOUNTING NEW YORK CLARK
     7782 CLARK    AB    ACCOUNTING NEW YORK CLARK

SQL>
```

You can query the USER_VIEWS data dictionary view to retrieve your view definitions, as shown in Listing 10-6.

■ **Note**   The two leading SQL*Plus commands in Listing 10-6 are used only to make the results more readable. Chapter 11 discusses these (and many other) SQL*Plus commands in more detail.

Listing 10-6. Retrieving View Definitions from the Data Dictionary

```
SQL> set     long 999
SQL> column text format a42 word wrapped

SQL> select view_name, text
  2  from    user_views;
```

VIEW_NAME	TEXT
DEPT20_V	select "EMPNO","ENAME","INIT","JOB", "MGR","BDATE","MSAL","COMM","DEPTNO" from employees where deptno=20

EMPDEPT_V	select e.empno
	, e.ENAME
	, e.init
	, d.dname
	, d.location
	, m.ENAME as MANAGER
	from · employees e
	        join
	        departments d using (deptno)
	        join
	        employees m on (m.empno = d.mgr)

```
SQL>
```

Apparently, if you define a view with a query starting with SELECT * FROM ..., the asterisk (*) gets expanded (and stored) as a comma-separated list of column names. Compare the query in Listing 10-1, where you created the DEPT20_V view, with the TEXT column contents in Listing 10-6. One might think that by using SELECT * FROM the view will become dynamic and will encompass any future columns added to the underlying table, but that is not the case exactly because the asterisk results in hardcoded column names in the data dictionary saved version of the view.

Replacing and Dropping Views

You cannot *change* the definition of an existing view. Oracle SQL offers an ALTER VIEW command, but you can use that command only to recompile views that became invalid, which would happen after for instance an alter command on the underlying table. You can *drop* a view definition only, with the DROP VIEW command.

The DROP VIEW command is very straightforward, and doesn't need additional explanation:

```
SQL> drop view <view_name>;
```

Alternatively, you can *replace* the definition of an existing view with the CREATE OR REPLACE VIEW command, as described earlier in this section.

10.3 What Can You Do with Views?

You can use views for many different purposes. This section lists and explains the most important ones: to simplify database retrieval, to maintain logical data independence, and to implement data security.

Simplifying Data Retrieval

Views can *simplify* database retrieval significantly. You can build up (and test) complex queries step by step for more control over the correctness of your queries. In other words, you will be more confident that your queries return the right results.

You can also store (hide) frequently recurring *standard queries* in a view definition, thus reducing the number of unnecessary mistakes. For example, you might define views based on frequently joined tables, UNION constructs, or complex GROUP BY statements.

Suppose we are interested in an overview showing all employees who have attended more course days than the average employee. This is not a trivial query, so let's tackle it in multiple phases. As a first step toward the final solution, we ask the question, "How many course days did everyone attend?" The query in Listing 10-7 provides the answer.

Listing 10-7. Working Toward a Solution: Step 1

```
SQL> select    e.empno
  2  ,          e.ename
  3  ,          sum(c.duration) as days
  4  from       registrations  r
  5             join courses   c on (c.code  = r.course)
  6             join employees e on (e.empno = r.attendee)
  7  group by e.empno
  8  ,          e.ename;

  EMPNO ENAME        DAYS
-------- -------- --------
    7900 JONES           3
    7499 ALLEN          11
    7521 WARD            1
    7566 JONES           5
    7698 BLAKE          12
    7782 CLARK           4
    7788 SCOTT          12
    7839 KING            8
    7844 TURNER          1
    7876 ADAMS           9
    7902 FORD            9
    7934 MILLER          4

12 rows selected.

SQL>
```

This is not the solution to our problem yet, but it is already quite complicated. We have a JOIN and a GROUP BY clause over a combination of two columns. If the result in Listing 10-7 were a real table, our original problem would be much easier to solve. Well, we can simulate that situation by defining a view. So we add one extra line to the query in Listing 10-7, as shown in Listing 10-8.

Listing 10-8. Working Toward a Solution: Step 2

```
SQL> create or replace view course_days as
  2  select     e.empno
  3  ,          e.ename
  4  ,          sum(c.duration) as days
  5  from       registrations  r
  6             join courses    c on (c.code = r.course)
  7             join employees e on (e.empno = r.attendee)
  8  group by e.empno
  9  ,          e.ename;

View created.

SQL> select *
  2  from    course_days
  3  where   days > 10;

   EMPNO ENAME       DAYS
-------- -------- --------
    7499 ALLEN         11
    7698 BLAKE         12
    7788 SCOTT         12

SQL>
```

Now, the original problem is rather easy to solve. Listing 10-9 shows the solution.

Listing 10-9. Working Toward a Solution: The Final Step

```
SQL> select *
  2  from    course_days
  3  where   days > (select avg(days)
  4                  from    course_days);

   EMPNO ENAME       DAYS
-------- -------- --------
    7499 ALLEN         11
    7698 BLAKE         12
    7788 SCOTT         12
    7839 KING           8
    7876 ADAMS          9
    7902 FORD           9

SQL>
```

Of course, you could argue that you could solve this query directly against the two base tables, but it is easy to make a little mistake. Moreover, your solution will probably be difficult to interpret. We could have used an inline view as well, or we could have moved the query in Listing 10-7 into a WITH clause, as described in Section 9.4 of Chapter 9. Inline views and subquery factoring (using the WITH clause) are good alternatives if you don't have the right system privileges to create views. A big advantage of using views, compared with inline views and subquery factoring, is the fact that view definitions are persistent; that is, you might benefit from the same view for more than one problem. Views occupy very little space (the DBMS stores the query text only), and there is no redundancy at all.

Maintaining Logical Data Independence

You can use views to change the (logical) external interface of the database, as exposed to database users and applications, without the need to change the underlying database structures themselves. In other words, you can use views to implement *logical data independency*. For example, different database users can have different views on the same base tables. You can rearrange columns, filter on rows, change table and column names, and so on.

Distributed databases often use views (or synonyms) to implement logical data independency and hide complexity. Synonyms are simple pointers, whereas views are (complex) SELECTs with a given name. See Chapter 7 for more about synonyms. For example, you can define (and store) a view as a "local" database object. Behind the scenes, the view query accesses data from other databases on the network, but this is completely transparent to database users and applications.

You can also provide *derivable information* via views; that is, you implement *redundancy* at the *logical* level. The COURSE_DAYS view we created in Listing 10-8 is an example, because that view derives the number of course days.

Implementing Data Security

Last, but not least, views are a powerful means to implement data *security*. Views allow you to hide certain data from database users and applications. The view query precisely determines which rows and columns are exposed via the view. By using the GRANT and REVOKE commands on your views, you specify in detail which actions against the view data are allowed. In this approach, you don't grant any privileges at all on the underlying base tables, since you obviously don't want database users or applications to bypass the views and access the base tables directly.

10.4 Data Manipulation via Views

As you've learned in this chapter, views are virtual tables, and they are supposed to behave like tables as much as possible. For retrieval, that's no problem. However, data manipulation via views is not always possible. A view is *theoretically updatable* if the DML command against the view can be unambiguously decomposed into corresponding DML commands against rows and columns of the underlying base tables.

Let's consider the three views created in Listings 10-10 and 10-11.

Listing 10-10. CRS_OFFERINGS View, Based on a Join

```
SQL> create or replace view crs_offerings as
  2  select o.course as course_code, c.description, o.begindate
  3  from   offerings o
  4         join
  5         courses   c
  6         on (o.course = c.code);

View created.

SQL>
```

Listing 10-11. Simple EMP View and Aggregate AVG_EVALUATIONS View

```
SQL> create or replace view emp as
  2  select empno, ename, init
  3  from   employees;

View created.
```

```
SQL> create or replace view avg_evaluations as
  2  select course
  3  ,         avg(evaluation) as avg_eval
  4  from    registrations
  5  group  by course;

View created.

SQL>
```

First, let's look at the simplest view: the EMP view. The Oracle DBMS should be able to delete rows from the EMPLOYEES table via this view, or to change any of the three column values exposed by the view. However, inserting new rows via this view is impossible, because the EMPLOYEES table has NOT NULL columns without a default value (such as the date of birth) outside the scope of the EMP view. See Listing 10-12 for some DML experiments against the EMP view.

Listing 10-12. Testing DML Commands Against the EMP View

```
SQL> delete from emp
  2  where  empno = 7654;

1 row deleted.

SQL> update emp
  2  set     ename = 'BLACK'
  3  where  empno = 7698;

1 row updated.

SQL> insert into emp
  2  values (7999,'NEWGUY','NN');
insert into e
*
ERROR at line 1:
ORA-01400: cannot insert NULL into ("BOOK"."EMPLOYEES"."BDATE")

SQL> rollback;
Rollback complete.

SQL>
```

Note that the ORA-01400 error message in Listing 10-12 actually reveals several facts about the underlying (and supposedly hidden) table:

- The schema name (BOOK)
- The table name (EMPLOYEES)
- The presence of a mandatory BDATE column

Before you think you've discovered a security breach in the Oracle DBMS, I should explain that you get this informative error message only because you are testing the EMP view while connected as BOOK. If you are connected as a different database user with INSERT privilege against the EMP view only, the error message becomes as follows:

```
ORA-01400: cannot insert NULL into (???)
```

Updatable Join Views

The CRS_OFFERINGS view (see Listing 10-10) is based on a join of two tables: OFFERINGS and COURSES. Nevertheless, you are able to perform some data manipulation via this view, as long as the data manipulation can be translated into corresponding actions against the two underlying base tables. CRS_OFFERINGS is an example of an *updatable join view*. The Oracle DBMS is getting closer and closer to the full implementation of Ted Codd's rule about views (see Chapter 1). Listing 10-13 demonstrates testing some DML commands against this view.

Listing 10-13. Testing DML Commands Against the CRS_OFFERINGS View

```
SQL> delete from crs_offerings where course_code = 'ERM';

1 row deleted.

SQL> insert into crs_offerings (course_code, begindate)
  2           values ('OAU' , trunc(sysdate));

1 row created.

SQL> rollback;
Rollback complete.

SQL>
```

There are some rules and restrictions that apply to updatable join views. Also, the concept of *key-preserved tables* plays an important role in this area. As the name indicates, a key-preserved table is an underlying base table with a one-to-one row relationship with the rows in the view, via the primary key or a unique key.

These are some examples of updatable join view restrictions:

- You are allowed to issue DML commands against updatable join views only if you change a *single* underlying base table.

- For INSERT statements, all columns into which values are inserted must belong to a key-preserved table.

- For UPDATE statements, all columns updated must belong to a key-preserved table.

- For DELETE statements, if the join results in more than one key-preserved table, the Oracle DBMS deletes from the first table named in the FROM clause.

- If you created the view using WITH CHECK OPTION, some additional DML restrictions apply, as explained a little later in this section.

As you can see in Listing 10-13, the DELETE and INSERT statements against the CRS_OFFERINGS updatable join view succeed. Feel free to experiment with other data manipulation commands. The Oracle error messages are self-explanatory if you hit one of the restrictions:

```
ORA-01732: data manipulation operation not legal on this view
ORA-01752: cannot delete from view without exactly one key-preserved table
ORA-01779: cannot modify a column which maps to a non key-preserved table
```

Nonupdatable Views

First of all, if you create a view with the WITH READ ONLY option (see Figure 10-1), data manipulation via that view is impossible by definition, regardless of how you defined the view.

The AVG_EVALUATIONS view definition (see Listing 10-11) contains a GROUP BY clause. This implies that there is no longer a one-to-one relationship between the rows of the view and the rows of the underlying base table. Therefore, data manipulation via the AVG_EVALUATIONS view is impossible.

If you use SELECT DISTINCT in your view definition, this has the same effect: it makes your view nonupdatable. You should try to avoid using SELECT DISTINCT in view definitions, because it has additional disadvantages; for example, each view access will force a sort to take place, whether or not you need it.

The set operators UNION, MINUS, and INTERSECT also result in nonupdatable views. For example, imagine that you are trying to insert a row via a view based on a UNION—in which underlying base table should the DBMS insert that row?

The Oracle documentation provides all of the details and rules with regard to view updatability. Most rules and exceptions are rather straightforward, and as noted earlier, most Oracle error messages clearly indicate the reason why certain data manipulation commands are forbidden.

The data dictionary offers a helpful view to find out which of your view columns are updatable: the USER_UPDATABLE_COLUMNS view. For example, Listing 10-14 shows that you cannot do much with the DESCRIPTION column of the CRS_OFFERINGS view. This is because it is based on a column from the COURSES table, which is not a key-preserved table in this view.

Listing 10-14. View Column Updatability Information from the Data Dictionary

```
SQL> select  column_name
  2  ,        updatable, insertable, deletable
  3  from     user_updatable_columns
  4  where    table_name = 'CRS_OFFERINGS';

COLUMN_NAME          UPD INS DEL
-------------------- --- --- ---
COURSE_CODE          YES YES YES
DESCRIPTION          NO  NO  NO
BEGINDATE            YES YES YES

SQL>
```

MAKING A VIEW UPDATABLE WITH INSTEAD-OF TRIGGERS

In a chapter about views, it's worth mentioning that PL/SQL (the standard procedural programming language for Oracle databases) provides a way to make any view updatable. With PL/SQL, you can define *instead-of triggers* on your views. These triggers take over control as soon as any data manipulation commands are executed against the view.

This means that you can make any view updatable, if you choose, by writing some procedural PL/SQL code. Obviously, it is your sole responsibility to make sure that those instead-of triggers do the "right things" to your database to maintain data consistency and integrity. Instead-of triggers should not be your first thought to solve data manipulation issues with views. However, they may solve your problems in some special cases, or they may allow you to implement a very specific application behavior.

The WITH CHECK OPTION Clause

If data manipulation is allowed via a certain view, there are two rather curious situations that deserve attention:

- You change rows with an UPDATE command against the view, and then the rows don't show up in the view anymore.

- You add rows with an INSERT command against the view; however, the rows don't show up when you query the view.

Disappearing Updated Rows

Do you still have the DEPT20_V view, created in Listing 10-1? Check out what happens in Listing 10-15: by updating four rows, they disappear from the view.

Listing 10-15. UPDATE Makes Rows Disappear

```
SQL> select * from dept20_v;

EMPNO ENAME     INIT  JOB       MGR  BDATE        MSAL  COMM DEPTNO
----- --------- ----- --------- ---- ----------- ----- ----- ------
 7369 SMITH     N     TRAINER   7902 17-DEC-1965   800           20
 7566 JONES     JM    MANAGER   7839 02-APR-1967  2975           20
 7788 SCOTT     SCJ   TRAINER   7566 26-NOV-1959  3000           20
 7876 ADAMS     AA    TRAINER   7788 30-DEC-1966  1100           20
 7902 FORD      MG    TRAINER   7566 13-FEB-1959  3000           20

SQL> update dept20_v
  2  set    deptno = 30
  3  where  job    ='TRAINER';

4 rows updated.

SQL> select * from dept20_v;

EMPNO ENAME     INIT  JOB       MGR  BDATE        MSAL  COMM DEPTNO
----- --------- ----- --------- ---- ----------- ----- ----- ------
 7566 JONES     JM    MANAGER   7839 02-APR-1967  2975           20

SQL> rollback;
Rollback complete.

SQL>
```

Apparently, the updates in Listing 10-15 are propagated to the underlying EMPLOYEES table. All trainers from department 20 don't show up anymore in the DEPT20_V view, because their DEPTNO column value is changed from 20 to 30.

Inserting Invisible Rows

The second curious scenario is shown in Listing 10-16. You insert a new row for employee 9999, and you get the message 1 row created. However, the new employee does not show up in the query.

Listing 10-16. INSERT Rows Without Seeing Them in the View

```
SQL> insert into dept20_v
  2  values ( 9999,'BOS','D', null, null
  3           , date '1939-01-01'
  4           , '10', null, 30);

1 row created.

SQL> select * from dept20_v;

EMPNO ENAME    INIT  JOB       MGR  BDATE        MSAL  COMM DEPTNO
----- -------- ----- -------- ----- ----------- ----- ----- ------
 7369 SMITH    N     TRAINER   7902 17-DEC-1965   800          20
 7566 JONES    JM    MANAGER   7839 02-APR-1967  2975          20
 7788 SCOTT    SCJ   TRAINER   7566 26-NOV-1959  3000          20
 7876 ADAMS    AA    TRAINER   7788 30-DEC-1966  1100          20
 7902 FORD     MG    TRAINER   7566 13-FEB-1959  3000          20

5 rows selected.

SQL> rollback;
Rollback complete.

SQL>
```

Listing 10-16 shows that you can insert a new employee via the DEPT20_V view into the underlying EMPLOYEES table without the new row showing up in the view itself.

Preventing These Two Scenarios

If the view behavior just described is undesirable, you can create your views with the WITH CHECK OPTION clause (see Figure 10-1). Actually, the syntax diagram in Figure 10-1 is not complete. You can assign a name to WITH CHECK OPTION constraints, as follows:

```
SQL> create [or replace] view ... with check option constraint <cons-name>;
```

If you don't provide a constraint name, the Oracle DBMS generates a rather cryptic one for you.

Listing 10-17 replaces the DEPT20_V view, using WITH CHECK OPTION, and shows that the INSERT statement that succeeded in Listing 10-16 now fails with an Oracle error message.

Listing 10-17. Creating Views WITH CHECK OPTION

```
SQL> create or replace view dept20_v as
  2  select * from employees where deptno = 20
  3  with check option constraint dept20_v_check;

View created.
```

```
SQL> insert into dept20_v
  2  values ( 9999,'BOS','D', null, null
  3         , date '1939-01-01'
  4         , '10', null, 30);
       , '10', null, 30)
    *
ERROR at line 4:
ORA-01402: view WITH CHECK OPTION where-clause violation

SQL>
```

Constraint Checking

In the old days, when the Oracle DBMS didn't yet support referential integrity constraints (which is a long time ago, before Oracle7), you were still able to implement certain integrity constraints by using WITH CHECK OPTION when creating views. For example, you could use subqueries in the view definition to check for row existence in other tables. Listing 10-18 gives an example of such a view. Nowadays, you don't need this technique anymore, of course.

Listing 10-18. WITH CHECK OPTION and Constraint Checking

```
SQL> create or replace view reg_view as
  2  select r.*
  3  from    registrations r
  4  where   r.attendee   in (select empno
  5                             from    employees)
  6  and     r.course     in (select code
  7                             from    courses 8 and    r.evaluation in (1,2,3,4,5)
  9  with check option;

View created.

SQL> select constraint_name, table_name
  2  from    user_constraints
  3  where   constraint_type = 'V';

CONSTRAINT_NAME        TABLE_NAME
--------------------   --------------------
SYS_C005979            REG_VIEW
DEPT20_V_CHECK         DEPT20_V

SQL>
```

Via the REG_VIEW view, you can insert registrations only for an existing employee and an existing course. Moreover, the EVALUATION value must be an integer between 1 and 5, or a null value. Any data manipulation command against the REG_VIEW view that violates one of the above three checks will result in an Oracle error message. CHECK OPTION constraints show up in the data dictionary with a CONSTRAINT_TYPE value V; notice the system generated constraint name for the REG_VIEW view.

10.5 Data Manipulation via Inline Views

Inline views are subqueries assuming the role of a *table expression* in SQL commands. In other words, you specify a subquery (between parentheses) in places where you would normally specify a table or view name. We already discussed inline views in the previous chapter, but we considered inline views only in the FROM component of queries.

You can also use inline views for data manipulation purposes. Data manipulation via inline views is especially interesting in combination with updatable join views. Listing 10-19 shows an example of an UPDATE command against an inline updatable join view.

Listing 10-19. UPDATE via an Inline Updatable Join View

```
SQL> update ( select  e.msal
  2               from    employees   e join
  3                       departments d using (deptno)
  4               where  location = 'DALLAS')
  5   set msal = msal + 1;

5 rows updated.

SQL> rollback;
Rollback complete.

SQL>
```

Listing 10-19 shows that you can execute UPDATE commands via an inline join view, giving all employees in Dallas a symbolic salary raise. Note that the UPDATE command does not contain a WHERE clause at all; the inline view filters the rows to be updated. This filtering would be rather complicated to achieve in a regular UPDATE command against the EMPLOYEES table. For that, you probably would need a correlated subquery in the WHERE clause.

At first sight, it may seem strange to perform data manipulation via inline views (or subqueries), but the number of possibilities is almost unlimited. The syntax is elegant and readable, and the response time is at least the same (if not better) compared with the corresponding commands against the underlying base tables. Obviously, all restrictions regarding data manipulation via updatable join views (as discussed earlier in this section) still apply.

10.6 Views and Performance

Normally, the Oracle DBMS processes queries against views in the following way:

1. The DBMS notices that views are involved in the query entered.

2. The DBMS retrieves the view definition from the data dictionary.

3. The DBMS merges the view definition with the query entered.

4. The optimizer chooses an appropriate execution plan for the result of the previous step: a command against base tables.

5. The DBMS executes the plan from the previous step.

In exceptional cases, the Oracle DBMS may decide to execute the view query from the data dictionary, populate a temporary table with the results, and then use the temporary table as a base table for the query entered. This happens only if the Oracle DBMS is not able to merge the view definition with the query entered, or if the Oracle optimizer determines that using a temporary table is a good idea.

In the regular approach, as outlined in the preceding five steps, steps 2 and 3 are the only additional overhead. One of the main advantages of this approach is that you can benefit optimally from indexes on the underlying base tables.

For example, suppose you enter the following query against the AVG_EVALUATIONS view:

```
SQL> select *
  2  from   avg_evaluations
  3  where  avg_eval >= 4
```

This query is transformed internally into the statement shown in Listing 10-20. Notice that the WHERE clause is translated into a HAVING clause, and the asterisk (*) in the SELECT clause is expanded to the appropriate list of column expressions.

Listing 10-20. Rewritten Query Against the REGISTRATIONS Table

```
SQL> select r.course
  2  ,      avg(r.evaluation) as avg_eval
  3  from   registrations r
  4  group  by r.course
  5  having avg(r.evaluation) >= 4;

COURSE AVG_EVAL
------ --------
JAV      4.125
OAU      4.5
XML      4.5

SQL>
```

Especially when dealing with larger tables, the performance overhead of using views is normally negligible. If you start defining views on views on views, the performance overhead may become more significant. And, in case you don't trust the performance overhead, you can always use diagnostic tools such as SQL *Plus or SQL Developer AUTOTRACE (see Chapter 7, Section 7.6) to check execution plans and statistics.

Complex views with many columns joined from several tables are sometimes misused for choosing data from just one of those tables—in which case, the performance will not be impressive. But then again, it might be the only choice when lacking privileges on the underlying tables.

10.7 Materialized Views

A brief introduction of *materialized views* makes sense in this chapter about views. The intent of this section is to illustrate the concept of materialized views using a simple example.

Normally, materialized views are mainly used in complex data warehousing environments, where the tables grow so big that the data volume causes unacceptable performance problems. An important property of data warehousing environments is that you don't change the data very often. Typically, there is a separate Extraction, Transformation, Loading (ETL) process that updates the data warehouse contents.

Materialized views are also often used with distributed databases. In such environments, accessing data over the network can become a performance bottleneck. You can use materialized views to replicate data in a distributed database.

To explore materialized views, let's revisit Listing 10-1 and add a third DDL command, as shown in Listing 10-21.

Listing 10-21. Comparing Views, Tables, and Materialized Views

```
SQL> create or replace VIEW dept20_v as
  2  select * from employees where deptno = 20;

View created.

SQL> create TABLE dept20_t as
  2  select * from employees where deptno = 20;

Table created.

SQL> create MATERIALIZED VIEW dept20_mv enable query rewrite as
  2  select * from employees where deptno = 20;

Materialized view created.

SQL>
```

You already know the difference between a table and a view, but what is a materialized view? Well, as the name suggests, it's a view for which you store both its definition *and* the query results. In other words, a materialized view has its own rows. Materialized views imply redundant data storage.

The materialized view DEPT20_MV now contains all employees of department 20, and you can execute queries directly against DEPT20_MV, if you like. However, that's not the main purpose of creating materialized views, as you will learn from the remainder of this section.

Properties of Materialized Views

Materialized views have two important properties in the areas of *maintenance* and *usage*:

- **Maintenance:** Materialized views are "snapshots." That is, they have a certain content at any point in time, based on "refreshment" from the underlying base tables. This implies that the contents of materialized views are not necessarily up-to-date all the time, because the underlying base tables can change. Fortunately, the Oracle DBMS offers various features to automate the refreshment of your materialized views completely, in an efficient way. In other words, yes, you have redundancy, but you can easily set up appropriate redundancy control.

- **Usage:** The Oracle optimizer (the component of the Oracle DBMS deciding about execution plans for SQL commands) is aware of the existence of materialized views. The optimizer also knows whether materialized views are up-to-date or stale. The optimizer can use this knowledge to replace queries written against regular base tables with corresponding queries against materialized views, if the optimizer thinks that approach may result in better response times. This is referred to as the *query rewrite* feature, which is explained in the next section.

■ **Note**　When you create materialized views, you normally specify whether you want to enable query rewrite, and how you want the Oracle DBMS to handle the refreshing of the materialized view. Those syntax details are used in Listing 10-21 but further usage information is omitted here. See *Oracle SQL Reference* for more information.

Query Rewrite

Let's continue with our simple materialized view, created in Listing 10-21. Assume you enter the following query, selecting all trainers from department 20:

```
SQL> select * from employees where deptno = 20 and job = 'TRAINER'
```

For this query, the optimizer may decide to execute the following query instead:

```
SQL> select * from dept20_mv where job = 'TRAINER'
```

In other words, the original query against the EMPLOYEES table is rewritten against the DEPT20_MV materialized view. Because the materialized view contains fewer rows than the EMPLOYEES table (and therefore fewer rows need to be scanned), the optimizer thinks it is a better starting point to produce the desired end result. Listing 10-22 shows query rewrite at work using the SQL*Plus AUTOTRACE feature.

Listing 10-22. Materialized Views and Query Rewrite at Work

```
SQL> set autotrace on explain
SQL> select * from employees where deptno = 20 and job = 'TRAINER';

EMPNO ENAME    INIT JOB       MGR  BDATE        MSAL COMM DEPTNO
------ -------- ---- -------- ----- ----------- ----- ---- ------
  7369 SMITH    N    TRAINER   7902 17-DEC-1965  800        20
  7788 SCOTT    SCJ  TRAINER   7566 26-NOV-1959 3000        20
  7876 ADAMS    AA   TRAINER   7788 30-DEC-1966 1100        20
  7902 FORD     MG   TRAINER   7566 13-FEB-1959 3000        20

Execution Plan
----------------------------------------------------------
Plan hash value: 2578977254

---------------------------------------------------------------------------------
| Id | Operation                    | Name      | Rows | Bytes | Cost (%CPU)| Time     |
---------------------------------------------------------------------------------
|  0 | SELECT STATEMENT             |           |    4 |   360 |    3   (0)| 00:00:01 |
|* 1 |  MAT_VIEW REWRITE ACCESS FULL| DEPT20_MV |    4 |   360 |    3   (0)| 00:00:01 |
---------------------------------------------------------------------------------

Predicate Information (identified by operation id):
---------------------------------------------------

   1 - filter("DEPT20_MV"."JOB"='TRAINER')

SQL>
```

Although it is obvious from Listing 10-22 that you write a query against the EMPLOYEES table, the execution plan (produced with AUTOTRACE ON EXPLAIN) shows that the materialized view DEPT20_MV is accessed instead.

Materialized views normally provide better response times; however, there is a risk that the results are based on stale data because the materialized views are out of sync with the underlying base tables. You can specify whether you tolerate query rewrites in such cases, thus controlling the behavior of the optimizer. If you want precise results, the optimizer considers query rewrite only when the materialized views are guaranteed to be up-to-date.

Obviously, the materialized view example we used in this section is much too simple. Normally, you create materialized views with relatively "expensive" operations, such as aggregation (GROUP BY), joins over multiple tables, and set operators (UNION, MINUS, and INTERSECT)—operations that are too time-consuming to be repeated over and over again. For more details and examples of materialized views, see *Data Warehousing Guide*.

10.8 Global Temporary Table

Another structure that can hold a query result is a global temporary table (GTT), which come in handy for instance in batch jobs.

In your session you may choose to keep some data in a table that you will first populate by doing a complex query against joined tables, then update the interim result a few times, then query into several different reports, and finally you drop the table.

Since you want to update, a view is seldomly an option. Since you end up by dropping the data, an ordinary table or a materialized view are unnecessarily permanent objects, and so we have Global Temporary Tables. Data in a GTT may last until the end of the transaction or until the end of the session. Notice in the syntax DELETE for transaction life time and PRESERVE for session life time.

```
CREATE GLOBAL TEMPORARY TABLE <table_name>
      (column specifications....)
    ON COMMIT { DELETE | PRESERVE } ROWS;
```

When you commit (or rollback to end the transaction) or exit the session, the data is removed, but the table definition remains in the data dictionary. Several concurrent sessions may use the same GTT since the data is owned exclusively by each session. Performance is better in a GTT exactly because the rows exclusively belong to your session and so need much less locking.

10.9 Invisible Columns

You may be planning for more columns in the next version of your application, but you don't want them to appear yet in SELECT * queries or to risk that INSERT INTO t VALUES... gets an error, so you make the columns INVISIBLE. For exactly this reason, we advise against using SELECT * as well as INSERT INTO... without the column list, so use explicit column selection and INSERT INTO t (x,y) VALUES (1,2), that is, with the column list before VALUES.

Let's make an example table with an invisible column:

```
SQL> create table t (x number, y number);
Table created.

SQL> alter table t add (newcol number INVISIBLE);
Table altered.

SQL> insert into t (x,y,newcol) values (1,2,3);
1 row created.
```

When addressing the column explicitly you of course see it.

```
SQL> select x, y, newcol from t;

         X          Y     NEWCOL
---------- ---------- ----------
         1          2          3
```

With SELECT * you don't see the column.

```
SQL> select * from t;

         X          Y
---------- ----------
         1          2
```

The new thing in 12c is that you can define a view where the column is visible, so you can address it more easily while testing it during development. Columns in views are visible regardless of their visibility in the base table.

```
SQL> create or replace view see_all as select x,y,newcol from t;

View created.
```

If we had specified SELECT * while creating the view, the invisible column from table t would never have made it to the view. The CREATE VIEW command hardcodes the columns it finds and explicitly lists them in the saved view text. Since we explicitly selected the newcol, it is part of the view see_all:

```
SQL> select * from see_all;

         X          Y     NEWCOL
---------- ---------- ----------
         1          2          3
```

In 12c it is possible to make the column INVISIBLE even in the view, if that, for some reason, is your wish. Normally the reason for making the view on top of a table with INVISIBLE columns would be to SEE them, but here is the syntax for making the column invisible even in the view.

```
SQL> create view see_all
2   (x, y, newcol INVISIBLE)
3   as select x, y, newcol from t;

View created.
```

10.10 Exercises

As in the previous chapters, we end this chapter with some practical exercises. See Appendix B for the answers.

1. Look at the example discussed in Listings 10-7, 10-8, and 10-9. Rewrite the query in Listing 10-9 without using a view by using the WITH operator.

2. Look at Listing 10-12. How is it possible that you can delete employee 7654 via this EMP view? There are rows in the HISTORY table referring to that employee via a foreign key constraint.

3. Look at the view definition in Listing 10-18. Does this view implement the foreign key constraints from the REGISTRATIONS table to the EMPLOYEES and COURSES tables? Explain your answer.

4. Create a SAL_HISTORY view providing the following overview for all employees based on the HISTORY table: for each employee, show the hire date, the review dates, and the salary changes as a consequence of those reviews. Check your view against the following result:

```
SQL> select * from sal_history;

EMPNO HIREDATE     REVIEWDATE   SALARY_RAISE
----- ----------- ----------- ------------
 7369 01-JAN-2000 01-JAN-2000
 7369 01-JAN-2000 01-FEB-2000         -150
 7499 01-JUN-1988 01-JUN-1988
 7499 01-JUN-1988 01-JUL-1989          300
 7499 01-JUN-1988 01-DEC-1993          200
 7499 01-JUN-1988 01-OCT-1995          200
 7499 01-JUN-1988 01-NOV-1999         -100
 ...
 7934 01-FEB-1998 01-FEB-1998
 7934 01-FEB-1998 01-MAY-1998            5
 7934 01-FEB-1998 01-FEB-1999           10
 7934 01-FEB-1998 01-JAN-2000           10

79 rows selected.

SQL>
```

■ ■ ■

SQL*Plus Basics and Scripting

Chapter 2 introduced SQL Developer. In this chapter, we introduce SQL*Plus.

■ **Note** SQL*Plus is the oldest Oracle tool still available. It was renamed from UFI (User Friendly Interface) in version 4 to SQL*Plus in Version 5 in the mid 1980s.

This chapter also covers some more advanced features of SQL*Plus for reporting, as well as some advanced uses of SQL*Plus for creating scripts for automation. Knowing how to use SQL*Plus and its features will enhance your SQL writing skills, thus increasing your satisfaction and productivity.

Section 11.1 introduces the SQL*Plus tool and the most essential commands required to get started with SQL, such as the SQL*Plus editor commands (LIST, INPUT, CHANGE, APPEND, DEL, and EDIT), file management (SAVE, GET, START, and SPOOL), and other commands (HOST, DESCRIBE, and HELP).

Section 11.2 introduces various variable types supported by SQL*Plus: substitution variables, user variables, and system variables. When dealing with SQL*Plus variables, the most important commands are SET, SHOW, DEFINE, and ACCEPT.

Section 11.3 explains SQL bind variables. These bind variables are crucial when developing mission-critical database applications if high performance and scalability are important goals.

Section 11.4 introduces the concept of SQL*Plus scripts, how they are created, how they are edited, and how they are executed.

In the previous chapters, the examples illustrate how to use SQL*Plus in an *interactive* way—you enter the commands, press the Enter key, and wait for the results to appear on your screen. Section 11.4 shows that you can also use SQL*Plus to make program modules by using script files, or simply to store something useful for repeated use.

In Section 11.5, you will see how you can use SQL*Plus as a reporting tool by enhancing the layout of the results with SQL*Plus commands such as the TTITLE, BTITLE, COLUMN, BREAK, and COMPUTE commands. You'll also learn how to use SQL*Plus as a *batch programming* environment for both retrieving information from the calling environment and passing information back.

Section 11.6 focuses on various ways you can use SQL*Plus as a database tool in an HTML (browser) environment.

Section 11.7 returns to the topic of SQL*Plus scripts, showing how a script can accept parameters from a calling program, handle error conditions, pass data from one SQL statement to another, and finally return an appropriate exit status to the calling program. This is useful for automating any special operations that your application or database requires.

■ **Note** For obvious reasons, listings in this chapter are all taken directly from SQL*Plus. They show the typical artifacts such as command prompts and substitution prompts that you'll encounter during a SQL*Plus session.

11.1 Introduction to SQL*Plus

SQL*Plus is a tool used to enter SQL commands and display the output. It is provided with every Oracle installation, whether on Windows, Unix, or Linux. It is a command line interface and supports editing, user input, and report formatting.

■ **Note**   In 11g, SQL*Plus for Windows (sqlplusw.exe) is no longer part of the client or database install. The command line version (sqlplus.exe) is still available. You can use an older version of SQL*Plus for Windows to connect to an 11g database, but some functionality may not be supported. SQL Developer, covered in Chapter 2, is a GUI interface that is shipped with 11g and should be considered the replacement for SQL*Plus for Windows.

To start SQL*Plus, simply type 'sqlplus' at the command prompt or after starting a DOS command session in Windows. Under normal circumstances, SQL*Plus prompts you for a username and corresponding password. If you are able to provide a valid username/password combination, the SQL> prompt appears on your screen to indicate that you have successfully established a session.

You can also start SQL*Plus with the username and password at the command line, as shown in Figure 11-1. In this case, if the username/password are valid, the SQL> prompt will appear. If not, you will be asked to enter a valid username and password.

```
SQL*Plus: Release 12.1.0.1.0 Production on Fri Jan 31 18:10:18 2014

Copyright (c) 1982, 2012, Oracle.  All rights reserved.

Enter user-name: book
Enter password:
Last Successful login time: Fri Jan 31 2014 18:08:49 -05:00

Connected to:
Oracle Database 12c Enterprise Edition Release 12.1.0.1.0 - 64bit Production
With the Partitioning, OLAP, Advanced Analytics and Real Application Testing options

SQL> █
```

Figure 11-1. *SQL*Plus screen after a successful connection using the username/password at the command line*

You can leave SQL*Plus with the commands EXIT or QUIT.

Entering Commands

SQL*Plus not only "understands" the SQL language, but it also supports and recognizes several tool-specific SQL*Plus commands. You must make sure to distinguish these SQL*Plus commands from SQL commands, because SQL*Plus treats these two command types differently, as you will see.

Let's start by entering an arbitrary (and rather simple) SQL command in SQL*Plus, as shown in Listing 11-1.

Listing 11-1. A Basic SQL SELECT Command

```
SQL> select *
  2  from    employees;
```

Notice that SQL commands are often spread over multiple lines and, by default, SQL*Plus automatically displays line numbers during SQL command entry. If your SQL command is fully entered and you want SQL*Plus to execute it for you, you should finish the last line with a semicolon (;) as a delimiter. If you forget the semicolon (this will probably happen quite often, initially), you can still enter that semicolon on the next (empty) line, as shown here:

```
SQL> select *
  2  from    employees
  3  ;
```

Either way, the command will execute. SQL*Plus will return all columns and all rows of the EMPLOYEES table, since the asterisk character (*) is used to denote your desire to show all columns of this table.

EMPNO	ENAME	INIT	JOB	MGR	BDATE	MSAL	COMM	DEPTNO
7369	SMITH	N	TRAINER	7902	17-DEC-65	800		20
7499	ALLEN	JAM	SALESREP	7698	20-FEB-61	1600	300	30
7521	WARD	TF	SALESREP	7698	22-FEB-62	1250	500	30
7566	JONES	JM	MANAGER	7839	02-APR-67	2975		20
7654	MARTIN	P	SALESREP	7698	28-SEP-56	1250	1400	30
7698	BLAKE	R	MANAGER	7839	01-NOV-63	2850		30
7782	CLARK	AB	MANAGER	7839	09-JUN-65	2450		10
7788	SCOTT	SCJ	TRAINER	7566	26-NOV-59	3000		20
7839	KING	CC	DIRECTOR		17-NOV-52	5000		10
7844	TURNER	JJ	SALESREP	7698	28-SEP-68	1500	0	30
7876	ADAMS	AA	TRAINER	7788	30-DEC-66	1100		20
7900	JONES	R	ADMIN	7698	03-DEC-69	800		30
7902	FORD	MG	TRAINER	7566	13-FEB-59	3000		20
7934	MILLER	TJA	ADMIN	7782	23-JAN-62	1300		10

Using the SQL Buffer

SQL*Plus stores your most recent SQL command in an area called the *SQL buffer*. The SQL buffer is an important SQL*Plus concept. You can display the contents of the SQL buffer using a SQL*Plus command called LIST, as shown in Listing 11-2.

Listing 11-2. The SQL*Plus LIST Command

```
SQL> L
  1  select *
  2* from employees

SQL>
```

The ability to retrieve the last SQL statement from the SQL buffer is often very useful when you need to correct errors and re-execute the SQL statement. You will see how to do this in the subsequent sections, where we'll also discuss some other SQL*Plus commands related to the SQL buffer.

If you enter a second SQL command, the SQL buffer is overwritten, and you lose the previous SQL command. In the "Saving Commands" section later in this chapter, you will see an easy method to save SQL commands for reuse in SQL*Plus.

Note from the example in Listing 11-2 that the SQL command returned from the SQL buffer did *not* include a semicolon at the end of it. The semicolon is *not* part of the SQL command itself, and it does not end up in the SQL buffer. If you enter a SQL command (or even a portion of a SQL command) and press the Enter key twice, without first adding a semicolon, the command will not be executed, but it will be saved in the SQL buffer.

The SQL*Plus commands you enter are *not* stored in the SQL buffer. You can run as many SQL*Plus commands as you like, but another SQL*Plus LIST command will display the same SQL command.

From the example in Listing 11-2, you can also note several other things about SQL*Plus commands:

- They are normally executed on a single line, unlike most SQL commands.

- You don't need to enter a semicolon to execute SQL*Plus commands. They execute immediately when you press the Enter key.

- SQL*Plus commands can be abbreviated (L stands for LIST), whereas SQL commands cannot.

Rather than just see what is in the buffer, it is often useful to be able to edit its contents and then re-execute the SQL, so let's now move on to discuss how to do that.

Using an External Editor

You can edit the contents of the SQL buffer in two ways:

- Use an external editor of your choice

- Use the built-in SQL*Plus editor

The main advantage of the SQL*Plus editor is that its functionality is always available in SQL*Plus, and the editor is totally independent of the underlying platform. The disadvantage of the SQL*Plus editor is its lack of user-friendliness and its very limited capabilities. This section explains how to use an external editor to edit your SQL commands. The next section will discuss the built-in SQL*Plus editor.

The default external editor under Microsoft Windows is Notepad.

You can also change or display the SQL*Plus external editor preference from the command line by using the DEFINE command, as shown in Listing 11-3.

Listing 11-3. Displaying and Changing the External Editor Preference

```
SQL> define _editor=Notepad

SQL> define _editor
DEFINE _EDITOR        = "Notepad" (CHAR)

SQL>
```

■ **Note** The SQL*Plus variable that holds the name of the external editor is _editor, with a leading underscore in its name.

You can invoke the external editor to change the contents of the SQL buffer. For this purpose, the SQL*Plus command is EDIT. You can invoke the external editor only when your SQL buffer is not empty. An empty buffer results in the error message "nothing to save."

Invoking the external editor starts a subprocess, which means that you cannot return to SQL*Plus until you have closed the external editor window. Alternatively, you may want to start a separate editor session from the operating system (that is, *not* from SQL*Plus) so you can switch between two windows. In that case, you must make sure to save the changes in your editor window before executing the changed SQL command in SQL*Plus.

Using the SQL*Plus Editor

Learning to use the SQL*Plus editing commands is key to being more proficient and efficient in scripting. Instead of starting over if you make a mistake entering a statement, you can make a quick edit and then execute the statement. The editing commands are the same in all versions of SQL*Plus on all platforms.

To explore the SQL*Plus editor, we begin with the same simple SQL SELECT command in the SQL buffer (from the "Entering Commands" section earlier in the chapter):

```
SQL> select *
  2  from    employees;
```

■ **Note**   Please follow all instructions in this section verbatim, even when you think there are some mistakes, because any mistakes are intentional.

It is important to realize that the SQL*Plus editor is line-oriented; that is, there is only one *current line* at any point in time. You can make changes only to that current line. (Perhaps you remember the good old EDLIN editor under MS-DOS?)

SQL*Plus marks the current line on screen with an asterisk (*) after the line number. Normally, it is the line you entered last; in our example, it is the second line.

If you want to change something on the first line, you must first activate that line with the L1 command. Let's try to change the asterisk into two column names. C is an abbreviation for the SQL*Plus command CHANGE. Listing 11-4 demonstrates how to use the LIST and CHANGE commands to make this change. SQL*Plus searches the current line for the first occurrence of an asterisk (*) and changes that character into eename, bdate.

Listing 11-4. Using the SQL*Plus LIST and CHANGE Commands

```
SQL> L
  1  select *
  2* from    employees

SQL> L1
  1* select *

SQL> c/*/eename, bdate/
  1* select eename, bdate

SQL> L
  1  select eename, bdate
  2* from    employees

SQL>
```

Instead of slashes (/), you can use any arbitrary character for the string delimiter (separator) in the CHANGE command. Also, a space character between the C and the first separator is not mandatory, and you can omit the last string delimiter, too.

Now, let's try to execute the SQL command in the buffer again. The SQL*Plus command to execute the contents of the SQL buffer is RUN, abbreviated to R. Apparently we made a mistake; we get an Oracle error message, as shown in Listing 11-5. Observe the error message. First, it shows a line number indication (ERROR at line 1), and within that line, an asterisk (*) indicates the position where the error was detected. Listing 11-5 also shows a first attempt to correct the error and the erroneous result of our CHANGE command.

Listing 11-5. Fixing Typos with the SQL*Plus CHANGE Command

```
SQL> R
  1  select eename, bdate
  2* from    employees
select eename, bdate
       *
ERROR at line 1:
ORA-00904: "EENAME": invalid identifier

SQL> c/e//
  1* slect eename, bdate

SQL>
```

We removed the first occurrence of an e on the first line, instead of the e in eename. This is the default (and only) way the CHANGE command works. This means that you must be careful with this command and be sure to specify appropriate search strings for replacement. In this case, it would have been better to issue the c/ee/e/ command instead.

You can also add text at the end of the current line using the SQL*Plus APPEND command, which is abbreviated A. Listing 11-6 demonstrates how we can first fix the mistake and then add one more column to the SELECT expression.

Listing 11-6. Appending Text with the SQL*Plus APPEND Command

```
SQL> L1
  1* slect eename, bdate

SQL> c/slect ee/select e/
  1* select ename, bdate

SQL> A , deptno
  1* select ename, bdate, deptno

SQL> L
  1  select ename, bdate, deptno
  2* from    employees

SQL>
```

Note that the SQL*Plus APPEND command does not insert a space by default. In this case, we don't need a space, but otherwise you should specify a second space character after the APPEND command.

You can also add one or more additional lines to the SQL buffer with the SQL*Plus INPUT command (abbreviated I), as shown in Listing 11-7. The lines you enter are added *below* the current line. If the current line is the last line in the buffer, the new lines are added at the end of the statement. This also means you need a "special trick" to add lines before the first line, as you'll learn in the next section. Notice the line numbering; SQL*Plus automatically generates appropriate line numbers while entering text. You can stop entering additional lines by pressing the Enter key twice, or by entering a semicolon when you are adding lines at the end of the buffer.

Listing 11-7. Inserting Text with the SQL*Plus INPUT Command

```
  1  select ename, bdate, deptno
  2* from    employees

SQL> I
  3  where  deptno = 30;

ENAME     BDATE         DEPTNO
--------  -----------   --------
ALLEN     20-FEB-1961       30
WARD      22-FEB-1962       30
MARTIN    28-SEP-1956       30
BLAKE     01-NOV-1963       30
TURNER    28-SEP-1968       30
JONES     03-DEC-1969       30

SQL>
```

■ **Note** The I is an abbreviation for INPUT, *not* for INSERT. INSERT is an SQL command (to add rows to a table in the database).

The SQL*Plus DEL command deletes the current line from the SQL buffer. You can optionally specify a line number with the DEL command to remove a certain line from the SQL buffer without making that line the current line first or a range of line numbers to remove several lines with a single DEL command. See Listing 11-8 for an example.

Listing 11-8. Deleting Lines with the SQL*Plus DEL Command

```
SQL> L
  1  select ename, bdate, deptno
  2  from    employees
  3* where  deptno = 30

SQL> DEL

SQL> L
  1  select ename, bdate, deptno
  2* from    employees

SQL>
```

■ **Note** DEL is *not* an abbreviation for DELETE, because DELETE is an SQL command (to remove rows from a table in the database.)

Using SQL Buffer Line Numbers

You can make any line the current one by just entering the line number, without the L (LIST) command, as shown in Listing 11-9.

Listing 11-9. Using Line Numbers to Change the Current Line

```
SQL> L
  1  select code, description
  2  from    courses
  3* where   category = 'DSG'

SQL> 2
  2* from    courses

SQL> 42
SP2-0226: Invalid line number

SQL>
```

Using line numbers, you can also *replace* any line in the SQL buffer without needing to use the SQL*Plus DEL command followed by a SQL*Plus INPUT command. Instead, simply enter the desired new line preceded by its line number. Listing 11-10 shows how to replace the first line and add a line at the end of the SQL buffer. Notice that the high line number (42) does not generate an error message, as it does in the example in Listing 11-9.

Listing 11-10. Using Line Numbers to Change the SQL Buffer

```
SQL> 1 select *

SQL> L
  1  select *
  2  from    courses
  3* where   category = 'DSG'

SQL> 42 order  by code

SQL> L
  1  select *
  2  from    courses
  3  where   category = 'DSG'
  4* order   by code

SQL>
```

As explained earlier, the SQL*Plus INPUT command always inserts lines *below* the current line. The trick to insert extra lines *before* the first line is to "overwrite" the artificial line zero, as demonstrated in Listing 11-11. This is a rather trivial example; however, this trick can be quite useful when creating views. Views are discussed in Chapter 10.

Listing 11-11. Inserting Text Before the First Line of the SQL Buffer

```
  1  select *
  2  from    courses
  3  where   category = 'DSG'
  4* order  by code

SQL> 0 /* this is just a comment */

SQL> L
  1  /* this is just a comment */
  2  select *
  3  from    courses
  4  where   category = 'DSG'
  5* order  by code

SQL>
```

Using the Ellipsis

If you are using the SQL*Plus CHANGE command, you might benefit from using three consecutive period characters, also known as the *ellipsis*. The examples in Listings 11-12 and 11-13 demonstrate the effect of using the ellipsis. First, we enter a new SQL command into the buffer and deliberately make a mistake.

Listing 11-12. Entering a SQL Command with a Deliberate Error

```
SQL> select mgr, department_name
  2  from    departments
  3  where   location = 'SCHIERMONNIKOOG';
select mgr, department_name
                *
ERROR at line 1:
ORA-00904: "DEPARTMENT_NAME": invalid identifier

SQL>
```

Normally, the last command line you entered into the SQL buffer is automatically the current line. However, if an error condition occurs (such as in Listing 11-12), the line where the error is found becomes the current line. This allows you to correct any mistakes with the SQL*Plus CHANGE command immediately, without activating any line with the SQL*Plus LIST command. Listing 11-13 demonstrates this phenomenon; the asterisk in the L* command is used to show the current line.

Listing 11-13. Using the SQL*Plus L* Command and the Ellipsis (. . .)

```
SQL> L*
  1* select mgr, department_name

SQL> c/d.../dname
  1* select mgr, dname
```

```
SQL> 3
  3* where  location = 'SCHIERMONNIKOOG'

SQL> c/s...g/BOSTON
  3* where  location = 'BOSTON'

SQL>
```

The last example in Listing 11-13 demonstrates that all CHANGE command searches are case-insensitive. As you can see, the ellipsis is powerful, but it's also dangerous. For example, the command c/d.../dname searches for the *first* occurrence of a d on the first line and then replaces everything to the end of the line.

SQL*Plus Editor Command Review

The SQL*Plus editor is a rather simple editor; nevertheless, it makes sense to spend some time to explore its possibilities. It might come in handy when you need to work with the Oracle DBMS in an environment that is completely unknown to you, or where you are not allowed to launch an external editor from the underlying operating system. The SQL*Plus editor is always available, and it's identical on all platforms supported by Oracle.

Table 11-1 summarizes all the SQL*Plus editor commands covered in this chapter, so far.

Table 11-1. *Some SQL*Plus Editor-Related Commands*

Command	Description
LIST	Show the complete SQL buffer.
LIST n (or just n)	Make line n the current line.
CHANGE/old/new/	Change the first occurrence of old into new on the current line.
APPEND txt	Append txt to the end of the current line.
INPUT	Insert line(s) below the current line.
DEL [x [y]]	Without arguments: remove current line. One argument: remove that line. Two arguments: remove range of lines (x and y can be line numbers, *, or LAST).
RUN (or /)	Execute the contents of the SQL buffer.
EDIT	Start an external editor on the current buffer contents.
DEFINE _EDITOR	Define your preferred external editor.

As Table 11-1 shows, you can use the forward slash (/) command as an alternative to the SQL*Plus RUN command. The difference between the two is that RUN always displays the SQL command *and* the results, whereas the forward slash (/) command displays the results only.

Saving Commands

As explained earlier in the chapter, the SQL buffer is overwritten with every new SQL command you enter in SQL*Plus. If you want to save the contents of the SQL buffer, you can use the SQL*Plus SAVE command. The SAVE command creates a script file containing the contents of the SQL buffer.

If a script file already exists, you can specify (with the options APPEND or REPLACE) what you want the SAVE command to do in that case. The APPEND option is useful if you want to save all your SQL commands in one single file, for example, to print that file later.

In Microsoft Windows, the options for saving the contents of the SQL buffer are also available via the File pull-down menu of SQL*Plus, as shown in Figure 11-2.

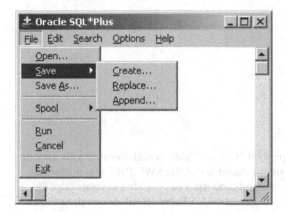

Figure 11-2. *The SQL*Plus options for saving the SQL buffer contents*

As an example of saving SQL commands, enter the commands shown in Listing 11-14.

Listing 11-14. The SQL*Plus SAVE Command

```
SQL> save result1

SQL> select * from departments;

DEPTNO DNAME      LOCATION  MGR
------ ---------- -------- -----
    10 ACCOUNTING NEW YORK  7782
    20 TRAINING   DALLAS    7566
    30 SALES      CHICAGO   7698
    40 HR         BOSTON    7839

SQL> save result2
Created file result2.sql

SQL> select * from courses;

CODE DESCRIPTION                    CAT DURATION
---- ------------------------------ --- --------
SQL  Introduction to SQL            GEN        4
OAU  Oracle for application users   GEN        1
JAV  Java for Oracle developers     BLD        4
PLS  Introduction to PL/SQL         BLD        1
XML  XML for Oracle developers      BLD        2
ERM  Data modeling with ERM         DSG        3
```

```
PMT  Process modeling techniques    DSG      1
RSD  Relational system design       DSG      2
PRO  Prototyping                    DSG      5
GEN  System generation              DSG      4

10 rows selected.

SQL> save result1
SP2-0540: File "result1.sql" already exists.
Use "SAVE filename[.ext] REPLACE".

SQL> save result1 replace
Created file result1.sql

SQL>
```

Note the error message after the second SAVE RESULT1 attempt; REPLACE (or APPEND) is mandatory if a file already exists. Since the SQL buffer is overwritten with each new SQL command issued, using the SAVE APPEND syntax when creating a script file can be useful if you would like any new SQL commands you issue to be added to your script file.

We have created two script files. These script files are assigned the extension, .SQL, by default. If you prefer to use a different file name extension, you can change it with the SQL*Plus SUFFIX setting.

Running SQL*Plus Scripts

You can load script files saved with the SAVE command back into the SQL buffer with the GET command, followed by the name of the script. For example, you might reload a script and then edit it. If you want to load a script file and immediately execute it, you can use the START command (to get and run the script), as shown in Listing 11-15.

Listing 11-15. Using the SQL*Plus GET and START Commands

```
SQL> GET result1
  1* select * from courses

SQL> START result2

DEPTNO DNAME        LOCATION   MGR
------ ----------   --------   -----
    10 ACCOUNTING  NEW YORK   7782
    20 TRAINING    DALLAS     7566
    30 SALES       CHICAGO    7698
    40 HR          BOSTON     7839

SQL>
```

Listing 11-16 shows how you can also use the @ symbol shortcut for the SQL*Plus START command.

Listing 11-16. Using the SQL*Plus @ Command

```
SQL> L
  1* select * from departments

SQL> @result1
CODE DESCRIPTION                    CAT DURATION
---- ------------------------------ --- --------
SQL  Introduction to SQL            GEN        4
OAU  Oracle for application users   GEN        1
JAV  Java for Oracle developers     BLD        4
PLS  Introduction to PL/SQL         BLD        1
XML  XML for Oracle developers      BLD        2
ERM  Data modeling with ERM         DSG        3
PMT  Process modeling techniques    DSG        1
RSD  Relational system design       DSG        2
PRO  Prototyping                    DSG        5
GEN  System generation              DSG        4

10 rows selected.

SQL>
```

Specifying Directory Path Specifications

The SQL*Plus commands SAVE, GET, and START can handle full file name specifications, with directory paths. In the absence of a directory path, these commands default to the current directory. In a Microsoft Windows environment, it is relatively simple to define the directory (or folder) in which you want SQL*Plus to start. This is one of the shortcut properties, which you can set in the Start In field of the Properties dialog box, shown in Figure 11-3. Right-click the SQL*Plus icon and select Properties to open this dialog box.

Figure 11-3. *SQL*Plus shortcut properties*

Through the Properties dialog box, you can also simplify the process to start SQL*Plus by specifying your username and password (such as book/book) in the Target field. In that case, the standard log on dialog will be skipped. However, this is a security risk, because anyone with access to your keyboard for more than two seconds will find out your database name and password.

■ **Tip**   Under Microsoft Windows, you can also set the SQLPATH Registry setting to define a default search path for all files that cannot be found in the current directory. For example, you could have this Registry setting point to a central directory where you maintain all your generic SQL scripts. Just open the Registry Editor with the REGEDIT command and search for SQLPATH. Under other operating systems, check out the SQLPATH environment variable.

Adjusting SQL*Plus Settings

You can modify the behavior of SQL*Plus in numerous ways, based on SQL*Plus variables or settings. This section provides some simple examples to give you an idea of how this works. Listing 11-17 demonstrates using the SET command to change some SQL*Plus settings.

Listing 11-17. Changing SQL*Plus Settings with the SET Command

```
SQL> set pagesize 22
SQL> set pause "Hit [Enter]... "
SQL> set pause on

SQL> run
  1* select * from courses

Hit [Enter]...
```

The effect of changing the PAUSE and PAGESIZE settings as shown in Listing 11-17 is that SQL*Plus now produces screen output per page, in this case, 22 lines at a time. The PAUSE setting is useful if the results of your SQL commands don't fit on your screen.

■ **Tip**   When using the PAUSE setting, don't just switch it on or off; make sure to specify a prompt string, too. Otherwise, SQL*Plus will just wait until you press the Enter key.

You can display the current values of SQL*Plus settings with the SHOW command, and you can revert to the default behavior with the SET command. Listing 11-18 shows examples of using these commands.

Listing 11-18. Displaying SQL*Plus Settings with the SHOW Command

```
SQL> show pages
pagesize 22

SQL> show pause
PAUSE is ON and set to "Hit [Enter]... "

SQL> set pause off

SQL> show pause
PAUSE is OFF

SQL>
```

Although we are discussing the SQL*Plus tool in this section, there is also another (client tool-independent) way to influence your database session behavior: by using the SQL command ALTER SESSION. With this command, you can set several NLS (National Language Support) session parameters, a selection of which are shown in Table 11-2.

Table 11-2. *Examples of NLS Session Parameters*

Parameter	Description
NLS_DATE_FORMAT	Default format to display dates
NLS_TIME_FORMAT	Default format to display timestamps
NLS_LANGUAGE	The language for SQL*Plus feedback and messages
NLS_NUMERIC_CHARACTERS	The decimal point and group separator characters
NLS_CURRENCY	The currency symbol

The most important parameter in this list is probably NLS_DATE_FORMAT, because this parameter influences the way date values are interpreted and displayed by your session, which is often a source of confusion. Listing 11-19 demonstrates an example of using the ALTER SESSION command to set some NLS session parameters.

Listing 11-19. Changing NLS Parameters with ALTER SESSION

```
SQL> alter session
  2   set   nls_date_format='dd-mm-yyyy'
  3         nls_language=Dutch
  4         nls_currency='Eur';

Sessie is gewijzigd.

SQL>
```

■ **Note**   Please note that the ALTER SESSION command, demonstrated in Listing 11-19, would work correctly only if your global database characterset, chosen during database creation, contained language settings for the Dutch language. The AL32UTF8 characterset is a universal characterset that contains, among many other language character settings, the character settings necessary for the Dutch language.

If you change settings with the ALTER SESSION command, or if you change certain SQL*Plus settings with the SQL*Plus SET command, you lose these changes as soon as you log off. On startup, SQL* Plus will use the default values again. If you want to avoid the hassle of applying the same changes over and over again, you can store these SQL and SQL*Plus commands in a file with the special name, login.sql. This file is automatically executed when you start SQL*Plus, or even when you change connections within a SQL*Plus session with the CONNECT command. Note that SQL*Plus must be able to find this file in the directory it starts in or via the SQLPATH Registry setting. login.sql is an example of a SQL*Plus script.

If the rows of a result table don't fit on a single line on your screen (and the line wrapping makes the result rather ugly), a solution might be to narrow the display of one or more columns with the SQL*Plus COLUMN command. By default, SQL*Plus displays all columns on the screen with a width derived from the corresponding column definitions found in the data dictionary. Listing 11-20 demonstrates how you can narrow (or widen) the display of alphanumeric columns on your screen by using the FORMAT option of the COLUMN command.

Listing 11-20. Changing the Width of Alphanumeric Columns

```
SQL> select * from courses
  2   where  category = 'BLD';

CODE DESCRIPTION                    CAT DURATION
---- ------------------------------ --- --------
JAV  Java for Oracle developers     BLD        4
PLS  Introduction to PL/SQL         BLD        1
XML  XML for Oracle developers      BLD        2

SQL> COLUMN description FORMAT a26
SQL> /
```

```
CODE DESCRIPTION                  CAT DURATION
---- --------------------------   --- --------
JAV  Java for Oracle developers   BLD        4
PLS  Introduction to PL/SQL       BLD        1
XML  XML for Oracle developers    BLD        2

SQL>
```

All SQL*Plus commands (and their optional components) can be abbreviated, as long as the abbreviation is unique. For example, the COLUMN command can be abbreviated to COL, and FORMAT can be abbreviated to FOR (see Listing 11-21).

You can influence the width of numeric columns in a similar way, as you can see in Listing 11-21.

Listing 11-21. Changing the Display of Numeric Columns

```
SQL> select * from salgrades
  2  where grade > 3;

GRADE LOWERLIMIT UPPERLIMIT BONUS
----- ---------- ---------- -----
    4       2001       3000   200
    5       3001       9999   500

SQL> COL bonus FOR 9999.99
SQL> /

GRADE LOWERLIMIT UPPERLIMIT    BONUS
----- ---------- ---------- --------
    4       2001       3000   200.00
    5       3001       9999   500.00

SQL>
```

If you want to save all your current SQL*Plus settings in a file (a SQL*Plus script file), use the STORE SET command. See Listing 11-22 for the syntax of this command.

Listing 11-22. SQL*Plus STORE SET Command Syntax

```
SQL> STORE SET <filename>[.sql] [REPLACE|APPEND]
```

The brackets in Listing 11-22 (around .sql and REPLACE|APPEND) are part of a common syntax notation convention to denote optional command clauses. This convention is also used in Appendix A of this book. In this convention, a vertical bar (|) can be used to separate optional choices, as in [REPLACE|APPEND]. Uppercase components such as SET and APPEND should be entered verbatim; lowercase components (such as <filename>) should be replaced (in this case) by a file name of your own choice. See Appendix A for more details.

If you have saved all SQL*Plus settings in a script file by using the STORE SET command, you can restore those settings at any time using the START (or @) command. This allows you to write SQL*Plus scripts that capture all SQL*Plus settings at the beginning, change various settings during script execution, and then restore the original settings at the end of the script.

Spooling a SQL*Plus Session

You can record the complete results (as displayed on your screen) of a SQL*Plus session in an operating system file, using the SQL*Plus SPOOL command. Listing 11-23 demonstrates this capability.

Listing 11-23. Using the SQL*Plus SPOOL Command

```
SQL> spool all_results.TXT [create|replace|append]
SQL> select * from employees;
...
SQL> select * from departments;
...
SQL> spool off
```

The ALL_RESULTS.TXT file, created in the same directory or folder where the SAVE command stores its script files, now contains a complete copy of all screen output. As Listing 11-23 shows, you can influence the behavior of the SPOOL command by specifying one of the following keywords: CREATE, REPLACE, or APPEND. With these three options, you can specify which behavior you want in case the specified file already exists. Just try these options for yourself; the error messages are self-explanatory.

Describing Database Objects

When formulating SQL commands, it is sometimes convenient to get a quick overview of the structure of a table, for example, to see the column names and the datatypes. In such cases, the SQL*Plus DESCRIBE command is what you need. See Listing 11-24 for an example.

Listing 11-24. The SQL*Plus DESCRIBE Command

```
SQL> descr employees

 Name                            Null?    Type
 ------------------------------- -------- --------------------
 EMPNO                           NOT NULL NUMBER(4)
 ENAME                           NOT NULL VARCHAR2(8)
 INIT                            NOT NULL VARCHAR2(5)
 JOB                                      VARCHAR2(8)
 MGR                                      NUMBER(4)
 BDATE                           NOT NULL DATE
 MSAL                            NOT NULL NUMBER(6,2)
 COMM                                     NUMBER(6,2)
 DEPTNO                                   NUMBER(2)

SQL>
```

Executing Commands from the Operating System

The HOST command (most implementations support a platform-specific shortcut, such as $ or !) allows you to temporarily leave your current SQL*Plus session to execute commands at the underlying operating system; for example, on a Microsoft Windows system, a command window is opened. Depending on the underlying operating system, you can finish the subsession and return to your SQL*Plus session with EXIT, LOGOUT, or a similar command.

Clearing the Buffer and the Screen

With the CLEAR BUFFER command, you can empty the SQL buffer in SQL*Plus. This is something you won't need to do too often, because the SQL buffer is overwritten each time by consecutive commands.

With the CLEAR SCREEN command, you can start at the top of a new, empty SQL*Plus screen.

SQL*Plus Command Review

Table 11-3 displays an overview of all SQL*Plus commands covered in this chapter thus far (including the SQL*Plus editor commands already listed in Table 11-2).

*Table 11-3. Some SQL*Plus Commands*

Command	Description
SAVE	Save the SQL buffer contents in a script file
GET	Read a saved script file back into the SQL buffer
START or @	Execute the contents of a script file
SPOOL	Copy all screen output to a file
SET	Change a SQL*Plus setting
SHOW	Show the current value of SQL*Plus settings
COLUMN ... FORMAT	Change screen display attributes of a column
STORE SET	Save the current SQL*Plus settings in a script file
DESCRIBE	Provide a description of a database object
HOST, $ or !	Start a subsession at the operating system level
CLEAR BUFFER	Empty the SQL buffer
CLEAR SCREEN	Start with an empty SQL*Plus screen

We also introduced the following SQL command in this section: ALTER SESSION. This command changes various settings for your session, such as NLS settings.

11.2 SQL*Plus Variables

SQL*Plus supports the following three variable types:

- Substitution variables
- User-defined variables
- System variables

SQL*Plus Substitution Variables

Substitution variables appear in SQL or SQL*Plus commands. SQL*Plus prompts for a value when you execute those commands. We have used substitution variables in earlier examples in this book (Listing 5-14, for example), to test certain commands multiple times with different literal values.

Substitution variable values are volatile; that is, SQL*Plus doesn't remember them and doesn't store them anywhere. This is what distinguishes substitution variables from the other two types. If you execute the same SQL or SQL*Plus command again, SQL*Plus prompts for a value again. The default character that makes SQL*Plus prompt for a substitution variable value is the ampersand (&), also known as the DEFINE character. Check out what happens in Listing 11-25.

Listing 11-25. Using the DEFINE Character (&)

```
SQL> select * from departments
  2  where dname like upper('%&letter%');

Enter value for letter: a
old   2: where dname like upper('%&letter%')
new   2: where dname like upper('%a%')

  DEPTNO DNAME      LOCATION     MGR
-------- ---------- -------- --------
      10 ACCOUNTING NEW YORK    7782
      20 TRAINING   DALLAS      7566
      30 SALES      CHICAGO     7698

SQL>
```

Actually, if a substitution variable occurs twice within a single command, SQL*Plus also prompts twice for a value, as demonstrated in Listing 11-26.

Listing 11-26. Prompting Twice for the Same Variable

```
SQL> select ename from employees
  2  where  empno between &x and &x+100;

Enter value for x: 7500
Enter value for x: 7500
old   2: where  empno between &x and &x+100
new   2: where  empno between 7500 and 7500+100

ENAME
--------
WARD
JONES

SQL>
```

You can use the period character (.) to mark the end of the name of a substitution variable, as shown in Listing 11-27. The period (.) is also known as the CONCAT character in SQL*Plus.

Normally, you don't need the CONCAT character very often, because white space is good enough to delimit variable names; however, white space in strings can sometimes be undesirable. See Listing 11-27 for an example.

Listing 11-27. Using the DEFINE and CONCAT Characters

```
SQL> select '&drink.glass' as result from dual;

Enter value for drink: beer
old   1: select '&drink.glass' as result from dual
new   1: select 'beerglass' as result from dual

RESULT
---------
beerglass

SQL>
```

Note that you can display the current settings of the DEFINE and CONCAT characters with the SQL*Plus SHOW command, and you can change these settings with the SQL*Plus SET command, as shown in Listing 11-28.

Listing 11-28. Displaying the DEFINE and CONCAT Character Settings

```
SQL> show define
define "&" (hex 26)

SQL> show concat
concat "." (hex 2e)

SQL>
```

If you don't want SQL*Plus to display the explicit replacement of substitution variables by the values you entered (as in Listings 11-25, 11-26, and 11-27), you can suppress this display with the SQL*Plus VERIFY setting, as shown in Listing 11-29.

Listing 11-29. Switching the VERIFY Setting ON and OFF

```
SQL> set  verify on
SQL> set  verify off
SQL> show verify
verify OFF

SQL>
```

If you change the VERIFY setting to OFF, as shown in Listing 11-29, and you execute the SQL command (still in the SQL buffer) with the SQL*Plus RUN command, you don't see the "old: ..." and "new: ..." lines anymore, as shown in Listing 11-30.

Listing 11-30. The Effect of VERIFY OFF

```
SQL> select ename from employees
  2  where  empno between &x and &x+100;

Enter value for x: 7500
Enter value for x: 7500
```

```
ENAME
--------
WARD
JONES

SQL>
```

SQL*Plus User-Defined Variables

If you want to store the value of a SQL*Plus variable (at least temporarily) so you can use it multiple times, you need the next category of SQL*Plus variables: *user-defined variables*.

You can use the SQL*Plus DEFINE command to declare user-defined variables and to assign values to them, as shown in Listing 11-31.

Listing 11-31. Assigning Values to User-Defined Variables with DEFINE

```
SQL> define x=7500

SQL> select ename from employees
  2  where   empno between &x and &x+100;

ENAME
--------
WARD
JONES

SQL>
```

The DEFINE command in Listing 11-31 stores the user-defined variable X with its value 7500. That's why SQL*Plus doesn't prompt for a value for X anymore in Listing 11-31.

The SQL*Plus DEFINE command not only allows you to *assign* values to user-defined variables, but also to display current values. Using the DEFINE command, you can display the value of a specific variable. You can also display a complete listing of all user-defined variables by not specifying a variable name and just entering the DEFINE command itself. The SQL*Plus UNDEFINE command allows you to remove a user-defined variable. Listing 11-32 demonstrates examples of DEFINE and UNDEFINE.

Listing 11-32. DEFINE and UNDEFINE Examples

```
SQL> def x
DEFINE X                = "7500" (CHAR)

SQL> def
DEFINE _DATE            = "02-FEB-2014" (CHAR)
DEFINE _CONNECT_IDENTIFIER = "orcl" (CHAR)
DEFINE _USER            = "BOOK" (CHAR)
DEFINE _PRIVILEGE       = "" (CHAR)
DEFINE _SQLPLUS_RELEASE = "1201000100" (CHAR)
DEFINE _EDITOR          = "vim" (CHAR)
DEFINE _O_VERSION       = "
Oracle Database 12c Enterprise Edition Release 12.1.0.1.0 - 64bit Production
With the Partitioning, OLAP, Advanced Analytics and Real Application Testing options" (CHAR)
```

```
DEFINE _O_RELEASE      = "1201000100" (CHAR)
DEFINE X               = "7500" (CHAR)

SQL> undefine x
SQL>
```

Implicit SQL*Plus User-Defined Variables

SQL*Plus also supports syntax allowing you to define variables implicitly. With this method, you start with *substitution variables* in your SQL and SQL*Plus commands, and you end up with *user-defined variables*; SQL*Plus prompts for a value only once. You can implement this behavior by using double ampersands (&&). Look at the experiments in Listing 11-33, showing that you start out without an ENR variable, you are prompted for a value only once, and then an implicit DEFINE is executed.

Listing 11-33. Using Double Ampersands (&&)

```
SQL> define enr
SP2-0135: symbol enr is UNDEFINED

SQL> select * from employees
  2  where  empno between &&enr and &enr+100;

Enter value for enr: 7500

EMPNO ENAME     INIT  JOB       MGR  BDATE       MSAL  COMM DEPTNO
----- --------  ----  --------  ---- ----------- ----- ----- ------
 7521 WARD      TF    SALESREP  7698 22-FEB-1962 1250   500     30
 7566 JONES     JM    MANAGER   7839 02-APR-1967 2975           20

SQL> define enr
DEFINE ENR             = "7500" (CHAR)
SQL>
```

If you now re-execute the contents of the SQL buffer (with / or RUN), there is no prompting at all; the stored ENR value (7500) is used. So if you use this technique, make sure to end (or start) your scripts with the appropriate UNDEFINE commands.

User-Friendly Prompting

SQL*Plus provides a more user-friendly method to create user-defined variables and prompt for values, while offering some more control over the values as well. This method is especially useful with SQL*Plus scripts (discussed in Section 11.4). User-friendly prompting uses a combination of the three SQL*Plus commands: PROMPT, PAUSE, and ACCEPT. Listing 11-34 demonstrates an example.

Note that you can split a SQL*Plus command over multiple lines, as shown in Listing 11-34 in the ACCEPT command example. Normally, the newline character is a SQL*Plus command delimiter, but you can "escape" from that special meaning of the newline character by ending your command lines with a minus sign (-).

Listing 11-34. Using PROMPT, PAUSE, and ACCEPT

```
SQL> prompt This is a demonstration.
This is a demonstration.

SQL> pause Hit the [Enter] key...
Hit the [Enter] key...

SQL> accept x number -
> prompt "Please enter a value for x: "
Please enter a value for x: 42

SQL> define x
DEFINE X                =        42 (NUMBER)
SQL>
```

The PROMPT command allows you to write text to the screen, the PAUSE command allows you to suspend script execution, and the ACCEPT command gives you full control over the datatype of the user-defined variable and the screen text prompting for a value. Just try to enter a nonnumeric value for variable X in Listing 11-34. You will get the following SQL*Plus error message:

```
Enter a value for x: monkey
SP2-0425: "monkey" is not a valid NUMBER
```

■ **Caution**   Splitting commands over multiple lines by using the minus sign as an escape character is relevant only for SQL*Plus commands, *not* for SQL commands.

SQL*Plus System Variables

The third category of SQL*Plus variables is *system variables*. The values of these system-defined SQL*Plus variables control the overall behavior of SQL*Plus. You already saw various examples of these system variables, such as PAGESIZE and PAUSE, in Section 11.1.

In the previous section, you learned that you need the SQL*Plus commands DEFINE and UNDEFINE to manage *user-defined* variables. For *system* variables, you need the SQL*Plus commands SET and SHOW to assign or retrieve values, respectively.

Listing 11-35 demonstrates some examples of system variables.

Listing 11-35. Some SQL*Plus System Variable Examples

```
SQL> show pagesize
pagesize 36

SQL> show pause
PAUSE is OFF
```

```
SQL> set   pause  '[Enter]... '
SQL> set   pause  on
SQL> set   pagesize 10

SQL> select * from employees;
[Enter]...

EMPNO ENAME     INIT  JOB       MGR BDATE        MSAL  COMM DEPTNO
----- --------  ----- --------  ----- ----------- ----- ----- ------
 7369 SMITH     N     TRAINER  7902 17-DEC-1965   800          20
 7499 ALLEN     JAM   SALESREP 7698 20-FEB-1961  1600   300    30
 7521 WARD      TF    SALESREP 7698 22-FEB-1962  1250   500    30
 7566 JONES     JM    MANAGER  7839 02-APR-1967  2975          20
 7654 MARTIN    P.    SALESREP 7698 28-SEP-1956  1250  1400    30
 7698 BLAKE     R     MANAGER  7839 01-NOV-1963  2850          30
 7782 CLARK     AB    MANAGER  7839 09-JUN-1965  2450          10
[Enter]...

EMPNO ENAME     INIT  JOB       MGR BDATE        MSAL  COMM DEPTNO
----- --------  ----- --------  ----- ----------- ----- ----- ------
 7788 SCOTT     SCJ   TRAINER  7566 26-NOV-1959  3000          20
 7839 KING      CC    DIRECTOR      17-NOV-1952  5000          10
 7844 TURNER    JJ    SALESREP 7698 28-SEP-1968  1500     0    30
 7876 ADAMS     AA    TRAINER  7788 30-DEC-1966  1100          20
 7900 JONES     R     ADMIN    7698 03-DEC-1969   800          30
 7902 FORD      MG    TRAINER  7566 13-FEB-1959  3000          20
 7934 MILLER    TJA   ADMIN    7782 23-JAN-1962  1300          10

14 rows selected.

SQL> set  pause off pagesize 42
SQL> show all
...
SQL>
```

If you execute the last command of Listing 11-35 (SHOW ALL), you will see that the number of SQL*Plus system variables is impressive. That's why the output in Listing 11-35 is suppressed.

Table 11-4 displays an overview of the SQL*Plus system variables, listing only the most commonly used SQL*Plus system variables. Where applicable, the third column shows the default values. In the first column, the brackets indicate abbreviations you may want to use.

Table 11-4. *Some Common SQL*Plus System Variables*

Variable	Description	Default
COLSEP	String to display between result columns	" " (space)
CON[CAT]	Character to mark the end of a variable name	. (period)
DEF[INE]	Character to refer to variable values	& (ampersand)
ECHO	Display or suppress commands (relevant only for scripts)	OFF
FEED[BACK]	Display ". . . rows selected" from a certain minimum result size	6
HEA[DING]	Display column names above results	ON
HEADS[EP]	Divide column headers over multiple lines	| (vertical bar)
LIN[ESIZE]	Line or screen width, in characters	80
LONG	Default width for LONG columns	80
NEWP[AGE]	Number of empty lines after every page break	1
NULL	Display of null values in the results	
NUMF[ORMAT]	Default format to display numbers	
NUM[WIDTH]	Default width for numeric columns, in digits	10
PAGE[SIZE]	Number of lines per page	14
PAU[SE]	Display results page by page, with pauses	OFF
RELEASE	Release or version of the RDBMS (cannot be set)	
SQLP[ROMPT]	SQL*Plus prompt string	SQL>
SQLT[ERMINATOR]	SQL command delimiter (execute the command)	; (semicolon)
TAB	Show tab characters, else display as spaces	ON
TIMI[NG]	Show elapsed time after each command	OFF
TRIMS[POOL]	Suppress trailing spaces in spool files	OFF
USER	Username for the current SQL*Plus session (cannot be set)	
VER[IFY]	Show command lines before/after variable substitution	ON

Let's look at some experiments with SQL*Plus system variables, beginning with the FEEDBACK variable. This variable is a switch (you can set it to ON or OFF) and also a threshold value, as shown in Listing 11-36 where we set it to 4.

Listing 11-36. Using the FEEDBACK System Variable

```
SQL> select * from departments;

    DEPTNO DNAME      LOCATION      MGR
    ------ ---------- --------  --------
        10 ACCOUNTING NEW YORK     7782
        20 TRAINING   DALLAS       7566
        30 SALES      CHICAGO      7698
        40 HR         BOSTON       7839
```

```
SQL> set feedback 4
SQL> /

DEPTNO DNAME       LOCATION      MGR
-------- ---------- --------- --------
    10 ACCOUNTING NEW YORK     7782
    20 TRAINING   DALLAS       7566
    30 SALES      CHICAGO      7698
    40 HR         BOSTON       7839

4 rows selected.                   <<<

SQL> select * from employees;
...
SQL> set  feedback off
SQL> show feedback
feedback OFF
SQL> /
...
SQL> set feedback 10
SQL>
```

■ **Note**   In order to save some trees, the listings don't repeat the query results each time. You can easily see the effects of the various system variable values yourself.

Using COLSEP and NUMWIDTH, as shown in Listing 11-37, the default space separating the result columns is replaced by a vertical line, and the GRADE and BONUS columns are now 10 digits wide.

Listing 11-37. Using the COLSEP and NUMWIDTH System Variables

```
SQL> select * from salgrades;

GRADE LOWERLIMIT UPPERLIMIT BONUS
------ ---------- ---------- ------
     1        700       1200      0
     2       1201       1400     50
     3       1401       2000    100
     4       2001       3000    200
     5       3001       9999    500

SQL> set colsep " | "
SQL> set numwidth 10
SQL> /
     GRADE | LOWERLIMIT | UPPERLIMIT |      BONUS
---------- | ---------- | ---------- | ----------
         1 |        700 |       1200 |          0
         2 |       1201 |       1400 |         50
         3 |       1401 |       2000 |        100
         4 |       2001 |       3000 |        200
         5 |       3001 |       9999 |        500

SQL>
```

Listing 11-38 demonstrates examples of using NULL and NUMFORMAT. The NULL system variable makes all null values more visible. The NUMFORMAT variable allows you to influence the layout of all numeric columns. It supports the same formats as the SQL*Plus COLUMN command (see Appendix A of this book or the *SQL*Plus User's Guide and Reference* in the online Oracle 12c documentation for details).

Listing 11-38. Using the NULL and NUMFORMAT System Variables

```
SQL> set numwidth 5
SQL> set null " [N/A]"

SQL> select ename, mgr, comm
  2  from    employees
  3  where   deptno = 10;

ENAME       MGR    COMM
--------- ------ ------
CLARK      7839  [N/A]
KING      [N/A]  [N/A]
MILLER     7782  [N/A]

SQL> set numformat 09999.99
SQL> select * from salgrades;

    GRADE LOWERLIMIT UPPERLIMIT     BONUS
--------- ---------- ---------- ---------
 00001.00   00700.00   01200.00  00000.00
 00002.00   01201.00   01400.00  00050.00
 00003.00   01401.00   02000.00  00100.00
 00004.00   02001.00   03000.00  00200.00
 00005.00   03001.00   09999.00  00500.00

SQL>
```

As Listing 11-39 demonstrates, you can use the DEFINE system variable as a switch (ON or OFF) and you can also change the DEFINE character, if you need the ampersand character (&) without its special meaning.

Listing 11-39. Using the DEFINE System Variable

```
SQL> select 'Miracle&Co' as result from dual;
Enter value for co: Breweries

RESULT
----------------
MiracleBreweries

SQL> set define off
SQL> run
  1* select 'Miracle&Co' as result from dual

RESULT
----------
Miracle&Co
```

```
SQL> set define !
SQL> select 'Miracle&Co' as result from !table;
Enter value for table: dual

RESULT
----------
Miracle&Co

SQL> set define &
SQL>
```

■ **Tip**   You have changed a lot of SQL*Plus settings in this section. In order to make a "clean" start, it is a good idea to exit SQL*Plus and start a new session. This will reset all SQL*Plus variables to their default values.

11.3 Bind Variables

The previous section discussed SQL*Plus variables, which are variables maintained by the *tool* SQL*Plus. The SQL*Plus client-side program replaces all variables with actual values *before* the SQL commands are sent to the Oracle DBMS.

This section discusses *bind variables*, an important component of the SQL language. To be more precise, bind variables are a component of *dynamic* SQL, a PL/SQL interface that allows you to build and process SQL statements at runtime. Bind variables are tool-independent.

Bind variables are extremely important if you want to develop database applications for critical information systems. Suppose you have a database application to retrieve employee details. Application users just enter an employee number in a field on their screen and then click the Execute button. For example, these SQL statements could be generated for two different database users, or for the same user using the same application twice:

```
SQL> select * from employees where empno = 7566;
SQL> select * from employees where empno = 7900;
```

These two SQL statements are obviously different, and the Oracle DBMS will also treat them as such. The optimizer will optimize them separately, and they will occupy their own memory structures (cursors). This approach can easily flood your internal memory, and it also forces the optimizer to produce execution plans over and over again. A much better approach would be to use a bind variable in the SQL command, instead of the literal employee number, and to provide values for the bind variable separately. In other words, all SQL commands coming from the application look like the following:

```
SQL> select * from employees where empno = :x;
```

Now, the Oracle DBMS is able to use cursor sharing, the optimizer can produce a single execution plan, and the SQL command can be executed many times for different values of the bind variable.

SQL*Plus offers support for bind variables with the VARIABLE and PRINTcommands. You will also use the SQL*Plus EXECUTE command, allowing you to execute a single PL/SQL statement.

Bind Variable Declaration

You can declare bind variables with the SQL*Plus VARIABLE command, and you can display bind variable values with the SQL*Plus PRINT command. Because SQL doesn't support any syntax to assign values to bind variables, we use the SQL*Plus EXECUTE command to execute a single PL/SQL command from SQL*Plus. Listing 11-40 demonstrates examples of using these commands.

Listing 11-40. Declaring Bind Variables and Assigning Values

```
SQL> variable x number
SQL> variable y varchar2(8)

SQL> execute :x := 7566
PL/SQL procedure successfully completed.

SQL> execute :y := 'ADMIN'
PL/SQL procedure successfully completed.

SQL> print x y

     X
------
  7566

Y
--------------------------------
ADMIN

SQL> variable
variable   x
datatype   NUMBER

variable   y
datatype   VARCHAR2(8)
SQL>
```

As you can see, we have created two variables, we have assigned values to them, and we can display those values. Note that := is the assignment operator in PL/SQL.

Bind Variables in SQL Statements

Now let's see whether we can retrieve the same two employees (7566 and 7900) using a bind variable. See Listing 11-41.

Listing 11-41. Using Bind Variables in SQL Commands

```
SQL> select * from employees where empno = :x;

 EMPNO ENAME     INIT  JOB        MGR BDATE         MSAL  COMM DEPTNO
------ --------- ----- -------- ----- ----------- ------ ----- ------
  7566 JONES     JM    MANAGER   7839 02-APR-1967   2975          20
```

```
SQL> execute :x := 7900
PL/SQL procedure successfully completed.

SQL> run
  1* select * from employees where empno = :x

 EMPNO ENAME    INIT  JOB       MGR BDATE         MSAL  COMM DEPTNO
------ -------- ----- -------- ----- ----------- ------ ----- ------
  7900 JONES    R     ADMIN     7698 03-DEC-1969    800          30

SQL>
```

Because EXECUTE is a SQL*Plus command, which means it is not stored in the SQL buffer, you can assign a new value and re-execute the query from the SQL buffer with the RUN command. If you want to see some evidence of the behavior of the Oracle DBMS, take a look at Listing 11-42.

Listing 11-42. Querying V$SQLAREA to See the Differences

```
SQL> select executions, sql_text
  2  from    v$sqlarea
  3  where   sql_text like 'select * from employees %';

EXECUTIONS SQL_TEXT
---------- --------------------------------------------
         2 select * from employees where empno = :x
         1 select * from employees where empno = 7566
         1 select * from employees where empno = 7900

SQL>
```

For more details about bind variables, refer to the *PL/SQL User's Guide and Reference*.

11.4 SQL*Plus Scripts

In Section 11.1, you learned that you can save SQL commands with the SQL*Plus SAVE command. Until now, we have written only single SQL commands from the SQL buffer to a file. However, you can also create files with multiple SQL commands, optionally intermixed with SQL*Plus commands. This type of file is referred to as a SQL*Plus *script*.

Script Execution

You can execute SQL*Plus scripts with the SQL*Plus START command, or with its shortcut, @. Listings 11-43 and 11-44 demonstrate examples of executing scripts.

Listing 11-43. Creating and Running SQL*Plus Scripts

```
SQL> select *
  2  from    employees
  3  where   deptno = &&dept_number
  4  and     job    = upper('&&job');
```

```
Enter value for dept_number: 10
Enter value for job: admin

EMPNO ENAME    INIT  JOB      MGR BDATE        MSAL  COMM DEPTNO
----- -------- ----- -------- ----- ----------- ----- ----- ------
 7934 MILLER   TJA   ADMIN    7782 23-JAN-1962  1300          10

SQL> save  testscript replace
Wrote file testscript.sql

SQL> clear buffer
SQL> start testscript
...
SQL> @testscript
...
SQL>
```

Listing 11-44. *Appending Commands to SQL*Plus Scripts*

```
SQL> select *
  2  from    departments
  3  where   deptno = &dept_number;

 DEPTNO DNAME      LOCATION    MGR
-------- ---------- -------- --------
     10 ACCOUNTING NEW YORK    7782

SQL> save testscript append
Appended file to testscript.sql

SQL> @testscript
...
SQL>
```

Listing 11-45 illustrates what happens if you use the GET command and you try to execute the script from the SQL buffer. You receive an Oracle error message, because the SQL buffer now contains multiple SQL commands (as a consequence of your GET command), which is a situation SQL*Plus cannot handle.

Listing 11-45. *What Happens If You Execute Scripts from the SQL Buffer*

```
SQL> get testscript
  1  select *
  2  from    employees
  3  where   deptno = &&dept_number
  4  and     job     = upper('&&job')
  5  /
  6  select *
  7  from    departments
  8* where   deptno = &dept_number
SQL> /
```

```
select *
*
ERROR at line 6:
ORA-00936: missing expression

SQL>
```

The SQL*Plus START command (or @) actually reads a script file *line-by-line*, as if those lines were entered interactively. At the end of the execution of a SQL*Plus script, you will see that only the SQL statement executed last is still in the SQL buffer.

This is also the reason why the SQL*Plus SAVE command always adds a forward slash (/) after the end of the contents of the SQL buffer. Check out what happens if you manually remove that forward slash, with an editor like Notepad. The script will wait for further input from the keyboard, as if the command were not finished yet.

By the way, you can also execute SQL*Plus scripts with a double at sign (@@) command. There is a subtle difference between the @ and @@ commands, which is relevant only if you invoke SQL*Plus scripts from other scripts. In such situations, @@ *always* searches for the (sub)script in the same folder (or directory) where the main (calling) script is stored. This makes the syntax to call subscripts fully independent of any local environment settings, without the risk of launching wrong subscripts (with the same name, from other locations) by accident.

Script Parameters

The next feature to explore is the ability to specify parameters (values for variables) when calling scripts. You can specify up to nine command-line parameter values immediately after the SQL*Plus script name, and you can refer to these values in your script with &1, &2, . . ., &9. To test this feature, open testscript.sql (the script you just generated in Listings 11-43 and 11-44) and make the changes shown in Listing 11-46.

Listing 11-46. Contents of the Changed testscript.sql Script

```
select *
from    employees
where   deptno = &&1        -- this was &&dept_number
and     job = upper('&2')   -- this was &&job
/
select *
from    departments
where   deptno = &1         -- this was &dept_number
/
undefine 1                  -- this line is added
```

Now you can call the script in two ways: with or without command-line arguments, as shown in Listings 11-47 and 11-48.

Listing 11-47. Calling a Script Without Command-Line Arguments

```
SQL> @testscript
Enter value for 1: 10
Enter value for 2: manager
```

EMPNO	ENAME	INIT	JOB	MGR	BDATE	MSAL	COMM	DEPTNO
-----	-----	----	-----	-----	-----	-----	-----	------
7782	CLARK	AB	MANAGER	7839	09-JUN-1965	2450		10

```
DEPTNO DNAME        LOCATION   MGR
------ ---------- -------- -----
    10 ACCOUNTING NEW YORK   7782

SQL>
```

As you can see in Listing 11-47, if you call the script without any arguments, SQL*Plus treats &1 and &2 just like any other substitution or user-defined variables, and prompts for their values—as long as earlier script executions didn't leave any variables defined. That's why we have added an UNDEFINE command to the end of our script, in Listing 11-46.

Listing 11-48 demonstrates what happens if you specify two appropriate values (30 and salesrep) on the command line calling the script.

Listing 11-48. Calling a Script with Command-Line Arguments

```
SQL> @testscript 30 salesrep

EMPNO ENAME      INIT JOB          MGR BDATE        MSAL  COMM DEPTNO
----- -------- ----- -------- ----- ---------- ----- ----- ------
 7499 ALLEN      JAM  SALESREP  7698 20-FEB-1961 1600   300     30
 7521 WARD       TF   SALESREP  7698 22-FEB-1962 1250   500     30
 7654 MARTIN     P    SALESREP  7698 28-SEP-1956 1250  1400     30
 7844 TURNER     JJ   SALESREP  7698 28-SEP-1968 1500     0     30

DEPTNO DNAME        LOCATION   MGR
------ ---------- -------- -----
    30 SALES        CHICAGO   7698

SQL>
```

SQL*Plus Commands in Scripts

SQL*Plus scripts may contain a mixture of SQL commands and SQL*Plus commands. This combination makes SQL*Plus a nice report-generating tool, as you will see in the next section of this chapter. One small problem is that SQL*Plus commands (entered interactively) don't go into the SQL buffer. Normally this is helpful, because it allows you to repeat your most recent SQL command from the SQL buffer, while executing SQL*Plus commands in between. However, this implies that you cannot add any SQL*Plus commands to your scripts with the SAVE . . . APPEND command.

To enter SQL*Plus commands into your scripts, you can use one of the following:

- An external editor

- A separate SQL*Plus buffer

Using an external editor is the most straightforward approach, in most cases. For example, you can use Notepad in a Microsoft Windows environment to maintain your SQL*Plus scripts. The charm of using a separate SQL*Plus buffer is that it is completely platform- and operating system-independent, and it is fully driven from the interactive SQL*Plus prompt. That's why we discuss using a separate buffer here.

Listing 11-49 demonstrates an example of using a separate SQL*Plus buffer to generate scripts. To try this out, execute the CLEAR BUFFER and SET BUFFER CUSTOMBUFFER commands, followed by the INPUT command, and enter the following 14 lines verbatim. Exit SQL*Plus input mode by entering another new line so that you return to the SQL*Plus prompt.

Listing 11-49. Using a Separate SQL*Plus Buffer to Generate Scripts

```
SQL> clear buffer
SQL> set buffer custombuffer
SQL> input
  1  clear screen
  2  set verify off
  3  set pause  off
  4  accept dept number -
  5  prompt "Enter a department number: "
  6  select *
  7  from    departments
  8  where   deptno = &dept;
  9  select ename, job, msal
 10  from    employees
 11  where   deptno = &dept;
 12  undefine dept
 13  set pause on
 14  set verify on
 15
SQL>
```

Now you can save the script and test it, as follows:

```
SQL> save testscript2
Created file testscript2.sql

SQL> @testscript2
Enter a department number: 20
...
```

The SET BUFFER command (choose any buffer name you like) creates a nondefault SQL*Plus buffer.

■ **Note** According to the SQL*Plus documentation, using additional buffers is a deprecated feature since the early 1990s, from SQL*Plus version 3.0 onward. However, it seems to be the only way to prevent the SQL*Plus SAVE command from appending a forward slash (/) at the end of the script, which would execute the last SQL command twice if you have a SQL*Plus command at the end, as in Listing 11-49.

You can only *manipulate* the contents of nondefault SQL*Plus buffers with the SQL*Plus editor commands, and use SAVE and GET for file manipulation. You cannot *execute* the contents of those buffers with the START or @ command, because these commands only on the SQL buffer. That's why you must save the script with the SAVE command before you can use it.

SQL*Plus commands are normally entered on a single line. If that is impossible, or if you want to make your scripts more readable, you must explicitly "escape" the newline character with a minus sign (-), as we did before with the ACCEPT command in Listing 11-34, and again in Listing 11-49.

■ **Note** The examples in the remainder of this chapter show only the contents of the SQL*Plus scripts. It is up to you to decide which method you want to use to create and maintain those scripts.

The login.sql Script

One special SQL*Plus script must be mentioned here: login.sql. SQL*Plus automatically executes this script when you start a SQL*Plus session, as long as the login.sql script is located in the folder (or directory) from where you start SQL*Plus, or if that script can be found via the SQLPATH environment variable (under Linux) or Registry setting (under Microsoft Windows).

Note that there is also a *global* SQL*Plus glogin.sql script. This script is executed for every user, and it allows you to have a mixture of global settings and personal settings in a multiuser environment. In a single-user Oracle environment, using both scripts is useless and can be confusing. The glogin.sql script is normally located in the sqlplus/admin subdirectory under the Oracle installation directory.

■ **Caution**   Starting with Oracle Database 10*g*, SQL*Plus also executes the glogin.sql and login.sql scripts if you execute a CONNECT command, without leaving SQL*Plus. This didn't happen with earlier releases of SQL*Plus.

You can use the glogin.sql and login.sql scripts to set various SQL*Plus system variables, user-defined variables, and column definitions. Listing 11-50 shows an example of a login.sql script, demonstrating that you can also execute SQL commands from this script. You can test it by saving this file to the right place and restarting SQL*Plus.

Listing 11-50. Example of a login.sql Script

```
--   ==========================================
--   LOGIN.SQL
--   ==========================================
set pause     "Enter... "
set pause     on
set numwidth 6
set pagesize 24
alter session set nls_date_format='dd-mm-yyyy';
-- define_editor=Notepad   /* for Windows */
-- define_editor=vi        /* for UNIX or Linux    */
clear screen
```

11.5 Report Generation with SQL*Plus

As you've learned in previous chapters, the SQL language enables you to write queries. Queries produce result tables. However, the default layout of those query results is often visually unappealing.

SQL*Plus offers many commands and features to enhance your query results into more readable reports. SQL*Plus is definitely the oldest and most traditional "quick-and-dirty" Oracle report generator; the original name in the 1980s was UFI (User Friendly Interface), before they renamed it to SQL*Plus. Several other Oracle reporting tools were developed and discarded over the years, but SQL*Plus is still here. Table 11-5 lists some of the SQL*Plus features you can use for enhancing your reports.

Table 11-5. *SQL*Plus Features to Enhance Reports*

Feature	Description
SET {LINESIZE|PAGESIZE|NEWPAGE}	Adjust the page setup; set to 0 suppresses page formatting
SET TRIMSPOOL ON	Suppress trailing spaces in SPOOL output
COLUMN	Adjust column layouts (header and contents)
TTITLE, BTITLE	Define top and bottom page titles
REPHEADER, REPFOOTER	Define report headers and footers
BREAK	Group rows (make sure the result is ordered appropriately)
COMPUTE	Add aggregate computations on BREAK definitions
SPOOL	Spool SQL*Plus output to a file

The SQL*Plus SET command was elaborated upon in Section 11.2, in the discussion of SQL*Plus system variables. Now we'll look at the other SQL*Plus commands that are useful for producing reports.

The SQL*Plus COLUMN Command

You also already saw some examples of the COLUMN command. However, the SQL*Plus COLUMN command has many additional features, as you will learn in this section.

The general syntax of the SQL*Plus COLUMN command is as follows:

```
SQL> column [<col-name>|<expression>] [<option>...]
```

If you don't specify any arguments at all, the COLUMN command produces a complete overview of all current column settings. If you specify <col-name>, you get only the settings for that column. Note that <col-name> is mapped with column aliases in the SELECT clause; that is, with the column headings of the final query result. You can use <expression> to influence SELECT clause expressions; make sure to copy the expression verbatim from the query. For <option>, you can specify various ways to handle the column. Table 11-6 displays a selection of the valid options for the COLUMN command.

Table 11-6. *Some SQL*Plus COLUMN Command Options*

Option	Description
ALI[AS]	Column alias; useful in BREAK and COMPUTE commands
CLE[AR]	Reset all column settings
FOLD_A[FTER]	Insert a carriage return after the column
FOR[MAT]	Format display of column values
HEA[DING]	Define (different) column title for display
JUS[TIFY]	Justify column header: LEFT, CENTER or CENTRE, RIGHT
LIKE	Copy settings over from another column
NEWL[INE]	Force a new line before this column

(continued)

Table 11-6. (*continued*)

Option	Description
NEW_V[ALUE]	Substitution variable to retain the last column value
NO[PRI[NT]]	Suppress (NOPRINT) or display (PRINT) specific columns
NUL[L]	Display of null values in specific columns
ON | OFF	Toggle to activate/deactivate column settings
WRA[PPED]	Wrap too-long column values to the following line
WOR[D_WRAPPED]	Wrap too-long column values to the following line, splitting the column value between words
TRU[NCATED]	Truncate too-long column values

The last three COLUMN options are mutually exclusive. In Table 11-6, the brackets indicate the abbreviations you can use. For example, you can abbreviate the first SQL*Plus command in Listing 11-51 as COL ENAME FOR A20 HEA LAST_NAME JUS C, if you like. If you do not specify a JUSTIFY value for a column, SQL*Plus uses the following alignment defaults:

- NUMBER column headings default to RIGHT.

- Other column headings default to LEFT.

Listings 11-51 through 11-53 demonstrate some examples of the SQL*Plus COLUMN command.

Listing 11-51. Using COLUMN FORMAT, HEADING, JUSTIFY, and LIKE

```
SQL> select empno, ename, bdate
  2  ,       msal        as salary
  3  ,       comm        as commission
  4  from    employees;

EMPNO ENAME     BDATE         SALARY COMMISSION
------ --------- ----------- -------- ----------
  7369 SMITH     17-DEC-1965    800
  7499 ALLEN     20-FEB-1961   1600        300
  7521 WARD      22-FEB-1962   1250        500
...
14 rows selected.

SQL> col ename       format  a20 heading last_name justify center
SQL> col salary      format  $9999.99
SQL> col commission  like    salary
SQL> col salary      heading month|salary
SQL> /
```

```
                                 month
    EMPNO      last_name       BDATE       salary COMMISSION
    ------ -------------------- ----------- --------- ----------
      7369 SMITH               17-DEC-1965  $800.00
      7499 ALLEN               20-FEB-1961 $1600.00     $300.00
      7521 WARD                22-FEB-1962 $1250.00     $500.00
    ...
    14 rows selected.

SQL>
```

Note the effects of the vertical bar (|) in the COL SALARY command and the LIKE option for the COMMISSION column.

Listings 11-51 and 11-52 illustrate an important property of the COLUMN command: you must always specify the column *alias*, not the original column name, as its argument.

Listing 11-52. Using COLUMN NOPRINT, ON, OFF

```
SQL> col COMM NOPRINT                  -- Note the column name
SQL> select empno, ename, bdate
  2  ,       msal         as salary
  3  ,       comm         as commission  -- and the column alias
  4  from    employees;
                                 month
    EMPNO      last_name       BDATE       salary COMMISSION
    ------ -------------------- ----------- --------- ----------
      7369 SMITH               17-DEC-1965  $800.00
      7499 ALLEN               20-FEB-1961 $1600.00     $300.00
      7521 WARD                22-FEB-1962 $1250.00     $500.00
    ...
    14 rows selected.
SQL> col COMMISSION NOPRINT -- Now you use the column alias instead
SQL> /
                                 month
    EMPNO      last_name       BDATE       salary
    ------ -------------------- ----------- ---------
      7369 SMITH               17-DEC-1965  $800.00
      7499 ALLEN               20-FEB-1961 $1600.00
      7521 WARD                22-FEB-1962 $1250.00
    ...
    14 rows selected.

SQL> col commission off
SQL> /
                                 month
    EMPNO      last_name       BDATE       salary COMMISSION
    ------ -------------------- ----------- --------- ----------
      7369 SMITH               17-DEC-1965  $800.00
      7499 ALLEN               20-FEB-1961 $1600.00         300
      7521 WARD                22-FEB-1962 $1250.00         500
    ...
```

```
SQL> col commission
COLUMN   commission OFF
FORMAT   $9999.99
NOPRINT
SQL> col commission on
SQL>
```

The NEW_VALUE feature of the COLUMN command is very nice, and you can use it for various tricks in SQL*Plus scripts. As you can see in Listing 11-53, the user-defined LAST_EMPNO variable remembers the last EMPNO value for you.

Listing 11-53. Using COLUMN NEW_VALUE

```
SQL> col empno new_value LAST_EMPNO
SQL> /
                                    month
 EMPNO    last_name       BDATE     salary
------ -------------------- ----------- ---------
  7369 SMITH            17-DEC-1965   $800.00
  7499 ALLEN            20-FEB-1961  $1600.00
  ...
  7934 MILLER           23-JAN-1962  $1300.00

14 rows selected.

SQL> def LAST_EMPNO
DEFINE LAST_EMPNO            =    7934 (NUMBER)

SQL> I
  5  where  deptno = 30;
                                    month
 EMPNO    last_name       BDATE     salary
------ -------------------- ----------- ---------
  7499 ALLEN            20-FEB-1961  $1600.00
  7521 WARD             22-FEB-1962  $1250.00
  7654 MARTIN           28-SEP-1956  $1250.00
  7698 BLAKE            01-NOV-1963  $2850.00
  7844 TURNER           28-SEP-1968  $1500.00
  7900 JONES            03-DEC-1969   $800.00

SQL> define LAST_EMPNO
DEFINE LAST_EMPNO            =    7900 (NUMBER)

SQL> undefine LAST_EMPNO
SQL>
```

The SQL*Plus TTITLE and BTITLE Commands

As you have seen so far, the SQL*Plus COLUMN command allows you to influence the report layout at the column level, and you can influence the overall page layout with the SQL*Plus SET PAGESIZE and SET LINESIZE commands. You can further enhance your SQL*Plus reports with the SQL*Plus TTITLE and BTITLE commands, which allow you to add page headers and footers to your report. The syntax is as follows:

```
SQL> ttitle [<print-spec> {<text>|<variable>}...] | [OFF|ON]
SQL> btitle [<print-spec> {<text>|<variable>}...] | [OFF|ON]
```

As Listing 11-54 demonstrates, you can also use these commands to display their current settings (by specifying no arguments) or to enable/disable their behavior with ON and OFF.

Listing 11-54. Using TTITLE and BTITLE

```
SQL> set     pagesize 22
SQL> set     linesize 80
SQL> ttitle left        'SQL*Plus report'        -
>            right       'Page: ' format 99 SQL.PNO -
>            skip center 'OVERVIEW'               -
>            skip center 'employees department 30' -
>            skip 2
SQL> btitle col 20 'Confidential' tab 8 -
>                   'Created by: ' SQL.USER
SQL> /
SQL*Plus report                                          Page:   1
                              OVERVIEW
                       employees department 30


                                      month
EMPNO      last_name       BDATE      salary
------  --------------------  -----------  ---------
  7499 ALLEN              20-FEB-1961 $1600.00
  7521 WARD               22-FEB-1962 $1250.00
  7654 MARTIN             28-SEP-1956 $1250.00
  7698 BLAKE              01-NOV-1963 $2850.00
  7844 TURNER             28-SEP-1968 $1500.00
  7900 JONES              03-DEC-1969  $800.00

            Confidential       Created by: BOOK
SQL> btitle off
SQL> btitle
btitle OFF and is the following 66 characters:
col 20 'Confidential' tab 8                 'Created by: ' SQL.USER
SQL> ttitle off
SQL>
```

The output in Listing 11-54 demonstrates the effects of the TTITLE and BTITLE commands. Note that we use two predefined variables: SQL.PNO for the page number and SQL.USER for the current username.

The TTITLE and BTITLE commands have several additional features. SQL*Plus also supports the REPHEADER and REPFOOTER commands, which allow you to add headers and footers at the report level, as opposed to the page level. See the *SQL*Plus User's Guide and Reference* for more information about these commands.

The SQL*Plus BREAK Command

You can add "breaks" to the result of your reports with the SQL*Plus BREAK command. Breaks are locations in your report: between certain rows, between all rows, or at the end of the report. You can highlight breaks in your reports by suppressing repeating column values, by inserting additional lines, or by forcing a new page.

Breaks are also the positions within your reports where you can add subtotals or other data aggregations. You can use the SQL*Plus COMPUTE command for these purposes. Let's investigate the possibilities of the BREAK command first.

The syntax of the SQL*Plus BREAK command is shown in Figure 11-4.

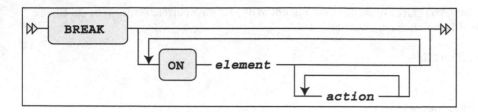

Figure 11-4. A BREAK command syntax diagram

For ELEMENT, you can specify a column name or a column expression, or a special report element, as discussed at the end of this section. The action values are listed in Table 11-7.

*Table 11-7. SQL*Plus BREAK Command Actions*

Action	Description
SKIP n	Skip n lines
SKIP PAGE	Insert a page break
[NO]DUPLICATES	Suppress or show duplicate values; NODUPLICATES is the default

Listing 11-55 shows an example of a BREAK command.

Listing 11-55. Using the BREAK Command

```
SQL> clear   columns

SQL> select deptno, job, empno, ename, msal, comm
  2  from    employees
  3  order   by deptno, job;

 DEPTNO JOB          EMPNO ENAME       MSAL     COMM
-------- -------- -------- -------- -------- --------
     10 ADMIN       7934 MILLER      1300
     10 DIRECTOR    7839 KING        5000
     10 MANAGER     7782 CLARK       2450
     20 MANAGER     7566 JONES       2975
     20 TRAINER     7369 SMITH        800
...
14 rows selected.

SQL> break on deptno skip 2
SQL> /
 DEPTNO JOB          EMPNO ENAME       MSAL     COMM
-------- -------- -------- -------- -------- --------
     10 ADMIN       7934 MILLER      1300
        DIRECTOR    7839 KING        5000
        MANAGER     7782 CLARK       2450
```

```
        20 MANAGER      7566 JONES         2975
           TRAINER      7369 SMITH          800
...
14 rows selected.

SQL> break
break on deptno skip 2 nodup

SQL> break on deptno page
SQL> set pause     "Enter... "
SQL> /
[Enter]...

  DEPTNO JOB        EMPNO ENAME        MSAL     COMM
-------- -------- -------- -------- -------- --------
      10 ADMIN       7934 MILLER       1300
         DIRECTOR    7839 KING         5000
         MANAGER     7782 CLARK        2450
[Enter]...

  DEPTNO JOB        EMPNO ENAME        MSAL     COMM
-------- -------- -------- -------- -------- --------
      20 MANAGER     7566 JONES        2975
         TRAINER     7369 SMITH         800
...
14 rows selected.
SQL>
```

Note the ORDER BY clause in the query in Listing 11-55. You need this clause for the BREAK command to work properly. The BREAK command itself does not sort anything; it just processes the rows, one by one, as they appear in the result.

Note also that you can have only one break definition at any time. Each break definition implicitly overwrites any current break definition. This implies that if you want two breaks for your report, at different levels, you must define them in a single BREAK command; for an example, see Listing 11-56.

Listing 11-56. Multiple Breaks in a Single BREAK Command

```
SQL> break on deptno skip page -
   >        on job    skip 1
SQL> /
[Enter]...

  DEPTNO JOB        EMPNO ENAME        MSAL     COMM
-------- -------- -------- -------- -------- --------
      10 ADMIN       7934 MILLER       1300

         DIRECTOR    7839 KING         5000

         MANAGER     7782 CLARK        2450
```

```
[Enter]...

DEPTNO JOB          EMPNO ENAME        MSAL      COMM
-------- -------- -------- -------- -------- --------
     20 MANAGER     7566 JONES        2975

        TRAINER     7369 SMITH         800
                    7902 FORD         3000
                    7788 SCOTT        3000
                    7876 ADAMS        1100
...
14 rows selected.
SQL> break
break on deptno page  nodup
        on job skip 1 nodup
SQL>
```

Note that you don't use any commas as break definition delimiters. Additionally, though you may include the NODUP option for the BREAK command, keep in mind that even if it is not listed explicitly, suppression of duplicate values (NODUP) is the default behavior of the BREAK command.

As you have seen so far, you can define breaks on columns or column expressions. However, you can also define breaks on two special report elements:

- ROW forces breaks on every row of the result.

- REPORT forces a break at the end of your report.

The SQL*Plus COMPUTE Command

The SQL*Plus COMPUTE command allows you to add aggregating computations on your break definitions. The syntax of the COMPUTE command is shown in Figure 11-5.

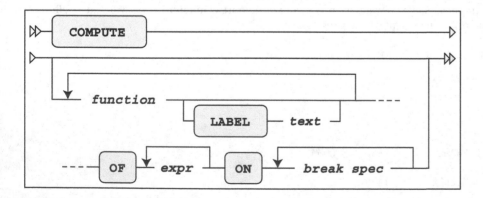

Figure 11-5. *A COMPUTE command syntax diagram*

Table 11-8 lists the various functions supported by the SQL*Plus COMPUTE command.

Table 11-8. *SQL*Plus COMPUTE Functions*

Function	Description
AVG	The average
COUNT	The number of NOT NULL column values
MAX	The maximum
MIN	The minimum
NUMBER	The number of rows
STD	The standard deviation
SUM	The sum
VAR	The variance

The expr indicates on which column you want the function to be applied. The break spec indicates at which points in the report you want this computation to happen. The break spec must be a column, column expression, or a report element (ROW or REPORT) on which you previously defined a BREAK.

Listing 11-57 demonstrates an example of using COMPUTE.

Listing 11-57. Using COMPUTE for Aggregation

```
SQL> set      pause off
SQL> break    on deptno skip page on job
SOL> compute sum label total of msal on deptno
SQL> compute count number    of comm on deptno
SQL> /
  DEPTNO JOB            EMPNO ENAME        MSAL      COMM
-------- -------- -------- -------- -------- --------
      10 ADMIN         7934 MILLER       1300
         DIRECTOR      7839 KING         5000
         MANAGER       7782 CLARK        2450
******** ********                    -------- --------
count                                               0
number                                              3
total                                    8750

  DEPTNO JOB            EMPNO ENAME        MSAL      COMM
-------- -------- -------- -------- -------- --------
      20 MANAGER       7566 JONES        2975
         TRAINER       7369 SMITH         800
                       7902 FORD         3000
                       7788 SCOTT        3000
                       7876 ADAMS        1100
******** ********                    -------- --------
count                                               0
number                                              5
total                                   10875
```

```
DEPTNO JOB           EMPNO ENAME        MSAL      COMM
-------- --------  -------- --------  -------- --------
      30 ADMIN       7900 JONES        800
         MANAGER     7698 BLAKE       2850
         SALESREP    7499 ALLEN       1600       300
                     7654 MARTIN      1250      1400
                     7844 TURNER      1500         0
                     7521 WARD        1250       500
******** ********                     -------- --------
count                                               4
number                                              6
total                                  9250

14 rows selected.

SQL> compute
COMPUTE sum LABEL 'total' OF msal ON deptno
COMPUTE count LABEL 'count' number LABEL 'number' OF comm ON deptno
SQL> clear computes
SQL> clear breaks
SQL>
```

As Listing 11-57 shows, you can issue multiple COMPUTE commands, and you can have multiple COMPUTE definitions active at the same time. The CLEAR COMPUTES command erases all compute definitions, and the CLEAR BREAKS command clears the current break definition.

If you are happy with the final report results on screen, you can store all SQL and SQL*Plus commands in a script, and add commands to spool the output to a text file, as described in the next section.

The Finishing Touch: SPOOL

If you look at the results in Listing 11-57, you see that this mixture of SQL and SQL*Plus commands produces a rather complete report. Now you can use the SQL*Plus SPOOL command to save the report into a file; for example, to allow for printing. The syntax is as follows:

```
SQL> spool [<file-name>[.<ext>] [CREATE|REPLACE|APPEND] | OFF | OUT]
```

If you specify no arguments, the SPOOL command reports its current status. The default file name extension <ext> is LST or LIS on most platforms. SPOOL OFF stops the spooling. SPOOL OUT stops the spooling *and* sends the result to your default printer.

Suppose you have saved the example of Listing 11-57 in a script, containing all SQL*Plus commands and the SQL query. You can turn this script into a complete report by changing the contents as indicated in Listing 11-58. For readability, the three lines to be added are highlighted. The TRIMSPOOL setting suppresses trailing spaces in the result, and the REPLACE option of the SPOOL command ensures that an existing file (if any) will be overwritten.

Listing 11-58. Using the SPOOL Command to Generate SQL*Plus Reports

```
set      pause off
break    on deptno skip page on job
compute  sum label total of msal on deptno
compute  count number    of comm on deptno
```

```
>>> set trimspool on                           <<< added line
>>> spool report.txt replace                   <<< added line
    -- The query
    select deptno, job, empno, ename, msal, comm
    from   employees
    order  by deptno, job;
>>> spool off                                  <<< added line
    -- Cleanup section
    undefine dept
    clear computes
    clear breaks
    set pause on
```

If you execute this script, it generates a text file named report.txt in the current folder/directory.

11.6 HTML in SQL*Plus

SQL*Plus supports the ability to generate reports in HTML format, allowing you to display the report results in a browser environment. *SQL Developer* has more features than SQL*Plus in this area, because it runs in a browser environment, itself. However, this chapter provides a look at how SQL*Plus can be used to help you perform this task.

HTML in SQL*Plus

The SQL*Plus MARKUP setting is very important if you want to work with HTML. Listing 11-59 demonstrates why this is the case.

Listing 11-59. The SQL*Plus MARKUP Setting

```
SQL> show markup
markup HTML OFF HEAD "<style type='text/css'> body
{font:10pt Arial,Helvetica,sans-serif; color:black; background:White;} p {font:1F
SQL> set markup
SP2-0281: markup missing set option
Usage: SET MARKUP HTML [ON|OFF] [HEAD text] [BODY text]
[TABLE text] [ENTMAP {ON|OFF}] [SPOOL {ON|OFF}] [PRE[FORMAT] {ON|OFF}]
SQL>
```

The SQL*Plus error message in Listing 11-59 (followed by the "Usage:" text) precisely indicates what you can do to fix the problem with the incomplete SET MARKUP command:

- SET MARKUP HTML is mandatory, followed by ON or OFF.

- HEAD allows you to specify text for the HTML <header> tag, BODY for the <body> tag, and TABLE for the <table> tag, respectively.

- ENTMAP allows you to indicate whether SQL*Plus should replace some special HTML characters (such as <, >, ', and &) with their corresponding HTML representations (<, >, ", and &).

- SPOOL lets you spool output to a file, without needing to use an additional SQL*Plus SPOOL command.

- PREFORMAT allows you to write output to a <pre> tag. The default value is OFF.

The HEADER option of the SET MARKUP command is particularly interesting, because it allows you to specify a *cascading style sheet*. Let's perform some experiments, as illustrated in Listing 11-60.

Listing 11-60. Using the SQL*Plus SET MARKUP Command

```
SQL> set markup html on head "<title>SQL*Plus demo</title>"
SQL&gt; select ename,init from employees where deptno = 10;
<br>
<p>
<table border='1' width='90%' align='center' summary='Script output'>
<tr>
<th scope="col">
last_name
</th>
<th scope="col">
INIT
</th>
</tr>
<tr>
<td>
CLARK
</td>
<td>
AB
</td>
</tr>
<tr>
<td>
KING
</td>
<td>
CC
</td>
</tr>
<tr>
<td>
MILLER
</td>
<td>
TJA
</td>
</tr>
</table>
<p>

SQL&gt; set markup html off
<br>
SQL>
```

As you can see in Listing 11-60, the screen output is in HTML format. Obviously, the MARKUP setting becomes truly useful in combination with the SQL*Plus SPOOL command, allowing you to open the result in a browser. The usefulness of the combination of the SQL*Plus MARKUP and SPOOL commands is so obvious that you are able to specify SPOOL ON as an option in the MARKUP setting (see Listing 11-60).

■ **Tip** You can also specify the MARKUP setting as a command-line argument when you launch SQL*Plus. This is useful for certain reports, because SQL*Plus then processes the <html> and <body> tags *before* the first command is executed.

If you execute the SQL*Plus script in Listing 11-61, you will note what happens as a consequence of the SET ECHO OFF TERMOUT OFF command: the SQL*Plus screen remains empty. SQL*Plus only writes the results to a file.

Listing 11-61. Contents of the htmldemoscript.sql Script

```
-- ================================
-- htmldemoscript.sql
-- ================================
SET ECHO off TERMOUT OFF
set markup html on spool on               -
    preformat off entmap on               -
    head "<title>HTML Demo Report</title>  -
          <link rel='stylesheet' href='x.css'>"

spool htmldemo.htm replace

select empno, ename, init, msal
from    employees
where   deptno = 20;

spool off
set markup html off
set echo on
```

Figure 11-6 illustrates what happens if you open the result in a browser. The example assumes that you have an x.css cascading style sheet document in the current folder/directory.

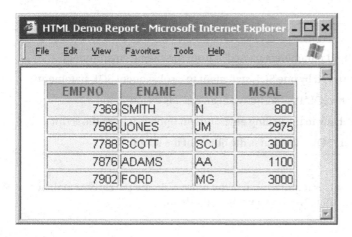

Figure 11-6. *The result of the htmldemoscript.sql in a browser*

315

One more tip: you can achieve various "special effects" by selecting HTML fragments as alphanumerical literals in your queries. Listing 11-62 demonstrates what happens if you add the following fragment to the htmldemoscript.sql script, just before the SPOOL OFF command.

Listing 11-62. Addition to the htmldemoscript.sql Script

```
set markup html entmap off preformat on
set heading off

select '<a href="http://www.naturaljoin.nl"> Visit this web site</a>'
from  dual;
```

11.7 Building SQL*Plus Scripts for Automation

Inevitably, as you work in SQL*Plus, you will want to create scripts containing SQL commands that do more than generate a nicely formatted report in text or HTML. You will want a script that has all the characteristics of a "batch" program: capturing input parameters, performing complex tasks, passing data values from one SQL statement to another, handling error conditions intelligently, and returning meaningful exit status codes to the calling environment. An amazing volume of these scripts exists on every database server in the world, and the power of SQL*Plus enables a developer or database administrator to do practically anything by means of SQL*Plus scripts.

What Is a SQL*Plus Script?

As introduced earlier in this chapter, a *SQL*Plus script* is a file containing SQL*Plus commands intermixed with SQL statements. Generally, SQL*Plus scripts have ".sql" file-extensions, but any type of file can be executed as a script using the SQL*Plus START command or its "@" abbreviation.

SQL*Plus scripts are often used simply to save useful SQL statements, to avoid having to re-type them again. But SQL*Plus scripts can also be used for automation purposes, to regularly run an important report or *batch program* from a job-scheduling program. This section is geared more toward learning SQL*Plus features for creating bullet-proof, automatable programs.

Besides containing one or more SQL statements, many scripts (like many batch programs) need to do one or more of the tasks listed in Table 11-9.

Table 11-9. *Tasks of a SQL*Plus Script*

Task	Description
Inputting parameters	Capturing and using input parameters passed in from the calling environment
Passing data values	Passing data values retrieved by one SQL statement to a subsequent SQL statement
Handling error conditions	Continuing or ending the SQL*Plus script when an error is encountered
Returning exit status	Passing a "status code" back to the calling environment upon exit from the script
Executing SQL or PL/SQL	Oh yeah—the SQL or PL/SQL code that is the object of the script!

Only the ability to execute SQL or PL/SQL statements is required—all of the other tasks are purely optional, but let's look at them one by one, so you'll know how to use them when you want to use them.

Capturing and Using Input Parameter Values

Input parameters are data values passed into a program when it starts. For a SQL*Plus script, data values can be specified within SQL*Plus using the START and @ commands. Listing 11-63 provides an example. Start and @ are each used to invoke a script named demoscript.sql (the .sql extension is the default). Two parameters are passed in for each invocation.

Listing 11-63. Two Input Parameters Passed in Using the START and @ Commands

```
start demoscript 01-FEB-2010 TRUE
@demoscript 01-FEB-2010 TRUE
```

Input parameter values can also be specified when SQL*Plus is started. You pass such parameters on the command line, following the name of the script. Listing 11-64 provides an example.

Listing 11-64. Passing Input Parameters to a SQL*Plus Script from a UNIX or Linux Shell or Windows Command Prompt

```
sqlplus book/<password> @demoscript ename 01-FEB-2010
```

In Listing 11-64, you see the SQL*Plus command connecting as BOOK (password BOOK or other password you may have chosen for your environment) and calling the demoscript.sql script with the two input parameter values of ENAME and 01-FEB-2010.

Inside the SQL*Plus script, these input parameters are accessed as ordinal substitution parameters. Use &1 to refer to the first parameter, &2 to refer to the second, and so forth. See Listing 11-65 for an example.

Listing 11-65. Retrieving Input Parameter Values Inside the SQL*Plus Script

```
select &1 from employees
where hire_date >= to_date('&2', 'DD-MON-YYYY')
and hire_date < to_date('&2','DD-MON-YYYY') + 1;
```

If you prefer more meaningful variable names, you can use the SQL*Plus DEFINE command to copy an input parameter value into a substitution variable of your choice. Listing 11-66 assigns the values from &1 and &2 to the more meaningfully named variables V_SELECTCOL and V_HIRE_DT.

Listing 11-66. Storing Input Parameter Values Within Substitution Variables

```
define V_SELECTCOL="&1"
define V_HIRE_DT="&2"
select &&V_SELECTCOL from employees
where hire_date >= to_date('&&V_HIRE_DT', 'DD-MON-YYYY')
and hire_date < to_date('&&V_HIRE_DT','DD-MON-YYYY') + 1;
```

Using meaningful variable names as shown in Listing 11-66 contributes to ease of maintenance down the road. Your SQL*Plus script is a little more readable and understandable, thus a little more maintainable.

When looking at the input parameters and how they are being used, please note that the first input parameter in the examples so far (ENAME) is not a data value, as is the second input parameter (01-FEB-2010). Instead, it is the name of a column in the EMPLOYEES table. In essence, substitution variables can be used to change the keywords, not just data values, in the SQL statement. In fact, a substitution variable can contain an entire clause or an entire SQL statement, if you so wish. Therefore, substitution variables are quite versatile in general, and they are the method by which data values and other directives are passed into a SQL*Plus script.

Passing Data Values from One SQL Statement to Another

More complex SQL*Plus scripts are likely to be comprised of several SQL statements, and sometimes it is useful to extract data from the database and pass that data to another SQL statement or SQL*Plus command. A good example of this type of data value passing might be naming an output file spooled from a script by including the name of the database instance used along with today's date. Another example might be when data is extracted with one query and passed to anther query.

Mechanism 1: The NEW_VALUE Clause

There are two mechanisms for passing values between SQL statements; the first uses SQL*Plus substitution variables and the second uses SQL*Plus bind variables. With substitution variables, you can use the COLUMN . . . NEW_VALUE command to save the last value retrieved from a SELECT statement into a substitution variable. Listing 11-67 illustrates an example of using the NEW_VALUE clause.

Listing 11-67. Passing Data Values from One SQL Statement to Another Using Substitution Variables

```
define V_BDATE="&1"
column empno new_value V_EMPNO
select empno from employees
where bdate >= to_date('&&V_BDATE', 'DD-MON-YYYY')
and bdate < to_date('&&V_BDATE','DD-MON-YYYY') + 1;

select ename from employees
where empno = &&V_EMPNO;
```

Here, the COLUMN EMPNO command specifies that the last value retrieved (NEW_VALUE) will be stored in a SQL*Plus substitution variable named V_EMPNO. So, in this example, we run the query against the EMPLOYEES table for the employees hired on the date specified by the substitution variable V_BDATE, then the last EMPNO column value retrieved is saved into the V_EMPNO substitution variable. Finally, the V_EMPNO substitution variable can be used in the WHERE clause of the subsequent SQL statement, as shown in Listing 11-67.

Obviously, there are limitations. If the first query returns more than one row, then only the value from the last row will be retained in the substitution variable and passed to the second query. So, it is far from perfect, but it has its uses. If all rows retrieved need to be passed to the second query then the best method would be either to rewrite the SQL so that both steps are performed in the same SQL statement or to "glue" the two SQL statements together within a PL/SQL program using PL/SQL collections.

Mechanism 2: Bind Variables

Another technique of passing data values between SQL statements in a SQL*Plus script involves the use of SQL*Plus *bind variables*. Unlike substitution variables, bind variables behave like bind variables in PL/SQL programs or other programming languages such as Java, C/C++, Perl, or others. That is, unlike substitution variables, which are resolved within SQL*Plus before a SQL statement is sent down to the database engine, bind variables are sent down to the database engine and resolved there. So, they can be used only for *bind values* in SQL statement SELECT, WHERE, GROUP BY, ORDER BY, SET, and VALUES clauses, and they cannot be used to replace the actual keywords or column names or table names in a SQL statement, as substitution variables can.

Bind variables must first be declared with a VARIABLE command. Once you've done that, you can use bind variables to generate data in one statement and use that data in another statement within a PL/SQL block, as shown in Listing 11-68.

Listing 11-68. Passing Data Values from One SQL Statement to Another Using Bind Variables

```
set serverout on
variable v_empno number
variable v_ename varchar2(8)

begin
   select empno into :v_empno from employees
    where bdate >= to_date('&&V_BDATE', 'DD-MON-YYYY')
      and bdate < to_date('&&V_BDATE','DD-MON-YYYY') + 1;

   select ename into :v_ename from employees
    where empno = :v_empno;

   dbms_output.put_line('v_empno = '||:v_empno||' and v_ename = '||:v_ename);
end;
/
```

So, in Listing 11-68, we declare a bind variable named V_EMPNO with a numeric datatype and a bind variable named V_ENAME with a VARCHAR2 datatype, and then populate them using the INTO clause of each SELECT statement that queries from the EMPLOYEES table. Please note the leading full-colon (:) character used to denote a bind variable.

Handling Error Conditions

When we run SQL statements interactively in SQL*Plus or SQL Developer or any other utility, we decide how to react to an error. If an SQL statement fails from a syntax error or from an unexpected data condition such as ORA-01403: no rows found, do we want to proceed and run the next SQL statement, or do we want to simply roll back all work that has been done and exit? When executing interactively, we can decide interactively. But what about when we're running a script?

SQL*Plus provides the WHENEVER command to direct SQL*Plus as to how to react to failures. WHENEVER is particularly useful when running a script. Table 11-10 describes two variations of the command.

Table 11-10. *WHENEVER Error-Handling Conditions*

Error condition	Description
WHENEVER OSERROR	Triggers whenever a SQL*Plus command like CONNECT, DISCONNECT, SPOOL, HOST, START, or any other command that interacts with the operating system fails
WHENEVER SQLERROR	Triggers whenever an SQL statement like SELECT, INSERT, UPDATE, DELETE, CREATE, ALTER, DROP, TRUNCATE, GRANT, REVOKE, or any other SQL command fails

Both of the commands in Table 11-10 have two possible directives: EXIT and CONTINUE. Each directive, in turn, implements two further directives describing how to handle an open transaction and (if necessary) which exit status to return to the operating system. Table 11-11 describes the options that you can pass to EXIT and CONTINUE.

Table 11-11. *WHENEVER Error-Handling Directives*

Error condition	Description
`EXIT [exit-status	txn-directive]`	Exit from SQL*Plus with the specified exit status after committing or rolling back the current transaction as directed.
`CONTINUE [ txn-directive ]`	Continue executing SQL*Plus after committing, rolling back, or doing nothing.
Exit-status	Can be one of: `[SUCCESS	FAILURE	n	substitution-variable	bind-variable]` where `SUCCESS` is an operating-system dependent exit status signifying successful completion, `FAILURE` is an operating-system dependent exit status signifying failure, and `n` is a number value. SQL*Plus substitution variables and SQL*Plus bind variables containing numeric values can also be used as return statuses. `SUCCESS` is the default.
Txn-directive	Can be one of: `[COMMIT	ROLLBACK	NONE]` where `NONE` can be used only with the `CONTINUE` directive. When used with the `EXIT` directive, `COMMIT` is the default and when used with the `CONTINUE` directive, `NONE` is the default.

Therefore, if a SQL*Plus script contains five UPDATE statements in a row and you want the script to stop executing, roll back any work already performed, and then exit to the operating system with a failure status, your script might look something like that shown in Listing 11-69.

Listing 11-69. Error-Handling in a SQL*Plus Script

```
whenever oserror exit failure rollback
whenever sqlerror exit failure rollback
set echo on feedback on timing on
spool update_script
update ...
update ...
update ...
update ...
update ...
exit success commit
```

In Listing 11-69, we see the use of the WHENEVER command directing SQL*Plus to exit back to the operating system with a FAILURE exit status, and perform a ROLLBACK as it does so, should any OS commands (such as SPOOL) or SQL commands (such as UPDATE) fail. If all of the commands are successful and we reach the very last line of the script, then the script will EXIT back to the operating system with a SUCCESS exit status and perform a COMMIT as it does so.

SQL*Plus Error Logging

If you wish to save the error messages you receive when running an SQL script, you can choose to have them written to an error log table. Having your errors written to an error log table provides you with flexibility in that you do not have to exit a script when you encounter an error if you do not want to, yet you can review any error messages at your convenience by querying the error log table. SQL*Plus Error Logging is turned off by default; but when it is turned on, errors are recorded whether a query is run interactively or from a script. Listing 11-70 demonstrates the default employment of this functionality.

Listing 11-70. Employing Default SQL*Plus Error Logging

```
SQL> SET ERRORLOGGING ON
SQL> select * from department;
select * from department
              *
ERROR at line 1:
ORA-00942: table or view does not exist

SQL> select first_name from employees;
select first_name from employees
       *
ERROR at line 1:
ORA-00904: "FIRST_NAME": invalid identifier

SQL> select empno into :v_emp_no from employees;

EMPNO
-----
 7369
  .
  .
  .

14 rows selected.

SQL> print :v_emp_no
SP2-0552: Bind variable "V_EMP_NO" not declared.

SQL> select timestamp, statement, message
  2    from sperrorlog;

TIMESTAMP                    STATEMENT
MESSAGE
----------------------------------------------------------------------
17-FEB-14 06.21.02.000000 PM    select * from department
ORA-00942: table or view does not exist
17-FEB-14 06.21.19.000000 PM    select first_name from employees
ORA-00904: "FIRST_NAME": invalid identifier
17-FEB-14 06.23.22.000000 PM    print :v_emp_no
SP2-0552: Bind variable "V_EMP_NO" not declared.
```

The output from Listing 11-70 illustrates the fact that when you turn on SQL*Plus error logging, if you do not already have a table in your schema called SPERRORLOG, then one is automatically created for you. Note that the example in Listing 11-70 is entirely interactive and all errors in your current session are logged to the SPERRORLOG table until you turn error logging off by issuing the command, SET ERRORLOGGING OFF, or by logging out of your current session. Such error logging capability is particularly useful for capturing errors during long-running queries and scripts. It avoids your having to capture all output using the SPOOL command.

Additionally, you may choose to use a user-defined error logging table provided the user-defined error logging table already exists and you have access to it.

11.8 Exercises

The following exercises allow you to practice using the commands covered in this chapter. See Appendix B for the answers.

1. Look at Listings 11-50 and 11-61. Apart from aesthetics, there is another important reason why the lines surrounding the script headers in those two listings switch from minus signs to equal signs. Obviously, the first two minus signs are mandatory to turn the lines into comments. What would be wrong with using only minus signs?

2. Create a SQL*Plus script to create indexes. The script should prompt for a table name and a column name (or list of column names), and then generate the index name according to the following standard: i_<tab-id>_<col-id>.

3. Create a SQL*Plus script to produce an index overview. The script should prompt for a table name, allowing you to specify any leading part of a table name. That is, the script should automatically append a % wildcard to the value entered. Then it should produce a report of all indexes, showing the table name, index name, index type, and number of columns on which the index is based.

4. Create a script that disables all constraints in your schema.

■ ■ ■

CHAPTER 12

Object-Relational Features

As promised in the introduction of this book, this final chapter discusses some object-relational features of the Oracle DBMS. For a proper understanding and appreciation of object-relational database features in general, you should consider those features in the context of an object-oriented development environment. Because this book is devoted to Oracle SQL, this chapter focuses on the consequences of these object-relational features for the SQL language.

The first step in setting up an object-relational environment is the definition of the appropriate collection of *object types* and *methods*. Once you have defined your object types, you can use them to create *object tables*, thus creating a truly object-relational environment. You can also use *object views* to create an object-relational layer on top of standard relational environments. This chapter mainly uses object types as a starting point for creating user-defined datatypes and then uses those datatypes in relational table structures.

Along with "regular" user-defined datatypes, there are two special user-defined datatypes, also referred to as *collection types* because they are multivalued: variable arrays and nested tables. Sections 12.1–12.4 of this chapter cover collection types and user-defined datatypes.

Section 12.5 introduces the ANSI/ISO standard multiset operators, which allow you to perform various sophisticated operations with nested tables. Note that the PL/SQL language normally plays an important role in creating an object-relational environment. PL/SQL is the programming language you need in the definition phase of such an environment. Because PL/SQL is not covered in this book, we assume some basic knowledge of this language.

■ **Note**   Instead of PL/SQL, you can also use the Java language to create an object-relational environment.

12.1 More Datatypes

So far in this book, we have used only the standard, built-in datatypes supported by Oracle, such as NUMBER, BINARY_FLOAT, BINARY_DOUBLE, DATE, TIMESTAMP [WITH [LOCAL] TIMEZONE], INTERVAL, [N]CHAR, and [N]VARCHAR2. This means that we haven't discussed the following two Oracle datatype categories:

- **Collection datatypes:** These are variable arrays (*varrays*) and *nested tables*. You are probably familiar with the concept of arrays from other programming languages, and nested tables are tables within a table.

- **User-defined datatypes:** These allow you (as the name indicates) to define your own complex datatypes.

Collection Datatypes

Collection datatypes are a special case of user-defined datatypes. Collection datatypes support attributes that can have multiple values. For example, you can store a list of phone numbers for each employee in a single column, or you can add a set of errata entries to every row in the COURSES table.

The first example (adding a list of phone numbers) is an obvious candidate for using a varray, because, in general, you know the maximum length of such a list of phone numbers in advance. Also, you probably want to assign some meaning to the order of the phone numbers in the list (office extension, home, mobile, fax, and so on).

It is probably better to implement the second example (maintaining course errata) with a nested table, because you don't have an idea beforehand about how many errata entries to expect.

■ **Note**   As you will see soon, you cannot create nested tables without using user-defined datatypes.

As a user-defined datatype, you might, for example, create an ADDRESS type, with STREET, NUMBER, POSTALCODE, and CITY components. You can create arrays of user-defined datatypes- and use ADDRESS type to add an array of addresses to the OFFERINGS table. That would allow you to store multiple alternative location addresses for course offerings. If you want to store only a single location address, you obviously don't need an array—a regular user-defined address type would be sufficient.

Methods

You can add *methods* to user-defined datatypes. Methods are operations specifically developed to work with your user-defined datatypes; for example, to specify how you want to *compare* two address type values, or how you want to *sort* address values.

Methods add a lot of semantic power to your user-defined datatypes. Unfortunately we can't spend much time on methods in this book, because you need a great deal of PL/SQL programming to create methods. If you want to see some method examples, check out the CUSTOMERS table of the OE schema, one of the standard sample schemas that ships with the Oracle software.

As you will see in the Section 12.2, as soon as you create a user-defined datatype in Oracle, you implicitly get one method "for free"—a method with the same name as the datatype itself. That method is the *constructor method*, which allows you to create occurrences of the datatype.

OBJECT-RELATIONAL VS. STANDARD RELATIONAL TECHNIQUES

For the examples mentioned so far in this chapter, you could argue that you could implement them very well with standard relational techniques, as discussed in previous chapters of this book. You could separate various phone numbers into separate columns, you could create a separate ERRATA table with a foreign key constraint referring to the COURSES table, and so on.

So when should you choose an object-relational approach rather than a pure relational approach? It might be a matter of taste, and discussions about taste are probably a waste of time in a technical book like this one. As the Romans said, "*De gustibus non disputandum est...*" (That phrase translates to "There is no disputing about tastes.")

It might be the case that you have a powerful object-oriented design and development environment. You may find that Oracle's object-relational features enable you to maintain an intuitive and straightforward mapping between that development environment and the Oracle database structures.

In any case, this book does not speculate about when one approach is better than the other. The examples in this chapter have a single purpose: to illustrate the object-relational features of the Oracle DBMS.

As you read about the techniques described in this chapter, you may wonder whether they violate the first normal form as one of the foundations of the relational model. That is *not* the case. The relational model does not forbid in any way storing complex or set-valued attributes in your rows. Data "atomicity" is a rather slippery concept. For example, if you consider DATE values, aren't you looking at a compound datatype? A DATE value has meaningful subcomponents, such as year, month, and day. For a thorough treatment of this subject, see *An Introduction to Database Systems, 8th Edition* by Chris Date (Addison-Wesley, 2003).

12.2 Varrays

We will begin to explore varrays by implementing the phone list example introduced in the previous section. To keep our EMPLOYEES table unimpaired, we create a copy of the EMPLOYEES table for our experiments in this final chapter of the book. We also leave out some of the columns of the original EMPLOYEES table. See Listing 12-1.

Listing 12-1. Creating a Copy of the EMPLOYEES Table

```
create table eas
select empno, ename, init, mgr, deptno
from    employees;
```

Creating the Array

Before we can add a list of phone numbers for every employee in the E table, we must create a corresponding type first, as shown in Listing 12-2.

Listing 12-2. Creating and Describing a Type

```
create or replace type numberlist_t
as varray(4) of varchar2(20);
/

describe numberlist_t
 numberlist_t VARRAY(4) OF VARCHAR2(20)

select type_name, typecode
from    user_types;

TYPE_NAME               TYPECODE
----------------------- -------------------------------
NUMBERLIST_T            COLLECTION
```

Note that you must end the CREATE TYPE command in Listing 12-2 with a slash (/) in the third line, although you ended the second line with a semicolon. The reason is that you are not entering an SQL or an SQL*Plus command; you're entering a PL/SQL command.

Note also that from now on, you can use this NUMBERLIST_T type as often as you like. It is known to the database, and its definition is stored in the data dictionary. You can query the USER_TYPES data dictionary view to see your own type definitions.

■ **Note**   To allow other database users to use your type definitions, you must grant them the EXECUTE privilege on those types.

In Listing 12-3, we add a column to the E table, using the NUMBERLIST_T type we created in Listing 12-2. Then, we execute a query.

Listing 12-3. Adding a Column Based on the NUMBERLIST_T Type

```
alter table e add (numlist numberlist_t);

describe e
Name            Null?          Type
------------    -------------  -------------
 EMPNO                         NUMBER(4)
 ENAME          NOT NULL       VARCHAR2(8)
 INIT           NOT NULL       VARCHAR2(5)
 MGR                           NUMBER(4)
 DEPTNO                        NUMBER(2)
 NUMLIST                       NUMBERLIST_T

select  empno, numlist from e;
  EMPNO NUMLIST
------- ----------------------------------------
   7369
   7499
   7521
   7566
   7654
   7698
   7782
   7788
   7839
   7844
   7876
   7900
   7902
   7934
```

The query results are not impressive. Obviously, the new NUMLIST column is still empty. So we have the following two problems to solve:

- How can we populate the NUMLIST column with phone numbers?

- After the column has these phone numbers, how can we retrieve them?

Populating the Array with Values

As mentioned earlier in the chapter, each user-defined object type implicitly has a function of the same name, allowing you to generate or construct values of that object type. This function is normally referred to as the *constructor method*. In other words, if you create a user-defined object type, you get a constructor method for free, with the same name as the object type.

Listing 12-4 shows how you can assign phone number lists to five employees in the E table. Note that you can skip elements, if you like, and you can also assign empty number lists.

Listing 12-4. Assigning Values to the NUMLIST Column

```
update e
set    numlist = numberlist_t('1234','06-78765432','029-8765432')
where  empno = 7839;

update e
set    numlist = numberlist_t('4231','06-12345678')
where  empno = 7782;

update e
set    numlist = numberlist_t('2345')
where  empno = 7934;

update e
set    numlist = numberlist_t('','06-23456789')
where  empno = 7698;
update e
set numlist = numberlist_t()
where  empno in (7566,7844);
```

Querying Array Columns

Now let's see what happens if we select the NUMLIST column, without applying any functions or operators to that column. In that case, we simply get the values back the same way we inserted them, including the constructor method, as shown in Listing 12-5.

Listing 12-5. Querying the NUMLIST Column

```
select empno, numlist
from   e
where  empno in (7566,7698,77832,7839,7934);

  EMPNO NUMLIST
------- --------------------------------------------------
   7566 NUMBERLIST_T()
   7698 NUMBERLIST_T(NULL, '06-23456789')
   7839 NUMBERLIST_T('1234', '06-78765432', '029-8765432')
   7934 NUMBERLIST_T('2345')
```

If you want to select individual phone numbers from the NUMLIST array, you need to "un-nest" the phone numbers first. You can un-nest arrays with the TABLE function. Listing 12-6 shows how you can use the TABLE function for that purpose. (For further details about the TABLE function, see *Oracle SQL Reference*.)

Listing 12-6. Using the TABLE Function to Un-Nest the NUMLIST Array

```
break on empno

select e.empno, n.*
from    e
,       TABLE(e.numlist) n;

   EMPNO COLUMN_VALUE
-------- ------------------
    7698
         06-23456789
    7782 4231
         06-12345678
    7839 1234
         06-78765432
         029-8765432
    7934 2345
```

Suppose that we want to go one step further and be able to select specific phone numbers from the array (for example, the second one). In that case, we need PL/SQL again, because the SQL language does not support a direct way to access array elements by their index value. It is not difficult to build a PL/SQL function to return a certain element from an array. Chapter 5 showed an example of a PL/SQL stored function to count the number of employees per department (Listing 5-31). Listing 12-7 shows how you can create a PL/SQL stored function to return the first phone number from the NUMLIST array, assuming that number represents the internal extension number.

Listing 12-7. Creating a PL/SQL Function to Return Array Elements

```
create or replace function ext
     (p_varray_in numberlist_t)
return varchar2
is
  v_ext varchar2(20);
begin
  v_ext := p_varray_in(1);
  return v_ext;
end;
/
Function created.

select ename, init, ext(numlist)
from    e
where   deptno = 10;

ENAME    INIT  EXT(NUMLIST)
-------- ----- ------------
CLARK    AB    4231
KING     CC    1234
MILLER   TJA   2345
```

The DEPTNO value (10) in the WHERE clause of this query is carefully chosen in order to avoid error messages. Just change the DEPTNO value in Listing 12-7, and you will see the corresponding Oracle error messages.

■ **Note** The EXT stored function is kept as simple as possible. For example, there is no code to handle situations where employees have no phone number list or an empty phone number list. It is relatively easy to enhance the EXT function definition with some proper exception handling. However, this is not a PL/SQL book, and the EXT function is meant only to illustrate the concept.

It is impossible to update specific elements of an array. You can only replace an entire array value with a new one.

12.3 Nested Tables

Nested tables offer you more flexibility than arrays. There are many similarities between arrays and nested tables. However, an important difference is that nested tables require one extra step. In the previous section, you saw that you create a type and then use it to define arrays. For nested tables, you first create a type, then you create a table type based on that type, and then you create a nested table based on that table type.

Creating Table Types

To demonstrate how to use nested tables we will implement the example of maintaining course errata, introduced in Section 12.1. Listing 12-8 shows how to create the two types we need for implementing the errata example as a nested table.

Listing 12-8. Creating a Table Type for a Nested Table

```
create or replace type erratum_t as object
( code varchar2(4)
, ch   number(2)
, pg   number(3)
, txt  varchar2(40)
) ;
/

create or replace type errata_tab_t as table of erratum_t;
/

describe errata_tab_t
 errata_tab_t TABLE OF ERRATUM_T
 Name                            Null?    Type
 ------------------------------- -------- ---------------
 CODE                                     VARCHAR2(4)
 CH                                       NUMBER(2)
 PG                                       NUMBER(3)
 TXT                                      VARCHAR2(40)
```

Creating the Nested Table

Listing 12-9 shows the next step of creating the nested table based on the ERRATA_TAB_T type. Just as we did in the previous section with the EMPLOYEES table, we first create a copy C of the COURSES table to keep that table unimpaired.

Listing 12-9. Creating a Table with a Nested Table Column

```
create table c
as
select * from courses;

alter table c
add (errata errata_tab_t)
nested table errata store as errata_tab;

update c
set    errata = errata_tab_t();
```

In Listing 12-9, the ALTER TABLE command adds an ERRATA nested table column to the C table, and the UPDATE command assigns an empty nested table to the ERRATA column for every row. Note that we use the ERRATA_TAB_T table type constructor method for that purpose.

Populating the Nested Table

Now we can add rows to the nested table, as shown in Listing 12-10. Note that you can access nested tables *only* within the context of the table they are part of; it is *impossible* to access them as independent tables. Listing 12-10 uses the TABLE function again, just as we did before in Listing 12-6, to un-nest the nested table.

Listing 12-10. Inserting Rows into the Nested Table

```
insert into table ( select errata
                    from   c
                    where  code = 'SQL')
values ('SQL'
       , 3
       , 45
       , 'Typo in last line.');
```

We inserted an erratum entry for the SQL course, Chapter 3, page 45. In a similar way, you can also delete rows from a nested table. As stated in the introduction to this section, nested tables offer more flexibility than arrays. For example, you can update individual column values of a nested table, whereas you can only replace arrays in their entirety.

Suppose we made a typo in Listing 12-10 while entering the chapter number: the erratum was not in Chapter 3, but rather in Chapter 7. Listing 12-11 shows how we can correct this mistake with an UPDATE command. Note that line 3 introduces tuple variable e ranging over the result of the TABLE function, allowing us to use that tuple variable on the fourth line to refer to its chapter (CH) column value.

Listing 12-11. Updating Individual Columns of Nested Tables

```
update table ( select errata
               from   c
               where  code = 'SQL') e
set    e.ch = 7;
```

Querying the Nested Table

If you want to retrieve all errata entries for the SQL course, you can join the course's table (C) with its nested table, as shown in Listing 12-12.

Listing 12-12. Selecting Errata for the SQL Course

```
select code
,      c.description
,      e.ch, e.pg, e.txt
from   c
       join
       table(c.errata) e
       using (code);

CODE    DESCRIPTION
------- ------------------------------
 CH  PG TXT
--- --- ------------------------------
SQL     Introduction to SQL
  7  45 Typo in last line.
```

As Listing 12-12 shows, this nested table join syntax is very similar to the syntax you use for regular joins (discussed in Chapter 8). The TABLE function un-nests its column-valued argument (c.errata) into a table.

Note that you can only refer to c.ERRATA because you specify the C table first in the FROM clause. The FROM clause order is important in this case. If you swap the two table expressions, you get the following Oracle error message:

```
select code
,      c.description
,      e.ch, e.pg, e.txt
from   table(c.errata) e
       join
       c
       using (code);
from   table(c.errata) e
            *
ERROR at line 4:
ORA-00904: "C"."ERRATA": invalid identifier
```

Listing 12-12 shows only a single row, because we inserted only a single erratum into the nested table. The last section of this chapter revisits nested tables, showing how you can use *multiset operators* on nested tables. These multiset operators could be a reason to consider using nested tables instead of regular (relational) tables with primary key and foreign key constraints. The multiset operators allow you to write elegant SQL statements that would need quite complicated syntax without them.

One additional thought: a nested table is a table like any other, and as the volume of data increases, it might help the performance of SQL statements against the nested table if the column used in the WHERE clause for searching were indexed.

So in summary, varrays and nested tables present similar solutions to the requirement for a complex column containing many elements. Varrays provide a faster solution needing only type definitions, but with restrictions such as only one column and a limit to the number of elements and fixed positions for the elements. Nested tables require more consideration involved in creating an actual table with its own storage requirements, but the rows in a nested table have no restrictions on quantity and they can be sorted any way on retrieval. Also, varrays can only be modified by writing a PL/SQL procedure, whereas nested tables can be accessed and updated more intuitively using SQL statements.

12.4 User-Defined Types

Your application may require a special, complex datatype. In that case, you would create a user-defined type.

Creating User-Defined Types

The third example mentioned in Section 12.1 was the compound ADDRESS type, used to store addresses with meaningful subcomponents into a single column. Listing 12-13 shows how you can create such a type.

Listing 12-13. Creating and Using User-Defined Types

```
create type address_t as object
( street varchar2(20)
, nr     varchar2(5)
, pcode  varchar2(6)
, city   varchar2(20)
) ;
/

describe address_t
```

Name	Null?	Type
STEET		VARCHAR2(20)
NR		VARCHAR2(5)
PCODE		VARCHAR2(6)
CITY		VARCHAR2(20)

```
select type_name, typecode
from   user_types;
```

TYPE_NAME	TYPECODE
NUMBERLIST_T	COLLECTION
ERRATUM_T	OBJECT
ERRATA_TAB_T	COLLECTION
ADDRESS_T	OBJECT

```
create table o
as
select course, begindate, trainer
from   offerings;

alter table o add (address address_t);

update o
set    o.address =
       address_t('','','',
              (select initcap(x.location)
               from   offerings   x
               where  x.course    = o.course
               and    x.begindate = o.begindate)
       )
;
```

Note that we now have four user-defined types, as shown by the query against the USER_TYPES data dictionary view. Then we create a copy O of the OFFERINGS table (again, to keep the original table unimpaired) and add an ADDRESS column to the O table. As a last step, Listing 12-13 updates the O table with some address values. The last command uses the ADDRESS_T function to generate address values, leaving the first three address fields empty and selecting the city name from the original OFFERINGS table with a subquery.

Showing More Information with DESCRIBE

If you use user-defined datatypes, you can change the behavior of the SQL*Plus DESCRIBE command to show more information by setting its DEPTH attribute to a value higher than 1 or to ALL. See Listing 12-14 for an example.

Listing 12-14. Setting the DEPTH Attribute of the DESCRIBE Command

```
describe o
Name                Null?    Type
------------------  -------- ------------
COURSE              NOT NULL VARCHAR2(4)
BEGINDATE           NOT NULL DATE
TRAINER                      NUMBER(4)
ADDRESS                      ADDRESS_T

set describe depth 2
describe o
Name                Null?    Type
------------------  -------- ----------------
COURSE              NOT NULL VARCHAR2(4)
BEGINDATE           NOT NULL DATE
TRAINER                      NUMBER(4)
ADDRESS                      ADDRESS_T
  STREET                     VARCHAR2(20)
  NR                         VARCHAR2(5)
  PCODE                      VARCHAR2(6)
  CITY                       VARCHAR2(20)
```

The DESCRIBE command now also shows the subcomponents of your user-defined types. If your object-relational tables have additional method functions, they are shown as well.

12.5 Multiset Operators

This section discusses the ANSI/ISO standard multiset operators of the SQL language. We will first look at a complete list of all SQL multiset operators with a brief description. You can use these operators *only* on nested tables. Therefore, to allow for some multiset operator examples in this section, we will enter some more nested table entries in the ERRATA nested table. You will also see how you can convert arrays into nested tables "on the fly," using the CAST and COLLECT functions.

Which SQL Multiset Operators Are Available?

If you are using nested tables in your table design, you can apply various SQL *multiset operators* against those tables. Multiset operators allow you to compare nested tables, check certain nested table properties, or derive new nested tables from existing ones.

■ **Note** The SQL language refers to *multisets* to indicate a rather important difference between these sets and "regular" sets. In mathematics, duplicate elements in sets are meaningless. In SQL, multisets may have meaningful duplicates; that is, you cannot ignore duplicates in multisets.

Table 12-1 shows an overview of the Oracle multiset operators. Note that these multiset operators are also part of the ANSI/ISO SQL standard. For completeness, Table 12-1 not only shows the SQL multiset operators, but also some other operations you can apply to nested tables.

Table 12-1. *SQL Multiset Operators and Functions*

Multiset Operator or Function	Description
nt1 MULTISET EXCEPT [DISTINCT] nt2	The difference of nt1 and nt2 (equivalent with the MINUS set operator)
nt1 MULTISET INTERSECT [DISTINCT] nt2	The intersection of nt1 and nt2
nt1 MULTISET UNION [DISTINCT] nt2	The union of nt1 and nt2
CARDINALITY(nt)	The number of rows in nt
nt IS [NOT] EMPTY	Boolean function to check whether nt is empty
nt IS [NOT] A SET	Boolean function to check whether nt contains duplicates
SET(nt)	Removes duplicates from nt
nt1 = nt2	Checks whether nt1 and nt2 are equal
nt1 IN (nt2, nt3, ...)	Checks whether nt1 occurs in a list of nested tables
nt1 [NOT] SUBMULTISET OF nt2	Checks whether nt1 a subset of nt2
r [NOT] MEMBER OF nt	Checks whether row r occurs in table nt
CAST(COLLECT(col))	Produces a nested table based on column col
POWERMULTISET(nt)	The set of all nonempty subsets of nt
POWERMULTISET_BY_CARDINALITY(nt,c)	The set of all nonempty subsets of nt with cardinality c

The following sections show a few typical examples of using multiset operators and functions. See the *Oracle SQL Reference* documentation for examples of all these operators and functions.

Preparing for the Examples

In Section 12.3, you learned how you can store errata entries for courses in a nested table. In Listing 12-10, we inserted only a single erratum. In Listing 12-15, we insert some more rows into the ERRATA nested table.

Listing 12-15. Inserting Some More Errata Rows

```
insert into table ( select errata
                     from   c
                     where  code = 'SQL' )
values ('SQL'
       , 3
       , 46
       ,'Layout illustration' );

insert into table ( select errata
                     from   c
                     where  code = 'SQL' )
values ('SQL'
       , 5
       , 1
       ,'Introduction missing.' );

insert into table ( select errata
                     from   c
                     where  code = 'XML' )
values ('XML'
       , 5
       , 1
       , 'Introduction missing.' );

insert into table ( select errata
                     from   c
                     where  code = 'XML' )
values ('XML'
       , 7
       , 3
       ,'Line 5: "succeeds" should read "fails"' );
```

Now we have five errata entries in total: three for the SQL course and two for the XML course. If you execute a "regular" query against the C table and select its ERRATA column without using any modifying functions, the structure of the ERRATA column (with the nested table) becomes clear from the query result, as shown in Listing 12-16.

Listing 12-16. Querying a Nested Table Without Using Modifying Functions

```
col errata format a80 word

select errata
from   c
where  code = 'SQL';
```

```
ERRATA(CODE, CH, PG, TXT)
---------------------------------------------------------------------
ERRATA_TAB_T(ERRATUM_T('SQL', 7, 45, 'Typo in last line.'),
             ERRATUM_T('SQL', 3, 46, 'Layout illustration'),
             ERRATUM_T('SQL', 5,  1, 'Introduction missing.'))
```

■ **Note** The query output in Listing 12-16 is formatted for readability.

The query result in Listing 12-16 consists of only a single row with a single column. In other words, you are looking at a complicated but *single* value. If you interpret that single value "inside out," you see that the ERRATUM_T constructor function (or method) appears three times to build individual erratum entries. These three erratum entries, in turn, are elements in a comma-separated list. The ERRATA_TAB_T constructor function takes that comma-separated errata list as an argument to convert it into a nested table.

Using IS NOT EMPTY and CARDINALITY

Listing 12-17 uses the IS NOT EMPTY operator to select only those courses that have at least one erratum entry, and it uses the CARDINALITY function to show the number of errata for those courses.

Listing 12-17. IS NOT EMPTY and CARDINALITY Example

```
select code, cardinality(errata)
from   c
where  errata is not empty;

CODE    CARDINALITY(ERRATA)
-------  -------------------
SQL                       3
XML                       2
```

A corresponding query against a "regular" relational errata table would need a COUNT(*), a GROUP BY, and a HAVING clause.

Using POWERMULTISET

Listing 12-18 shows how you can produce the *powermultiset* of the ERRATA column for the SQL course. To increase the readability of the results in Listing 12-18, we issue a SQL*Plus BREAK command, which highlights the fact that the query result contains seven rows. Every row is a subset of the ERRATA nested table for the SQL course.

Listing 12-18. POWERMULTISET Example

```
break on row page

select *
from   table ( select powermultiset(errata)
               from   c
               where  code = 'SQL' );
```

```
ERRATA_TAB_T(ERRATUM_T('SQL', 7, 45, 'Typo in last line.'))
ERRATA_TAB_T(ERRATUM_T('SQL', 3, 46, 'Layout illustration'))
ERRATA_TAB_T(ERRATUM_T('SQL', 7, 45, 'Typo in last line.'),
             ERRATUM_T('SQL', 3, 46, 'Layout illustration'))
ERRATA_TAB_T(ERRATUM_T('SQL', 5,  1, 'Introduction missing.')
ERRATA_TAB_T(ERRATUM_T('SQL', 7, 45, 'Typo in last line.'),
             ERRATUM_T('SQL', 5,  1, 'Introduction missing.'))
ERRATA_TAB_T(ERRATUM_T('SQL', 3, 46, 'Layout illustration'),
             ERRATUM_T('SQL', 5,  1, 'Introduction missing.'))
ERRATA_TAB_T(ERRATUM_T('SQL', 7, 45, 'Typo in last line.'),
             ERRATUM_T('SQL', 3, 46, 'Layout illustration'),
             ERRATUM_T('SQL', 5,  1, 'Introduction missing.'))
```

■ **Note**   In mathematics, the powerset of a set X is the set consisting of all possible subsets of X.

The result contains seven rows because we have three SQL errata; see also Listing 12-17. Why seven rows for three errata? Well, there are the following possible subsets:

- Three possible subsets with cardinality 1 (rows 1, 2, and 4)

- Three possible subsets with cardinality 2 (rows 3, 5, and 6)

- One possible subset with cardinality 3 (row 7; that is, the nested table itself)

In mathematics, we would also expect the empty set to show up as an element of the powerset. However, the definition of the POWERMULTISET operator (see Table 12-1) explicitly excludes that subset, by stating that only *nonempty* subsets are considered.

Using MULTISET UNION

Listing 12-19 shows how you can use the MULTISET UNION operator to merge two nested tables into a single one. The query result is manually formatted to enhance readability, allowing you to see that the result is a single nested table, containing five errata entries. Without manual formatting, the query result will show up as one unstructured string.

Listing 12-19. MULTISET UNION Example

```
select c1.errata
       MULTISET UNION
       c2.errata
       as result
from   c c1,
       c c2
where  c1.code = 'SQL'
and    c2.code = 'XML';
```

```
RESULT(CODE, CH, PG, TXT)
-----------------------------------------------------------------------------
ERRATA_TAB_T( ERRATUM_T('SQL', 7, 45, 'Typo in last line.')
            , ERRATUM_T('SQL', 3, 46, 'Layout illustration')
            , ERRATUM_T('SQL', 5, 1, 'Introduction missing.')
            , ERRATUM_T('XML', 5, 1, 'Introduction missing.')
            , ERRATUM_T('XML', 7, 3, 'Line 5: "succeeds" should read "fails"')
            )
```

Converting Arrays into Nested Tables

For the last example, we revisit the E table with the phone number array (see Listings 12-1 through 12-6). Listing 12-20 shows how you can use the COLLECT and CAST operators to convert an array into a nested table. To be able to capture the result, we first create a new numBer_tab_t type using the existing numBerlist_t type.

Listing 12-20. CAST and COLLECT Example to Convert an Array into a Nested Table

```
create type number_tab_t
as table of numberlist_t;
/

select cast(collect(numlist) as number_tab_t) as result
from   e
where  empno in (7839, 7782);

RESULT
---------------------------------------------------------------------
NUMBER_TAB_T(NUMBERLIST_T('4231', '06-12345678'),
             NUMBERLIST_T('1234', '06-78765432', '029-8765432'))
```

This final chapter gave you a high-level introduction to the object-relational features of the Oracle DBMS, focusing on the way you can use those features in SQL. You learned how you can create object types, and how you can use those types as user-defined datatypes. You also learned about the Oracle collection types: variable arrays and nested tables. If your tables contain nested tables, you can use SQL multiset operators on those tables.

If you want to learn more about the object-relational features of Oracle, refer to the Oracle documentation. *Application Developer's Guide: Object-Relational Features* is an excellent starting point for further study in this area.

12.6 Exercises

You can do the following exercises to practice using the object-relational techniques covered in this chapter. The answers are in Appendix B.

1. The SALGRADES table has two columns to indicate salary ranges: LOWERLIMIT and UPPERLIMIT. Define your own SALRANGE_T type, based on a varray of two NUMBER(6,2) values, and use it to create an alternative SALGRADES2 table.

2. Fill the new SALGRADES2 table with a single INSERT statement, using the existing SALGRADES table.

3. Create a table TESTNEST with two columns: column X and column MX. Column X is NUMBER(1,0) with values 2, 3, 4, …, 9. Column MX is a nested table, based on a MX_TAB_T type, containing all multiples of X less than or equal to 20.

4. Use multiset operators to solve the following problems, using the TESTNEST table you created and populated in the previous exercise:

    a. Which rows have a nested table containing value 12?

    b. Which nested tables are *not* a subset of any other subset?

    c. Which nested tables have more than 42 different nonempty subsets?

■ ■ ■

The Seven Case Tables

This appendix offers an overview of the seven case tables used throughout this book, in various formats. Its main purpose is to help you in writing SQL commands and checking your results.

The first section shows an Entity Relationship Modeling (ERM) diagram, indicating the entities of the underlying data model, including their unique identifiers and their relationships. Then you can find descriptions of the seven case tables, with names and datatypes of all their columns and short explanations, when necessary. The next section shows a table diagram, focusing on all primary key and foreign key constraints. This diagram may be especially helpful when you are writing joins.

The biggest component of this appendix (with the highest level of detail) is a complete listing of the seven case tables with all their rows. This overview may be useful to check your query results for correctness.

At the end of this appendix, you will find two alternative representations of the case table data, showing the table rows in a compact format. The first diagram shows an overview of the 14 employees. It clearly shows the department populations and the hierarchical (manager/subordinate) relationships. The second illustration shows a matrix overview of all course offerings, with starting dates, locations, attendees (A), and trainers (T). Again, these representations may be useful to check your query results for correctness.

ERM Diagram

The ERM diagram, shown in Figure A-1, shows the seven entities (the rounded-corner boxes) with their unique identifiers and their mutual relationships.

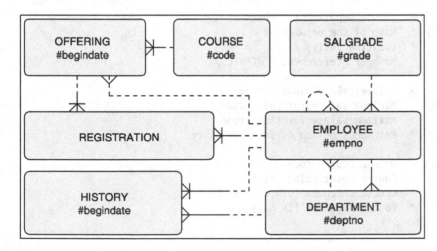

Figure A-1. ERM diagram of the case entities

The ten crow's feet indicate one-to-many relationships. The diagram shows two types of one-to-many relationships: three relationships are *completely* optional (indicated by all dashed lines) and the remaining ones are mandatory in one direction (indicated by the solid part of the line).

Hash signs (#) in front of an attribute mean that the attribute is part of the unique identifier; relationship cross-lines indicate that the relationship is part of the unique identifier. Note that the diagram shows only attributes that are part of unique identifiers, for enhanced readability.

You can interpret the relationships in this diagram as follows:

- Every employee has *at most one* manager (and employees may have multiple subordinates).

- Every employee belongs to *precisely one* salary grade and is employed by *at most one* department (employees without a department are allowed).

- Each department has *precisely one* manager (and employees may be manager of multiple departments).

- Each course offering refers to *precisely one* existing course, with *at most one* employee as trainer.

- Each registration is for *precisely one* employee and for *precisely one* course offering.

- Each history record refers to *precisely one* employee and *precisely one* department.

Table Structure Descriptions

This section presents descriptions of the table structures. In the listings, * means NOT NULL and P means primary key.

```
EMPLOYEES:    EMPNO        N(4)    P   Unique employee number
              ENAME        VC(8)   *   Last name
              INIT         VC(5)   *   Initials (without punctuation)
              JOB          VC(8)       Job description
              MGR          N(4)        Manager (references EMPLOYEES)
              BDATE        DATE    *   Date of birth
              MSAL         N(6,2)  *   Monthly salary (excluding net bonus)
              COMM         N(6,2)      Commission (per year, for sales reps)
              DEPTNO       N(2)        Department (references DEPARTMENTS)

DEPARTMENTS:  DEPTNO       N(2)    P   Unique department number
              DNAME        VC(10)  *   Name of the department
              LOCATION     VC(8)   *   Location (city)
              MGR          N(4)        Manager (references EMPLOYEES)

SALGRADES:    GRADE        N(2)    P   Unique salary grade number
              LOWERLIMIT   N(6,2)  *   Minimum salary for this grade
              UPPERLIMIT   N(6,2)  *   Maximum salary for this grade
              BONUS        N(6,2)  *   Net bonus on top of monthly salary

COURSES:      CODE         VC(6)   P   Unique course code
              DESCRIPTION  VC(30)  *   Course description (title)
              CATEGORY     C(3)    *   Course category (GEN,BLD, or DSG)
              DURATION     N(2)    *   Course duration (in days)
```

```
OFFERINGS:      COURSE      VC(6)   P  Course code      (references COURSES)
                BEGINDATE   DATE    P  First course day
                TRAINER     N(4)       Instructor       (references EMPLOYEES)
                LOCATION    VC(8)      Location of the course offering

REGISTRATIONS:  ATTENDEE    N(4)    P  Attendee         (references EMPLOYEES)
                COURSE      VC(6)   P  Course code      (references OFFERINGS)
                BEGINDATE   DATE    P  First course day (references OFFERINGS)
                EVALUATION  N(1)       Attendee's opinion (scale 1 - 5)

HISTORY:        EMPNO       N(4)    P  Employee         (references EMPLOYEES)
                BEGINYEAR   N(4)    *  Year component of BEGINDATE
                BEGINDATE   DATE    P  Begin date interval
                ENDDATE     DATE       End date interval
                DEPTNO      N(2)    *  Department       (references DEPARTMENTS)
                MSAL        N(6,2)  *  Monthly salary during the interval
                COMMENTS    VC(60)     Free text space
```

Columns and Foreign Key Constraints

Figure A-2 shows the columns and foreign key constraints in the case tables. The primary key components have a dark-gray background, and all arrows point from the foreign keys to the corresponding primary keys. Boxes surrounding multiple columns indicate composite keys.

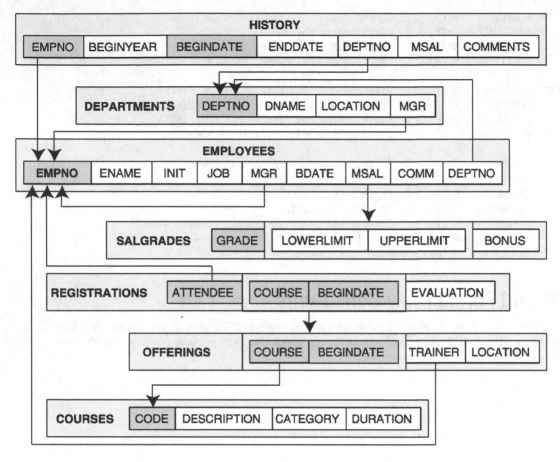

Figure A-2. *Columns and foreign key constraints*

Contents of the Seven Tables

This section lists the contents of each of the seven case tables.

EMPLOYEES

EMPNO	ENAME	INIT	JOB	MGR	BDATE	MSAL	COMM	DEPTNO
7369	SMITH	N	TRAINER	7902	17-12-1965	800		20
7499	ALLEN	JAM	SALESREP	7698	20-02-1961	1600	300	30
7521	WARD	TF	SALESREP	7698	22-02-1962	1250	500	30
7566	JONES	JM	MANAGER	7839	02-04-1967	2975		20
7654	MARTIN	P	SALESREP	7698	28-09-1956	1250	1400	30
7698	BLAKE	R	MANAGER	7839	01-11-1963	2850		30
7782	CLARK	AB	MANAGER	7839	09-06-1965	2450		10
7788	SCOTT	SCJ	TRAINER	7566	26-11-1959	3000		20
7839	KING	CC	DIRECTOR		17-11-1952	5000		10
7844	TURNER	JJ	SALESREP	7698	28-09-1968	1500	0	30
7876	ADAMS	AA	TRAINER	7788	30-12-1966	1100		20

7900 JONES	R	ADMIN	7698	03-12-1969	800	30
7902 FORD	MG	TRAINER	7566	13-02-1959	3000	20
7934 MILLER	TJA	ADMIN	7782	23-01-1962	1300	10

14 rows selected.

DEPARTMENTS

DEPTNO	DNAME	LOCATION	MGR
10	ACCOUNTING	NEW YORK	7782
20	TRAINING	DALLAS	7566
30	SALES	CHICAGO	7698
40	HR	BOSTON	7839

SALGRADES

GRADE	LOWERLIMIT	UPPERLIMIT	BONUS
1	700	1200	0
2	1201	1400	50
3	1401	2000	100
4	2001	3000	200
5	3001	9999	500

COURSES

CODE	DESCRIPTION	CATEGORY	DURATION
JAV	Java for Oracle developers	BLD	4
PLS	Introduction to PL/SQL	BLD	1
XML	XML for Oracle developers	BLD	2
ERM	Data modeling with ERM	DSG	3
GEN	System generation	DSG	4
PMT	Process modeling techniques	DSG	1
PRO	Prototyping	DSG	5
RSD	Relational system design	DSG	2
OAU	Oracle for application users	GEN	1
SQL	Introduction to SQL	GEN	4

10 rows selected.

OFFERINGS

COURSE	BEGINDATE	TRAINER	LOCATION
SQL	12-04-1999	7902	DALLAS
OAU	10-08-1999	7566	CHICAGO
SQL	04-10-1999	7369	SEATTLE
SQL	13-12-1999	7369	DALLAS
JAV	13-12-1999	7566	SEATTLE
JAV	01-02-2000	7876	DALLAS
XML	03-02-2000	7369	DALLAS

```
PLS   11-09-2000    7788 DALLAS
XML   18-09-2000         SEATTLE
OAU   27-09-2000    7902 DALLAS
ERM   15-01-2001
PRO   19-02-2001         DALLAS
RSD   24-02-2001    7788 CHICAGO
```

13 rows selected.

REGISTRATIONS

ATTENDEE	COURSE	BEGINDATE	EVALUATION
7499	SQL	12-04-1999	4
	JAV	13-12-1999	2
	XML	03-02-2000	5
	PLS	11-09-2000	
7521	OAU	10-08-1999	4
7566	JAV	01-02-2000	3
	PLS	11-09-2000	
7698	SQL	12-04-1999	4
	SQL	13-12-1999	
	JAV	01-02-2000	5
7782	JAV	13-12-1999	5
7788	SQL	04-10-1999	
	JAV	13-12-1999	5
	JAV	01-02-2000	4
7839	SQL	04-10-1999	3
	JAV	13-12-1999	4
7844	OAU	27-09-2000	5
7876	SQL	12-04-1999	2
	JAV	13-12-1999	5
	PLS	11-09-2000	
7900	OAU	10-08-1999	4
	XML	03-02-2000	4
7902	OAU	10-08-1999	5
	SQL	04-10-1999	4
	SQL	13-12-1999	
7934	SQL	12-04-1999	5

26 rows selected.

HISTORY (formatted, and without COMMENTS column values)

EMPNO	BEGINYEAR	BEGINDATE	ENDDATE	DEPTNO	MSAL
7369	2000	01-01-2000	01-02-2000	40	950
	2000	01-02-2000		20	800

7499	1988	01-06-1988	01-07-1989	30	1000
	1989	01-07-1989	01-12-1993	30	1300
	1993	01-12-1993	01-10-1995	30	1500
	1995	01-10-1995	01-11-1999	30	1700
	1999	01-11-1999		30	1600
7521	1986	01-10-1986	01-08-1987	20	1000
	1987	01-08-1987	01-01-1989	30	1000
	1989	01-01-1989	15-12-1992	30	1150
	1992	15-12-1992	01-10-1994	30	1250
	1994	01-10-1994	01-10-1997	20	1250
	1997	01-10-1997	01-02-2000	30	1300
	2000	01-02-2000		30	1250
7566	1982	01-01-1982	01-12-1982	20	900
	1982	01-12-1982	15-08-1984	20	950
	1984	15-08-1984	01-01-1986	30	1000
	1986	01-01-1986	01-07-1986	30	1175
	1986	01-07-1986	15-03-1987	10	1175
	1987	15-03-1987	01-04-1987	10	2200
	1987	01-04-1987	01-06-1989	10	2300
	1989	01-06-1989	01-07-1992	40	2300
	1992	01-07-1992	01-11-1992	40	2450
	1992	01-11-1992	01-09-1994	20	2600
	1994	01-09-1994	01-03-1995	20	2550
	1995	01-03-1995	15-10-1999	20	2750
	1999	15-10-1999		20	2975
7654	1999	01-01-1999	15-10-1999	30	1100
	1999	15-10-1999		30	1250
7698	1982	01-06-1982	01-01-1983	30	900
	1983	01-01-1983	01-01-1984	30	1275
	1984	01-01-1984	15-04-1985	30	1500
	1985	15-04-1985	01-01-1986	30	2100
	1986	01-01-1986	15-10-1989	30	2200
	1989	15-10-1989		30	2850
7782	1988	01-07-1988		10	2450
7788	1982	01-07-1982	01-01-1983	20	900
	1983	01-01-1983	15-04-1985	20	950
	1985	15-04-1985	01-06-1985	40	950
	1985	01-06-1985	15-04-1986	40	1100
	1986	15-04-1986	01-05-1986	20	1100
	1986	01-05-1986	15-02-1987	20	1800
	1987	15-02-1987	01-12-1989	20	1250
	1989	01-12-1989	15-10-1992	20	1350
	1992	15-10-1992	01-01-1998	20	1400
	1998	01-01-1998	01-01-1999	20	1700
	1999	01-01-1999	01-07-1999	20	1800
	1999	01-07-1999	01-06-2000	20	1800
	2000	01-06-2000		20	3000

7839	1982	01-01-1982	01-08-1982	30	1000
	1982	01-08-1982	15-05-1984	30	1200
	1984	15-05-1984	01-01-1985	30	1500
	1985	01-01-1985	01-07-1985	30	1750
	1985	01-07-1985	01-11-1985	10	2000
	1985	01-11-1985	01-02-1986	10	2200
	1986	01-02-1986	15-06-1989	10	2500
	1989	15-06-1989	01-12-1993	10	2900
	1993	01-12-1993	01-09-1995	10	3400
	1995	01-09-1995	01-10-1997	10	4200
	1997	01-10-1997	01-10-1998	10	4500
	1998	01-10-1998	01-11-1999	10	4800
	1999	01-11-1999	15-02-2000	10	4900
	2000	15-02-2000		10	5000
7844	1995	01-05-1995	01-01-1997	30	900
	1998	15-10-1998	01-11-1998	10	1200
	1998	01-11-1998	01-01-2000	30	1400
	2000	01-01-2000		30	1500
7876	2000	01-01-2000	01-02-2000	20	950
	2000	01-02-2000		20	1100
7900	2000	01-07-2000		30	800
7902	1998	01-09-1998	01-10-1998	40	1400
	1998	01-10-1998	15-03-1999	30	1650
	1999	15-03-1999	01-01-2000	30	2500
	2000	01-01-2000	01-08-2000	30	3000
	2000	01-08-2000		20	3000
7934	1998	01-02-1998	01-05-1998	10	1275
	1998	01-05-1998	01-02-1999	10	1280
	1999	01-02-1999	01-01-2000	10	1290
	2000	01-01-2000		10	1300

79 rows selected.

Hierarchical Employees Overview

Figure A-3 illustrates an overview of the employees and management structure. Note that department 40 has no employees.

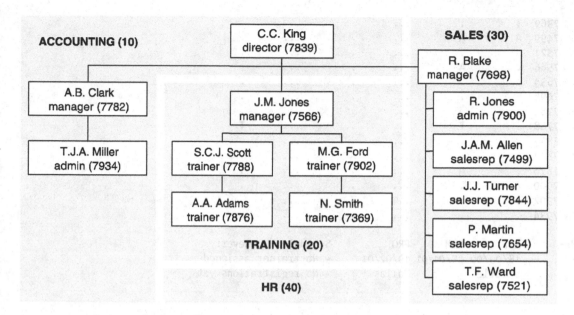

Figure A-3. *Employee overview with management structure*

Course Offerings Overview

This section shows an overview of the course offerings. In the listing A stands for Attendee and T stands for Trainer.

Course code:	SQL	OAU	SQL	JAV	SQL	JAV
Begindate:	12/04/99	10/08/99	04/10/99	13/12/99	13/12/99	01/02/00
Location:	Dallas	Chicago	Seattle	Seattle	Dallas	Dallas

		SQL	OAU	SQL	JAV	SQL	JAV
Smith, N	7369	.	.	T	.	T	.
Allen, JAM	7499	A	.	.	A	.	.
Ward, TF	7521	.	A	.	.	.	.
Jones, JM	7566	.	T	.	T	.	A
Martin, P	7654	.	.	.	.	.	.
Blake, R	7698	A	.	.	.	A	A
Clark, AB	7782	.	.	.	A	.	.
Scott, SCJ	7788	.	.	A	A	.	A
King, CC	7839	.	.	A	A	.	.
Turner, JJ	7844	.	.	.	.	.	.
Adams, AA	7876	A	.	.	A	.	T
Jones, R	7900	.	A	.	.	.	.
Ford, MG	7902	T	A	A	.	A	.
Miller, TJA	7934	A	.	.	.	.	.

Course code:	XML	PLS	...	OAU	...	RSD
Begindate:	03/02/00	11/09/00	...	27/09/00	...	24/02/01
Location:	Dallas	Dallas	...	Dallas	...	Chicago

Smith, N	7369	**T**	.	...	.	...	.
Allen, JAM	7499	A	A	...	.	...	.
Ward, TF	7521	.	.	...	.	...	.
Jones, JM	7566	.	A	...	.	...	.
Martin, P	7654	.	.	...	.	...	.
Blake, R	7698	.	.	...	.	...	.
Clark, AB	7782	.	.	...	.	...	**T**
Scott, SCJ	7788	.	**T**	...	.	...	**T**
King, CC	7839	.	.	...	.	...	.
Turner, JJ	7844	.	.	...	A	...	.
Adams, AA	7876	.	A	...	.	...	.
Jones, R	7900	A	.	...	.	...	.
Ford, MG	7902	.	.	...	**T**	...	.
Miller, TJA	7934	.	.	...	.	...	.

Course code:	XML	ERM	PRO		Scheduled; however:
Begindate:	18/09/00	15/01/01	19/02/01		- No trainer assigned
Location:	Seattle		Dallas		- No registrations yet

■ ■ ■

Answers to the Exercises

This appendix provides answers and solutions to the chapter-ending exercises presented earlier in this book. In some cases, we have presented multiple (alternative) solutions for a single exercise. Sometimes you will see warnings for possible *incorrect* solutions, in case of known pitfalls.

Of course, it is impossible to list all correct solutions for each exercise; the SQL language is too rich (or redundant?) for such an attempt. This implies that it is perfectly possible for you to approach and solve certain exercises in a completely different way. In that case, you can compare your results with the results listed in this appendix. However, always keep the following warning in mind.

■ **Caution** Although a query may produce the correct result, this doesn't imply that you wrote the right query. Incorrect SQL statements sometimes produce the correct results by accident. These are the most treacherous queries, because they can start producing wrong results at any point in the future, based on the actual contents of the tables involved.

Some exercises in this book are quite tough. For some of them, it may be challenging to fully appreciate and understand the given solutions. The reasoning behind including such exercises is the following: to test your SQL knowledge, you can look at the abundance of relatively simple examples in Oracle's online documentation – the *Oracle Database SQL Language Reference*, and you can easily come up with simple SQL experiments yourself.

Chapter 1, 2 and 3: No exercises
Chapter 4 Exercises

1. Provide the code and description of all courses with an exact duration of four days.

    Solution 4-1.

    ```
    SQL> select code, description
      2  from    courses
      3  where   duration = 4;
    CODE DESCRIPTION
    ---- -------------------------------
    SQL  Introduction to SQL
    JAV  Java for Oracle developers
    GEN  System generation
    ```

2. List all employees, sorted by job, and per job by age (from young to old).

Solution 4-2.

```
SQL> select *
  2  from    employees
  3  order   by job, bdate desc;
```

EMPNO	ENAME	INIT	JOB	MGR	BDATE	MSAL	COMM	DEPTNO
7900	JONES	R	ADMIN	7698	03-DEC-1969	800		30
7934	MILLER	TJA	ADMIN	7782	23-JAN-1962	1300		10
7839	KING	CC	DIRECTOR		17-NOV-1952	5000		10
7566	JONES	JM	MANAGER	7839	02-APR-1967	2975		20
7782	CLARK	AB	MANAGER	7839	09-JUN-1965	2450		10
7698	BLAKE	R	MANAGER	7839	01-NOV-1963	2850		30
7844	TURNER	JJ	SALESREP	7698	28-SEP-1968	1500	0	30
7521	WARD	TF	SALESREP	7698	22-FEB-1962	1250	500	30
7499	ALLEN	JAM	SALESREP	7698	20-FEB-1961	1600	300	30
7654	MARTIN	P	SALESREP	7698	28-SEP-1956	1250	1400	30
7876	ADAMS	AA	TRAINER	7788	30-DEC-1966	1100		20
7369	SMITH	N	TRAINER	7902	17-DEC-1965	800		20
7788	SCOTT	SCJ	TRAINER	7566	26-NOV-1959	3000		20
7902	FORD	MG	TRAINER	7566	13-FEB-1959	3000		20

14 rows selected.

3. Which courses have been held in Chicago and/or in Seattle?

Solution 4-3.

```
SQL> select distinct course
  2  from    offerings
  3  where   location in ('CHICAGO','SEATTLE');
```

```
COURSE
------
JAV
OAU
RSD
SQL
XML
```

Notice the DISTINCT keyword in the SELECT clause, to ensure that a course code doesn't show up more than once. This way, you get the correct answer to the question if the same offering should be listed in both locations in the future.

4. Which employees attended both the Java course and the XML course? (Provide their employee numbers.)

Solution 4-4.

```
SQL> select attendee
  2  from    registrations
  3  where   course   = 'JAV'
  4  and     attendee in (select attendee
  5                       from    registrations
  6                       where  course = 'XML');

ATTENDEE
--------
    7499
```

You might want to add the DISTINCT keyword to the SELECT clause here, too, just as you did in the previous exercise; otherwise, what happens if someone attends the XML course once and attends the Java course twice?

This fourth exercise has many different solutions. For example, you can also use two subqueries instead of one. Obviously, the following solutions with AND or OR at the row level are wrong:

```
where course = 'JAV' and course = 'XML'   -- Wrong: Gives "no rows selected."
where course = 'JAV' or  course = 'XML'   -- Wrong: Gives too many results.
```

5. List the names and initials of all employees, except for R. Jones.

Solution 4-5a. Using Parentheses

```
SQL> select ename, init
  2  from    employees
  3  where   not (ename = 'JONES' and init = 'R');

ENAME     INIT
--------  -----
SMITH     N
ALLEN     JAM
WARD      TF
JONES     JM
MARTIN    P
BLAKE     R
CLARK     AB
SCOTT     SCJ
KING      CC
TURNER    JJ
ADAMS     AA
FORD      MG
MILLER    TJA

13 rows selected.
```

Solution 4-5b. Without Parentheses (Note the OR)

```
SQL> select ename, init
  2  from    employees
  3  where   ename <> 'JONES' OR init <> 'R';
```

6. Find the number, job, and date of birth of all trainers and sales representatives born before 1960.

   Solution 4-6a. First Solution

   ```
   SQL> select empno, job, bdate
     2  from    employees
     3  where   bdate < date '1960-01-01'
     4  and     job in ('TRAINER','SALESREP');

       EMPNO JOB      BDATE
   -------- -------- -----------
       7654 SALESREP 28-SEP-1956
       7788 TRAINER  26-NOV-1959
       7902 TRAINER  13-FEB-1959
   ```

Here is an alternative solution; note the parentheses to force operator precedence.

Solution 4-6b. Second Solution

```
SQL> select empno, job, bdate
  2  from    employees
  3  where   bdate < date '1960-01-01'
  4  and     (job = 'TRAINER' or job = 'SALESREP');
```

7. List the numbers of all employees who do not work for the training department.

   Solution 4-7.

   ```
   SQL> select empno
     2  from    employees
     3  where   deptno <> (select deptno
     4                      from    departments
     5                      where   dname = 'TRAINING');

       EMPNO
   --------
       7499
       7521
       7654
       7698
       7782
       7839
       7844
       7900
       7934
   ```

───

■ **Note**   This solution assumes that there is only one training department. And, indeed, in this table the DNAME column has a unique constraint. You could also use NOT IN instead of <>.

───

8. List the employee numbers of all employees who did not attend the Java course.

Solution 4-8a. Correct Solution

```
SQL> select empno
  2  from    employees
  3  where   empno not in (select attendee
  4                        from   registrations
  5                        where  course = 'JAV');

    EMPNO
--------
    7369
    7521
    7654
    7844
    7900
    7902
    7934
```

The following two solutions are *wrong*.

Solution 4-8b. Wrong Solution 1

```
SQL> select distinct attendee
  2  from    registrations
  3  where   attendee not in (select attendee
  4                           from   registrations
  5                           where  course = 'JAV');

ATTENDEE
--------
    7521
    7844
    7900
    7902
    7934
```

This result shows only five employees because employees 7369 and 7654 never attended any course; therefore, their employee numbers do not occur in the REGISTRATIONS table. So this is the answer to the question: Who attended courses other than the Java course?

Solution 4-8c. Wrong Solution 2

```
SQL> select distinct attendee attendee
  2  from    registrations
  3  where   course <> 'JAV';

ATTENDEE
--------
    7499
    7521
    7566
```

```
7698
7788
7839
7844
7876
7900
7902
7934
```

11 rows selected.

This result shows too many results, because it also shows employees who attended the Java course *and* at least one non-Java course; for example, employee 7566 attended the Java and the PL/SQL courses.

9a. Which employees have subordinates?

Solution 4-9a. Employees with Subordinates

```
SQL> select empno, ename, init
  2  from    employees
  3  where   empno in (select mgr
  4                    from    employees);

    EMPNO ENAME    INIT
-------- -------- -----
     7566 JONES    JM
     7698 BLAKE    R
     7782 CLARK    AB
     7788 SCOTT    SCJ
     7839 KING     CC
     7902 FORD     MG
```

9b. Which employees *don't* have subordinates?

Solution 4-9b. Employees Without Subordinates

```
SQL> select empno, ename, init
  2  from    employees
  3  where   empno not in (select mgr
  4                        from    employees
  5                        where   mgr is not null);

    EMPNO ENAME    INIT
-------- -------- -----
     7369 SMITH    N
     7499 ALLEN    JAM
     7521 WARD     TF
     7654 MARTIN   P
     7844 TURNER   JJ
     7876 ADAMS    AA
     7900 JONES    R
     7934 MILLER   TJA
```

■ **Note**   The WHERE clause on the fifth line of Solution 4-9b is necessary for a correct result, assuming that null values in the MGR column always mean "not applicable." See Solution 4-12, as well.

10. Produce an overview of all general course offerings (course category GEN) in 1999.

Solution 4-10.

```
SQL> select *
  2  from    offerings
  3  where   begindate between date '1999-01-01'
  4                        and date '1999-12-31'
  5  and     course in (select code
  6                      from   courses
  7                      where  category = 'GEN');

COURSE BEGINDATE    TRAINER LOCATION
------ ----------- -------- --------
OAU    10-AUG-1999    7566 CHICAGO
SQL    12-APR-1999    7902 DALLAS
SQL    04-OCT-1999    7369 SEATTLE
SQL    13-DEC-1999    7369 DALLAS

SQL>
```

You can solve the "1999 condition" in many ways by using SQL functions (see Chapter 5). Here are some valid alternatives for lines 3 and 4:

```
where to_char(begindate,'YYYY') = '1999'
where extract(year from begindate) = 1999
where begindate between to_date('01-JAN-1999','DD-MON-YYYY')
                    and to_date('31-DEC-1999','DD-MON-YYYY')
```

■ **Caution**   Avoid using column names as function arguments if it is possible to express the same functional result without having to do that, because it may have a negative impact on performance. In this case, Solution 4-10 and the last alternative are fine; the first two alternatives should be avoided.

11. Provide the name and initials of all employees who have ever attended a course taught by N. Smith. Hint: Use subqueries, and work "inside out" toward the result; that is, retrieve the employee number of N. Smith, search for the codes of all courses he ever taught, and so on.

Solution 4-11.

```
SQL> select ename, init
  2  from    employees
  3  where   empno in
  4          (select attendee
```

```
 5              from   registrations
 6              where (course, begindate) in
 7                     (select course, begindate
 8                      from   offerings
 9                      where  trainer =
10                             (select empno
11                              from   employees
12                              where  ename = 'SMITH'
13                              and    init  = 'N'
14                             )
15                     )
16           );
```

```
ENAME     INIT
--------  -----
ALLEN     JAM
BLAKE     R
SCOTT     SCJ
KING      CC
JONES     R
FORD      MG
```

12. How could you redesign the EMPLOYEES table to avoid the problem that the COMM column contains null values meaning *not applicable*?

    Answer: By dropping that column from the EMPLOYEES table and by creating a separate SALESREPS table, with the following rows:

    ```
    EMPNO     COMM
    --------  --------
       7499       300
       7521       500
       7654      1400
       7844         0
    ```

In this table, the EMPNO column is not only the primary key, but it is also a foreign key referring to the EMPLOYEES table.

13. In Section 4.9, you saw the following statement: In SQL, NOT is not "not." What is this statement trying to say?

    Answer: In three-valued logic, the NOT operator is not the complement operator anymore:

    ```
    NOT TRUE is equivalent with FALSE
    not TRUE is equivalent with FALSE OR UNKNOWN
    ```

    Referring to the brain-twister at the end of Section 4.9, what is the explanation of the result "no rows selected" in Listing 4-43?

    Answer: The following WHERE clause:

    ```
    2  where evaluation not in (1,2,3,NULL)
    ```

is logically equivalent with the following "iterated AND" condition:

```
2   where  evaluation <> 1
3   AND    evaluation <> 2
4   AND    evaluation <> 3
5   AND    evaluation <> NULL
```

If you consider a row with an EVALUATION value of 1, 2, or 3, it is obvious that out of the first three conditions, one of them returns FALSE, and the other two return TRUE. Therefore, the complete WHERE clause returns FALSE.

If the EVALUATION value is NULL, all four conditions return UNKNOWN. Therefore, the end result is also UNKNOWN. So far, there are no surprises.

If the EVALUATION value is 4 or 5 (the remaining two allowed values), the first three conditions all return TRUE, but the last condition returns UNKNOWN. So you have the following expression:

```
(TRUE) and (TRUE) and (TRUE) and (UNKNOWN)
```

This is logically equivalent with UNKNOWN, so the complete WHERE clause returns UNKNOWN.

14. At the end of Section 4.5, you saw the following statement.

The following two queries are logically equivalent:

```
select * from employees where NOT (ename = 'BLAKE' AND init = 'R')
select * from employees where     ename <> 'BLAKE' OR init <> 'R'
```

Prove this, using a truth table.

Answer: First, we assign names to the two WHERE clause components.

- Let's represent ename = 'BLAKE' with P.

- Let's represent init = 'R' with Q.

Then we must show that NOT(P AND Q) and NOT(P) OR NOT(Q) are logically equivalent. The truth tables for both expressions look as follows:

P	Q	P AND Q	--	NOT(P AND Q)
TRUE	TRUE	TRUE	--	FALSE
TRUE	FALSE	FALSE	--	TRUE
TRUE	UNK	UNK	--	UNK
FALSE	TRUE	FALSE	--	TRUE
FALSE	FALSE	FALSE	--	TRUE
FALSE	UNK	FALSE	--	TRUE
UNK	TRUE	UNK	--	UNK
UNK	FALSE	FALSE	--	TRUE
UNK	UNK	UNK	--	UNK

P	Q	NOT(P)	NOT(Q)	NOT(P) OR NOT(Q)
TRUE	TRUE	FALSE	FALSE	FALSE
TRUE	FALSE	FALSE	TRUE	TRUE
TRUE	UNK	FALSE	UNK	UNK
FALSE	TRUE	TRUE	FALSE	TRUE
FALSE	FALSE	TRUE	TRUE	TRUE
FALSE	UNK	TRUE	UNK	TRUE
UNK	TRUE	UNK	FALSE	UNK
UNK	FALSE	UNK	TRUE	TRUE
UNK	UNK	UNK	UNK	UNK

As you can see, the last columns in the two truth tables are identical. This proves that the two expressions are logically equivalent.

Chapter 5 Exercises

1. For all employees, provide their last name, a comma, followed by their initials.

   Solution 5-1.

   ```
   SQL> select ename ||', '||init
     2         as full_name
     3  from   employees;

   FULL_NAME
   ---------------
   SMITH, N
   ALLEN, JAM
   WARD, TF
   JONES, JM
   MARTIN, P
   BLAKE, R
   CLARK, AB
   SCOTT, SCJ
   KING, CC
   TURNER, JJ
   ADAMS, AA
   JONES, R
   FORD, MG
   MILLER, TJA

   14 rows selected.

   SQL>
   ```

2. For all employees, list their last name and date of birth, in a format such as April 2nd, 1967.

Solution 5-2.

```
SQL> select ename
  2  ,       to_char(bdate,'fmMonth ddth, yyyy')
  3  from    employees;

ENAME     TO_CHAR(BDATE,'FMMON
--------- --------------------
SMITH     December 17th, 1965
ALLEN     February 20th, 1961
WARD      February 22nd, 1962
JONES     April 2nd, 1967
MARTIN    September 28th, 1956
BLAKE     November 1st, 1963
CLARK     June 9th, 1965
SCOTT     November 26th, 1959
KING      November 17th, 1952
TURNER    September 28th, 1968
ADAMS     December 30th, 1966
JONES     December 3rd, 1969
FORD      February 13th, 1959
MILLER    January 23rd, 1962

14 rows selected.

SQL>
```

■ **Note**   You can change the language to display the month names in this result with the NLS_LANGUAGE parameter setting, as in this example:

```
SQL> alter session set nls_language=dutch;
Sessie is gewijzigd.
SQL>
```

3a. On which day are (or were) you exactly 10,000 days old?

Solution 5-3a.

```
SQL> select date '1954-08-11' + 10000
  2         as "10,000 days"
  3  from   dual;

10,000 days
-----------
27-DEC-1981

SQL>
```

3b. On which day of the week is (was) this?

Solution 5-3b.

```
SQL> select to_char(date '1954-08-11' + 10000,'Day')
  2          as "On a:"
  3  from    dual;

On a:
---------
Sunday

SQL>
```

4. Rewrite the example in Listing 5-23 using the NVL2 function.

Solution 5-4.

```
SQL> select ename, msal, comm
  2  ,       nvl2(comm,12*msal+comm,12*msal) as yearsal
  3  from    employees
  4  where   ename like '%T%';

ENAME        MSAL     COMM  YEARSAL
--------  --------  -------- --------
SMITH         800              9600
MARTIN       1250     1400    16400
SCOTT        3000             36000
TURNER       1500        0    18000

SQL>
```

5. Rewrite the example in Listing 5-24 to remove the DECODE functions using CASE expressions, both in the SELECT clause and in the ORDER BY clause.

Solution 5-5.

```
SQL> select job, ename
  2  ,       case
  3            when msal <= 2500
  4            then 'cheap'
  5            else 'expensive'
  6          end         as class
  7  from    employees
  8  where   bdate < date '1964-01-01'
  9  order   by case job
 10            when 'DIRECTOR' then 1
 11            when 'MANAGER'  then 2
 12                            else 3
 13            end;
```

```
JOB       ENAME     CLASS
--------  --------  ---------
DIRECTOR  KING      expensive
MANAGER   BLAKE     expensive
SALESREP  ALLEN     cheap
SALESREP  WARD      cheap      .
ADMIN     MILLER    cheap
TRAINER   FORD      expensive
TRAINER   SCOTT     expensive
SALESREP  MARTIN    cheap

SQL>
```

■ **Note**   The TO_DATE function expression is also replaced by a DATE literal.

---

6. Rewrite the example in Listing 5-20 using DATE and INTERVAL constants, in such a way that they become independent of the NLS_DATE_FORMAT setting.

Solution 5-6.

```
SQL> select date '1996-01-29' + interval '1' month as col_1
  2  ,      date '1997-01-29' + interval '1' month as col_2
  3  ,      date '1997-08-11' - interval '3' month as col_3
  4  from   dual;
,        date '1997-01-29' + interval '1' month as col_2
                              *
ERROR at line 2:
ORA-01839: date not valid for month specified

SQL> select date '1996-01-29' + interval '1' month as col_1
  2  ,      date '1997-01-28' + interval '1' month as col_2
  3  ,      date '1997-08-11' - interval '3' month as col_3
  4  from   dual;

COL_1        COL_2        COL_3
-----------  -----------  ---------
29-FEB-1996  28-FEB-1997  11-MAY-1997

SQL>
```

As you can see, January 29 plus a month causes problems for 1997, which is not a leap year. If you change 1997-01-29 to 1997-01-28 on the second line, there is no longer a problem.

7. Investigate the difference between the date formats WW and IW (week number and ISO week number) using an arbitrary date, and explain your findings.

Solution 5-7.

```
SQL>  1  select date '2005-01-01' as input_date
   2  ,      to_char(date '2005-01-01', 'ww') as ww
   3  ,      to_char(date '2005-01-01', 'iw') as iw
   4* from   dual

INPUT_DATE  WW IW
----------- -- --
01-JAN-2005 06 07

SQL>
```

If you don't get different results, try different dates within the same week. The difference between WW and IW has to do with the different definitions of week numbers. The WW format starts week number 1 on January 1, regardless of which day of the week that is. The ISO standard uses different rules: an ISO week *always* starts on a Monday. The rules around the new year are as follows: if January 1 is a Friday, a Saturday, or a Sunday, the week belongs to the previous year; otherwise, the week fully belongs to the new year. Similar rules apply for the ISO year numbering.

8. Look at Listing 5-15, where we use the REGEXP_INSTR function to search for words. Rewrite this query using REGEXP_LIKE. Hint: You can use {n,} to express "at least n times."

Solution 5-8a. First Solution

```
SQL> select comments
  2  from   history
  3  where  regexp_like(comments, '([^ ]+ ){8,}');

COMMENTS
------------------------------------------------------------
Not a great trainer; let's try the sales department!
Sales also turns out to be not a success...
Hired as the new manager for the accounting department
Junior sales rep -- has lots to learn... :-)

SQL>
```

You could make your solution more readable by using character classes.

Solution 5-8b. Second Solution, Using Character Classes

```
SQL> select comments
  2  from   history
  3  where  regexp_like(comments, '([[:alnum:]+[:punct:]]+[[:space:]]+){8,}');

COMMENTS
------------------------------------------------------------
Not a great trainer; let's try the sales department!
Sales also turns out to be not a success...
Hired as the new manager for the accounting department
Junior sales rep -- has lots to learn... :-)

SQL>
```

Chapter 6: No exercises.

Chapter 7 Exercises

1. Listing 7-5 defines the constraint E_SALES_CHK in a rather cryptic way. Formulate the same constraint without using DECODE and NVL2.

    Solution 7-1a. Solution 1

    ```
    check ((job = 'SALESREP' and comm is not null) or
           (job <>'SALESREP' and comm is null)          )
    ```

    Solution 7-1b. Solution 2

    ```
    check ((job = 'SALESREP' or  comm is null) and not
           (job = 'SALESREP' and comm is null)          )
    ```

2. Why do you think the constraint E_DEPT_FK (in Listing 7-7) is created with a separate ALTER TABLE command?

    Answer: You must define this constraint with an ALTER TABLE command because you have a "chicken/egg" problem. A foreign key constraint can refer to only an *existing* table, and you have two tables (EMPLOYEES and DEPARTMENTS) referring to each other.

3. Although this is not covered in this chapter, try to come up with an explanation of the following phenomenon: when using sequences, you cannot use the pseudo column CURRVAL in your session without first calling the pseudo column NEXTVAL.

    Answer: In a multiuser environment, multiple database users can use the same sequence generator at the same time. Therefore, they will be using *different* CURRVAL values at the same time; that is, there is no database-wide "current" CURRVAL value. On the other hand, NEXTVAL is always defined as the next available sequence value.

4. Why is it better to use sequences in a multiuser environment, as opposed to maintaining a secondary table with the last/current sequence values?

    Answer: A secondary table will become a performance bottleneck. Each update to a sequence value will lock the corresponding row. The next update can take place only after the first transaction has committed. In other words, all transactions needing a sequence value will be serialized. Sequences are better because they don't have this problem. With sequences, multiple transactions can be served simultaneously and independently.

5. How is it possible that the EVALUATION column of the REGISTRATIONS table accepts null values, in spite of the constraint R_EVAL_CHK (see Listing 7-11)?

    Answer: This is caused by three-valued logic. A CHECK constraint condition can result in TRUE, FALSE, or UNKNOWN. Moreover, a CHECK constraint reports a violation *only* if its corresponding condition returns FALSE.

■ **Note** This implies that you always need an explicit NOT NULL constraint if you want your columns to be mandatory; a CHECK constraint as shown in Listing 7-11 is not enough.

---

6. If you define a PRIMARY KEY or UNIQUE constraint, the Oracle DBMS normally creates a unique index under the covers (if none of the existing indexes can be used) to check the constraint. Investigate and explain what happens if you define such a constraint as DEFERRABLE.

   Answer: If you define PRIMARY KEY or UNIQUE constraints as DEFERRABLE, the Oracle DBMS creates nonunique indexes. This is because indexes must be maintained immediately. Therefore, indexes for deferrable constraints must allow for temporary duplicate values until the end of your transactions.

7. You can use function-based indexes to implement "conditional uniqueness" constraints. Create a unique function-based index on the REGISTRATIONS table to check the following constraint: employees are allowed to attend the OAU course only once. They may attend other courses as many times as they like. Test your solution with the following command (it should fail):

   ```
   SQL> insert into registrations values (7900,'OAU',trunc(sysdate),null);
   ```

   Hint: You can use a CASE expression in the index expression.

   Solution 7-7.

   ```
   SQL> create unique index oau_reg on registrations
     2  ( case course when 'OAU' then attendee else null end
     3  , case course when 'OAU' then course   else null end );

   Index created.

   SQL>
   ```

The trick is to create a function-based index on (ATTENDEE, COURSE) combinations, while ignoring all non-OAU course registrations.
Here's the test:

```
SQL> insert into registrations values (7900,'OAU',sysdate,null);
insert into registrations values (7900,'OAU',sysdate,null)
*
ERROR at line 1:
ORA-00001: unique constraint (BOOK.OAU_REG) violated

SQL>
```

■ **Note** Notice the Oracle error message number for the unique constraint violation: 00001. This must have been one of the first error messages implemented in Oracle!

Chapter 8 Exercises

1. Produce an overview of all course offerings. Provide the course code, begin date, course duration, and name of the trainer.

Solution 8-1a. First Solution

```
SQL> select  c.code
  2  ,        o.begindate
  3  ,        c.duration
  4  ,        e.ename    as   trainer
  5  from     employees e
  6  ,        courses    c
  7  ,        offerings  o
  8  where    o.trainer = e.empno
  9  and      o.course  = c.code;

CODE BEGINDATE    DURATION TRAINER
---- ----------- -------- --------
XML  03-FEB-2000        2 SMITH
SQL  13-DEC-1999        4 SMITH
SQL  04-OCT-1999        4 SMITH
OAU  10-AUG-1999        1 JONES
JAV  13-DEC-1999        4 JONES
RSD  24-FEB-2001        2 SCOTT
PLS  11-SEP-2000        1 SCOTT
JAV  01-FEB-2000        4 ADAMS
SQL  12-APR-1999        4 FORD
OAU  27-SEP-2000        1 FORD

10 rows selected.

SQL>
```

If you also want to see all course offerings with an unknown trainer, you can change the solution as follows:

Solution 8-1b. Second Solution, Also Showing Course Offerings with Unknown Trainers

```
SQL> select DISTINCT c.code
  2  ,        o.begindate
  3  ,        c.duration
  4  ,        case when o.trainer is not null
  5              then e.ename
  6              else null
  7          end  as trainer
  8  from     employees e
  9  ,        courses    c
 10  ,        offerings  o
 11  where    coalesce(o.trainer,-1) in (e.empno,-1)
 12  and      o.course = c.code;
```

```
CODE BEGINDATE   DURATION TRAINER
---- ----------- -------- --------
ERM  15-JAN-2001        3
JAV  13-DEC-1999        4 JONES
JAV  01-FEB-2000        4 ADAMS
OAU  10-AUG-1999        1 JONES
OAU  27-SEP-2000        1 FORD
PLS  11-SEP-2000        1 SCOTT
PRO  19-FEB-2001        5
RSD  24-FEB-2001        2 SCOTT
SQL  12-APR-1999        4 FORD
SQL  04-OCT-1999        4 SMITH
SQL  13-DEC-1999        4 SMITH
XML  03-FEB-2000        2 SMITH
XML  18-SEP-2000        2

13 rows selected.

SQL>
```

Line 11 might look curious at first sight. It "relaxes" the join between OFFERINGS and EMPLOYEES a bit. Instead of –1, you can use any other arbitrary numeric value, as long as it could not be an existing employee number. Note also that this trick makes the addition of DISTINCT necessary.

2. Provide an overview, in two columns, showing the names of all employees who ever attended an SQL course, with the name of the trainer.

Solution 8-2.

```
SQL> select a.ename    as attendee
  2  ,        t.ename    as trainer
  3  from    employees    t
  4          join
  5          offerings    o on  (o.trainer = t.empno)
  6          join
  7          registrations r using (course, begindate)
  8          join
  9          employees    a on (r.attendee = a.empno)
 10  where   course = 'SQL';

ATTENDEE TRAINER
-------- --------
ALLEN    FORD
BLAKE    FORD
ADAMS    FORD
MILLER   FORD
SCOTT    SMITH
KING     SMITH
FORD     SMITH
BLAKE    SMITH
FORD     SMITH

SQL>
```

This solution uses the new ANSI/ISO join syntax, just for a change.

3. For all employees, list their name, initials, and yearly salary (including bonus and commission).

Solution 8-3.

```
SQL> select e.ename, e.init
  2  ,      12 * (e.msal + s.bonus)
  3         + nvl(e.comm,0) as yearsal
  4  from   employees e
  5         join
  6         salgrades s
  7         on (e.msal between s.lowerlimit
  8                        and s.upperlimit);

ENAME    INIT  YEARSAL
-------- ----- --------
SMITH    N        9600
JONES    R        9600
ADAMS    AA      13200
WARD     TF      16100
MARTIN   P       17000
MILLER   TJA     16200
TURNER   JJ      19200
ALLEN    JAM     20700
CLARK    AB      31800
BLAKE    R       36600
JONES    JM      38100
SCOTT    SCJ     38400
FORD     MG      38400
KING     CC      66000

14 rows selected.

SQL>
```

4. For all course offerings, list the course code, begin date, and number of registrations. Sort your results on the number of registrations, from high to low.

Solution 8-4.

```
SQL> select    course
  2  ,          begindate
  3  ,          count(r.attendee) as reg_count
  4  from       offerings   o
  5             left outer join
  6             registrations r
  7             using (course, begindate)
  8  group by course
  9  ,          begindate
 10  order by reg_count desc;
```

```
    COURSE BEGINDATE    REG_COUNT
    ------ -----------  ---------
    JAV    13-DEC-1999          5
    SQL    12-APR-1999          4
    JAV    01-FEB-2000          3
    OAU    10-AUG-1999          3
    PLS    11-SEP-2000          3
    SQL    04-OCT-1999          3
    SQL    13-DEC-1999          2
    XML    03-FEB-2000          2
    OAU    27-SEP-2000          1
    ERM    15-JAN-2001          0
    XML    18-SEP-2000          0
    PRO    19-FEB-2001          0
    RSD    24-FEB-2001          0

    13 rows selected.

    SQL>
```

You need an outer join here, to see all courses without registrations in the result as well. Note also that COUNT(*) in the third line would give you wrong results.

5. List the course code, begin date, and the number of registrations for all course offerings in 1999 with at least three registrations.

Solution 8-5.

```
SQL> select    course
  2  ,          begindate
  3  ,          count(*)
  4  from       registrations
  5  where      extract(year from begindate) = 1999
  6  group by course
  7  ,          begindate
  8  having     count(*) >= 3;

COURSE BEGINDATE    COUNT(*)
------ -----------  --------
JAV    13-DEC-1999         5
OAU    10-AUG-1999         3
SQL    12-APR-1999         4
SQL    04-OCT-1999         3

SQL>
```

In this case, accessing the REGISTRATIONS table is enough, because you are not interested in offerings without registrations. The solution would have been more complicated if the question were "... with *fewer than* three registrations," because zero is also less than three.

6. Provide the employee numbers of all employees who ever taught a course as a trainer, but never attended a course as an attendee.

Solution 8-6a. First Solution

```
SQL> select trainer  from offerings
  2  minus
  3  select attendee from registrations;

   TRAINER
   --------
      7369

SQL>
```

This solution looks good; however, if you look very carefully, the solution is suspect. You don't see it immediately, but this result doesn't contain a single row, but two rows, as becomes apparent if you set FEEDBACK to 1:

```
SQL> set feedback 1
SQL> /

 TRAINER
 --------
    7369

2 rows selected.

SQL>
```

Because a null value obviously doesn't represent a valid trainer, you need to exclude null values in the TRAINER column explicitly.

Solution 8-6b. Second Solution, Excluding Null Values

```
SQL> select trainer  from offerings
  2  where  trainer  is not null
  3  minus
  4  select attendee from registrations;

 TRAINER
 --------
    7369

1 row selected.

SQL>
```

371

7. Which employees attended a specific course more than once?

Solution 8-7.

```
SQL> select    attendee,course
  2  from       registrations
  3  group by attendee,course
  4  having     count(*) > 1 ;

ATTENDEE COURSE
-------- ------
    7698 SQL
    7788 JAV
    7902 SQL

SQL>
```

8. For all trainers, provide their name and initials, the number of courses they taught, the total number of students they had in their classes, and the average evaluation rating. Round the evaluation ratings to one decimal.

Solution 8-8.

```
SQL> select    t.init, t.ename
  2  ,          count(distinct begindate) courses
  3  ,          count(*)                  attendees
  4  ,          round(avg(evaluation),1)  evaluation
  5  from       employees    t
  6  ,          registrations r
  7             join
  8             offerings    o
  9             using (course, begindate)
 10  where     t.empno = o.trainer
 11  group by t.init, t.ename;

INIT  ENAME      COURSES ATTENDEES EVALUATION
----- --------  -------- --------- ----------
N     SMITH           3         7          4
AA    ADAMS           1         3          4
JM    JONES           2         8        4.3
MG    FORD            2         5          4
SCJ   SCOTT           1         3

SQL>
```

■ **Note**   While counting courses, this solution assumes that trainers cannot teach more than one course on the same day.

---

9. List the name and initials of all trainers who ever had their own manager as a student in a general course (category GEN).

Solution 8-9.

```
SQL> select distinct e.ename, e.init
  2  from    employees    e
  3  ,       courses      c
  4  ,       offerings    o
  5  ,       registrations r
  6  where   e.empno    = o.trainer
  7  and     e.mgr      = r.attendee
  8  and     c.code     = o.course
  9  and     o.course   = r.course
 10  and     o.begindate = r.begindate
 11  and     c.category = 'GEN';

ENAME    INIT
-------- -----
SMITH    N

SQL>
```

10. Did we ever use two classrooms at the same time in the same course location?

Solution 8-10.

```
SQL> select o1.location
  2  ,       o1.begindate, o1.course, c1.duration
  3  ,       o2.begindate, o2.course
  4  from    offerings    o1
  5  ,       offerings    o2
  6  ,       courses      c1
  7  where   o1.location = o2.location
  8  and     (o1.begindate < o2.begindate or
  9           o1.course   <> o2.course    )
 10  and     o1.course   = c1.code
 11  and     o2.begindate between o1.begindate
 12                       and o1.begindate + c1.duration;

LOCATION BEGINDATE   COUR DURATION BEGINDATE   COURSE
-------- ----------- ---- -------- ----------- ------
DALLAS   01-FEB-2000 JAV         4 03-FEB-2000 XML

SQL>
```

The solution searches for two *different* course offerings (see lines 8 and 9) at the same location (see line 7) overlapping each other (see lines 11 and 12). Apparently, the Java course starting February 1, 2000, in Dallas overlaps with the XML course starting two days later (note that the Java course takes four days).

11. Produce a matrix report (one column per department, one row for each job) where each cell shows the number of employees for a specific department and a specific job. In a single SQL statement, it is impossible to dynamically derive the number of columns needed, so you may assume you have three departments only: 10, 20, and 30.

Solution 8-11.

```
SQL> select   job
  2  ,         count(case
  3                  when deptno <> 10
  4                  then null
  5                  else deptno
  6                  end                   ) as dept_10
  7  ,         sum(case deptno
  8                  when 20
  9                  then 1
 10                  else 0
 11                  end                   ) as dept_20
 12  ,         sum(decode(deptno,30,1,0)) as dept_30
 13  from      employees
 14  group by job;

JOB        DEPT_10  DEPT_20  DEPT_30
--------   -------- -------- --------
ADMIN            1        0        1
DIRECTOR         1        0        0
MANAGER          1        1        1
SALESREP         0        0        4
TRAINER          0        4        0

SQL>
```

This solution shows three different valid methods to count the employees: for department 10, it uses a searched CASE expression; for department 20, it uses a simple CASE expression and a SUM function; and for department 30, it uses the Oracle DECODE function, which is essentially the same solution as for department 20.

12. Listing 8-26 produces information about all departments with *more* than four employees. How can you change the query to show information about all departments with *fewer* than four employees?

Solution 8-12a. Incorrect Solution

```
SQL> select deptno, count(empno)
  2  from    employees
  3  group   by deptno
  4  having count(*) < 4;

DEPTNO COUNT(EMPNO)
-------- ------------
     10            3

SQL>
```

This solution is *not* correct, because it does not show departments with zero employees. You can fix this in several ways; for example, by using an outer join.

Solution 8-12b. Correct Solution

```
SQL> select deptno, count(empno)
  2  from    departments
  3          left outer join
  4          employees
  5          using (deptno)
  6  group   by deptno
  7  having count(*) < 4;

 DEPTNO COUNT(EMPNO)
-------- ------------
     10            3
     40            0

SQL>
```

13. Look at Listings 8-44 and 8-45. Are those two queries logically equivalent? Investigate the two queries and explain the differences, if any.

Solution 8-13. Making the Difference Visible with FEEDBACK

```
SQL> set feedback 1

SQL> select o.location from offerings   o
  2  MINUS
  3  select d.location from departments d;

LOCATION
--------
SEATTLE

2 rows selected.

SQL> select DISTINCT o.location
  2  from    offerings o
  3  where   o.location not in
  4          (select d.location
  5           from    departments d);

LOCATION
--------
SEATTLE

1 row selected.

SQL>
```

If you change the SQL*Plus FEEDBACK setting to 1, the difference becomes apparent.

We have one course offering with unknown location, and (as you know by now) you cannot be too careful with null values. The first query produces two rows. The null value appears in the result because the MINUS operator does not remove the null value. However, if the second query checks the ERM course offering (with the null value) the WHERE clause becomes:

```
... where NULL not in ('NEW YORK','DALLAS','CHICAGO','BOSTON');
```

This WHERE clause returns UNKNOWN. Therefore, the row does not pass the WHERE clause filter, and as a consequence the result contains only one row.

Chapter 9 Exercises

1. It is normal practice that (junior) trainers always attend a course taught by a senior colleague before teaching that course themselves. For which trainer/course combinations did this happen?

   Solution 9-1.

   ```
   SQL> select o.course, o.trainer
     2  from    offerings o
     3  where   exists
     4          (select r.*
     5           from    registrations r
     6           where   r.attendee   = o.trainer
     7           and     r.course     = o.course
     8           and     r.begindate  < o.begindate)
     9  and     not exists
    10          (select fo.*
    11           from    offerings fo
    12           where   fo.course    = o.course
    13           and     fo.trainer   = o.trainer
    14           and     fo.begindate < o.begindate);

   COURSE  TRAINER
   ------  --------
   JAV        7876
   OAU        7902
   ```

This exercise is not an easy one. You can solve it in many ways. The solution shown here uses the EXISTS and the NOT EXISTS operators. You can read it as follows:

"Search course offerings for which (1) the trainer attended an *earlier* offering of the same course as a student, and for which (2) the trainer is teaching that course for the first time."

■ **Note** The second condition is necessary, because otherwise you would also get "teach/attend/teach" combinations.

---

2. Actually, if the junior trainer teaches a course for the first time, that senior colleague (see the previous exercise) sits in the back of the classroom in a supporting role. Try to find these course/junior/senior combinations.

Solution 9-2.

```
SQL> select o1.course
  2  ,         o1.trainer    as senior
  3  ,         o2.trainer    as junior
  4  from      offerings     o1
  5  ,         registrations r1
  6  ,         offerings     o2
  7  ,         registrations r2
  8  where  o1.course    = r1.course     -- join r1 with o1
  9  and    o1.begindate = r1.begindate
 10  and    o2.course    = r2.course     -- join r2 with o2
 11  and    o2.begindate = r2.begindate
 12  and    o1.course    = o2.course     -- o1 and o2 same course
 13  and    o1.begindate < o2.begindate  -- o1 earlier than o2
 14  and    o1.trainer   = r2.attendee   -- trainer o1 attends o2
 15  and    o2.trainer   = r1.attendee   -- trainer o2 attends o1
 16  ;

COURSE   SENIOR   JUNIOR
-------  -------  --------
JAV        7566      7876
```

This solution uses a join, for a change.

3. Which employees never taught a course?

Solution 9-3a. Using NOT IN

```
SQL> select e.*
  2  from    employees e
  3  where   e.empno not in (select o.trainer
  4                          from   offerings o);

no rows selected
```

Solution 9-3b. Using NOT EXISTS

```
SQL> select e.*
  2  from    employees e
  3  where   not exists (select o.trainer
  4                      from   offerings o
  5                      where  o.trainer = e.empno);
```

```
EMPNO ENAME     INIT  JOB        MGR BDATE         MSAL  COMM DEPTNO
----- --------  ----- --------  ----- -----------  ----- ----- ------
 7499 ALLEN     JAM   SALESREP   7698 20-FEB-1961  1600   300    30
 7521 WARD      TF    SALESREP   7698 22-FEB-1962  1250   500    30
 7654 MARTIN    P     SALESREP   7698 28-SEP-1956  1250  1400    30
 7698 BLAKE     R     MANAGER    7839 01-NOV-1963  2850          30
 7782 CLARK     AB    MANAGER    7839 09-JUN-1965  2450          10
 7839 KING      CC    DIRECTOR        17-NOV-1952  5000          10
 7844 TURNER    JJ    SALESREP   7698 28-SEP-1968  1500     0    30
 7900 JONES     R     ADMIN      7698 03-DEC-1969   800          30
 7934 MILLER    TJA   ADMIN      7782 23-JAN-1962  1300          10

9 rows selected.
```

At first sight, you might think that both of these solutions are correct. However, the results are different. Now, which one is the correct solution?

You can come up with convincing arguments for both solutions. Note that you have three course offerings with a null value in the TRAINER column.

- If you interpret these null values as "trainer unknown," you can never say *with certainty* that an employee never taught a course.

- The second query obviously treats the null values differently. Its result (with nine employees) is what you probably expected.

The different results are *not* caused by an SQL bug. You simply have two SQL statements with different results, so they must have a different meaning. In such cases, you must revisit the query in natural language and try to formulate it more precisely in order to eliminate any ambiguities.

Last but not least, our OFFERINGS table happens to contain only data from the past. If you want a correct answer to this exercise under all circumstances, you should also add a condition to check the course dates against SYSDATE.

4. Which employees attended all build courses (category BLD)? They are entitled to get a discount on the next course they attend.

Solution 9-4a. Using NOT EXISTS Twice

```
SQL> select   e.empno, e.ename, e.init
  2  from      employees e
  3  where     not exists
  4            (select c.*
  5             from    courses c
  6             where   c.category = 'BLD'
  7             and     not exists
  8                     (select r.*
  9                      from    registrations r
 10                      where   r.course   = c.code
 11                      and     r.attendee = e.empno
 12                     )
 13            );
```

```
   EMPNO ENAME    INIT
-------- -------- -----
    7499 ALLEN    JAM
```

Solution 9-4b. Using GROUP BY

```
SQL> select    e.empno, e.ename, e.init
  2  from       registrations r
  3             join
  4             courses    c on (r.course = c.code)
  5             join
  6             employees e on (r.attendee = e.empno)
  7  where      c.category = 'BLD'
  8  group by e.empno, e.ename, e.init
  9  having     count(distinct r.course)
 10             = (select count(*)
 11                 from    courses
 12                 where  category = 'BLD');

   EMPNO ENAME    INIT
-------- -------- -----
    7499 ALLEN    JAM
```

This is not an easy exercise. Both of these solutions are correct.

5. Provide a list of all employees having the same monthly salary and commission as (at least) one employee of department 30. You are interested in only employees from other departments.

Solution 9-5.

```
SQL> select e.ename
  2  ,        e.msal
  3  ,        e.comm
  4  from     employees e
  5  where    e.deptno <> 30
  6  and      (        e.msal,coalesce(e.comm,-1) ) in
  7           (select x.msal,coalesce(x.comm,-1)
  8             from    employees x
  9             where  x.deptno = 30              );

ENAME        MSAL    COMM
-------- -------- --------
SMITH         800
```

Note that this solution uses the COALESCE function, which you need to make comparisons with null values evaluate to true, in this case. The solution uses the value –1 based on the reasonable assumption that the commission column never contains negative values. However, if you check the definition of the EMPLOYEES table, you will see that there actually is *no* constraint to allow only nonnegative commission values. It looks like you found a possible data model enhancement here. Such a constraint would make your solution—using the negative value in the COALESCE function—correct under all circumstances.

6. Look again at Listings 9-4 and 9-5. Are they really logically equivalent? Just for testing purposes, search on a nonexisting job and execute both queries again. Explain the results.

Solution 9-6.

```
SQL> select e.empno, e.ename, e.job, e.msal
  2  from    employees e
  3  where   e.msal > ALL (select b.msal
  4                        from    employees b
  5                        where   b.job = 'BARTENDER');
```

```
EMPNO ENAME    JOB        MSAL
-------- -------- -------- --------
   7369 SMITH    TRAINER     800
   7499 ALLEN    SALESREP   1600
   7521 WARD     SALESREP   1250
   7566 JONES    MANAGER    2975
   7654 MARTIN   SALESREP   1250
   7698 BLAKE    MANAGER    2850
   7782 CLARK    MANAGER    2450
   7788 SCOTT    TRAINER    3000
   7839 KING     DIRECTOR   5000
   7844 TURNER   SALESREP   1500
   7876 ADAMS    TRAINER    1100
   7900 JONES    ADMIN       800
   7902 FORD     TRAINER    3000
   7934 MILLER   ADMIN      1300
```

```
14 rows selected.
```

```
SQL> select e.empno, e.ename, e.job, e.msal
  2  from    employees e
  3  where   e.msal >    (select MAX(b.msal)
  4                       from    employees b
  5                       where   b.job = 'BARTENDER');
```

```
no rows selected
```

This example searches for BARTENDER. The subquery returns an empty set, because the EMPLOYEES table contains no bartenders. Therefore, the > ALL condition of the first query is *true* for every row of the EMPLOYEES table. This outcome complies with an important law derived from mathematical logic. The following statement is always true, regardless of the expression you specify following the colon:

-   For all elements x of the empty set: . . .

This explains why you see all 14 employees in the result for the first query.

The second query uses a different approach, using the MAX function in the subquery. The maximum of an empty set results in a null value, so the WHERE clause becomes WHERE E.MSAL > NULL, which returns *unknown* for every row. This explains why the second query returns no rows.

7. You saw a series of examples in this chapter about all employees that ever taught an SQL course (in Listings 9-9 through 9-11). How can you adapt these queries in such a way that they answer the negation of the same question (...all employees that *never*...)?

Solution 9-7a. Negation of Listing 9-9

```
SQL> select e.*
  2  from    employees e
  3  where   NOT exists (select o.*
  4                      from    offerings o
  5                      where   o.course = 'SQL'
  6                      and     o.trainer = e.empno);
```

EMPNO	ENAME	INIT	JOB	MGR	BDATE	MSAL	COMM	DEPTNO
7499	ALLEN	JAM	SALESREP	7698	20-FEB-1961	1600	300	30
7521	WARD	TF	SALESREP	7698	22-FEB-1962	1250	500	30
7566	JONES	JM	MANAGER	7839	02-APR-1967	2975		20
7654	MARTIN	P	SALESREP	7698	28-SEP-1956	1250	1400	30
7698	BLAKE	R	MANAGER	7839	01-NOV-1963	2850		30
7782	CLARK	AB	MANAGER	7839	09-JUN-1965	2450		10
7788	SCOTT	SCJ	TRAINER	7566	26-NOV-1959	3000		20
7839	KING	CC	DIRECTOR		17-NOV-1952	5000		10
7844	TURNER	JJ	SALESREP	7698	28-SEP-1968	1500	0	30
7876	ADAMS	AA	TRAINER	7788	30-DEC-1966	1100		20
7900	JONES	R	ADMIN	7698	03-DEC-1969	800		30
7934	MILLER	TJA	ADMIN	7782	23-JAN-1962	1300		10

```
12 rows selected.
```

Solution 9-7b. Negation of Listing 9-10

```
SQL> select e.*
  2  from    employees e
  3  where   e.empno NOT in (select o.trainer
  4                          from    offerings o
  5                          where   o.course = 'SQL');
```

EMPNO	ENAME	INIT	JOB	MGR	BDATE	MSAL	COMM	DEPTNO
7499	ALLEN	JAM	SALESREP	7698	20-FEB-1961	1600	300	30
7521	WARD	TF	SALESREP	7698	22-FEB-1962	1250	500	30
...								
7934	MILLER	TJA	ADMIN	7782	23-JAN-1962	1300		10

```
12 rows selected.
```

This looks good—you get back the same 12 employees. However, you were lucky, because all SQL course offerings happen to have a trainer assigned. If you use the NOT IN and NOT EXISTS operators, you should *always* investigate whether your subquery could possibly produce null values and how they are handled.

The following negation for Listing 9-11 is *wrong*.

Solution 9-7c. Wrong Negation for Listing 9-11

```
SQL> select DISTINCT e.*
  2  from     employees e
  3           join
  4           offerings o
  5           on e.empno = o.trainer
  6  where    o.course <> 'SQL';
```

EMPNO	ENAME	INIT	JOB	MGR	BDATE	MSAL	COMM	DEPTNO
7369	SMITH	N	TRAINER	7902	17-DEC-1965	800		20
7566	JONES	JM	MANAGER	7839	02-APR-1967	2975		20
7788	SCOTT	SCJ	TRAINER	7566	26-NOV-1959	3000		20
7876	ADAMS	AA	TRAINER	7788	30-DEC-1966	1100		20
7902	FORD	MG	TRAINER	7566	13-FEB-1959	3000		20

It is not an easy task to transform this join solution into its negation.

8. Check out your solution for Exercise 4 in Chapter 8: "For all course offerings, list the course code, begin date, and number of registrations. Sort your results on the number of registrations, from high to low." Can you come up with a more elegant solution now, without using an outer join?

Solution 9-8. A More Elegant Solution for Exercise 4 in Chapter 8

```
SQL> select    course
  2  ,          begindate
  3  ,          (select count(*)
  4              from    registrations r
  5              where   r.course = o.course
  6              and     r.begindate = o.begindate)
  7              as      registrations
  8  from        offerings o
  9  order by registrations desc;
```

COURSE	BEGINDATE	REGISTRATIONS
JAV	13-DEC-99	5
SQL	12-APR-99	4
SQL	04-OCT-99	3
OAU	10-AUG-99	3
PLS	11-SEP-00	3
JAV	01-FEB-00	3
XML	03-FEB-00	2
SQL	13-DEC-99	2
OAU	27-SEP-00	1
RSD	24-FEB-01	0
XML	18-SEP-00	0
ERM	15-JAN-01	0
PRO	19-FEB-01	0

```
13 rows selected.
```

9.   Who attended (at least) the same courses as employee 7788?

Solution 9-9.

```
SQL> select e.ename, e.init
  2  from    employees e
  3  where   e.empno <> 7788
  4  and     not exists
  5          (select r1.course
  6           from    registrations r1
  7           where   r1.attendee = 7788
  8           MINUS
  9           select r2.course
 10           from    registrations r2
 11           where   r2.attendee = e.empno);

ENAME     INIT
--------  -----
ALLEN     JAM
BLAKE     R
KING      CC
ADAMS     AA
```

This is not an easy exercise. The elegant solution shown here uses the MINUS set operator and a correlated subquery. Note the correct position of the negation on the fourth line. You can read the solution as follows:

"List all employees (except employee 7788 himself/herself) for which you cannot find a course attended by employee 7788 and not attended by those employees."

The first subquery (see lines 5 through 7) is not correlated, and it results in all courses attended by employee 7788. The second subquery (see lines 9 through 11) is correlated, and it produces all courses attended by employee e.

■ **Note**   This exercise is similar to Exercise 4 in this chapter. Both exercises belong to the same category of "subset problems." This means that the solutions of Chapter 9's Exercises 4 and 9 are interchangeable (not verbatim, of course, because the exercises are different; however, they can be solved with the same approach).

---

10.   Give the name and initials of all employees at the bottom of the management hierarchy, with a third column showing the number of management levels above them.

Solution 9-10.

```
SQL> select     ename, init
  2  ,           (level - 1) as levels_above
  3  from        employees
  4  where       connect_by_isleaf = 1
  5  start with mgr is null
  6  connect by prior empno = mgr;
```

```
ENAME     INIT  LEVELS_ABOVE
--------  ----- ------------
ADAMS     AA               3
SMITH     N                3
ALLEN     JAM              2
WARD      TF               2
MARTIN    P                2
TURNER    JJ               2
JONES     R                2
MILLER    TJA              2

8 rows selected.
```

Chapter 10 Exercises

1. Look at the example discussed in Listings 10-7, 10-8, and 10-9. Rewrite the query in Listing 10-9 without using a view, by using the WITH operator.

    Solution 10-1. Listing 10-9 Rewritten to Use the WITH Operator

```
SQL> with    course_days as
  2          (select   e.empno, e.ename
  3          ,         sum(c.duration) as days
  4          from      registrations r
  5          ,         courses        c
  6          ,         employees      e
  7          where     e.empno  = r.attendee
  8          and       c.code   = r.course
  9          group by e.empno, e.ename)
 10  select *
 11  from    course_days
 12  where   days > (select avg(days)
 13                     from    course_days);

   EMPNO ENAME        DAYS
-------- --------  --------
    7499 ALLEN           11
    7698 BLAKE           12
    7788 SCOTT           12
    7839 KING             8
    7876 ADAMS            9
    7902 FORD             9

SQL>
```

2. Look at Listing 10-12. How is it possible that you can delete employee 7654 via this EMP view? There are rows in the HISTORY table, referring to that employee via a foreign key constraint.

    Answer: You can delete that employee because you created the foreign key constraint with the CASCADE DELETE option, so all corresponding HISTORY rows are deleted implicitly.

3. Look at the view definition in Listing 10-18. Does this view implement the foreign key constraints from the REGISTRATIONS table to the EMPLOYEES and COURSES tables? Explain your answer.

Answer: No, it doesn't. The view checks insertions and updates, but it doesn't prevent you from deleting any rows from the EMPLOYEES and COURSES tables; that is, the view implements only one side of those foreign key constraints.

■ **Tip** Don't try to program your own referential integrity constraint checking. Your solution will probably overlook something, and it will always be less efficient than the declarative constraints of the Oracle DBMS.

---

4. Create a SAL_HISTORY view providing the following overview for all employees, based on the HISTORY table: For each employee, show the hire date, the review dates, and the salary changes as a consequence of those reviews.

Solution 10-4. The SAL_HISTORY View

```
SQL> create or replace view sal_history as
  2  select empno
  3  ,        min(begindate) over
  4           (partition by empno)
  5             as hiredate
  6  ,        begindate as reviewdate
  7  ,        msal - lag(msal) over
  8           (partition by empno
  9               order by empno, begindate)
 10             as salary_raise
 11  from    history;

View created.

SQL> break on empno on hiredate
SQL> select * from sal_history;

EMPNO HIREDATE     REVIEWDATE   SALARY_RAISE
----- -----------  -----------  ------------
 7369 01-JAN-2000  01-JAN-2000
                   01-FEB-2000          -150
 7499 01-JUN-1988  01-JUN-1988
                   01-JUL-1989           300
                   01-DEC-1993           200
                   01-OCT-1995           200
                   01-NOV-1999          -100
 7521 01-OCT-1986  01-OCT-1986
 ...
```

```
7934 01-FEB-1998 01-FEB-1998
              01-MAY-1998              5
              01-FEB-1999             10
              01-JAN-2000             10

79 rows selected.

SQL>
```

Chapter 11 Exercises

1. Look at Listings 11-26 and 11-37. Apart from aesthetics, there is another important reason why the lines surrounding the script headers in those two listings switch from minus signs to equal signs. Obviously, the first two minus signs are mandatory to turn the lines into comments. What would be wrong with using only minus signs?

   Answer: It is the last minus sign that causes trouble. It will make SQL*Plus interpret the next line as a continuation of the current line. Since the current line is a comment, the next line will be considered a continuation of that comment. Therefore, the SQL or SQL*Plus command on the next line will be *ignored* by SQL*Plus.

2. Create a SQL*Plus script to create indexes. The script should prompt for a table name and a column name (or list of column names), and then *generate* the index name according to the following standard: i_<tab-id>_<col-id>.

   Solution 11-2. SQL*Plus Script to Create Indexes

```
accept table_name              -
       default &&table_name    -
       prompt 'Create index on table [&table_name]: '
accept column_name             -
       default &&column_name -
       prompt 'on column(s) [&column_name]: '
set    termout off
store  set sqlplus_settings replace
save   buffer.sql replace
column dummy new_value index_name
set    heading off feedback off verify off
set    termout on

select 'Creating index'
,       upper(substr( 'i_'                    ||
                     substr('&table_name',1,3) ||
                     '_'                       ||
                     translate
                     ( replace
                       ( '&column_name'
                       , ' ', '')
                     , ',', '_')
                     , 1, 30)
       ) as dummy
,       '...'
from    dual;
```

```
create index &index_name
on &table_name(&column_name);

get    buffer.sql nolist
@sqlplus_settings
set    termout on
```

The following are some comments on this solution:

- The script "remembers" table names and column names, and offers them as default values on consecutive executions. This may save you some time when creating multiple indexes.

- The script saves all current SQL*Plus settings before changing the SQL*Plus environment. This enables the script to restore the original SQL*Plus environment at the end of the script.

- The script saves the current contents of the SQL buffer, and then restores the contents at the end with the GET ... NOLIST command. This way, you can resume working on that SQL statement.

- The COLUMN DUMMY NEW_VALUE INDEX_NAME command captures the result of the query against the DUAL table, which generates the index name.

- The index name generation contains many SQL functions. It takes the first three characters of the table name as the table identifier. The script removes all spaces from the column name list, and then replaces the commas with underscores. To avoid error messages for too-long index names, the script truncates the result to a maximum length of 30.

3. Create a SQL*Plus script to produce an index overview. The script should prompt for a table name, allowing you to specify any leading part of a table name. That is, the script should automatically append a % wildcard to the value entered. Then, it should produce a report of all indexes, showing the table name, index name, index type, and number of columns on which the index is based.

Solution 11-3. SQL*Plus Script to Produce an Index Overview

```
set    termout off
store  set sqlplus_settings.sql replace
save   buffer.sql replace
set    verify off feedback off
set    termout on
break  on table_name skip 1 on index_type

accept table_name default &&table_name -
       prompt 'List indexes on table [&table_name.%]: '

select ui.table_name
,      decode(ui.index_type
              ,'NORMAL', ui.uniqueness
              ,ui.index_type) as index_type
,      ui.index_name
,      (select count(*)
        from   user_ind_columns uic
        where  uic.table_name = ui.table_name
        and    uic.index_name = ui.index_name) as col_count
```

```
from      user_indexes  ui
where     ui.table_name like upper('&table_name.%')
order by  ui.table_name
,         ui.uniqueness desc;

get       buffer.sql nolist
@sqlplus_settings
set       termout on
```

Many SQL*Plus tricks in this script are similar to the ones used in the script for the previous exercise. Here are some additional comments on this solution:

- The BREAK command enhances the readability.

- You use the same default value trick for the table name.

- You need the period character in the ACCEPT command as a separator between the TABLE_NAME variable and the percent sign.

4. Create a script that disables all constraints in your schema.

    Answer: First, you must find out which SQL statement allows you to disable constraints, because your script is going to generate that statement. The following SQL command is the most obvious choice:

```
SQL> ALTER TABLE <table-name> DISABLE CONSTRAINT <constraint-name> [CASCADE]
```

As the next step, you must figure out how to retrieve relevant information about your constraints. The SQL*Plus DESCRIBE command is useful:

```
SQL> describe user_constraints
Name                                    Null?     Type
--------------------------------------- --------  ------------
OWNER                                   NOT NULL  VARCHAR2(30)
CONSTRAINT_NAME                         NOT NULL  VARCHAR2(30)
CONSTRAINT_TYPE                                   VARCHAR2(1)
TABLE_NAME                              NOT NULL  VARCHAR2(30)
SEARCH_CONDITION                                 LONG
R_OWNER                                           VARCHAR2(30)
R_CONSTRAINT_NAME                                 VARCHAR2(30)
DELETE_RULE                                       VARCHAR2(9)
STATUS                                            VARCHAR2(8)
DEFERRABLE                                        VARCHAR2(14)
DEFERRED                                          VARCHAR2(9)
VALIDATED                                         VARCHAR2(13)
GENERATED                                         VARCHAR2(14)
BAD                                               VARCHAR2(3)
RELY                                              VARCHAR2(4)
LAST_CHANGE                                       DATE
INDEX_OWNER                                       VARCHAR2(30)
INDEX_NAME                                        VARCHAR2(30)
INVALID                                           VARCHAR2(7)
VIEW_RELATED                                      VARCHAR2(14)
```

By executing some test queries, it becomes apparent which columns of the USER_CONSTRAINTS view you need. Let's look at a first attempt to generate the ALTER TABLE commands.

Solution 11-4a. First Attempt to Generate the Correct SQL

```
SQL> select 'ALTER TABLE '||table_name||' DISABLE CONSTRAINT
  2            '||constraint_name||';'
  3  from   user_constraints;
```

However, if you capture the output from this query in a script file and execute it, you will discover that there is room for improvement. Some ALTER TABLE commands may fail with the following message:

```
ORA-02297: cannot disable constraint (BOOK.xxx) - dependencies exist
```

You can fix this problem in two ways:

- Add the CASCADE keyword to the generated ALTER TABLE commands.

- Sort the ALTER TABLE commands in such a way that all primary keys are disabled before the foreign key constraints.

Let's implement both fixes. Also, let's add a WHERE clause to the query to avoid generating ALTER TABLE commands for constraints that are disabled already.

Solution 11-4b. Second Attempt to Generate the Correct SQL

```
SQL> select 'ALTER TABLE '||table_name||' DISABLE CONSTRAINT '||constraint_name
  2            ||' CASCADE;'
  3  from   user_constraints
  4  where  status <> 'DISABLED'
  5  order  by case constraint_type when 'P' then 1 else 2 end;
```

Finally, now that you are satisfied with the result of the query, you add the appropriate SQL*Plus commands to capture and execute the query result. The final script looks like the following.

Solution 11-4c. SQL*Plus Script to Disable All Constraints of a Schema

```
set    pagesize 0 verify off feedback off trimspool on
spool  doit.sql replace
select 'ALTER TABLE '||table_name||
       ' DISABLE CONSTRAINT '||constraint_name||' CASCADE;'
from   user_constraints
where  status <> 'DISABLED'
order  by case constraint_type when 'P' then 1 else 2 end;
spool off
@doit
exit
```

You can build many useful SQL*Plus scripts, once you have discovered how you can use SQL*Plus as a command generator.

Chapter 12 Exercises

1. The SALGRADES table has two columns to indicate salary ranges: LOWERLIMIT and UPPERLIMIT. Define your own SALRANGE_T type, based on a varray of two NUMBER(6,2) values, and use it to create an alternative SALGRADES2 table.

   Solution 12-1.

   ```
   SQL> create or replace type salrange_t
     2  as varray(2) of number(6,2);
     3  /

   Type created.

   SQL> create table salgrades2
     2  ( grade      number(2)  constraint S2_PK
     3                          primary key
     4  , salrange   salrange_t constraint S2_RANGE_NN
     5                          not null
     6  , bonus      NUMBER(6,2) constraint S2_BONUS_NN
     7                          not null
     8  ) ;

   Table created.

   SQL>
   ```

2. Fill the new SALGRADES2 table with a single INSERT statement, using the existing SALGRADES table.

   Solution 12-2.

   ```
   SQL> insert into salgrades2
     2  select grade
     3  ,      salrange_t(lowerlimit,upperlimit)
     4  ,      bonus
     5  from   salgrades;

   5 rows created.

   SQL> col salrange format a25
   SQL> select * from salgrades2;

       GRADE SALRANGE                     BONUS
   --------- ------------------------- --------
           1 SALRANGE_T(700, 1200)            0
           2 SALRANGE_T(1201, 1400)          50
           3 SALRANGE_T(1401, 2000)         100
           4 SALRANGE_T(2001, 3000)         200
           5 SALRANGE_T(3001, 9999)         500

   5 rows selected.

   SQL>
   ```

3. Create a table TESTNEST with two columns: column X and column MX. Column X is NUMBER(1,0) with values 2, 3, 4, ..., 9. Column MX is a nested table, based on a MX_TAB_T type, containing all multiples of X less than or equal to 20.

Solution 12-3a. Table TESTNEST Creation

```
SQL> create or replace type mx_tab_t
  2  as table of number(2);
  3  /

Type created.

SQL> create table testnest
  2  ( x    number(1,0)
  3  , mx   mx_tab_t
  4  ) nested table mx store as mx_tab;

Table created.

SQL>
```

You can use pure INSERT statements to populate the TESTNEST table. The following solution uses PL/SQL to insert all rows in an efficient way. The PL/SQL syntax is straightforward.

Solution 12-3b. Table TESTNEST Population

```
SQL> declare
  2     i number;
  3     j number;
  4  begin
  5     for i in 2..9 loop
  6       insert into testnest (x, mx)
  7                    values (i, mx_tab_t());
  8       for j in 1..20 loop
  9         exit when i*j > 20;
 10         insert into table (select mx from testnest where x=i)
 11                    values (i*j);
 12       end loop;
 13     end loop;
 14  end;
 15  /

PL/SQL procedure successfully completed.

SQL>
```

Now, let's check the contents of the TESTNEST table.

Solution 12-3c. Table TESTNEST Query

```
SQL> col x  format 9
SQL> col mx format a80
SQL> select * from testnest;

 X  MX
 -- -------------------------------------------
 2  MX_TAB_T(2, 4, 6, 8, 10 ,12, 14, 16, 18, 20)
 3  MX_TAB_T(3, 6, 9, 12, 15, 18)
 4  MX_TAB_T(4, 8, 12, 16, 20)
 5  MX_TAB_T(5, 10, 15, 20)
 6  MX_TAB_T(6, 12, 18)
 7  MX_TAB_T(7, 14)
 8  MX_TAB_T(8, 16)
 9  MX_TAB_T(9, 18)

8 rows selected.

SQL>
```

4. Use multiset operators to solve the following problems, using the TESTNEST table you created and populated in the previous exercise:

    a. Which rows have a nested table containing value 12?

        Answer: 2, 3, 4, 6

        Solution 12-4a.

```
SQL> select *
  2  from    testnest
  3  where   12 member of mx;

 X MX
 -- -------------------------------------------
 2 MX_TAB_T(2, 4, 6, 8, 10, 12, 14, 16, 18, 20)
 3 MX_TAB_T(3, 6, 9, 12, 15, 18)
 4 MX_TAB_T(4, 8, 12, 16, 20)
 6 MX_TAB_T(6, 12, 18)

SQL>
```

    b. Which nested tables are *not* a subset of any other subset?

        Answer: 2, 3, 5, 7

        Solution 12-4b.

```
SQL> select t1.*
  2  from    testnest t1
  3  where   not exists
  4          (select t2.*
  5           from    testnest t2
```

```
6          where  t2.x <> t1.x
7          and    t1.mx submultiset of t2.mx);

 X MX
-- ----------------------------------------------
 2 MX_TAB_T(2, 4, 6, 8, 10, 12, 14, 16, 18, 20)
 3 MX_TAB_T(3, 6, 9, 12, 15, 18)
 5 MX_TAB_T(5, 10, 15, 20)
 7 MX_TAB_T(7, 14)

SQL>
```

c. Which nested tables have more than 42 different nonempty subsets?

Answer: 2, 3

Solution 12-4c.

```
SQL> select x
  2  ,       cardinality(powermultiset(mx))
  3  from    testnest
  4  where   cardinality(powermultiset(mx)) > 42;

 X CARDINALITY(POWERMULTISET(MX))
-- ------------------------------
 2                           1023
 3                             63

SQL>
```

Index

Get the eBook for only $10!

Now you can take the weightless companion with you anywhere, anytime. Your purchase of this book entitles you to 3 electronic versions for only $10.

This Apress title will prove so indispensible that you'll want to carry it with you everywhere, which is why we are offering the eBook in 3 formats for only $10 if you have already purchased the print book.

Convenient and fully searchable, the PDF version enables you to easily find and copy code—or perform examples by quickly toggling between instructions and applications. The MOBI format is ideal for your Kindle, while the ePUB can be utilized on a variety of mobile devices.

Go to www.apress.com/promo/tendollars to purchase your companion eBook.